PHILOSOPHY AND GERMAN LITERATURE 1700–1990

Although the importance of the interplay of literature and philosophy in Germany has often been examined within individual works or groups of works by particular authors, little research has been undertaken into the broader dialogue of German literature and philosophy as a whole. Philosophy and German Literature 1700–1990 offers six chapters by leading specialists on the dialogue between German literary writers and philosophers through their works. The volume shows that German literature, far from being the mouthpiece of a dour philosophical culture dominated by the great names of Leibniz, Kant, Hegel, Marx, Heidegger and Habermas, has much more to offer: while possessing a high affinity with philosophy it explores regions of human insight and experience beyond philosophy's ken.

NICHOLAS SAUL is Professor of German and Head of Department at the University of Liverpool. He is the author of *Poetry and History in Novalis and in the Tradition of the German Enlightenment* (1984) and *Literature and Pulpit Oratory in the German Romantic Age* (1999). He is a contributor to the *Cambridge History of German Literature*. He has also edited volumes on literature and science, and the body in German literature.

CAMBRIDGE STUDIES IN GERMAN

General editors
H. B. Nisbet, University of Cambridge
Martin Swales, University of London
Advisory editor
Theodore J. Ziolkowski, Princeton University

PHILOSOPHY AND GERMAN LITERATURE
1700–1990

EDITED BY

NICHOLAS SAUL
University of Liverpool

CAMBRIDGE
UNIVERSITY PRESS

PUBLISHED BY THE PRESS SYNDICATE OF THE UNIVERSITY OF CAMBRIDGE
The Pitt Building, Trumpington Street, Cambridge, United Kingdom

CAMBRIDGE UNIVERSITY PRESS
The Edinburgh Building, Cambridge CB2 2RU, UK
40 West 20th Street, New York, NY 10011-4211, USA
477 Williamstown Road, Port Melbourne, VIC 3207, Australia
Ruiz de Alarcón 13, 28014 Madrid, Spain
Dock House, The Waterfront, Cape Town 8001, South Africa

http://www.cambridge.org

First published 2002

Printed in the United Kingdom at the University Press, Cambridge

Typeface Baskerville Monotype 11 / 12.5 pt.   *System* LaTeX 2$_\varepsilon$ [TB]

A catalogue record for this book is available from the British Library

Library of Congress Cataloguing in Publication data
Philosophy and German literature 1700–1990 / edited by Nicholas Saul.
p.   cm. – (Cambridge studies in German)
Includes bibliographical references and index.
ISBN 0-521-66052-1
1. German literature – History and criticism.   2. Literature and philosophy.
3. Philosophy, German.   I. Saul, Nicholas.   II. Series.
PT111 .M63 2002
830.9′384 – dc21   2001043838

ISBN 0 521 66052 1 hardback

Contents

Contributors

JOHN A. MCCARTHY is Professor of German and Comparative Literature, and Co-Director of German Studies at Vanderbilt University.
His teaching and research focus on Enlightenment, *Sturm und Drang*,
Weimar Classicism, Nietzsche, science and literature, the essay genre,
and the history of Germanics. Among his book publications are
*Crossing boundaries: a theory and history of essayistic writing in German 1680–
1815* (1989) and *Disrupted patterns: on chaos and order in the Enlightenment*
(2000). Currently McCarthy is researching his next major project: the
reception of the *Sturm und Drang* movement, 1770–1990.

NICHOLAS SAUL is Professor of German and Head of Department at the
University of Liverpool. He is the author of *Poetry and history in Novalis
and the German Enlightenment* (1984) and '*Prediger aus der neuen romantischen
Clique.*' *Zur Interaktion von Romantik und Homiletik um 1800* (1999). He has
also edited volumes on literature and science, threshold metaphors,
and the body in German literature, and published on authors from
Frederick the Great of Prussia to Hugo von Hofmannsthal and Botho
Strauß. He contributed the section on German literature 1790–1830
to the *Cambridge history of German literature* (1997).

JOHN WALKER is lecturer in German at Birkbeck College, University
of London, where he served as Chair of Department in 1996–9. His
research interests focus on the interrelation between philosophy and
literary form in German literature 1770–1900. He has published a
book on Hegel's religious and historical thought, *History, spirit and
experience* (1995), and edited the collection of essays *Thought and faith
in the philosophy of Hegel* (1991). He has also contributed to books on
Hegel and Nietzsche, and published several articles on Lessing, Kleist,
Büchner and Böll.

RITCHIE ROBERTSON is Professor of German at Oxford University and a Fellow of St John's College. His publications include *Kafka: Judaism, politics, and literature* (1985), *Heine* (1988), *The 'Jewish Question' in German literature, 1749–1939* (1999), and an anthology of texts in translation, *The German Jewish dialogue, 1749–1993* (1999). He contributed the section on German literature 1890–1945 to the *Cambridge history of German literature* (1997).

RUSSELL A. BERMAN holds the Walter A. Haas Professorship in the Humanities at Stanford University, with appointments in German Studies and Comparative Literature. He has written widely on topics in modern German literature, culture and theory. His major publications include *The rise of the modern German novel* (1986), *Modern culture and Critical Theory* (1989), *Cultural studies of Modern Germany* (1993), and *Enlightenment or Empire* (1998).

ROBERT C. HOLUB teaches intellectual, cultural and literary history in the German Department at the University of California, Berkeley. Among his publications on these topics are books on Heinrich Heine, reception theory, nineteenth-century realism, Jürgen Habermas, recent literary theory, and Friedrich Nietzsche. He has also edited five volumes on various topics from the Enlightenment to the present.

Acknowledgements

I have many debts of gratitude to acknowledge. The *Deutscher Akademischer Austauschdienst* (*German Academic Exchange Service*, London Office) generously funded a term's leave at the University of Würzburg in spring 1998, without which my own contributions to this volume could not have been written. During this time I profited from unlimited access to the minds (and wine cellars) of Helmut Pfotenhauer and Wolfgang Riedel. Thanks go also to Kate Brett, from whose original suggestion this book is descended. Finally, no project of this kind ever reaches fruition without the teamwork of all the contributors. I thank them for their energy, cognitive skills both analytic and synthetic, and their *Langmut*.

Nicholas Saul
University of Liverpool

Abbreviations

CD	Johann Jakob Breitinger, *Critische Dichtkunst*, 2 vols., Zürich: Orell, 1740; facsimile reprint, ed. Wolfgang Bender, Stuttgart: Metzler, 1966.
Ethics	Baruch de Spinoza, *Ethics*, trans. Andrew Boyle, revised G. H. R. Parkinson, London: J. M. Dent, 1995.
F	Theodor Fontane, *Romane, Erzählungen, Gedichte*, ed. Walter Keitel, 6 vols., Munich: Hanser, 1962.
H	Hugo von Hofmannsthal, *Gesammelte Werke in Einzelbänden*, ed. Bernd Schoeller, 10 vols., Frankfurt: Fischer, 1979.
HA	Johann Wolfgang von Goethe, *Werke* (Hamburger Ausgabe), ed. Erich Trunz et al., 14 vols., Munich: Beck, 1948–60.
Hinske-Specht	Raffaele Ciafardone, *Die Philosophie der deutschen Aufklärung. Texte und Darstellung*, ed. Norbert Hinske and Rainer Specht, Stuttgart: Reclam, 1990.
JGH	Johann Gottfried Herder, *Sämtliche Werke*, ed. Bernhard Suphan, 33 vols., Berlin: Weidmann, 1891; repr. Hildesheim: Georg Olms, 1967.
K	Immanuel Kant, *Werke*, ed. Wilhelm Weischedel, 10 vols., Darmstadt: Wissenschaftliche Buchgesellschaft, 1983.
KFSA	Friedrich Schlegel, *Kritische Friedrich-Schlegel-Ausgabe*, ed. Ernst Behler, Hans Eichner and Jean-Jacques Anstett, 35 vols., Paderborn, Munich, Vienna and Zürich: Schöningh, 1958–.
KrV	Immanuel Kant, *Kritik der reinen Vernunft*, in *Werkausgabe*, ed. Wilhelm Weischedel, 12 vols.,

	Frankfurt am Main: Suhrkamp, 1977, vols. III–IV (pages numbered consecutively).
L	Leibniz, *Philosophical writings*, trans. Mary Morris and G. H. R. Parkinson, ed. G. H. R. Parkinson, London: J. M. Dent, 1997.
LW	G. E. Lessing, *Lessings Werke*, ed. Kurt Wölfel, 3 vols., Frankfurt am Main: Insel, 1967.
M	Thomas Mann, *Gesammelte Werke*, 13 vols., Frankfurt: Fischer, 1974.
N	Friedrich Nietzsche, *Werke*, ed. Karl Schlechta, 3 vols., Munich: Hanser, 1956.
NS	Hardenberg, Friedrich von, *Novalis. Schriften*, ed. Paul Kluckhohn, Richard Samuel et al., 6 vols., Stuttgart, Berlin, Cologne and Mainz: Kohlhammer, 1960–.
PW	Immanuel Kant, *Philosophical writings*, ed. Ernst Behler, New York: Continuum, 1992.
R	Rainer Maria Rilke, *Werke*, ed. Manfred Engel et al., 4 vols., Frankfurt and Leipzig: Insel, 1996.
S	Arthur Schopenhauer, *Sämtliche Werke*, ed. Julius Frauenstädt, 6 vols., Leipzig: Brockhaus, 1923.
SE	*The Standard edition of the complete psychological works of Sigmund Freud*, ed. James Strachey, 24 vols., London: Hogarth Press, 1953–74.

Introduction: German literature and philosophy

Nicholas Saul

'[T]he intermingling of philosophical and literary ideas', Peter Stern once wrote, is a 'commonplace of German literary history'. Apart from his own studies of the 'traffic between literature and philosophy',[1] a long list might be compiled of studies which aim somehow to explain German literature since 1700 in philosophical terms, from (to name but a few) Hermann August Korff's *Geist der Goethezeit* (1923–53; *Spirit of the Goethean age*),[2] via Nicholas Boyle's philosophical reading of Goethe's 'Vermächtniß' (1979; 'Testament')[3] to Géza von Molnár's *Goethes Kantstudien* (1993; *Goethe's Kant studies*).[4] The list of studies which look at German philosophy from a literary angle of some kind might not be quite as long, but would still be impressive.[5] Now such lists would scarcely prove that German literature, by comparison with literature in other languages, exhibits some special relationship with philosophy (however defined), still less an intrinsic one. And yet how often do modern German writers signal that their literary works were prompted by reading philosophy. Johann Christoph Gottsched (not a great writer, but an important one) builds the early eighteenth-century reform of German literature on the intellectual reforms of Leibniz-Wolffian philosophy. Schiller is the very paradigm of the *poeta philosophus*. The Romantic Friedrich von Hardenberg (Novalis) founds his entire literary *œuvre* on an intensive study of Fichte. Kleist becomes a poet only after having endured a crisis of knowledge in the name of Kant. Thomas Mann is habitually read through Nietzsche and Schopenhauer. And this is not to mention other well-known or popularly accredited cases such as Goethe and Spinoza (or Leibniz), Heine and Hegel, Hofmannsthal and Mach, Brecht and Marx, Bernhard and Wittgenstein, Jelinek and Freud (or Marx), Botho Strauß and Adorno.

But even if we allow for heuristic purposes the claim of a special relationship between German literature and philosophy, of what kind might their relation be? Co-operation between equals on the basis of an agreed division of intellectual labour? Subordination of one discourse

to another? Criticism of one by another? Mutual antagonism? Irreducibly occasionalistic interaction? Final incommensurability, despite
everything? Stern for his part dismissed the 'distinction between "literature" and "thought"' as 'the source of much pedantry'. For him,
that distinction became 'less than self-evident where ideas are treated
as living things' and should be kept 'relative . . . to the overall creative
achievement, which is . . . an exploration of human possibilities in a given
historical setting'.[6]

Since those words were written by a leading exponent of the intellectual history of literature, and weighty as that judgement is, many
landmarks have shifted on our intellectual horizon – yet not, perhaps,
towards positions he would have approved. Much has been done on literature and philosophy in individual writers and works. In particular a
great deal of work has been done on the *general* aspect of the relation,
beyond the confines of any national literature. But it seems nonetheless
that till now a major scholarly task has remained undone. If many have
examined the interplay of literary and philosophical discourse at the
level of the individual writer and work and at the level of philosophical
aesthetics, little research has yet been conducted into the *concrete dialogue
of literature and philosophy in Germany, as a whole, through the history of modernity*.
This volume thus seeks for the first time, not merely to reflect philosophically on what literature is, and so make one more contribution to
literary theory, but to reconstruct, analyse and evaluate how poets and
philosophers in Germany really *did* interact with one another through
their writings, epoch by epoch, in the modern period as a whole. The
authors of the chapters in this book neither followed nor rejected any
particular theory or method, but rather allowed argument to flow unpredictably from concrete engagement with the material. It is not the
purpose of this introduction to pre-empt the findings of the following
chapters, but certain patterns do emerge.

The dominant of John A. McCarthy's opening chapter, 'Criticism and
experience: philosophy and literature in the German Enlightenment',
is co-operation, a term that precludes any easy division of labour between literature and philosophy in the German eighteenth century. It
is hardly surprising that this epoch is the cradle of modern aesthetics –
as one possible synthesis of the two discourses. But the main achievement of the German Enlightenment in the context of our question is
to ally philosophy and literature in the first place. The thrust of the
German Enlightenment consists, as McCarthy shows, in the use of literature and philosophy alike as the 'epistemic tools' (p. 27) of a grand,

fundamentally anthropocentric project: the systematic exploration of the self in its manifold relationships with inner self, community, nature and God, and the concomitant translation of those abstract findings into practical human fact in the cause of perfection. But it is clear that here philosophy is constantly *primus inter pares*, leaving aesthetics and literature with the role of executor. Leibniz, for example, formulates principles which *inter alia* explain the structure of the world as the realisation of maximum unity in multiplicity and the journey of the soul as progress to perfection. Bodmer's and Breitinger's aesthetics translate the former into the model of modern (organic) aesthetic form; Wieland's novels the latter into the model form of human existence. Similarly Wolff's notion of human reason as analogous to divine creativity underlies not only the theory of creative artistry in the didactic poetics of Gottsched, Bodmer and Breitinger, but also the full-blown theory of artistic genius in Klopstock, Hamann, Herder, and the *Sturm und Drang* (Storm and Stress). Haller's idylls, Gellert's sentimental comedies, Laroche's novel, Wieland's comic narratives, all serve the end of human improvement through imaginative instantiations of philosophical ideals which appeal to the reason, will and feeling of their recipients. Even Hamann's and Herder's ideals of greatness of personality, energy and enthusiasm are less counter-Enlightenment programmes than critical radicalisations of the original project; indeed, the literature of the Classic-Romantic epoch, as exemplified by Goethe's reception of Spinoza, Leibniz and Kant, represents but a refinement of these optimistic ideals.

Nicholas Saul's 'The pursuit of the subject. Literature as critic and perfecter of philosophy 1790–1830' argues by contrast for the growing divergence of philosophers' and poets' self-understanding in the Classic-Romantic epoch, as intellectuals struggle to explain the disproportion between the ideals of Enlightenment and the reality of the French Revolution, and to assess the consequences of this for Germany. With Schiller and Goethe, literature emerges for the first time as a discourse which gives voice to something philosophy silences. Kant had replaced the Enlightenment notion of the unitary self with something fragmented and deficient. Knowledge of the world of appearances is securely founded by analogy with empirical science, but only at the price of a dualism which leaves the essential nature of the self – and things – unknowable. The categorical imperative offers comfort. As moral autonomy realised, it is the foundation of a postulated metaphysic. But as Schiller sees, moral action in Kant's dictatorial style is not only liberation (of intellect) but also enslavement (of sense) – thus entailing a further division of human nature. All this is the signature of a modernity in which Enlightenment has missed its path, and the untrammelled exercise even of critical reason has failed to realise reason's project. Philosophy, Schiller concludes, is no longer up to the job, and he advances aesthetic experience, with its characteristic harmonious synthesis of intellect and sense, as the sole restorer of human wholeness. Literature is thus no longer quite what it was, the amicable executor of a project primarily defined by philosophy. Schiller accepts the authority of Kantian criticism. But he also suggests much more strongly than Kant that philosophical reflection faces strict limits, and places the entire practical sphere, in particular corporeality, under the legislation of art. With the Romantics, this divergence of literature and philosophy deepens. Rejecting Fichte's compromise solution to the problem of grounding absolute subjectivity in reflection, they far exceed Schiller's promotion of aesthetic experience. For Hardenberg, Friedrich Schlegel and the rest, the ground of subjectivity can only be intuited, only aesthetic discourse will serve as the means to re-present the lost ground of the subject in the phenomenal world, and even then only as self-consciously experimental, ironically self-relativising constructions which symbolise unending progress to perfection. Thus the Enlightenment project stands until Hegel under the influence of Romantic aestheticism and its faith in redemptive intuitions of wholeness. Not philosophy but literature takes on the task of healing the divided modern subject, with ever-increasing cognitive ambition and finally mythical status. The Romantic faith in redemptive intuitions reaches its height in the popular philosophy of G. H. Schubert, who rejects all philosophical reflection in favour of clairvoyant-oneiric revelations of nature's hidden truth. But the Romantic consensus eventually erodes. Kleist not only becomes a poet following his philosophical crisis, but also deconstructs the cognitive hubris of Romantic poesy in his own variant of Romanticism. Hegel represents the philosophical backlash. For him, the Romantics as modernist writers are not so much the cure as the symptom of modernity's sickness, division. Purporting to heal the rift of absolute and world in the construct of a truly self-knowing subjectivity, they in fact mix vague intuition with empirical fact in an exhibition of formalist shallowness, thus perpetuating the division. Not intuition but thought, rightly understood as the subject that is concretely, fully and transparently in and for itself, is the sole legitimate means to work through contradiction to resolution. The epoch of art as this function of absolute consciousness is by definition past.

John Walker, in his chapter 'Two realisms: German literature and philosophy 1830–1890', finds that the unfolding dialogue of philosophy and literature fails to confirm Hegel's prognosis of the future of Romantic art and deepens the discursive rift. The tradition of German idealist thought had always assumed the reality reflectively treated by philosophy and philosophical aesthetics to be co-extensive with the reality imaginatively treated by the works of art themselves, so that both discursive domains in this sense share a common 'realistic' focus. This fundamental idealist tenet, Walker shows, loses its validity over the course of the nineteenth century, and a dichotomy emerges between the 'reality' of the philosophers and that of the writers. Thus whilst the Hegelian tradition continues to dominate German official philosophy for much of the nineteenth century, it increasingly fails to reflect the relation of the modern subject to reality and so to achieve reconciliation. In the 1830s and 1840s alternative modes are sought. They turn out in the work of Heine and the writers of *Das junge Deutschland* (Young Germany) to be aesthetic, and to aim more at social and ideological criticism than philosophical reconciliation. There occurs a concomitant shift in the dominant productive mode of creative writers, from drama to novel. For Hegel the drama resolves substantive private–public conflicts without unsettling contradictory residues. Yet in this drama conspicuously fails. Grabbe's work modulates philosophy into satire, Hebbel's functions as social critique against the grain of its would-be Hegelian framework. Büchner analyses the profound disproportion between philosophico-political discourse and reality in *Dantons Tod* (1835; *Danton's death*). Meanwhile the novel develops its own, autonomous mode of *aesthetic* reflection on reality. Keller's and Stifter's socio-semiotic anatomisations offer analysis of society *as* representation (typically German in this politically retarded century) and a critical assessment of the *validity* of such representations of the underlying (modern) realities. It is this internal reflective dynamic of literature, built not on Hegelian thought but on the Classic-Romantic achievement, which marks German literature in the nineteenth century as characteristically German. German literary realism of this century may reflect a social reality different from that in other great western European cultures, in that Germany was less urbanised, centralised and industrialised, and German culture thus perhaps in terms of content more provincial, particularist and inward-looking. Yet the characteristic inwardness does not reflect an ideologically unquestioning aesthetic retreat from reality, so much as the insight *that* reality is a construct, and a deeply reflective critical questioning *of* that construct, which finally performs the Hegelian task of modern self-understanding in a deeply un-Hegelian way. Fontane's novels mark the apogee of literary development in an epoch when school philosophy such as that of Dilthey renounces the possibility of grasping the sense of society and is increasingly dissociated from public life.

Ritchie Robertson's 'Modernism and the self 1890–1924' reveals two shifts in the received terms of negotiation between philosophy and literature. Attention is focused as before on problems of representation. But now, in a neo-Romantic turn, it is again directed to the individual subject, which is seen in isolation from the community and held to be in crisis. Moreover contemporary philosophy – in Enlightenment, Romanticism and the first half of the nineteenth century always volubly present in the public sphere – is now, in the guise of Marburg and Heidelberg neo-Kantianism and following the late nineteenth-century trend, confined increasingly to the school. Literary writers around 1900 engage in dialogue less with Frege and Husserl than latecomers unrecognised in their own time (Schopenhauer and Nietzsche) or still-influential thinkers of earlier generations (Darwin) and their popularisers. In this constellation, literary writers tend to absorb intellectual and imaginative models rather than crisply defined concepts from philosophical sources, and to challenge philosophy by asking how its claims would look if one lived by them. The terms of engagement between philosophy and literature around 1900 consist, then, in the testing by writers of several current philosophical models of the self. Confronted by the materialism and determinism of the impersonal universe invoked by positivist natural science, some writers of the early phase (Hauptmann) propagate a popularised social Darwinism. Impressionism tests the 'punctual self' (Charles Taylor) of Cartesian reason in its modern Viennese realisation. Where Mach and Bahr see identity as the illusion of a coherent subject only seeming to underlie the ultimate reality of impressions blossoming and fading, Hofmannsthal emphasises memory as the substrate of the self's inner continuity and explores the ethical consequences of his counter-vision. Other writers experiment with the construct of the embattled self they find in Schopenhauer and Nietzsche, which strives to overcome the threat to its existence by exertion of will. Mann's Thomas Buddenbrook battles heroically against the tide of change for institutions he knows to be doomed but will neither change nor allow to die, never understanding that his struggle masks the failure to encounter the fact of his own mortality. At the centre of the interaction between philosophy and literature in this epoch is however a discourse neither quite philosophy, nor quite literature (though it partakes richly of both), Freud's psychoanalytic theory of the enfeebled self perched atop the unconscious like a rider on his horse. Mann, Hofmannsthal and Beer-Hofmann use literary dreams in their Freudian significance (regressions to the pre-civilised state) as moral warnings to their dreamers. Others from Buber to Heym extend the notion of dream far beyond Freud's intention, to encompass the modern mysticism of the literary epiphany: a compensatory vision of oneness with a meaningless universe. Only rarely does school philosophy impinge on the literary quest for modern selfhood, as when Hofmannsthal encounters the icily abstract phenomenology of Husserl in 1906. Rilke's 'Dinggedichte' ('thing-poems') and Hofmannsthal's privileged object intuitions seem strangely to resemble the reduction to the pure contents of consciousness practised by phenomenological investigation – even if the poet's aim (sensual enrichment) is hardly that of the austere philosopher.

In 'The subjects of community. Aspiration, memory, resistance 1918–1945' Russell Berman shows official German culture after the First World War to have ossified into a life lie. Philosophy still inhabits the private world of the schools. Thus literature, allied with Freudian and Nietzschean tendencies on the wilder shores of thought, leads the assault on the Wilhelmine organisation of the landscape of meaning. Rejecting high modernism's introspection, writers and thinkers identify community as the locus of reflection on alternative sources of meaning. Max Weber stands for compromise with the old order. He sees rationalistic modern culture as having fragmented into unmediated spheres of specialised knowledge. But he defends official culture against the charge of total bureaucratisation, defends the received dichotomy of aesthetic and political institutions, and warns against irrationalist, 'prophetic' short-cuts to found new structures of public meaning. Traditional and legal sources of legitimate renewal are nonetheless exhausted, so that Weber, whether intentionally or not, opens the way for 'charismatic', aesthetic discourse to design a vast variety of redemptive models of meaning, in which the liberal subjective tradition is slowly submerged. Expressionism urges connection with a vitalistic totality, but fails to achieve concrete conceptual clarity and too often accepts the socio-political establishment it ostensibly opposes. Dada's radical anti-logocentrism rejects all dichotomies of aesthetic and public institutions (especially art and politics) in the name of the identity of life and art. But its decentred anarcho-communist tendencies are countered by the inheritors of the Nietzschean tradition of the embattled self, figures loosely allied under the banner of a 'conservative revolution'. Gundolf insists in stark contrast to Dada that charismatic poetic language is the source of authentic cultural life in alienated and mechanistic modernity. Only a poetic leader such as George can re-instil authentic spirituality into art, and so Gundolf finally promotes a spiritualised and personalised yet apolitical cult of the aesthetic. Bertram's musical nationalism, Jünger's battlefield existentialism, Thomas Mann's *Betrachtungen eines Unpolitischen* (1919; *Considerations of an unpolitical man*) are variations on this theme. The left meanwhile radicalises these received positions. Brecht marks Marxism's aesthetic turn. He rejects bourgeois individualism and propagates an engaged, if highly complex literature addressed to a collective subject. But if his self-consciously experimental art reveals Brecht's affinity with modernism, Lukács makes the break between this great aesthetic trend and Marxism. The modernist acceptance of cognitive fragmentation and subjectivist perspectivism is, he says, incompatible with the Marxist demand for objective totality and singular intelligibility as evidenced by the nineteenth-century realist tradition. Benjamin, by contrast, reveals the continued influence of Romanticism. Like Brecht, he denies the auratic status of the work of art, the emancipatory energies of which are unfolded in Romantic style through philosophical-critical reception. But Benjamin also rejects the Marxian belief in art's influence on political development. History is modernistically discontinuous, and change is occasioned by epiphanic irruptions from another domain into time's immanent flow. Mann's *Der Zauberberg* (1924; *The magic mountain*) and Döblin's *Berlin Alexanderplatz* (1929), with their scepticism of any received developmental model and postponement of redemption, exemplify the resultant diminished status of the modern individual. Psychoanalysis and the related work of Schnitzler seal its fate. Finally, even philosophy looks to art for semantic redemption. Heidegger, in another recourse to the Romantic position, argues authentic art to be the only medium capable of disclosing the irreducibly agonistic situation of existence in a modernity dominated by redundant critical chatter. The *Dialektik der Aufklärung* (1944–7; *Dialectic of Enlightenment*) of Horkheimer and Adorno formulates perhaps the most influential diagnosis of the fate of philosophy in German modernity: Enlightenment, the mainstream occidental tradition of thought, is in crisis. Its great achievement, the concept, has turned into its opposite, a means of control and eradication of difference. Only high, formally difficult art contains in hermetically sealed form a source of utopian energy and truth. Thomas Mann's *Doktor Faustus* (1947) contains the retrospective sum of these tendencies of the epoch. Leverkühn's Adornian espousal of rebarbative, difficult art and abandonment of the liberal humanistic tradition is the only way forward for the aesthetic recovery of the subject.

Robert C. Holub's 'Coming to terms with the past in postwar literature and philosophy' captures the break and continuity of German culture after World War Two. If the self-consciousness of writers and thinkers in earlier parts of the modern era had been informed above all by the sentimental recall of something positive lost (individual wholeness, the immediate relation of individual and community) in the name of a future which might recreate it, this time is dominated by the necessity to remember something deeply negative – the collective shame of National Socialism and the Holocaust – and the recuperation of its meaning in the name of a future which must be different. It was a task performed under contrasting conditions in West and East Germany, and, in contrast to the preceding epoch, it has been equally shared by philosophy and literature. At first it was failure they shared. On the philosophical side, Horkheimer and Adorno had proposed with the *Dialektik der Aufklärung* a philosophical framework capable of accounting, if not specifically for fascism, then at least for the rise of totalitarian systems of cultural control in modernity through the domination of the concept. But these exiled voices were heard in Germany only in the 1960s. Until then, the astonishingly thin public discourse on the heritage of shame in Germany was dominated by the ambivalent responses of Jaspers and Heidegger. Jaspers's ready acceptance of Germany's political and criminal responsibility for the war also involved rejection of any substantive concept of collective guilt, in the sense of that which might be legitimately punished by authority, so that individual Germans were left to their own devices in facing up to the past. Heidegger, continuing an amoral tradition of German thought and letters, avoided the issue. Until Grass, the early postwar literature of Böll and Borchert mirrors this asymmetry of grief, in that the returning soldiers are ultimately presented from the standpoint of immediate singular experience, as victims rather than as somehow complicit. Even Celan's celebrated 'Todesfuge' (1948, 'Death fugue'), which attempts to write the experience of the Holocaust from the Jewish standpoint in musical figures transcending conventional semantics, runs the risk of unwittingly transfiguring horror. Only with Grass's *Blechtrommel* (1959; *The tin drum*) is a literary language – that of a deranged dwarf in an anti-*Bildungsroman* – found in which the Nazi past might be captured, and Grass's sequel *Katz und Maus* (1961; *Cat and mouse*) figures the collective complicity of the Germans for the first time through its thematisation of denial and subtle perspectivist entwining of the fellow traveller's and victim's views. With the generational divide of the 1960s and especially in the semi-documentary and historically ambitious works of Hochhuth and Weiss, the accusation of complicity and the location of the Holocaust in wider contexts of understanding dominates the literary scene. If the spirit of Adorno is discernible in these literary developments, it is only with the rise of the philosopher of the public sphere, Jürgen Habermas, that German philosophy proper seeks critically to come to terms with its inheritance. Any philosophy which fails to address this issue, from Gadamer's ideologically indifferent hermeneutics to Luhmann's value-free systems theory, is engaged by Habermas in a public dialogue. This, true to the premises of his own philosophy, seeks to expose received arguments to the process of open, intersubjective legitimation, criticism and consensus-building which is the utopian engine of his own thought, the counter-image of National Socialist totality, and his alternative to the dialectic of Enlightenment. In the East, the issue of fascism was simply equated with capitalism and exported to West Germany, later to return. Philosophy (predictably in real-existing socialism) was silent, and early East German literature focused almost exclusively on building socialism. Only with Becker's *Jakob der Lügner* (1968; *Jacob the liar*) is the Jewish Holocaust experience posed as a common German heritage, and only with Christa Wolf's *Kindheitsmuster* (1976; *Patterns of childhood*) does a German, who is also an East German and a German woman, critically reconstruct the past and present reality of her damaged subjectivity, the saturation with National Socialist, anti-Semitic values, in a framework beyond that offered by East German ideological orthodoxy. The unification of Germany sealed a trend which had begun in the early 1980s with Helmut Kohl's self-proclaimed 'grace of a late birth' and the increasing desire for the normalisation of German cultural life. Following this trend, the attention of German intellectuals turned away from the ethical and political issues raised by the catastrophe of modernity and towards postmodern, 'new subjectivist' forms of aesthetic and existential experimentation. These gravitated naturally towards easy nationalism and cultural conservatism. Habermas has been prominent among philosophers in defending the positive inheritance of modernity, in particular the autonomy of the modern spheres of rationality in Weber's tradition, against the use of aesthetic categories to elide their legitimacy and erect an anti-Enlightenment. Both, for him, derive ultimately from the Hegelian tendency to devalue individuality and critique. He and Manfred Frank share suspicion of any attempt to undermine the foundations of autonomous subjectivity. In the work of Ransmayr and Schlink it is evident that writers of fiction also share Habermas's view that the past, despite everything, has yet to be mastered.

We lack space to reflect fully on the lessons of the literary-philosophical dialogue in Germany as reconstructed here. But perhaps a few suggestive theses can be ventured in conclusion. The relation of literary and philosophical discourse in Germany cannot in fact be reduced to some single principle or tendency. It changes unpredictably. It responds sometimes to purely internal dynamics, sometimes to external influences – social, political and other. Sometimes, as in the Enlightenment, philosophical and literary discourse pursue common cognitive interests. At other times, as when the early Romantics propound their doctrine of aesthetic cognition against received philosophical wisdom, literature claims insight where philosophical discourse cannot reach. This Romantic tradition certainly exercises a pervasive influence over subsequent epochs of German literary and intellectual history. Even realists such as Keller and Fontane are part of this tradition when they use literature to explore a social world accepted by idealist philosophy to be beyond its own purview. When Brecht places the official celebration of his soldier's death under the perspective of the stars and the carnival, when Grass exposes Pilenz's complicity through narrative sleight of hand, when East German writers alone recover the repressed history of their country, they too continue the tradition of literature's claim to special cognitive power. Yet this is far from being always so. The eighteenth century as a whole shows philosophy to be a dominant and benevolent emancipatory force, literature's guide in many ways. The same is true after the Second World War. Official philosophy may have failed in the task of *Vergangenheitsbewältigung*, but so too, and equally, did literature. And if Adorno attacks the rationalistic tradition of philosophy, then Habermas's interdiscursive-communicative utopia is a living demonstration of Adorno's tendentiousness.

Thus it seems that if we examine the cognitive dimension of the relation between philosophy and literature, there may be observable tendencies in the relation of the two discourses over our period, but these cannot be easily generalised. The contributions to this volume suggest rather the practical validation of a position occupied recently by Andrew Bowie in *From Romanticism to Critical Theory*.[7] Himself arguing from both the Adornian and the analytical perspectives on aesthetics, Bowie suggests in an argument aimed primarily against Eagleton's Marxist dismissal of the aesthetic as ideological compensation[8] that the aesthetic does indeed possess the dignity of critical and philosophical cognition. This is thanks to the tradition of metaphorical disclosure of truth which Bowie finds in the early Romantics, and it is this mode of meta-philosophical aesthetic cognition which he argues to be the basis of Adorno's theory.

But this does not lead Bowie to the Adornian position. Rather, he – in concert with others such as Arthur Danto[9] – argues for the existence of a *spectrum* of cognitive potential *across* generic speech-act divisions between philosophy and literature, so that conceivably literary texts may offer philosophical insights and philosophical texts literary embodiments of truth. It is a latitudinarian stance of which Peter Stern would thoroughly have approved.

NOTES

1 J. P. Stern, *Re-interpretations. Seven studies in nineteenth-century German literature*, 2nd edn (Cambridge: Cambridge University Press, 1981; 1st edn 1964), p. 158.
2 Hermann August Korff, *Geist der Goethezeit. Versuch einer ideellen Entwicklung der klassisch-romantischen Literaturgeschichte*, 4 vols. (Leipzig: Weber, 1923; Leipzig: Koehler und Amelang, 1953).
3 Nicholas Boyle, 'Kantian and other elements in Goethe's "Vermächtniß"', *MLR* 73 (1978), 532–49.
4 Géza von Molnár, *Goethes Kantstudien* (Weimar: Hermann Böhlaus Nachfolger, 1994).
5 See for example Malcolm Pasley (ed.), *Nietzsche. Imagery and thought* (Berkeley: University of California Press, 1984), Manfred Frank, *Einführung in die frühromantische Ästhetik* (Frankfurt am Main: Suhrkamp, 1989) and Andrew Bowie, *From Romanticism to Critical Theory. The philosophy of German literary theory* (London, New York: Routledge, 1997).
6 Stern, *Re-interpretations*, pp. 3f.
7 See note 5.
8 See Terry Eagleton, *The ideology of the aesthetic* (Oxford: Blackwell, 1990).
9 See Arthur C. Danto, 'Philosophy as/and/of literature', in *The philosophical disenfranchisement of art* (New York: Columbia University Press, 1986), pp. 135–61.

CHAPTER ONE

Criticism and experience: philosophy and literature in the German Enlightenment

John A. McCarthy

Selbst die philosophische Wahrheit, die auf die Erleuchtung des Verstandes zielet, kan uns nicht gefallen, wenn sie nicht neu und unbekannt ist.[1]

Was endlich die *Deutlichkeit* betrifft, so hat der Leser ein Recht, zuerst die *diskursive* (logische) *Deutlichkeit, durch Begriffe*, denn aber auch eine *intuitive* (ästhetische) *Deutlichkeit*, durch *Anschauungen*, d. i. Beispiele oder andere Erläuterungen, in concreto zu fodern.[2]

PREAMBLE: MAPPING THE TERRAIN

To write an introductory chapter on philosophy, literature, and Enlightenment in the eighteenth century is a daunting task. Realistically, one can offer at best a blueprint for reading individual works of the eighteenth century. Since Pythagoras, Aristotle and Plato, thinkers have had a direct and above all an indirect impact on the intellectual life of subsequent generations in every sphere. It was no different for René Descartes (1596–1650), John Locke (1632–1704), Anthony Ashley Cooper, Earl of Shaftesbury (1671–1713), Benedictus de Spinoza (1632–77), Gottfried Wilhelm Leibniz (1646–1714), Charles de Montesquieu (1689–1755), Jean-Jacques Rousseau (1712–88) or Claude Adrien Helvétius (1715–71). These thinkers launched scholarly debates which spilled over into the more general realm of literature and the public sphere, giving birth to what the Swiss aesthetician Johann Jacob Breitinger (1701–76) labelled *ars popularis* (popular art) around 1740. Fifty years later Christian Garve (1742–98) lauded this style and tone as the best approach for reaching the majority of educated readers – whether of literature or philosophy.[3] Popularity in this sense was grounded in the desire to be read outside the academy and to be of practical use.

Moreover, the easy conjoining of philosophy–literature–Enlightenment masks certain residual difficulties. Of course, philosophy is a branch of literature in as far as philosophy is written. But philosophy does not have to be written, while literature does. Even when it is committed to paper (which is most often), we would not readily describe philosophy as being literary. Philosophy does not *eo ipso* involve communication, while literature can hardly dispense with an actual or imaginary reader in the realisation of its intent. A philosopher philosophises first and foremost alone; the writer writes in the hope of communication with an other. Minimally, Enlightenment is the search for truth and the endeavour to express it in words. Metaphorically, it is an incandescence and the diffusion of light into previously dark corners. The process of *éclairer* – inherent in the common designations for the era: Enlightenment, *Aufklärung, les Lumières* – can occur either via philosophy or via literature. In the first case (as seen from the perspective of the solitary seeker) it is likely to be self-enlightenment, in the second (seen from the perspective of the writer) enlightenment of others. Rarely, however, do the two occur separately, even though philosophy in the Age of Reason took a big step towards professionalisation as an independent discipline just as literature captured a large share of the public sphere and evolved towards an autonomous ideal of its own function. The combination of philosophy and literature in the project of the *Aufklärung* amounts basically to a kind of messy mathematics: rigorous logic is coupled with explanatory metaphor. The supreme example of this is Gotthold Ephraim Lessing's (1729–81) early theory of the fable, and its reincarnation in his final plea for religious and cultural tolerance in the fairy-tale-like parable of the three rings situated at the centre of his didactic play, *Nathan der Weise* (1779; *Nathan the wise*). The latter epitomises the epoch.

'Philosophy' derives from the Greek 'philo' and 'sophia': love of wisdom. Wisdom is essentially related to the art of living so as to maximise happiness. It requires conscious reflection. It did not originally refer to formalistic logic and abstract reasoning, but rather precisely to that which Adolph von Knigge (1751–96) offered up with his popular book on social conduct, *Über den Umgang mit Menschen* (1788; *On human conduct*): philosophy as practical wisdom. Literature derives from the Latin 'littera' and 'litteratura'. The former means 'letter', 'mark' or 'sign'; the latter the alphabet, lettered writing. Of course lettered writing can be used to express philosophical thought, although the modern understanding of literature in the narrower sense emphasises not merely acquaintance with letters and books, but polite or human learning and, more essentially, literary culture. In short, enhanced sociability ('Geselligkeit'). While systematic philosophy in its pure form focuses on the (closed) system and often remains distant from practical matters and inaccessible to a wider audience, literature embraces practical needs and seeks a broader public. Occasionally, the latter celebrates an inquisitive indeterminacy and complexity of meaning in an aesthetically pleasing manner. This is due, at least in part, to the new connotations of 'littera' as 'cipher' or 'hieroglyph' or 'signature' of something concealed or not fully present. One commonly ascribes the origins of this semantic shift to Johann Georg Hamann (1730–88), Johann Gottfried Herder (1744–1803), Lessing and especially Karl Philipp Moritz (1756–93).[4] Whereas one normally turns to philosophy for truth, literature is the preferred choice for the pleasure of its heuristic encirclements and self-reflexive ramifications. Moreover, philosophy has split into a practical and a theoretical branch, the latter enjoying greater prestige today. However, the actual praxis of doing philosophy in the eighteenth century was not very far removed from composing literature. Philosophers wrote literature; writers engaged in philosophical discourse.[5]

The demarcation between the two fields of agency is therefore not always distinct. This is due not just to the attitudes of the writer but also to the metaphorical style adopted and the genre preferred (dialogue, letter, review, essay, fable, narrative). The best-known representative of the Enlightenment in Germany, Immanuel Kant (1724–1804), merely summarised a basic trait of the epoch when he decisively argued against a separation of procedure and style in the doing of philosophy. Strikingly, he argued the point in the preface to one of his most difficult prose works, the *Kritik der reinen Vernunft* ([1]1781, [2]1787; *Critique of pure reason*). There he saliently remarked that his reader could expect conceptual clarity through discursive logic in tandem with intuitive or aesthetic clarity based on concrete examples and metaphors.[6] In short, strategies of abstract conceptualisation and aesthetic expression are drawn upon equally. The quotations at the head of this chapter are chosen to draw attention to the fundamental fact of a 'messy mathematics' when exploring the relationships among philosophy, literature and Enlightenment. The rapprochement between critical inquiry and literary expression is a chief hallmark of eighteenth-century intellectual and literary life with its maxim of intuitive thinking.[7] It was in many ways the 'business' of the Enlightenment.[8] In any event, philosophy was enlightenment.

The mission of the Enlightenment was to spread light through the use of print media: the light of reason was inscribed in books, books influenced books, readers began to see more clearly, and hopefully to act more reasonably, that is, wisely, prudently. The goal of philosophy in this sense was happiness here on earth, not the prospect of some transcendental reward.[9] The Enlightenment was driven by an inherent optimism and belief in the goodness of the human being as it drew on the past and spread through the present working towards a better future by combating ignorance and prejudice. It was, to adapt a term of the German Romantics, a kind of progressive universalisation, but based in reason.[10]

Yet true Enlightenment is not canonically encapsulated in the culture of the printed word, which the young Herder and the *Sturm und Drang* Storm and Stress) writers of 1767–82 abhorred. Strikingly, that protest came precisely at the moment when the *Aufklärung* was about to reach full expression in Immanuel Kant's *Kritik der reinen Vernunft*, and specifically in his seminal essay 'Beantwortung der Frage: was ist Aufklärung?' (1784; 'Answer to the question: what is Enlightenment?'). As a radical form of *Aufklärung*, the *Sturm und Drang* movement represented an emphatic turn to the original Enlightenment ideal of individual self-determination and a turning away from the more ideologically tinged mission of a self-enlightened person actively seeking to educate others to self-determination. It could draw inspiration from the young Lessing's indictment of bookishness and the exhortation to study real life in his early comedy, *Der junge Gelehrte* (1748; *The young scholar*). That insistence upon individual experience could also draw upon the liberating emotional thrust of Pietism (a subjectivist form of Christian devotion) and its later secular cousin, *Empfindsamkeit* (1740–80; sentimentality), which gave rise to such psychological (auto)biographies as Adam Bernd's *Eigene Lebensbeschreibung* (1738; *Description of my life*) and Johann Heinrich Jung-Stilling's *Lebensgeschichte* (1777–8; *Heinrich Stilling's life story*). The original exhortation to release oneself from the shackles of prejudice and habit evolved into the call to enlighten others through literature and through one's own experience. Yet inherent in the extension of philosophy to literature was the threat to 'true' philosophy and 'true' Enlightenment. Committed to print, once-vital concepts flattened out and lent themselves to dogmatic misuse. The discursive nature of literary culture was supposed to serve as an antidote against ideological rigidity, because the dynamism of the bond between writer and reader (especially after around 1760) demanded flexibility. As mere theory or merely insistent information without true communication, philosophy ceases to be philosophy in the Enlightenment's meaning of an active quest for truth. Lessing aptly formulated the nature of that dynamic quest at the beginning of his *Eine Duplik* (1778; *A riposte*). That is why Kant himself defined his times as the 'age of Enlightenment' and not as an 'enlightened age' in his famous essay of 1784, that is, an age of progressing toward a goal, not one of having attained it. Thus, Peter Gay concludes, 'philosophy as criticism demanded constant vigilance'.[11]

Aimed at self-determination and at the spread of this ideal to others, the Enlightenment thus had (and still has) a dual mission. Essentially ethical in nature, it entails a pedagogical, political, even a militant dimension. The path to the goal also has a dual focus: on reason (with both faculties of 'Vernunft' and 'Verstand'), and on virtue. While reason ('Vernunft') represented for the Enlighteners the highest mental faculty, the understanding ('Verstand') had more immediate practical application. Enlightenment was thus a matter of reasoning (albeit with a shift from the primitive reasoning faculty of 'Verstand' to the discursive reasoning faculty of 'Vernunft') and consequently a question of norms. Virtue in its original meaning of fitness as human being and citizen of the state gave way in the late Enlightenment to the notion of freedom framed both in terms of duty ('Pflicht') and right ('Recht').[12] Friedrich Schiller's (1759–1805) aesthetic project in the 1790s adds the concept of inclination ('Neigung') in emphatic fashion so that the confluence of duty and inclination leads to the idea of the beautiful soul, the most perfect union of virtue and freedom. Whether expressed in terms of the good burgher, the enlightened despot, the poetic genius, the wise Jew or the beautiful soul, the common root is traceable to an overriding message of virtue.[13]

Kant's dubbing of his epoch the 'age of criticism' in the preface to his *Kritik der reinen Vernunft* – he meant the art of critical self-reflection according to the rules of logic and open discourse – is well known. Less well known is Johann Gottfried Herder's formulation in his programmatic *Journal meiner Reise im Jahr 1769* (1810–20/1846; *Journal of my travels in the year 1769*) to characterise his times: the 'age of experience'.[14] Herder meant the term negatively, to designate received notions inherent in the social structures, civil administration, religious customs and social conventions of his day. From these tired practices and intractable forms he wished to move the focus back to organic processes as the source of personal and even cultural development. Echoing Spinoza, he argued that everything was rooted in nature. It was human creative genius as much as empirical observation which promised to unlock the secrets of existence. Because of his insistence on personal experience over received 'experience', he placed great emphasis on the reading act as an animated conversation with the author. If reading is not dialogical and inspired, 'it is nothing!' (JGH IV, 461). It was a typical assessment of the age.

Both Herder and Kant struggled to correlate body and mind in understanding nature and in cultivating the human spirit. These two labels – reason and experience, one by the dominant systematic philosopher of the eighteenth century, the other by one of its most iconoclastic thinkers – capture the philosophical and literary tensions of the German Enlightenment. Resonating with both Cartesian rationalism ('cogito, ergo sum'; 'I reflect, therefore I am') and Charles Bonnet's (1720–93) sensibility ('je sens, donc je suis'; 'I feel, therefore I am'), Kant's critique of reason and Herder's focus on the human experience of nature highlight the individual subject ('ego', 'je') as the centre of scrutiny and the agent of reform. These tendencies of rationalism and sensualism – of the theoretical and the practical – are discernible throughout the age. That epoch was marked not by the human understanding alone, but also by the heart, which had its own reasons to believe in a better future and had its own access to knowledge. Even Kant admitted his project was rooted in a '*belief*' in the ultimate power of reason. As Pascal put it: 'Nous connaissons la vérité, non seulement par la raison, mais encore par le cœur'.[15] These major tendencies form the basis of the two greatest novels of development from the era, Christoph Martin Wieland's (1733–1813) *Die Geschichte des Agathon* (1766–7; *The history of Agathon*) and Goethe's *Wilhelm Meisters Lehrjahre* (1795–6; *Wilhelm Meister's years of apprenticeship*).

The literary and aesthetic revolution with its far-reaching consequences began with Christian Thomasius (1655–1728), reached an early zenith with literary theorists Johann Christoph Gottsched (1700–66), Johann Jacob Bodmer (1698–1783) and Johann Jacob Breitinger, was radicalised by Hamann and Herder, and found classic expression in Lessing, Wieland, Moses Mendelssohn (1729–86), Moritz, Goethe and Schiller. Those literary developments as seen against the philosophical thought of early (1680–1740), middle (1740–80) and late Enlightenment (1780–1800) are the focus of this chapter. History (the Glorious Revolution in Great Britain in 1688, the American War of Independence in 1776, and the French Revolution of 1789), philosophy and New Science all led to new ways of seeing in philosophy, art and literature. While there may not be a direct path leading from the Hamburg patrician-poet Barthold Heinrich Brockes (1680–1747) to the quintessential poet of the age, Goethe, there is a connection between the empirically inspired *Irdisches Vergnügen in Gott* (1721–48; *Earthly pleasure in God*) of the former, where he reads nature like a book, and the nature poetry of the latter, where nature mirrors the poet's inner being. 'Really to know something', Goethe averred in the introduction to his journal *Propyläen* (1797), 'one must look very carefully' ('Was man weiß, sieht man erst!'). To be sure, Brockes saw in natural phenomena signs directing the observer outward to the transcendental, while Goethe interpreted those signs as directing us inward deeper into nature itself and back into the soul of the observer. This apprehension of nature as sign is related to Moritz's concept of signature in the essay 'Die Signatur des Schönen' (1788–9; 'The signature of the beautiful'), which he also expressed in different terms in his seminal essay 'Über die bildende Nachahmung des Schönen' (1788; 'On the imitation of the beautiful in the fine arts'): as the experience of that which is complete unto itself. If nature was the crucible, *seeing* was the art.

The emphasis on seeing and reflecting which emerged from that fundamentally new epistemology led to the founding at mid-century of a separate discipline of aesthetics. One readily thinks of Georg Friedrich Meier's (1718–77) *Anfangsgründe aller schönen Wissenschaften* (1748; *The elements of belles lettres*), Alexander Gottlieb Baumgarten's (1714–62) *Aesthetica* (1750–8), Johann Joachim Winckelmann's (1717–68) *Gedanken über die Nachahmung griechischer Werke in der Malerei und Bildhauerei* (1755; *Thoughts on the imitation of Greek works in the plastic arts*), Moses Mendelssohn's *Betrachtungen über die Quellen und die Verbindungen der schönen Künste und Wissenschaften* (1757; *Reflections on the origins and the interconnections of the fine arts and belles lettres*), Lessing's *Laokoon* (1766) and Johann Georg Sulzer's (1720–79) *Allgemeine Theorie der schönen Künste* (1771–4; *General theory of the fine arts*). Widely received, these works occasioned a long and vigorous debate. Aesthetics arose in response to French, English and German theorists such as Charles Batteux (1713–80), Rousseau, Helvétius, Shaftesbury, Joseph Addison (1672–1719), Edward Young (1683–1765), David Hume (1711–76), Francis Hutcheson (1694–1746), Christian Wolff (1679–1754), Breitinger and many others. The debates on the nature of the beautiful and the sublime, on the differences between literature and the plastic arts, on the Aristotelian concepts of fear and pity in tragedy, on the wondrous and the monstrous took place concurrently with the rise of the modern domestic novel, the evolution of the bourgeois drama (e.g. *Emilia Galotti*, 1772), and the popularity of 'Erlebnisdichtung' ('poetry of personal experience').

Meier, for example, combined Baumgarten's rational aesthetics with the evocativeness of sensibility in a move towards what we now call reception aesthetics. Mendelssohn grounded pleasure both in the beauty of external arrangement and in the perfection of inner moral ordering; he thus provided an initial argument for the autonomy of the aesthetic experience. Especially influential were Winckelmann and Lessing. Winckelmann re-established *kalokagathia* ('the good and the beautiful') as the anthropological ideal with its qualities of 'edle Einfalt und stille Größe' ('noble simplicity and quiet grandeur'). Lessing identified the essence of aesthetic experience, whether in the fine arts or belles lettres, as residing in movement either implicit or explicit, since nature is always changing. Thus it is incumbent upon the artist to allow the imagination free reign in order to experience the full effect of emotional evocation.[16] This insight marks a major juncture in the general history of aesthetics; namely, construction ('Werkästhetik') on the one hand and textual reception ('Wirkungsästhetik') on the other.[17]

As a consequence, Lessing urges the artist to think 'in transitions' ('transitorisch denken'), in keeping with the movement of nature (*LW* III, 22). In literature this appears in the chronological sequence of action. In the fine arts it is embodied in the configuration of shapes and colours in space. Because of the lack of overt movement in the fine arts, the artist must focus on the moment most pregnant with significance, one which insinuates foregoing and succeeding action frozen in the moment chosen for portrayal (89–90). Dramatic art is thus 'die lebendige Malerei des Schauspielers' (25, 'the living painting of the actor'); utilising time and space to realise its movement, dramatic art stands between the fine arts and poetry (*LW* II, 144). The suffering of the tragic hero is not physical but spiritual – the very point made in regard to the Laokoon group. Thus Emilia Galotti's suffering, for example, is not physical but moral. From this it follows that the sensations of 'Furcht' (fear) and 'Mitleid' (compassion) – which as Lessing argues must be combined in the same individual and conjoined with love in order for the observer to experience their full effect – are essentially related to the dynamic principle. Compassion is aroused at the sight of undeserved suffering; fear is possible only if we can see ourselves in the tragic figure; that is, if the tragic figure is a mixed character, neither a paragon of virtue nor a black-hearted villain (*LW* II, 420, 446). The purpose of fear and compassion in tragedy is to bring about a cathartic response in the spectator, to purify the emotions and transform passion into virtuous acts: Aristotle's 'philanthropy' (427, 434).

The awareness of the moment of receptivity and the importance of the recipient's interactive response to the aesthetic stimulus to realise its full intent is amply obvious in Lessing's now classic interpretation. One commonly speaks of 'productive reception'. However, there is a prehistory leading up to the innovative moves by Meier, Mendelssohn and

Lessing. That prehistory – largely ignored, yet intriguing and innovative in its own right – is the focus of the remainder of this chapter. What one should not expect, however, is an exclusive focus on the aesthetic debates of the era. Our topic is much broader. Moreover, the reader will search in vain for a discussion of the 'underside' of the Enlightenment. The monstrous, the un-beautiful, the terrifying as aesthetic categories belong to a different discussion, the participants in which no longer believe in the salutary powers of reason and imagination and have lost confidence in man's goodness and nature's benevolence.[18]

In what follows the central themes revolve around the poles of criticism and experience and are summed up by the three guiding principles of Enlightenment inquiry as expressed in Kant's *Kritik der reinen Vernunft*: 'Was kann ich wissen?' ('What can I know?'); 'Was soll ich tun?' ('What should I do?'); 'Was darf ich hoffen?' ('What may I hope for?') (K IV, 677). The first ('kann') is speculative in nature and underscores epistemological limits. The second ('soll') is practical and foregrounds the ethical component of human actions. The third ('darf') is both theoretical and practical, because the inquiry into what one should do is premised on the assumption that there is some transcendental good which answers the query: 'What should I do?' These queries should act as a beacon, lighting the path from start to finish. The goal of human development is the attainment of happiness and inner tranquillity. In the following, then, the German philosophers Thomasius, Leibniz, Wolff, Hamann and Herder will be highlighted.

To pre-empt our conclusion: philosophy and literature in the Age of Enlightenment were epistemic tools for exploring the self, the limits of knowledge, the vocation of man, the inner workings of nature, for explaining the body–mind problematic and for establishing the appropriate relationship between individual freedom and social duty. The vocation or destiny of man remained a primary concern from Johann Joachim Spalding's (1714–1804) *Betrachtung über die Bestimmung des Menschen* (1748; *Observations on the vocation of humankind*) to Johann Gottlieb Fichte's (1762–1814) *Bestimmung des Menschen* (1800; *Vocation of humankind*).[19] Unlike previous philosophical schools, the Enlightenment possessed a sustained, self-critical attitude which proved to be part and parcel of what it means to be human and what the limits of man's control of nature are. Since the German *Aufklärung* was initially centred at universities, (Halle, Leipzig, Göttingen), it succeeded in educating whole generations of lawyers, doctors, municipal administrators, court advisors, educators, professors, publishers and journalists to the new way of conceptualising the self and the world. That Enlightenment project of education and aestheticisation began in Saxony in the late seventeenth century with Christian Thomasius, the 'father' of the German Enlightenment; it found characteristic expression in Lessing's *Die Erziehung des Menschengeschlechts* (1781; *The education of the human race*) and continues into the present day as a 'significant force' (Troeltsch), as a *philosophia perennis* (Améry), a learning process aimed at studying the 'energies of the mind' (Cassirer), and as 'trust' (Schneiders) in the powers of reason.[20] An 'attitude of mind rather than a course in science and philosophy', the Enlightenment permeated all levels of intellectual pursuits.[21] Thus Norbert Hinske speaks of its 'programmatic character', whereas Peter Gay emphasises that the Enlightenment was more a 'Revolt against Rationalism' than an 'Age of Reason'.[22]

MONADOLOGY: A MODERN ONTOLOGY

A certain continuity from the Reformation to the *Aufklärung* is discernible. For one thing, the Protestant work ethic remained intact. For another, the humanistic emphasis on education and development of human potential lost none of its attractiveness. From Leibniz, Thomasius, Wolff and Spalding to Kant and Fichte, the Enlightenment sought to define human destiny in clear, universally valid, anthropological terms, and not in psychologically individualistic ones. Two cardinal models held sway: that of the quietist and that of the activist. Through contemplation and meditation on the transcendental good and denial of the material body, the introverted quietist sought to move closer to the divine and thus achieve human perfection. The activist sought to achieve perfection through wilful engagement with the world. This duality is reminiscent of Martin Luther's distinction between the inner and the outer man, whereby the outer must be subordinate to the inner. That goal is to be achieved by abstinence, fasting, and denial of the flesh in general. A primary duty of humankind on earth was to love and serve one's fellows. That service was an end in itself, not a means to an end. Similarly, as a citizen of a particular state, one's task was to be a good and useful citizen by executing one's duties and professional responsibilities for the general welfare. The individual's value as a Christian was measured by the degree of empathetic love for one's neighbour, while the individual's value as a citizen was measured in terms of utility within the community.[23] In the seventeenth century it was the courtier, not the burgher, who felt a need for *Bildung* (education, development). The latter was consigned to obedience. At the turn of the century, there was not yet any philosophical justification for a civil vocation of humankind. Neither courtly philosophy, with its disdain of bourgeois values, nor academic scholasticism, with its speculative thrust, proved to be appropriate guides for the emergent ideals of practicality and productivity within the growing middle classes. The early Enlightenment thus had a dual objective: to recast the vocation of the human race as *vita activa* and to legitimise middle-class virtues as the higher values. The attempt at legitimisation has a speculative moment in Leibniz's theory of monads and a practical side in Thomasius's concept of wisdom.

Leibniz was the most significant pre-Kantian German philosopher, and the influence of his system was magnified thanks to its popularisation by the Leipzig professors Wolff and Gottsched. Wieland, Lessing, Herder, Goethe and Schiller were among those who acknowledged their debt to him. Combining theological concepts of teleology with natural philosophy, Leibniz constructed a rationalistic system to resolve the Cartesian duality of the body–soul problem. By positing a pre-established harmony since the birth of the universe between spirit and matter which is rooted in the dynamic principle of becoming ('Werden'), Leibniz ushered in a new union between mechanistic nature and Christian belief. His is a systematic undertaking to reveal the unity of the world by conjoining theodicy, ethics, metaphysics and natural philosophy in a single vision.[24]

Perhaps Leibniz's most seminal and representative work is the *Monadology* (L, 179–94), written in 1714. It contains the culmination of his thinking about substance, and provides the basis for a powerful reductionist metaphysics underlying his entire philosophical system.[25] Penned as a succinct introduction to his longer and more elaborate treatise on the place of evil in a divinely ordained universe, *Theodicy* (1710; *Essais de théodicée sur la bonté de Dieu, la liberté de l'homme et l'origine du mal*), the *Monadology* was first published posthumously in a German translation in 1720. The main themes elaborated in this slim work are central to understanding the entire following epoch: (1) the concept of organic growth; (2) the notion of perfectibility; (3) optimism or the notion of the best of all possible worlds; (4) the idea that being is actually becoming; (5) the concept of diversity as a fundamental characteristic of unity; and (6) self-reflexivity as the telos (goal or purpose) of human existence. The inherent optimism of this theory is grounded on the one hand in the principle of self-determination of each monad (and therefore of each individual human being) and on the other in the positing of a telos toward which all monads evolve. That telos is anchored in a transcendent being with which the individual sentient monads are in contact.

Defined as indivisible substance, the smallest in creation, the monad is so to speak without windows (§7). Each is marked by its own unique characteristics (individuality) and evolves according to its own internal principle at its own pace towards the fulfilment of its internal principle (§§10–11). Although simple, i.e. without parts, the monad nonetheless contains a plethora of internal affections and relations. These explain the principle of internal transformations, i.e., the degrees by which a thing changes and a thing remains the same (§13) without direct influence on its internal workings from another monad.[26] A dialectic of exertion and passivity characterises that process (§52). Neither essentially material in nature nor subject to externally deterministic laws, the monad thus appears as the expression of the principle of self-realisation. Leibniz uses garden, plant and animal metaphors to illustrate this (§§67, 74). While every monad is different (§9), operating like organic matter (§§71–3) or germinating seeds (§74), its nature is representative, and is thus a mirror of the universe as a whole. As such the individual monads are connected directly to God, 'who is the cause of this correspondence between their phenomena', and thus are indirectly connected to one another. Otherwise 'there would be no interconnexion' (L, 27).

Actually, there is no completely new beginning in nature, 'for monads can only begin or end all at once' – by creation or annihilation (§6). Rather, a non-linear rejuvenation obtains, so that living forms constitute an encompassing unity of the whole: 'not only will there be no birth, but also no complete destruction, no death' in the world (§76). That is because 'there is no waste, nothing sterile, nothing lifeless in the universe; no chaos, no confusion, save in appearance' (§69). When body and soul are conjoined, each functions independently according to its own evolutionary principles; yet each acts as if its 'twin' did not exist (§81), for body and soul co-operate according to a pre-established harmony (§78). In its self-conscious form, the monad is more properly an 'entelechy' (§18) and as such is a reflection of the primary unity (§47), of the Deity or formative energy expressed as knowledge and will (§48), which is the final grounding of all existence (§§39–44). Knowledge of necessary and eternal truths leads via a process of abstraction to 'reflexive acts'. These reflexive acts are the chief objects of reason and distinguish humans from other sentient beings. By directing perception at the self, humans form an awareness of an 'I'. Leibniz equates this self-consciousness to the essence of humanity, its 'substance': 'in thinking of ourselves, we think of being, of substance, of the simple and the compound, of the immaterial and of God himself' (§30). As the 'Supreme Substance' (§40) or 'Necessary Being' (§45), God is the unlimited expression of all that is finite in us. These sections are an echo of his earlier essay, 'Of an *organum* or *ars magna* of thinking' (c. 1679), where Leibniz had asserted: 'The most powerful of human faculties is the *power of thinking*'. Indeed, the cultivation of self-reflexive reason constitutes 'the supreme happiness of man', because fully developed reason equates to 'the greatest possible increase in his perfection' (L, 1). Virtue and happiness are thus equated with 'an active progressive attitude', in which we not only apprehend the world's inherent tendency toward ever greater perfection, but also replicate it through our own deeds and interactions with others to advance them toward perfection as well.[27] In this regard, Leibniz echoes a main tenet of Spinoza (*Ethics*, pp. 93, 199). He also clearly provides a basis of the later *Bildungsroman*.

While God is necessary, humans are 'accidental'. Because the mind of God is the region whence all essences and realised manifestations spring and in which all future imaginable manifestations reside (§43), it guarantees the legitimacy of the imagination and the wondrous (§44). In fact, that which is thinkable, imaginable and possible has the right to insist upon its realisation (§54). Given that supposition, Leibniz concludes that polyperspectivity – diversity – is the hallmark of creation, although there is but one universe (§57). Thus the greater the diversity, the higher the degree of order (§58). Perfection is nothing other than the relative magnitude of the positive realisation of an infinite potential, because the absolute realisation of that infinite potential is possible in God alone (§41).[28] In 'A résumé of metaphysics' (c. 1697), which summarises the main theses of *On the ultimate origination of things* (1697), Leibniz had averred: '*everything possible demands existence*, inasmuch as it is founded on a necessary being which actually exists, and without which there is no way by which something possible may arrive at actuality' (L, 145). The 'dominant Unity of the universe', he adds, 'not only rules the world, but also constructs or makes it; and it is higher than the world and, if I may so put it, extramundane; it is thus the ultimate reason of things' (L, 136). Subsequently, this principle of the unity in the multiplicity of all actual and especially possible worlds becomes the cornerstone of the new eighteenth-century aesthetics with its emphasis on the quantifiability of unity in multiplicity.[29] The direct link to the Deity (and thus the Unity) is the intellect with its unique faculty of imagination. The repeated process of endeavouring to reveal the infinitely possible leads through Bodmer's

and Breitinger's theory of the imagination around 1730 to its literary realisation in Wieland's novel, *Don Sylvio von Rosalva* (1764), and his *Komische
Erzählungen* (1762; *Comic tales*), to Goethe's quintessential truth seeker,
Faust, at century's end. The notion of God as the site of all manifestations past, present and future points forward to the myth of the eternally
creative Mothers in *Faust II* (1831; lines 6283–9).

Transposed to the political realm, the monadology suggests a model
for enlightened monarchy. Sentient beings are related to the Deity like
the sons to the father or the subjects to the monarch. The assemblage
of all sentient beings under the leadership of the most perfect of rulers
would constitute the City of God (§85). In that perfect state, the moral
world and the natural world would exist in harmony (§86). As architect
of the world-machine and as the lawgiver in the spiritual realm of grace,
God has created a unified system which necessarily leads from the realm
of nature to grace, forgiveness, salvation and unity (§88). If we emphasise
the moral freedom of each subject in the state so that no one is used
instrumentally and all are equal, we can recognise here the framework
for Schiller's aesthetic state as formulated in his *Über die ästhetische Erziehung
des Menschen* (1795; *On the aesthetic education of humankind*). Moreover Leibniz
suggests, in a manner seemingly anticipating Schiller's view of nemesis
in his philosophical poem 'Resignation' (1782) or his classical trilogy
Wallenstein (1799), that world history passes its own moral judgement
by containing its own rewards and punishments (§89). Even Wieland's
philosophical novels, *Agathon* and *Agathodämon* (1799; *Agathodaemon*) could
be approached from the perspective of Leibnizian ontology.

The final article of the *Monadology* gives rise to perhaps the greatest
legacy, for it is here that Leibniz speaks of the best of all possible worlds,
stating: 'if we could sufficiently understand the order of the universe, we
should find that it surpasses all the desires of the most wise, and that it is
impossible to make it better than it is' (§90). Ignoring the disclaimer at the
beginning of this statement, first Voltaire in *Candide* (1759), then Johann
Karl Wezel in his novel, *Belphegor oder die unwahrscheinlichste Geschichte der
Welt* (1776; *Belphegor or the most unlikely tale in the world*) bitingly satirised the
Leibnizian concept of the best of all possible worlds.[30]

Moreover, Leibniz argues that love forms the cornerstone of his optimistic ontology (§90). The Deity has created the world just as it should
be and He has done so out of pure love, the kind that allows participation
in the joy of the loved one. The wise and virtuous, Leibniz avers, will
attend to all that which appears to coincide with the suspected or predetermined Divine Will, but will nonetheless be content with that which

God actually provides in his mysterious ways (§90). Inherent in this view are the keystone virtues of happiness and contentment which mark Enlightenment literature from Haller's didactic poem *Die Alpen* (1729; *The Alps*), Schnabel's 'Robinsonade' *Insel Felsenburg* (1731; *Felsenburg Island*), Hagedorn's narrative poem 'Johann der muntere Seifensieder' (1738; 'Johann the cheerful soapmaker'), Gellert's novel *Das Leben der schwedischen Gräfin von G**** (1747; *The life of the Swedish Countess of G****), Sophie von La Roche's *Das Fräulein von Sternheim* (1771; *Miss Sternheim*), to Lessing's epoch-making play *Nathan der Weise* and Wieland's aforementioned novels of development. Even Schiller's early philosophical essay 'Theosophie des Julius' (1786; 'Julius's theosophy') echoes these fundamental views of sympathetic response to others as the cornerstone of happiness in the realisation of human potential.

Leibniz's ontology also underlies Schiller's concept of the historical moment as the product of all that has gone before and the result of no simple linear causal relationship. It would be fascinating to do a comparison of the concepts of history in the *Monadology* (§22) and Schiller's inaugural Jena lecture as Professor of History, 'Was heißt und zu welchem Ende studiert man Universalgeschichte?' (1789; 'What is and to what purpose does one study universal history?'). One could, of course, point to Kant's 'Idee zu einer allgemeinen Geschichte in weltbürgerlicher Absicht' (1784; 'Idea for a universal history from a cosmopolitan point of view') as the immediate catalyst, yet Kant himself stands in a tradition dating from Leibniz, as is obvious from the opening passage of that famous essay (*PW*, 249).

Then too the polyvalence of Goethe's *Wilhelm Meister* might be seen through the lens of Leibniz's monadology. Wilhelm Meister's self-directed development evolves according to its own inner inscription, yet is nudged along or distracted momentarily from its predestined course by the great array of characters Wilhelm meets along the way (the Abbé, Marianne, Lothario, Jarno, the beautiful soul, Natalie, Mignon, the Harper, Theresa, Friedrich, etc.). The centrepiece of the novel, 'Bekenntnisse einer schönen Seele' ('Confessions of a beautiful soul'; Book 6), contains some of the clearest formulations on the concept of development (*Bildung*), the dynamic principle, the inherent goodness of the instinct for perfectibility and the revelation of God in nature. Even granting the usual reference to Schiller to explain the confluence of 'Pflicht' (duty) and 'Neigung' (inclination) in the 'schöne Seele' (beautiful soul), it is difficult to ignore the echoes of Leibnizian ethics. All the while, however, the secret Tower Society is pulling the strings, so to speak, to ensure that each encounter contributes to Wilhelm's education, advancing him toward his ultimate destiny and integration into society. In this sense, the 'Turmgesellschaft' acts much like the 'Urmonade' in Leibniz's speculative system.

REASON, SENTIMENT AND THE *SUMMUM BONUM*

Christian Thomasius studied law and philosophy and lectured for ten years in philosophy at the University of Leipzig until he was censored for his views and forced to leave. Thus he experienced a fate similar to Pierre Bayle (1647–1706) in The Hague. Thomasius is important because of his popularising influence, but also because he did not separate reason and revelation as Bayle did, although theology and philosophy were kept separate. In 1687 he caused a minor furore in Leipzig by lecturing in German rather than in the traditional Latin of the scholar. His topic was one of immediate concern: 'In welcher Gestalt solle man denen Frantzosen im gemeinen Leben und Wandel nachahmen?' ('What is the proper form for imitating the French in the round of everyday life?'). Thomasius's response is to foreground the ideal of the *honnête homme* who is marked by all that is good, noble, and honest in human interaction. Aligned with the ideal man is the essence of gallantry, the *bon sens*. Strikingly – and this point is little noted in research on women's history – Thomasius offers the admission of women to university studies as the best prospect for achieving a reform of the German academy, for they, he says, have not been spoiled or misled as have their male counterparts.

Yet more significant for our particular purposes with regard to the spread of Enlightenment and the popularisation of its ideals is Thomasius's eclectic approach to style and content. Rejecting the scholastic philosophy of his day as too speculative, he pleaded for an entertaining approach in doing philosophy. This new model he developed through reading and criticising narrative literature. In his journalistic *Lustige und ernsthaffte Monats-Gespräche* (1688–90; *Witty and earnest monthly conversations*) he characterised his new, more effective style as being simultaneously useful and entertaining, thereby sounding the Horatian directive *prodesse et delectare*. Such works are the best because they 'could be read by the greatest number of readers' (Hinske-Specht, 107). This exhortation echoed throughout the literature of the Enlightenment. Strikingly, Gottsched included his translation of Horace's *Ars poetica* (*The art of poetry*) in place of a preface to the fourth edition of his *Versuch einer critischen Dichtkunst* (1752, first edition 1730; *Essay on a theory of literature*), the first to have a more general impact. Hagedorn and Lange viewed Horace as the supreme authority around mid-century. Later in the century, Wieland turned to Horace's reflections on the aesthetic ideal in his epistle to the Pisones, translating it for a modern audience. The result was published in 1782 as *Horaz. Über die Dichtkunst (Horace. On poetry)* and quickly became the classical translation. In many ways it laid the groundwork for the aesthetic ideals of the emergent period of Weimar Classicism.

To be sure, Thomasius's more academic work is not composed in such a popular style. His *Vernunftlehre* (1691; *Logic*) contains his philosophical system. Perceiving that the parameters of philosophical knowledge have been set too wide, so that the results are unproductive, Thomasius proposes to redirect attention to the practical, ethical knowledge needed for a *vita activa*. In doing so, he redefined scholarly erudition ('Gelehrtheit') and transformed it into *Bildung*: 'Erudition is a recognition by means of which an individual is enabled to distinguish the true from the false, the good from evil. It makes him capable of understanding the essence of the true or, as the case may be, of proffering probable causes of it in order to advance his own temporal and eternal welfare and that of others in the flux of social life.'[31] Consequently, knowledge is not supposed to be its own end. Rejecting the notion of innate ideas, Thomasius sets aside deductive in favour of inductive logic based on experience and practicality. In this he echoes John Locke's rejection of innate ideas in his *Essay on human understanding* (1690) and points forward to Andreas Rüdiger's similar move in his *Philosophia pragmatica* (1723; *Pragmatic philosophy*).[32] Whatever is not manifest in nature itself is inaccessible to the mind. The essence of God cannot therefore be grasped by the intellect. The latter must be directed at problems of a practical and empirical kind in an effort to enhance one's usefulness and productivity. So employed, reason appears as 'sound or salubrious' ('gesund'). For this reason, Thomasius retains a belief in revelation as being separate from the operations of the mind. Obviously, then, he neither anticipates nor participates in the ensuing physico-theological movement which gripped many writers in the first decades of the eighteenth century, notably Brockes.

Yet the notion of sound reason forms the basis of much of Enlightenment thought. It evolved as the personal ideal promulgated in the literature of the era and served as the source of 'Popularphilosophie' which later took hold and held sway for decades. Sound reason knows its limits, seeks not to query abstract problems, and concerns itself only with those issues having an immediate bearing on one's functioning in society. In short, Thomasius's intention is to make philosophy socially acceptable by transforming it into an instrument of efficacy. As worldly wisdom ('Weltweisheit'), it is a matter of education through knowledge. Everything is subject to the scrutiny of reason except for logic itself and belief in external reality. As such salubrious reason cannot err. Errors arise rather through the moral degeneracy of humankind, through arrogance. Nonetheless, reason is not set up as the absolute guide, for Thomasius warns us against radical scepticism, pointing to an inner, deep-lying feeling of certainty. That inner, non-rational guide keeps the seeker on even keel. Here one is reminded of Agathon's pivotal response to the materialistic sceptic Hippias, who has just argued in the best Sophist tradition against the existence of God. Agathon does not need a long-drawn-out rational explanation; an inner instinct assures him that the Deity does exist, just as his senses convince him that the sun is warm and that his body is his. His conclusion? 'I feel, therefore I am.'[33] The presence of this innate feeling of certitude reveals that the Enlightenment did have an inherent proclivity to sensibility.[34]

By prioritising 'gesunde Vernunft' over speculative reason, Thomasius believed that he had created a transition from Spinoza's ethics of knowledge to an ethic of the active life. In his *Einleitung zur Sittenlehre* (1696; *Introduction to ethics*) Thomasius laid the foundation for the new ethic. Its highest goal is inner contentment or 'Ruhe des Gemütes', which he labels the *summum bonum* (Hinske-Specht, 49). Unlike Spinoza, who posited a harmony between the insights of reason and the action of the will (*Ethics*, 76; prop. xvix), Thomasius declared that the intellect could only show the way to the supreme good, whereas human will led man astray. Reason is good, while the will is deleterious or evil. Man lives up to his vocation, that is, actualises the *summum bonum*, when he seeks his freedom in nothing other than the service and advancement of his fellows.[35] Thomasius's characterisation of the supreme good contains a series of objectives aligned with the Enlightenment project in general: the fundamental sociability of the age, love of and service to one's fellow man as the leading principle in this sociability, the resultant obligation of tolerance, and the call for compassion.

Awareness of the social dependency of humankind Thomasius calls love. Anticipating Rousseau's reflections on the refinement of *amour de soi* through the sentiment of natural compassion by half a century (but setting the accents somewhat differently), Thomasius claims that love of one's fellow man is stronger than self-love, since one cannot do without one's fellow man. From this he concludes that love, not reason, is the true hallmark of humankind. Again the role of emotion, of feeling, in defining the human destiny is manifest. It is not a trait to be relegated simply to the sentimentalists, Lessing, Wieland or the *Sturm und Drang* generation. Everyone partakes of this sentiment, even the villainous. The difference between the villainous and the virtuous lies in the fact that the former erroneously believe that they prefer themselves to everyone else, whereas the virtuous know full well that others are more important than the self (Hinske-Specht, 50). The individual is obligated to nurture the villainous in the hope of transforming him into an instrument for the good in society at large. Presented with the choice between being a good citizen and a self-absorbed individual, the human being has a moral obligation to choose the former. Yet this decision cannot be imposed from without; it must be one's own personal choice. From this foregrounding of the social function follows the principle of equality of all burghers. For Thomasius, then, reason alone cannot lead to an active life; virtue requires brotherly love to motivate the will. Consequently, he retracts in the *Sittenlehre* (1696) his previous position in the *Vernunftlehre* (1691). Philanthropy, which is now identified with virtue, does not exist as such in the world. But it is a concept which dovetails with the socio-economic reality of the emergent middle classes. Bound to the ego, the will is necessarily instinct-driven. This situation caused a dilemma in that the will was constantly drawn to self-love ('Selbstliebe') and away from brotherly love ('Nächstenliebe'). To overcome this problem, Thomasius substituted the dictate to serve others ('Nächstendienst') for brotherly love. The *service* of one's fellow man foregrounded the active engagement for the general welfare as opposed to the more passive – and perhaps self-indulgent – *love* of one's fellow beings. By philosophically grounding human destiny in the active principle, Thomasius laid the foundation for the ensuing century.

This envisioning of the functions of reason and the will finds literary expression in early Enlightenment novels such as Schnabel's *Insel Felsenburg* and Gellert's *Leben der schwedischen Gräfin von G****. Moreover, the call to empathise with the suffering of others leads to Lessing's positing 'Mitleid' (compassion, pity) as the cornerstone of his new theory of tragedy developed in his correspondence with Mendelssohn and Friedrich Nicolai (1733–1811), *Briefwechsel über das Trauerspiel* (1759; *Letters on tragedy*). In November 1756 Lessing wrote to Nicolai: 'the most compassionate person is the best person, one who is most inclined to all social virtues and all kinds of generosity. Thus, whoever makes us compassionate makes us better and more virtuous, and tragedy that does the former, also accomplishes the latter, or – does the former in order to bring about the latter.'[36] For him compassion is the quintessentially social virtue. In making this move he rejects the classicistic view of the passions as dangerous without the guidance of reason and ascribes constitutive powers to sympathetic love, for it leads to benevolent acts.

In its sentimental form this ideology of compassion appears in Lessing's *Miß Sara Sampson* (1755), in Sophie La Roche's Richardsonian narrative of seduction *Das Fräulein von Sternheim*, and – in destructive form – in Goethe's *Die Leiden des jungen Werthers* (1774; *The sufferings of young Werther*). Lessing's *Nathan* is perhaps the definitive expression in a balanced form, for Nathan is the paragon of quiet understanding, selfless service, unconditional love of his fellow humans, insistence on inner tranquillity, and preference for the active over the contemplative life. Like Job before him – and in compliance with the subjection of the individual will to the Divine will – Nathan is wise because he finally recognises the inadequacy of human understanding in the face of inscrutable mysteries. Fittingly, both Agathon and Wilhelm Meister conclude their 'apprenticeships' with the knowledge that they can best fulfil their human destiny by applying their study of nature and of the human psyche in the service of others. While Agathon has aspirations of government service in Tarentum (despite his disastrous experiences in Syracuse), Wilhelm Meister ultimately decides upon a medical profession. Miss Sternheim devotes herself to the education of children and the betterment of women. All can be seen as literary formulations of the fundamental concept of the *summum bonum* advocated by Thomasius and others.

Spinoza had similarly expressed the supreme ideal of human perfection in his *Tractatus de intellectus emendatione* (1677; *Treatise on the correction of the intellect*), which is really a piece on how to use one's intellect. He averred that all humans yearn for more constancy in the search for perfection. The movement to that goal depends on individual and collaborative effort. Spinoza writes:

The supreme good, however, is to reach a point such that he, together with other individuals if possible, enjoys such a [constant] nature. What that nature is . . . is the knowledge of the union that the mind has with the whole of nature. This, then, is the end towards which I strive: namely, to endeavour to acquire such a nature, and to endeavour that many others should acquire it with me. That is, it also belongs to my happiness that I should take pains to ensure that many other people should understand what I understand, so that their intellect and desire agree with mine. (Preface, *Ethics*, 226)

Thus, only that knowledge of nature is valued which is crucial in achieving sociable perfection: namely, moral philosophy, the education of children, the science of medicine and the mechanical arts. Above all, 'we must think out a way of healing the intellect and purifying it . . . so that it understands things successfully and without error' (227). Only through such attention to the useful sciences and to the cultivation of critical thought for practical application can humankind realise its vocation to be perfect beings. Spinoza concludes his argument by specifying three general rules: 1) speak in a broadly accessible manner so as to be understood by the general public; 2) partake of luxuries only in so far as they are necessary to maintaining human health; 3) enjoy everything (money, honour) in moderation and imitate those customs not opposed to the ultimate goal (227).

An analogy to Spinoza's vision of a cooperative effort in propelling humankind through individual engagement to perfection of the genus is apparent in Leibniz's theory of the monads, which is grounded in the individual substance but networked via the links to the original unity of God. The insistence upon the importance of society in advancing the individual to perfection is everywhere evident in the literature of the eighteenth century. Lessing made that conception the *sine qua non* of his theological views in *Die Erziehung des Menschengeschlechts*. And the supportive role of the community functions as the capstone in the rendition of a perfect civic society at Tarentum under the wise leadership of Archytas in the third, final version of Wieland's *Bildungsroman, Agathon* (1794, Book 16). Without that cooperative effort, humankind would remain as imperfect and egoistic as Hippias describes it, although the destiny of the human race is to be as Archytas envisions it: compassionate, wise, tolerant, moderate. In order for this fundamental revolution in thought, action and social reform to come about so that a civil society could be based on just laws and their just administration, the project of education must be universal. But the *sine qua non* of the transformation in the public realm is the effort of each individual to become better and wiser. The larger revolution is premised on a whole series of individually small ones. Each person must begin with him or herself.

The influence of Kant's thinking on this concluding vision of a wise and just people is manifest. In his 'Idee zu einer allgemeinen Geschichte in weltbürgerlicher Absicht' Kant addresses the role of a telos in human history which guides the evolution of the race despite all the obvious deviations from a common objective. In §5 Kant notes:

Da nur in der Gesellschaft, und zwar derjenigen, die die größte Freiheit, mithin einen durchgängigen Antagonism ihrer Glieder, und doch die genauste

Bestimmung und Sicherung der Grenzen dieser Freiheit hat, damit sie mit der Freiheit anderer bestehen könne, – da nur in ihr die höchste Absicht der Natur, nämlich die Entwickelung aller ihrer Anlagen, in der Menschheit er-reicht werden kann, die Natur auch will, daß sie diesen, so wie alle Zwecke ihrer Bestimmung, sich selbst verschaffen solle. (K IV, 39)

The highest purpose of Nature, which is the development of all the capacities which can be achieved by humankind, is attainable only in society, and more specifically in the society with the greatest freedom. Such a society is one in which there is mutual opposition among the members, together with the most exact definition of freedom and fixing of its limits so that it may be consistent with the freedom of others. Nature demands that humankind should itself achieve this goal like all its other destined goals. (*PW*, 254)

This 'great revolution' can come about only gradually and over many generations. The establishment of a universal cosmopolitan condition would then serve 'as the womb wherein all the original capacities of the human race can develop' (*PW*, 260). The idea of a perfectly just civic society based on moral values proved to be a motivating factor for the project of the Enlightenment from the start. Thomasius argued that the human race must be educated to achieve sociability, happiness and wisdom through the process of communication,[37] whereas Spinoza opined that each person should 'take pains to ensure that many other people should understand what I understand' (*Ethics*, 226). The view that humankind must be educated to bring out the good culminates in Kant's conviction, expressed prominently in 'Beantwortung der Frage: Was ist Aufklärung?', that Enlightenment occurs via the printed word and public discourse. It is emphatically reiterated in his *Anthropologie in pragmatischer Hinsicht* (1798; *Anthropology from a pragmatic point of view*): 'Man is destined by reason to a social existence among men, and there to *cultivate, civilise and moralise himself* through art and science (K XII, 678).[38] Schiller lent the concept an aesthetic twist in his *Über die ästhetische Erziehung des Menschen*.

WIDENING CIRCLES: USEFUL AND POTENTIALLY USEFUL KNOWLEDGE

A number of thinkers in the early eighteenth century began to adopt and adapt Thomasius's philosophy. Among them is Johann Adolph Hoffmann (1676–1731) in Hamburg, who published a popular treatise on how to achieve contentment: *Zwei Bücher der Zufriedenheit* (1722; *Two books on contentment*). Between its first publication and 1745 this work went through ten official printings. Hoffmann's point of departure is

Thomasius's doctrine of moral inadequacy. Decisive is the insight that the instincts (lust, ambition, avarice) must be brought under control in order for man to achieve contentment. That is the function of the understanding. The objective is achieved with the onset of inner tranquillity. A positive attitude, moderation in one's longing for earthly goods and social recognition, modesty in dress and acceptance of what cannot be changed are the keys to attaining composure. Practical usefulness is the prerequisite of contentment. Contrary to it is idleness ('Müßiggang'), because an idle life increases the power of desire while weakening the body and thereby contributing to discomfort, discontentedness and unhappiness. The inevitable outcome is the rise of vice. From this Hoffmann concludes that professional specialisation is the best safeguard to achieving the highest good. Although no opponent of general education, he was thus an outspoken advocate of specialised knowledge and service. 'Do everything necessary and demanded by reason for the good of humankind' was his motto. Negation of personal desires for the sake of the general welfare required strict asceticism and devotion to the material and spiritual wellbeing of others. The purpose of the *Zwei Bücher der Zufriedenheit* was to promulgate this ethical ideal of social asceticism. In this urban form, the early German Enlightenment urged the individual to give up his or her individuality in order to become the ideal burgher. As with George Lillo's (1693–1739) *The London merchant* (1731), the German ideal citizen also had an economic vein.[39]

However, the major disseminator of these new ideas and ideals was the Leipzig philosopher Christian Wolff, the so-called dogmatist of the Enlightenment. His notable achievement was the creation of a philosophic system written in German and capable of reaching beyond an academic audience.[40] His own specific goal was to render philosophy a practical tool in advancing humankind toward ever more perfect self-definition. He wished to demonstrate that humankind had control over its own fate through the salubrious use of reason. What Kant did for the second half of the century – conjoining rationalism and empiricism, the two major thrusts of philosophical thinking, into a unified system of inquiry and self-critique with consequences for the rest of philosophy – Wolff did for the first half of the era: he synthesised in his system the speculative theory of Leibniz's *Monadology* and Thomasius's *Vernunftlehre* and *Sittenlehre*. Wolff's efforts also had significant consequences for philosophy, aesthetics and literature. More than any other philosopher of the day, Wolff had a truly broad impact. His influence was even felt in the numerous moral weeklies published between approximately 1720 and 1760 which schooled the mind and refined interpersonal skills in an entertaining format. Deserving of special note are Gottsched's *Die vernünftigen Tadlerinnen* (*Reasonable female critics*) in Leipzig, and Bodmer and Breitinger's *Die Discourse der Mahlern* in Zürich (1721–3; *Discourses of artists*). They are of special note because Gottsched and Breitinger also penned two of the most important poetics of the early century which had a lasting impact on broad segments of the educated classes. The literary critics specifically cite Wolff as their source of inspiration; the Swiss even dedicate some of their works to the Leipzig philosopher.

If the general achievement of Wolff was to synthesise Leibniz and Thomasius, his specific contribution was to insist that humankind had a moral obligation to cultivate its use of reason much more fully than Thomasius had suggested. Wolff saw in reason a creative faculty, the power to imagine clearly what was virtual. Drawing upon the Leibnizian conception of the mind of God as containing all possible worlds and insights far beyond those possible within the universe as created, Wolff emphasised the notion of general education and of potentially useful knowledge. If the human mind is essentially related to the Divine Mind, then humans could also be actively creative because by definition the Divine Mind is eternally creative. In setting these new expectations in his so-called *Deutsche Logik* (1713; *German logic*) and *Deutsche Metaphysik* (1720; *German metaphysics*), Wolff gave emphatic expression to the ideal of *Bildung* in the German philosophical tradition. His insistence that all individuals are capable of development and that each individual has an obligation to assist in the advancement of humankind toward the full realisation of its intellectual potential capitalised on what had gone before, while popularising key elements of the new school of thought. With his philosophical grounding of man as a second creator (*alter deus*) he also smoothed the way for more radical claims by subsequent thinkers for the creative genius: Friedrich Gottlieb Klopstock (1724–1803), Hamann, Herder, and Heinrich Wilhelm von Gerstenberg (1737–1823). Wolff's entire theory of psychology is based on the imaginative power of the soul, which manifests itself in a passive state as sensation ('Empfindung'). In the case of self-reflective entelechies ('Geister') the behaviour of the being in question is determined through the implementation of the imagination or other faculties of the active mind (*intellectus agens*). The seat of pleasure shifts for Wolff from animal instinct to the mental sphere. Perceptions of perfection give rise to pleasure while views of the imperfect and distorted cause displeasure. With that shift he moves the 'pleasure principle' into the realm of the Divine, since only God is perfect, humans being weak reflections of infinite plenitude (*Deutsche Metaphysik*, §956). Yet man's vocation is to strive for ever clearer comprehension of perfection and its inner workings.[41] Moreover, we can readily see the foundation stone for the new reception aesthetics ('Wirkungsästhetik') of the *Aufklärung* in the Leibniz-Wolffian concepts of plenitude and unity in multiplicity (*Deutsche Metaphysik*, §§56, 178), sentiment as a balance to the insufficiency of reason (§98 and §§103–5), and the special ability of the poetic work to render totality (§114).

LITERARY THEORY AND THE THOMASIAN-WOLFFIAN AXIS

The Leipzig professor of rhetoric Johann Christoph Gottsched, together with the independent Zürich scholars Bodmer and Breitinger, popularised main tenets of early Enlightenment philosophy in their compendia on the role of literature in advancing humankind toward the full realisation of its potential. Most famous is Gottsched's insistence, in *Versuch einer critischen Dichtkunst*,[42] that a poet's first move must be to choose a moral thesis for a poetic work (161). The plot, action, and characterisation of a work should all be set in relation to that basic thesis. Citing Aristotle as his authority, Gottsched determines the function of literature to be more philosophical than mere historical chronicles and more entertaining than straight philosophy. The reason is the position poetry occupies between philosophical contemplation and external action. Because of its hybrid nature, literature is as instructive as treatises on the human spirit but also as entertaining as historical tales, for 'it teaches and entertains [simultaneously] and is [thus] equally suitable for the erudite and the non-erudite' (167). In characterising the nature of the ideal poet, Gottsched had earlier remarked that he (or she) must be conversant in philosophical thought and possess refined aesthetic judgement (108), both of which are expressed as common sense ('gesunder Menschenverstand'; 97). At the outset he defines philosophy as a 'thorough knowledge of all things', thereby concluding that only a philosopher is actually able to offer a full accounting of the essential characteristics of the poet. Shaftesbury, whose *Characteristics of men, manners, and times* (1711) with its 'Advice to an author' had just been translated into German, is cited as a model of the new caste of 'philosophical poets' or the 'poetically inclined philosophers' (96).

If the basic nature of literature is its mimetic impulse (97f.), its quintessential element is the 'Fabel' which Gottsched initially defines as 'the combination or interconnection of things' (149). The fable must be based on a moral point and include examples of both virtue and vice (although he does not allow their intermingling in one and the same person). However, Gottsched does refine his initial definition to allow for different kinds of imitation, for deviation from a mechanical imitation of nature as one might experience it on a quotidian level. His fuller definition reads: 'a fable . . . is the narration of an event possible under certain circumstances, but one that has not actually occurred . . . Philosophically, one could say it is a tale from another world' (150). For his part, Breitinger remarks that the origins of the fable mark it as an instructive tale wrapped in a wondrous garb (*CD* I, 166). To be sure, this fantastic tale must also be based on a moral. The justification for the expansion of imitation to possible worlds is provided by Wolff himself, whom Gottsched immediately cites (151). Gottsched thus underscores the relationship between philosophy and literature, as well as the advantages of literary descriptions over abstract and metaphysical philosophical arguments. What Gottsched wanted to accomplish with his *Versuch einer critischen Dichtkunst* was to provide an introduction to young would-be writers with the fruits of his reading of old masters from Aristotle to Opitz and Shaftesbury (221–2). While he provides *in nuce* an opening for fantastic writing and the exploration of all possible kinds of universes, it was left to Bodmer and Breitinger to explore those openings more fully and perhaps even more radically. Whereas nature remained the touchstone of truth in poetry for Gottsched, the wondrous assumed a greater role in Breitinger's poetic system, and had far-reaching consequences.[43]

The mother of the wondrous according to Breitinger is novelty. While evident in the infinite expanse and complex operations of nature itself, that novelty is due primarily to the imagination, which mines hidden natural riches by reaching beyond actual phenomena to their formative forces. Inspired by Addison's 'On the pleasures of the imagination' and Leibniz's concept of possible worlds, Breitinger elevates the imagination to the pivotal role in the making of literature. The new and unusual emerge, therefore, as the single most important source of aesthetic pleasure (*CD*, 110–14). Literary imagination is likened to a magnifying glass which is capable of revealing deep structures in the microscopic and macroscopic dimensions, especially since its operations are attuned to the creative forces in nature itself rather than limited to an imitation of its surface phenomena (122–5). The wondrous is then definable as the most extreme form of novelty and is a kind of 'cloaked verisimilitude' (130–2).[44] As with Gottsched, the wondrous must be aligned with nature; yet unlike the Leipzig professor, Breitinger shifts the weight of his argument to the

Leibnizian concept of possible worlds. Although ostensibly removed from the truth of manifest nature, the wondrous participates fully in the truths of nature. Breitinger demonstrates this connection by focusing on the seemingly endless creative possibilities of nature ('Schöpferkraft'). This process of discovery and revelation accounts for the special powers of poetic enchantment (134–7). Poetic – even fanciful – renderings sharpen the understanding and improve the will, transforming a staid treatise on right and wrong, truth and deception, good and evil into popular art. And as Breitinger states in full compliance with the tradition since Thomasius: 'without these two components... no genuine enjoyment fitting for creatures of reason is possible'. Literature then is a 'school for the reader', a 'mirror of middle-class life' (104–6).

FROM THEORY TO PRACTICE

From Gottsched, Bodmer and Breitinger the way leads in direct fashion to the Saxon comedies of Adelgunde von Culmus-Gottsched, Johann Elias Schlegel and young Lessing, then to Gellert's sentimental comedies, Wieland's *Don Sylvio* (1764), Johann Michael Reinhold Lenz's *Der Hofmeister oder Vorteile der Privaterziehung* (1774; *The tutor, or the advantages of private education*), Mozart's *Die Zauberflöte* (1791; *The magic flute*), and even to Friedrich Schlegel's *Athenaeums-Fragmente* (1797–8; *Athenaeum Fragments*). While references to the correlation between philosophical and literary formulations of Enlightenment thought have been made at previous junctures of this argument, a more in-depth analysis of pivotal works is provided in the following to bring the issues into sharper focus. I begin with Haller's *Die Alpen*, which originated simultaneously with the early stages of literary theory in both Leipzig and Zürich and out of the same Swiss spirit as was later to inform Rousseau's cultural critique.

Albrecht von Haller (1708–77) introduced philosophical reflection to German poetry, although he was certainly far removed from the Romantics' programme as it was to emerge two generations later. He did not tire of addressing the major themes of the German Enlightenment, to which his extremely popular anthology, *Versuch Schweizerischer Gedichte* (1732; *Essay in Swiss poetry*), gives ample testimony. Not only does he here provide a compendium of popular philosophical concepts of his day, he even goes beyond them by exploring the nihilistic tendencies generated by the problem of evil in such philosophical poems as 'Unvollkommenes Gedicht über die Ewigkeit' (1736; 'Incomplete poem on eternity') and by

pointing forward to the ideal of the 'beau savage' and the more perfect
state of untainted nature in the most famous of his poems, *Die Alpen*. That
poem became a central point of dissension in the famous feud between
Leipzig (Gottsched) and Zürich (Bodmer, Breitinger), later also becoming an object of critique for Lessing in *Laokoon*. Personally, he sided with
his Swiss compatriots, but Haller actually stood closer to Gottsched's
more conservative interpretation of the aesthetic implications of Wolff's
philosophical position. While Brockes, Hagedorn and Johann Peter Uz
(1720–96) reacted favourably in their own nature poetry to Haller's realistic descriptions, Lessing sharply criticised the botanical and floral
descriptions in the *Alpen* as uninspired and hollow (see *LW* II, 97–9). For
his part, Schiller admired the Bernese writer, praising him in *Über naive
und sentimentalische Dichtung* (1795–6; *On naive and reflective poetry*) and imitating him in his own philosophical poetry such as 'Der Spaziergang' (1795;
'The walk'). Nature as stimulus for philosophical reflection is also evident
in Goethe's lyrical 'Gesang der Geister über den Wassern' (1779; 'Song
of the spirits over the waters'). Haller was also one of Kant's favourite
authors.

Inspired by his travels in the high mountains outside Berne, Haller
presented rugged and monstrous nature in an appealing light. In the
process he succeeded in radically altering the general view of the Alps
as forbidding, as the source of 'delightful horrour', in the words of John
Dennis (1657–1734).[45] Ontologically speaking, the poem is in praise of
the simple life in complete harmony with nature, imitating its rhythms
in back-breaking work and simple pleasures. The local inhabitants live a
hard yet contented and happy life because they have gained the insight
that 'moderate nature alone can convey happiness' (line 450).[46] In contrast to Brockes, whose nature reflections are theocentric, Haller's nature
descriptions are aimed at defining the *summum bonum* of humankind itself
in Thomasian terms. Although the poem participates in the tradition
of bucolic poetry, Haller emphasises the role of the work ethic as the
best way to guard against such vices as avarice, envy and overwrought
ambition (lines 127f., 455–60), thus echoing Wolff and Hoffmann. The
incidence of work, let alone hard work, was unknown in the bucolic tradition and is also not a part of the idyllic tradition following *Die Alpen*,
such as Johann Heinrich Voß's (1751–1826) *Der siebzigste Geburtstag* (1781;
The seventieth birthday) or *Luise* (1783–4).[47] Nonetheless, Haller's poem is
clearly idyllic in its rendering of the inhabitants as being undefiled by
the advances of urban culture. They are as innocent as the day they
came forth from the hand of God and know only inner peace (lines 93,

97, 489–90). In this sense, Haller offers an answer to the question later posed by Rousseau, who urged a return to an unspoiled state of nature in his rejection of the civilising process as morally degenerative. In as far as Haller emphasises here the principle of usefulness and simultaneously acknowledges the right to and value of aesthetic pleasure (lines 271–80), he inaugurates, with Brockes and Hagedorn, a movement which finally extends into Weimar Classicism.

Furthermore, Haller is critical of urban life: refined art, the sciences, commerce and luxurious wealth. Against these he holds up the model of innocent love which he encounters among the mountain people. In doing so, Haller emphasises love as a positive force, one different from the urban view of it as a passion contrary to the ethical dictates of utilitarianism (lines 1–10, 81–6, 270). Thus the poem is transformed into a call to the simple yet joyous life. The goal of observation – of really 'seeing' – is to establish the ground rules for achieving wisdom by turning the gaze inward to study one's own soul (lines 461–90). One might want to see the foregrounding of the idyllic life as a prefiguring of the private sphere in opposition to the public realm of urban existence with its deceit, corruption and false 'seeing'. Later, in his play *Sturm und Drang* (1776), Friedrich Maximilian Klinger (1751–1831) would use the depiction of close family ties in untamed America to underscore the contrast to polite society in the Old World.

Christian Fürchtegott Gellert (1715–69), one of the most successful writers of the era, began his literary career as a disciple of Gottsched, viewing literature as a vehicle for enlightening ever more readers. He did this using different literary genres, ranging from the fable and the epistle to the *comédie larmoyante* and the novel. Notably in the sentimental comedy *Die zärtlichen Schwestern* (1747; *The tender sisters*) and the novel *Das Leben der schwedischen Gräfin von G**** he draws heavily upon early Enlightenment ethics and aesthetics. The main topic in both is the need for passion (here called love) to be moderated by reason. The urban middle classes found reflections of themselves in Gellert's novel and dramatic works, not, as tradition and Gottsched prescribed, as participants in a comedy but as models for emulation in serious drama and in tragic yet ennobling circumstances. The new attitudes toward happiness, reason, book learning and benevolence found consummate expression here. But above all, Gellert was interested in depicting true love as driven by the dictates of reason and aligned with the inner worth of an individual. It was a matter of the head and heart working in concert rather than reason and passion being at loggerheads.

virtues of 'Nächstenliebe' and 'Nächstendienst' are everywhere extolled in this novel, a favourite of the *Sturm und Drang*. A 'munterer Geist' and 'Mäßigkeit' – those very qualities which distinguish the rococo Musarion – are equally the trademarks of Sophie Sternheim at the conclusion of her travels. Not lacking is the distinct formulation of the highest ideal of the tranquil spirit which has been achieved through love, service and education (315). It is a fuller formulation of the ideal of the active life, communal service and inner peace contained in Haller's *Die Alpen* forty years earlier (lines 161–6; 471–90).

One of the most successful literary realisations of Breitinger's theory of the wondrous and its relationship to the truths of nature and of the human mind (i.e., imagination) is the story of Prince Biribinker imbedded in Wieland's *Don Sylvio*. Wieland's theoretical discussion of that tale in chapter three of book six is a direct echo of Breitinger's own theory. So too is the preface to his three-volume collection of fairy tales, *Dschinnistan* (1786–9). In carrying out that aesthetic premise, Wieland also fulfilled the purpose of literature as a tool in advancing truth and virtue while opposing vice. Similarly, Mozart fully utilises elements of fantasy and fable in his and Emanuel Schikaneder's popular opera *Die Zauberflöte*. Far from being a mere whimsical fairy tale set to music, the opera draws upon Enlightenment thought and mirrors political events, while presenting a plea for virtue, tolerance, equality and common sense.[52] These works substantiate Breitinger's claim that 'the enchanting power of poesy arises from the special way the poetic imagination combines the wondrous with the plausible' (*CD* I, 141).

RADICALISING THE ENLIGHTENMENT: HAMANN AND HERDER

The *Sturm und Drang* movement represents a radicalisation of tendencies inherent in both the rational and sentimental sides of Enlightenment thought. It also shares roots with the anti-orthodox religious reform movement, Pietism. Moreover, Rousseau was as much a fixed star for Wieland and Wezel as he was for the young Goethe and Lenz.[53] Moritz's *Anton Reiser* combines all these elements into a vibrant whole. What sets the *Sturm und Drang* apart, however, is its insistence that passion, action and decisiveness are needed to counteract the presumed debilitating effects of the Enlightenment, with its emphasis on equality, tolerance and sympathetic love. Greatness of personality and audacity of desire – whether good or bad – became the new aesthetic and moral ideal. In holding up Shakespeare as the model of the modern genius, *Sturm und*

Drang writers such as Gerstenberg, Herder, Goethe and Lenz could draw upon Lessing's extolling of his virtues in the seventeenth letter of *Briefe, die neueste Litteratur betreffend* (1759; *Letters on contemporary literature*) and use Wieland's prose translation of twenty-two of Shakespeare's plays (1762). Within the German tradition, Hamann and Herder provided the most immediate impulse to rethink the Enlightenment programme.

Known as the Magus of the North, Hamann is the acknowledged 'father' of the *Sturm und Drang*. His philosophy derives from his inner conviction that knowledge of the divine is possible only through a purely personal and subjective certainty; it is not the result of rational thought. This explains Hamann's typically rhapsodic and hypotactic style in the series of compositions dating from the late 1750s. He developed his ideas and issued his call for a new kind of philosophy primarily in *Sokratische Denkwürdigkeiten* (1759; *Socratic memorabilia*) and *Kreuzzüge eines Philologen* (1762; *Philological crusades*).[54] Turning his back on the intellectualism and logic of the Enlightenment, Hamann believed language to be of divine origin. Marked by a strong irrational element and born along by metaphor, image and symbol – the medium of the passions – language and its rhythms are expressions of individual perceptions and sensations in need of deciphering. Since God reveals Himself only indirectly through the dynamic of clouded passions mirrored in language, humankind must learn to interpret the signs of divine presence. Hamann never tired of designating poesy, moreover, as the 'mother tongue of all humankind' (121).[55] Nature appears to him to be a second book of Revelation after the Bible, a coded text in which the deity reveals itself ('ein versiegelt Buch'; 68). Speaking is thus a kind of translation of nature (123). Essentially hieroglyphic, nature cries out for interpretation, for a 'Hebammenkunst' (midwifery) as practised by Socrates (69). If the priest is charged with the exegesis of the Bible, the poet's role is to reveal the mysteries of God in nature throughout history. Thus, Hamann calls upon humankind to become prophets of the divine in the natural dynamics of nature and language, for what we know is determined by language itself (108–10).

Equally important as an innovative thrust is Hamann's elevation of the unconventional thinker and social outsider to the status of leader and prophet. He does this by privileging intuition over reason and by locating genius in the unconscious. In his *Sokratische Denkwürdigkeiten* he argues for the right of poetic expression and then – against the wont of the times – transforms Socrates into the great representative of irrationalism, for his wisdom (like that of Lessing's Nathan) was that truth is obscured and that one must act out one's inner *daimon* (78–9). He even cites the Jews as the source of salvation. Here too rhapsodic language, a plastic and formative style (82), is the unmediated expression of feeling. Drawing upon English empiricism, he assigns the senses a key role in interpretation: one must speak not so much to be heard as to be 'seen' in images and similes. Hamann here anticipates the synaesthesia of the Romantics.

If Hamann's strength lay in the areas of hermeneutics and critique, Herder's specific contribution was a re-evaluation of cultural history through a questioning of the hegemony of Greek and Roman antiquity as models for eighteenth-century culture, as advanced by Winckelmann. Like Giovanni Battista Vico (1668–1744), Herder was an advocate of cultural relativism, assigning to each epoch in cultural history (Oriental, Egyptian, Phœnician, Greek, Roman, Northern European) its own intrinsic value and valuing each cultural heritage as a unique contribution to the evolution of humankind as a whole. By maintaining a dual focus on the concepts of *humanitas* and of 'organic' development (*Bildung*), Herder was able to provide for continuity despite the national emphasis he gave to each cultural tradition as a result of its geographical, climatic and linguistic determinants. The influence of Shaftesbury, Leibniz, Montesquieu and Rousseau as well as that of Hamann and Kant is everywhere evident in his thought. From Shaftesbury he adopted the doctrine of enthusiasm, the view of the poet as a second creator, and the idea that human interaction is to be modelled on the harmony of the cosmos. From Leibniz he derived a dynamic concept of nature and the notion of perfectibility of the monad. Montesquieu's grounding of the spirit of the laws in local conditions and customs proved fruitful for his own sense of place. In concert with Rousseau, Herder favoured a return to the immediacy of nature with its simplicity and directness over the debilitating influence of luxury and idleness of contemporary urban society. Like Hamann, he privileged the genius as the source of all energy, valued the arousing affect of diction, tone, rhythm and image in language, and placed intuition above reason. Similarly he saw the cultural historian as prophet and poet. Yet unlike Hamann, Herder emphasised that language was a human rather than a divine development, for it was tied inherently to the natural conditions of human existence: the soil, the climate, daily routine and regional customs. For this reason, Herder is credited with having introduced the concept of 'folk art', 'folk song' and 'folk poetry' into German literature. These ideas are developed in a series of pioneering works: *Fragmente über die neuere deutsche Literatur* (1767; *Fragments on recent German literature*), *Journal meiner Reise im Jahr 1769*, *Kritische Wälder* (1769; *Critical forests*), *Über den Ursprung der Sprache* (1771; *On the origin of language*), *Von deutscher Art und Kunst* (edited by Herder in 1773; *On the German character and art*), *Älteste Urkunde des Menschengeschlechts* (1774; *On the oldest document of the human race*), *Auch eine Philosophie der Geschichte zur Bildung der Menschheit* (1774; *Another philosophy of history for the education of humankind*) and *Vom Erkennen und Empfinden der menschlichen Seele* (1778; *On cognition and sensation in the human soul*).

Best known is the essay collection *Von deutscher Art und Kunst*. It is celebrated as the *Sturm und Drang* manifesto because of its emphasis on folk poesy, gothic architecture and the heroic personalities of German national history. All these qualities found expression in Goethe's dramatised history of *Götz von Berlichingen mit der eisernen Hand* (1773; *Götz of Berlichingen with the iron hand*) modelled on Shakespeare's dramatic technique. Of Shakespeare – the general model for the new history and character plays of the 1770s – Herder exclaims that he is the greatest poet simply because he was 'only and always a servant of nature', asserting: 'Here is no mere poet! This is a creator! This is world history!' (JGH V, 223). In addition to its rhapsodic tribute to Shakespeare as an alternative model of creative genius to that of the ancient Greeks, *Von deutscher Art und Kunst* also contains Herder's pioneering analysis of Ossian and ancient folk songs ('Auszug aus einem Briefwechsel über Ossian und die Lieder alter Völker'), Goethe's tribute to Erwin Steinbach concerning gothic architecture ('Von deutscher Baukunst') and Justus Möser's piece on German history ('Deutsche Geschichte').

In *Auch eine Philosophie* he lauds 'sound, Nordic reason' (JGH V, 515), while generally rejecting the professional philosophers of his day as cold and short-sighted (482) and as having fostered consumptive contemporaries and debilitating practices (556–7). Herder thus echoes Goethe's critique of the ossified German juridical culture in *Götz von Berlichingen* and engenders Schiller's later indictment of the eighteenth century as the age of wimpish eunuchs ('das schlappe Kastratenjahrhundert') in *Die Räuber* (1781; *The robbers*). Here Herder also expresses his view of history as a dialectical process between being and becoming, as the progressive revelation and realisation of the divine in humankind, in individual cultural epochs and stages of national genesis. However, since he did not here view history as a linear and coordinated development toward a predetermined state of perfection, he broke decisively with Enlightenment historiography.

The course of history was analogous to the cycles of creativity and destruction evident in nature. Herder speaks of a 'movement of God across the nations' of the world (JGH V, 565). Here he elaborates upon his concepts of the individuality of all peoples ('Völker'), the contingency of epochal trends, the *autopoiesis* of living organisms (with clear allusions to Leibniz and Shaftesbury), the experience of tragically agonistic contests in life (Shakespeare, Ossian), ancient Greece as but one highpoint in human history, and his judgement that his own age was in crisis. With bitter irony he castigates his own time as lacking in spirit, for imposing its culture of excess on distant colonies (alchohol, arrogance), for having banished slavery at home only to enslave the other three corners of the earth (546–50). As in his essays on Shakespeare and Ossian, he looks to the creative individual for salvation, the one who draws upon his own cultural traditions and history to renew culture and the human spirit generally (583–4). Although he readily grants that truly remarkable gains in the flow of history are due to the actions of extraordinary individuals, he emphasises the fact that the whole is still more important than the individual trapped in time and space: 'the whole is an ocean where waves and undulations strike out with force and amid great din in no particular direction' (581). Yet all individuals are chained together around the globe and throughout history, affecting one another even when each acts as if its own local position were the centre of the universe. The contingencies of life are complex and non-linear. To render 'the entire vital portrait' of the contingencies of experience requires a new art of depiction ('das ganze lebendige Gemälde von Lebensart, Gewohnheiten, Bedürfnissen, Landes- und Himmelseigenheiten'; 502). Nonetheless, in resonance with the underlying ideals of the Enlightenment, Herder posits as the ultimate goal of all this movement the recognition of truth, self-awareness, the exercise of benevolence, and the achievement of human happiness (584). In like manner, Lenz offers a critical portrait of life ('Gemälde des Lebens') around 1770 in his *Der Hofmeister*, adding a plea for general educational reform to advance humankind towards the ultimate goal of happiness. Schiller too promotes the cause by having the rebellious robber leader, Karl Moor, turn himself over to the authorities in order to benefit the unfortunate head of a large family.

ECHOES: A CONCLUSION ... AND AN OPENING

In his *Erkennen und Empfinden* Herder argues in Leibnizian fashion for the unity of body, soul and spirit; knowledge is inherently tied to aroused passions which take in the world intuitively, metamorphosing it into visions. This analysis of the limits of knowledge proves to be a transition piece between the rhapsodic enthusiasm of the young Herder and the more philosophically reflective mature Herder. Herder's progression from the early *Sturm und Drang* philosophy to a more classically rounded and harmonious stance is especially manifest in his *Ideen zur Philosophie der Geschichte der Menschheit* (1784–91; *Ideas on the philosophy of the history of humankind*), the title of which clearly connects it to *Auch eine Philosophie*. A comparison of *Auch eine Philosophie* and the *Ideen* would amply demonstrate the lines of continuity from Leibniz and Thomasius through Wolff and Gottsched, Lessing and Wieland, the *Sturm und Drang* and the classical era of the late eighteenth century. At the centre of his *Ideen* stands the calling of humankind to fulfil its destiny. This requires the joining of the individual and unique expression of human aspirations with a universal concept of 'Humanität' (*humanitas*) valid across the ages and throughout the cultural spectrum. 'Humanität' signifies here for Herder the cultivation of humankind's intellectual and moral vocation. All individuals share in this potential and the charge to bring it to fruition. Herder subsumes under this term not only the notions of tolerance, altruism, sympathy and respect for others but also all specifically human faculties and potentialities. As a manifesto of Weimar Classicism, Herder's *Ideen* mirror ideas found in Lessing's *Nathan*, Goethe's *Iphigenie auf Tauris* (1779), Wieland's *Oberon* (1780) and Schiller's *Don Carlos* (1787). (Like *Iphigenie*, *Don Carlos* went through revisions transforming it from a *Sturm und Drang* work into a classical one.)

Connections to later developments are evident in Goethe's own theoretical writings, which demonstrate many parallels to Herder. The key is perhaps Goethe's reading of Spinoza (especially the *Ethics*), which occurred in three stages: first around 1773, when Goethe published his essay on Shakespeare; then around 1785, when he had begun his natural scientific studies, and Friedrich Heinrich Jacobi published *Über die Lehre des Spinoza* (*On Spinoza's teaching*) which stamped Spinoza an atheist; and finally around 1812, in connection with his morphological studies. On 7 November 1816 Goethe remarked in a letter to the composer Carl Friedrich von Zelter (1758–1832) that Spinoza ranked with Shakespeare and Linné as one of the three thinkers who had most influenced him (HA XIII, 564).[56] The alignment of the philosopher (Spinoza), the creative genius (Shakespeare) and the natural scientist (Linné) has to do, I think, in general with the overall contour of the age of Enlightenment, in particular its re-evaluations of the historical, philosophical and scientific traditions. In his address 'Zum Schäkespears Tag' (1773; 'On Shakespeare's birthday') Goethe formulated early on his belief that great men are inherently related to creative nature itself. And Shakespeare was the poet who best succeeded in drawing such great characters who in turn helped to shape history. He concludes: 'all his works revolve around a mysterious point – which no philosopher has seen or identified – in which the essence of our being, the presumed freedom of our will, collides with the necessary course of the whole' (HA XII, 226). This contestation and struggle of the individual 'I' to express and maintain itself echoes Herder's view of history.

In his 'Studie nach Spinoza' (1784; 'Study after Spinoza') Goethe takes up the idea that the parts are inextricably intertwined with the whole, but in such a way that the whole is not the measure of the parts nor the parts the measure of the whole (HA XIII, 8). As such the pantheistic quality of nature was maintained. Spinoza's *hen kai pan* clearly resonates in Goethe's thinking – even if he disagreed with Jacobi's interpretation of Spinoza as an atheist (HA XIII, 564). The complex interactions of nature and humankind are further addressed in an essay from 1823, 'Probleme'. There Goethe avers that nature does not follow a linear system but is marked rather by life processes themselves which evolve from 'an unknown centre' and move toward 'an unknown boundary' (HA XIII, 35). The mysteriousness of the divine presence in nature which revolves about a mysterious point and radiates outward from an unknown centre to expanding borders is a poignant echo of Herder's view of the movement of the divine throughout the histories of nations which in turn are rooted in the physical conditions of life. 'Nature! Nature! Nothing so natural as Shakespeare's characters' (HA XII, 226).

In an essay from 1820, 'Über die Einwirkung der neueren Philosophie' ('On the effects of contemporary philosophy' (HA XIII), Goethe transfers his insights from the study of nature to an evaluation of Kant (with remarks on Moritz and Schiller). He decides that he can follow neither the late Herder nor Kant's analytic method in *Kritik der reinen Vernunft*. Nature is too strongly marked by the dialectic of diastole and systole, 'never separate, always pulsating'. This Goethe found in the introduction to the *Kritik* (as well as in F. W. J. Schelling), but his own poetic nerve would not allow him to follow Kant's further argument, although he does grant that a priori knowledge and synthetic judgements seemed to provide the philosophical language for what he had long held to be true. Essentially, Goethe suggests he had no 'organ' for philosophy (HA XIII, 25). By contrast, his reaction to the *Kritik der Urteilskraft* (1790; *Critique of judgement*) was very positive; it marked the beginning of a 'most happy period in his life' (HA XIII, 27). Although he did not entirely understand Kant's argument, he did discover in the *Kritik der Urteilskraft* ideals and principles analogous to his own. What he found to be familiar was the acknowledgement that art and nature each have an 'inner life', the idea that their mutual activities emanate from an internal source and that each realm – art and nature – 'was to exist for its own sake and [to exist] for one another but not intentionally *because* of one another'; that is, they are contingent, but not mutually determined (HA xiii, 28). This surely echoes both Leibniz's notion of pre-established harmony, which links body and soul while ensuring their mutual autonomy, and Moritz's 'signature of the beautiful'. Is it, then, more than wishful thinking to see in Goethe's project a continuance of the dual focus of Enlightenment culture on reason and experience?

We have come, perhaps, full circle. Not that the movement toward aesthetic or moral perfection is necessarily circular, linear, steady or absolute. Inherent in Leibniz's concept of perfectibility is the insistence upon the dynamic principle. Whether that principle will ever play itself out fully, so that it eventually deprives itself of its own justification, becomes increasingly an intriguing question for subsequent philosophers and writers. Always and everywhere it is the exploration of ever new possibilities of construction and re-configuration which fascinated Wolff, then Breitinger, then Wieland and ultimately Goethe and the Romantics. Friedrich Schlegel, for example, calls in his *Gespräch über die Poesie* (1800; *Conversation on poesy*) for a 'new' mythology as a 'hieroglyphics' of nature. Poesy leads away from the movement and the laws of rationally operative reason ('vernünftig denkende Vernunft'), through the pleasant confusions of the imagination and back to the originary state of chaos in human affairs. The paths back to the origins of contemporary existence are individual and thus innumerable. Schlegel finds a fitting representation of that chaotic state in the colourful array of the ancient gods (195).[57] On the one hand, Schlegel's roots in Enlightenment thought are discernible when he values Kant in the *Athenaeums-Fragmente* as the 'Copernicus of philosophy' (101); on the other, his vision of a 'new' mythology – of a 'symphilosophy' – might have roots in Spinoza, whom he designates 'the universal foundation and anchor of every individual type of mysticism' (196). It could prove valuable to pursue these analogies in greater detail.

In the foregoing there is no mention of the 'underside' of Enlightenment aesthetics upon which Carsten Zelle has frequently commented, especially as regards 'pleasurable horror'. This represents a decoupling of the ethical impulse inherent in the Enlightenment from the outset, an autonomisation of the imagination and a trivialisation of the demand for a popular style. As such it could easily mark the end of the era.[58] Yet the focus throughout has been on the essentiality of the link between ethics and aesthetic pleasure for an understanding of 'true' Enlightenment. Without the belief in the perfectibility of human beings, the Enlightenment would indeed no longer be the Enlightenment.[59] The key to progress despite – or perhaps because of – the non-linear movement is the practice of criticism. That practice includes the critique of reason and the critique of experience. It is animated by an inward impulse emanating from an unknown centre outward toward unknown limits. But yet it is held together by a bonding agent, a benevolent force. That is why the Enlightenment is aptly labelled a *philosophia perennis*. With their discursive style and metaphorical language, its popular texts aimed to be accessible to the many. Breitinger and Kant are cited at the masthead of this chapter to underscore that intent. Indeed, the legacy of the *Aufklärung* consists in determining what the possibilities and limits of Enlightenment are.[60] It is – and should be – a pleasurable undertaking.

NOTES

1 Johann Jacob Breitinger, *CD* I, 110.
2 Immanuel Kant, *Kritik der reinen Vernunft*, A xviii, in K III, 16.
3 See *CD* I, 9; also Christian Garve, 'Von der Popularität des Vortrages', in Kurt Wölfel (ed.), *Popularphilosophische Schriften über literarische, ästhetische und gesellschaftliche Gegenstände*, 2 vols. (Stuttgart: Metzler, 1974), vol. II, pp. 1041, 1058.
4 Georg Braungart, *Leibhafter Sinn. Der andere Diskurs der Moderne* (Tübingen: Niemeyer, 1995) examines the prehistory of Derrida's 'trace' ('Spur'), succeeding admirably in highlighting the emergence of the concept (albeit with different content) in late eighteenth-century aesthetics. In the following I will argue that the theory of linguistic and corporeal traces begins with Leibniz.
5 Susan Manning demonstrates this crossing over in her study 'Literature and philosophy', in H. B. Nisbet and Claude Rawson (eds.), *The Cambridge history of literary criticism*, vol. IV: *The eighteenth century* (Cambridge: Cambridge University Press, 1997), pp. 587–613.
6 See K III, 16. Willi Goetschel, *Constituting critique. Kant's writing as critical praxis* (Durham and London: Duke University Press, 1994), demonstrates the continuity of Kant's method and style dating from the 1750s (see pp. 115–43).
7 The close proximity of philosophy and literature is the topic of much research. Peter Gay wrote in *The eighteenth century: an interpretation* (New York: Random House, 1968): 'Yet the most characteristic mode of its expression was witty, informed, and didactic at once' (p. 197). See also Robert Ginsberg (ed.), *The philosopher as writer: The eighteenth century* (London and Toronto: Associated University Presses, 1987); *Eighteenth-century German authors and their*

aesthetic theories: Literature and the other arts, ed. Richard Critchfield and Wulf Koepke (Columbia SC: Camden House, 1988); John A. McCarthy, *Crossing boundaries: A theory and history of the essay in German 1680–1815* (Philadelphia: University of Pennsylvania Press, 1989); Goetschel, *Constituting critique*; Peter-André Alt, *Aufklärung. Ein Lehrbuch* (Stuttgart and Weimar: Metzler, 1996). Nisbet and Rawson (eds.), *The Cambridge history of literary criticism*, vol. IV: *The eighteenth century*, contains numerous useful essays, esp. Douglas Lane Perry, 'The institution of criticism in the eighteenth century', pp. 3–31, a perceptive rendering of the topic.

8 Werner Schneiders, *Hoffnung auf Vernunft. Aufklärungsphilosophie in Deutschland* (Hamburg: Meiners, 1990), pp. 67–8. Schneiders offers here an excellent survey of the complex lines of influence, especially in the first half of the eighteenth century in the wake of Thomasius und Wolff (pp. 111–56).

9 On the Enlightenment as 'mission' see Werner Schneiders (ed.), *Aufklärung als Mission. La mission des Lumières. Akzeptanzprobleme und Kommunikationsdefizite (Das achtzehnte Jahrhundert.* Supplementa, 1) (Marburg: Hitzeroth, 1993), pp. 11–21.

10 Peter Pütz, *Die deutsche Aufklärung*, 4th edn (Darmstadt: Wissenschaftliche Buchgesellschaft, 1991), p. 5.

11 Peter Gay, *The Enlightenment: an interpretation. The rise of modern paganism* (New York: Random House, 1968).

12 Schneiders, *Hoffnung auf Vernunft*, pp. 14–15.

13 See Wolfgang Martens, *Die Botschaft der Tugend. Die Aufklärung im Spiegel der deutschen Moralischen Wochenschriften* (Stuttgart: Metzler, 1968).

14 See JGH IV, 342–461, here p. 455 ('Jahrhundert der Erfahrungen').

15 *Pascal: Pensées. Texte de l'édition Brunschvicg*, introduction and notes by ch.-M. des Granges (Paris: Garnier, 1948), p. 147 (no. 282).

16 G. E. Lessing, *Laokoon oder über die Grenzen der Malerei und die Poesie, LW* III, 21.

17 Armand Nivelle, *Literaturästhetik der europäischen Aufklärung* (Wiesbaden: Athenaion, 1977), p. 40.

18 For a review of aesthetic trends in the eighteenth century see John A. McCarthy, 'Aufklärung des ästhetischen Scheins – die Ästhetisierung der Aufklärung', *Das achtzehnte Jahrhundert* 15/2 (1991) 147–69; Nivelle, *Literaturästhetik*; Silvio Vietta, *Literarische Phantasie. Theorie und Geschichte – Barock und Aufklärung* (Stuttgart: Metzler, 1986); Alt, *Aufklärung*, pp. 60–125. On the category of the 'Nicht-Schön' see especially Carsten Zelle, *'Angenehmes Grauen'. Literarhistorische Beiträge zur Ästhetik des Schrecklichen im achtzehnten Jahrhundert* (Hamburg: Meiner, 1987).

19 See the essays in *Aufklärung. Internationale Halbjahresschrift zur Erforschung des 18. Jahrhunderts und seiner Wirkungsgeschichte* 11/1 (1999), ed. by Norbert Hinske (esp. pp. 3–107), which trace the history of the debate on the vocation and destiny of humankind.

20 The quotations are drawn respectively from Ernst Troeltsch, 'Aufklärung', *Realenzyklopädie für protestantische Theologie und Kirche* 2 (1897), 273; Jean Améry, 'Aufklärung als *philosophia perennis*', in Paul Raabe and Wilhelm Schmitt-Biggemann (eds.), *Aufklärung in Deutschland* (Bonn: Hohwacht, 1979), pp. 231–8; Ernst Cassirer, *Philosophy of the Enlightenment*, trans. Fritz C. A. Koelln and

James P. Pettegrove (Boston: Beacon P, 1966), pp. 121, 127; and Schneiders, *Hoffnung auf Vernunft*, pp. 185–6.

21 Norman Hampson, *The Enlightenment* (Baltimore: Penguin, 1968), p. 146.

22 Norbert Hinske, 'Die tragenden Grundideen der deutschen Aufklärung. Versuch einer Typologie', in Hinske-Specht, 415; Peter Gay, *The Enlightenment*, p. 141.

23 Panajotis Kondylis, *Die Aufklärung im Rahmen des neuzeitlichen Rationalismus* (Munich: Deutscher Taschenbuch Verlag, 1986), emphasises the interconnections with Protestantism as a unique marker of the German version of Enlightenment (pp. 538–43).

24 Cassirer, *Enlightenment*, pp. 35–6. For a more recent, superb treatment of Leibniz see Donald Rutherford, *Leibniz and the rational order of nature*, 3rd edn (New York: Cambridge University Press, 1998). On Leibniz's significance for high and late *Aufklärung* see Kondylis, *Aufklärung*, pp. 576–649.

25 Donald Rutherford, *Leibniz and the rational order of nature* (New York: Cambridge University Press, 1998), p. 159.

26 See also Leibniz, *Discourse on metaphysics*, L, 26–7.

27 Rutherford, *Leibniz*, p. 61.

28 Spinoza also emphasises diversity and multiplicity as a sign of enhanced perfection because they bring one closer to God, the Unity of all things. See *Ethics*, pp. 203, 209, 211, 240–1.

29 Eberhard Reichmann, 'Die Begründung der deutschen Aufklärungsästhetik aus dem Geist der Zahl', *Monatshefte* 59/3 (1967), 193–203.

30 Wezel is one of those authors who cannot be treated in detail here. He remained an adherent of the *Aufklärung*, radicalising many of its tenets. See Franz Futterknecht, *Infantiles Bewußtsein. Johann Karl Wezels Kritik der Moderne* (Munich: Iudicium, 1999).

31 Christian Thomasius, *Vernunftlehre* (1791), in *Deutsche Literaturdenkmäler des 18. und 19. Jahrhunderts* 52/2, new series 2/3 (Nendeln: Krauss, 1968), pp. 75–6; also in Schneiders, *Hoffnung auf Vernunft*, p. 113.

32 On Rüdiger see Schneiders, *Hoffnung auf Vernunft*, pp. 67–71, 117–19 (passage cited by Schneiders, p. 118). The *Philosophia pragmatica* is the third version of Rüdiger's main treatise, first published as *Philosophia synthetica* (1707), then reincarnated as *Institutiones eruditionis seu philosophia synthetica* (1711). Each version of the work appeared in two or more editions, thus attesting to Rüdiger's popularity.

33 Christoph Martin Wieland, *Werke*, 5 vols., ed. Fritz Martini and Hans Werner Seiffert (Munich: Hanser, 1964–66), vol. I, p. 422.

34 See for example John Mullen, 'Sensibility and literary criticism', in Nisbet and Rawson (eds.), *The Cambridge history of literary criticism*, vol. IV, pp. 419–33. What Mullen has to say about the English and French traditions is also applicable to the German.

35 See Hans M. Wolff, *Die Weltanschauung der deutschen Aufklärung in geschichtlicher Entwicklung* (Bern: Francke, 1949), p. 33.

36 See Hans-Jürgen Schings, *Der mitleidigste Mensch ist der beste Mensch. Poetik des Mitleids von Lessing bis Büchner* (Munich: Beck, 1980), pp. 34–45.

37 Thomasius, *Von der Kunst Vernünfftig und Tugendhaft zu lieben* (1692), 2. Hauptstück, §71–76, pp. 79f.; Hinske-Specht, 51.

38 On the essentiality of the communicative act for the Enlightenment project see, e.g., Hans Eric Bödeker, 'Aufklärung als Kommunikationsprozeß', *Aufklärung* 2/2 (1987), 89–111; Jürgen Habermas, *Strukturwandel der Öffentlichkeit* (Frankfurt am Main: Suhrkamp, 1961); *Von Almanach bis Zeitung. Ein Handbuch der Medien in Deutschland 1700–1800*, ed. Ernst Fischer, Wilhelm Haefs and York-Gothart Mix (Munich: C. H. Beck Verlag, 1999).

39 See John W. Van Cleve, *The merchant in German literature of the Enlightenment* (Chapel Hill and London: University of North Carolina Press, 1986).

40 For an excellent discussion of Wolff see Thomas P. Saine, *Von der kopernikanischen bis zur Französischen Revolution. Die Auseinandersetzung der deutschen Frühaufklärung mit der neuen Zeit* (Berlin: Schmidt, 1987), pp. 116–44, or in English: *The problem of being modern or the German pursuit of Enlightenment from Leibniz to the French Revolution* (Detroit: Wayne State University Press, 1997), pp. 120–45.

41 Saine, *Von der kopernikanischen bis zur Französischen Revolution*, p. 176; *The Problem of being modern*, p. 137.

42 Johann Christoph Gottsched, *Versuch einer critischen Dichtkunst* (Darmstadt: Wissenschaftliche Buchgesellschaft, 1962), p. 161.

43 On these far-reaching consequences see Hans Blumenberg, 'Nachahmung der Natur. Zur Vorgeschichte der Idee des schöpferischen Menschen' (1957), in *Wirklichkeiten in denen wir leben. Aufsätze und eine Rede* (Stuttgart: Reclam, 1985), pp. 55–103; Helga Madland, 'Imitation to creation: the changing concept of mimesis from Bodmer and Breitinger to Lenz', in Critchfield and Koepke (eds.), *Eighteenth-century German authors and their aesthetic theories*, pp. 29–43; Sven Aage Jørgensen, Klaus Bohnen and Per Øhrgaard, *Aufklärung, Sturm und Drang, Frühe Klassik 1740–1789* (Munich: C. H. Beck, 1990), pp. 101–23; Jill Anne Kowalik, *The poetics of historical perspectivism: Breitinger's 'Critische Dichtkunst' and the neoclassic tradition* (Chapel Hill and London: University of North Carolina Press, 1992); Alt, *Aufklärung*, pp. 68–92.

44 Breitinger makes many such claims. See e.g.: 'Da nun die Poesie eine Nachahmung der Schöpfung und der Natur nicht nur in dem Würcklichen, sondern auch in dem Möglichen ist, so muß ihre Dichtung, die eine Art der Schöpfung ist, ihre Wahrscheinlichkeit entweder in der Uebereinstimmung mit den gegenwärtigen Zeit eingeführten Gesetzen und dem Laufe der Natur gründen, oder in den Kräften der Natur, welche sie bey andern Absichten nach unsern Begriffen hätte ausüben können' (*CD* I, 136–7). Cf. also: 'Denn die Natur ist in ihrem Vermögen unerschöpflich und in dem Fleiß ihrer Arbeit gantz unermüdet' (*CD* I, 113–14).

45 Alt, *Aufklärung*, p. 140.

46 References are to Albrecht von Haller, *Die Alpen und andere Gedichte*, ed. Adalbert Elschenbroich (Stuttgart: Philipp Reclam jun., 1984), pp. 3–22.

47 See Helmut J. Schneider, 'Naturerfahrung und Idylle in der deutschen Aufklärung', in *Erforschung der deutschen Aufklärung*, ed. Peter Pütz (Königstein im Taunus: Hanstein, 1980), pp. 289–316.

48 Christian Fürchtegott Gellert, 'Abhandlung für das rührende Lustspiel', in *Die zärtlichen Schwestern*, ed. Horst Steinmetz (Stuttgart: Reclam, 1988), pp. 129–30.

49 See Wieland, *Werke*, vol. IV, p. 364: 'die reitzende Philosophie, / Die, was Natur und Schicksal uns gewährt, / Vergnügt genießt, und gern den Rest entbehrt' (verses 1409–11). On the ideal of the 'galant homme' cf. Thomasius, *Discours*, in Hinske-Specht, pp. 13–14, 32–3.

50 Sophie La Roche, *Die Geschichte des Fräuleins von Sternheim*, ed. Barbara Becker-Cantarino (Stuttgart: Reclam, 1983).

51 The father's view is as follows: 'Die Liebe und Übung der Tugend und der Wissenschaften ... geben ihrem Besitzer eine von Schicksal und Menschen unabhängige Glückseligkeit, und machen ihn zugleich, durch das Beispiel, das seine edle und gute Handlungen geben, durch den Nutzen und das Vergnügen, das sein Rat und Umgang schaffen, zu einem moralischen Wohltäter an seinen Mitmenschen' (40).

52 See Helmut Perl, *Der Fall 'Zauberflöte'. Mozarts Oper im Brennpunkt der Geschichte* (Darmstadt: Wissenschaftliche Buchgesellschaft, 2000).

53 Johann Karl Wezel, 'Vorrede', *Robinson Crusoe* (1781) in *Kritische Schriften*, facsimile reprint, ed. Albert R. Schmitt (Stuttgart: Metzler, 1975), vol. III, pp. 5, 41.

54 The *Kreuzzüge* contain among others the essays, 'Das Kleeblatt hellenistischer Briefe' (1759; 'A trio of hellenic letters'), 'Aesthetica in nuce' (1762; 'Aesthetics in a nutshell').

55 Hamann is cited according to *Sturm und Drang. Kritische Schriften*, ed. Erich Loewenthal and Lambert Schneider (Heidelberg: Verlag Lambert Schneider, 1963). For a general, useful account of Hamann see James C. O'Flaherty, *Johann Georg Hamann* (Boston: Twayne, 1979).

56 See also Ernst Cassirer, 'Goethe and the Kantian Philosophy', in *Rousseau, Kant and Goethe* (New York: Harper Torchbooks, 1963), pp. 61–98, here pp. 68–70. Kant emerges here as the fourth more modern thinker to impact upon Goethe's thinking.

57 References are to Friedrich Schlegel, *Kritische und theoretische Schriften*, ed. Andreas Huyssen (Stuttgart: Reclam, 1978), pp. 165–224.

58 E.g., Zelle, 'Angenehmes Grauen', pp. 139, 356, 418 and Carsten Zelle, 'Enlightenment or aesthetics? The aesthetic boundary of the Enlightenment in poetological texts from the second half of the eighteenth century', in *Impure reason: dialectic of Enlightenment in Germany*, ed. W. Daniel Wilson and Robert C. Holub (Detroit: Wayne State University Press, 1993), pp. 109–25.

59 On this issue see McCarthy, 'Aufklärung des ästhetischen Scheins', pp. 151–5 and John A. McCarthy, 'Verständigung and Dialektik: on consensus theory and the Dialektik of Enlightenment', in Wilson and Holub (eds.), *Impure Reason*, pp. 13–33.

60 See Werner Schneiders, *Das Zeitalter der Aufklärung* (Munich: Beck, 1997), p. 131.

CHAPTER TWO

The pursuit of the subject: literature as critic and perfecter of philosophy 1790–1830

Nicholas Saul

In 1798 the Romantic writer Friedrich Schlegel (1772–1829) boldly reduced the age in which he lived to three dominant tendencies.[1] That the French Revolution, the most significant single political and cultural development in modernity, should be written large no one then or now would dispute. Alongside this historical cataclysm, however, Schlegel ranks phenomena from the republic of letters: a philosophy, Johann Gottlieb Fichte's 'Wissenschaftslehre' (theory of knowledge); and a literary work, the novel *Wilhelm Meisters Lehrjahre* (1795–6; *Wilhelm Meister's years of apprenticeship*) by Johann Wolfgang Goethe (1749–1832). Schlegel's intention, of course, is to emphasise and provoke. But he clearly intends a fundamental relation between the Revolution, philosophy and literature in our epoch. Of what kind? The age around 1800, it will be argued with Schlegel, was one in which literature and philosophy self-consciously co-operated and competed for Germany's intellectual leadership. The Revolution ultimately determined their relationship. Both literature and philosophy sought words to express its meaning. Both hoped to launch actions out of those words.

The Revolution then as now was in fact seen philosophically – as the fulfilment of the project of Enlightenment, which Immanuel Kant (1724–1804) had famously defined as the emergence of humanity from its self-imposed tutelage, that is, as a race of fully self-conscious free beings. Concretely, as Kant said, Enlightenment meant rampant criticism – of all received forms of thought and action – by the new authority in matters of truth: human reason (*KrV*, 13n). The public sphere, in which matters of dispute might be settled not by appeal to received authority (religion, the state, tradition) but according to agreed, transparent rules of rational debate, had for the first time in Germany begun to constitute itself in the life of the middle classes,[2] in the form of literary and philosophical journals, reading clubs and the like. Here, and not just in the universities, the thinking of knowledge, morality, art, politics and above all religion was cast for the first time in recognisably modern form. With its replacement of the traditional form of the state by a representative constitution and a republic, and of Christian religion by the official cult of the supreme being *qua* reason, the Revolution in France (if not in Germany) seemed to mark the translation of Enlightenment theory into practice. It seemed to fulfil the long-cherished project of the French *philosophes*, to embody the final, anthropocentric re-ordering of human affairs. The full significance of this – perhaps because of the widespread Burkean rejection of political violence – was only beginning to be grasped in Germany. All this Schlegel encapsulates in his dictum. But where did Fichte and Goethe, philosophy and literature, seek to lead the tendencies of the Revolution? To share their common yet divergent vision, only hinted at in Schlegel's lapidary commentary, we must first turn to the unnamed authority on whose monumental achievement their work rests, and through whom the significance of the Revolution was mediated to Germany: Kant.

Kant had not only included the term 'critical' in his philosophy's title, suggesting that it drew the sum of Enlightenment philosophical endeavour, but also characterised his system metaphorically (and with calculated political implications) as a Copernican revolutionary shift in philosophical thought (*KrV*, 23, 25, 28). His philosophy is revolutionary in that he grounds three major fields of philosophical endeavour – epistemology, ethics and aesthetics – in a radically new way which provides the intellectual signature of the epoch around 1800 and of modernity: in *subjectivity*.[3] But for his successors Kant's account of subjectivity – despite its axial function in the system – raised as many problems as it solved. Fichte and Goethe represent the main philosophical and literary tendencies of the age not only because they take up the pursuit of the subject as the key to humanity's self-understanding in our epoch of Revolution, but also because they see philosophical and aesthetic discourse, with their distinctively differing modes of talk, as competing for the prize. This chapter charts the progress of that chase – as a dialogue between the epoch's great philosophical movement, the idealism of Kant, Fichte and Schelling, and its literary counterparts, the classicism and Romanticism of Goethe, Schiller, Schlegel, Hardenberg-Novalis and others. At the end of that dialogue stands the system of perhaps the ultimate philosopher of subjectivity, Hegel.

The problem of subjectivity arises for Kant because of his dissatisfaction with traditional metaphysics, which he thought relied on excessively self-confident use of deductive rationality. He therefore submitted reason itself to criticism and the subject to unprecedented logical dissection. In order to guarantee the scientific status of knowledge claims (including metaphysical ones), an alternative, more reliable epistemological model was required. In the *Kritik der reinen Vernunft* (1780, 1787; *Critique of pure reason*) the experimental procedures of truth finding in mathematics and natural science seemed to offer just that, and so to reveal the conditions under which propositions might claim necessarily to be true. The geometrician Thales had for example understood that all certain knowledge of the triangle's properties derived paradoxically not from empirical (a posteriori) investigation of the thing, but from the concepts he himself had already formulated independently of experience (a priori); indeed, triangles not being given in nature, he had to refer to a priori concepts to construct the thing in the first place (*KrV*, 22). Galileo knew empirical observation to be indispensable in natural science. But he also knew that observation can only be adequately judged by principles of enquiry grounded in reason. Reason in natural science is to this extent counter-intuitive: not the pupil, but the judge of nature. Reason dictates theoretical questions for nature to answer, secure in the knowledge that, as in geometry, reason can only grasp that which reason itself has already projected (23f.) – even if only nature can answer the questions. Before any metaphysical enquiry can begin, then, the task of the *Kritik der reinen Vernunft* is to explain the conditions under which a priori cognition, with its characteristic certainty, general validity and independence of experience, is possible: how the laws of nature are founded not in nature, but in the structure of human reason, not in the object, but in the *subject*.

Obviously, the key to transcendental philosophy lies in the functions attributed to the thinking subject, but precisely here problems arise. The first task is to clarify the relation of the a priori and the empirical in the constitution of experience, which Kant briskly defines as having cognitive character. He sees only two sources of knowledge: sensuality and conceptuality. Sensuality gives us objects to experience, conceptuality thinks them. But sensuality, if we try to consider it free of interference by concepts, only gives us objects in a certain way, as material sensations. Abstracting from material sensuality in order to arrive at its transcendental condition (a priori principle), we arrive at the notion of a pure (irreducible) form of sensuality, pure intuition. Time and space are the two pure forms of intuition; they offer the subject two channels of intuitive experience, inner and outer, self and world. But experience so constituted concerns things only as they appear, not in themselves. This exploration of a priori conditions relates only to the possibility of things' reception, not their intrinsic possibility: a rose's redness appears different to different subjects, is not a feature of the rose in itself. Kant thus obtains conditions of the possible reality and objectivity of experience at the level of sensuality at the price of a fundamental dualism: the supposition of a stratum of cognitively inaccessible ideality.

Problems also arise with the understanding. Here cognition functions not intuitively but discursively, through concepts. If intuition is fundamentally receptive, understanding is fundamentally spontaneous. But if intuition gives us material sensation immediately, understanding operates only through mediation, in unifying judgements which subsume particular, indefinite, multifarious inputs under general concepts according to deep-structural, logical rules in the understanding, categories. Now judgement can only function if sensual inputs (which would otherwise be chaotic) are synthesised a priori into a singular order of representations, on which the understanding does its work. This pre-cognitive task is performed by the imagination. Only application of the categories, as a priori concepts of the understanding, can constitute intuitions as knowledge. But categories achieve this only in so far as an intuition actually *does* correspond to the concept. Anything can be *thought*, but it does not thereby automatically attain cognitive value. Concepts without intuitions are empty, intuitions without concepts are blind (*KrV*, 98). Experience, then, or knowledge, is only possible in that field of representation constituted by the imagination (transcendental synthesis of apperception), and in which judgements are formed by the action of concepts on intuitions, a process of interfacing which Kant terms the schematism. This is also where the subject, considered as consciousness, resides. There must be some stable instance which acts spontaneously upon the manifold representations in the synthesis of apperception. An 'I think', a primal or pure apperception (to distinguish it from empirical input), the transcendental unity of self-consciousness, accompanies all work of cognition (136ff.). This is what acts through time, the inner sense, in the process of making judgements. The difficulty is that Kant's critical project, which rests on accountability to reason and which proudly proclaims the defining role of subjectivity in the constitution of knowledge, at this crucial point avoids accountability. For when we ask for an explanation of the 'I think' (self-knowledge), we receive an answer analogous to that for questions in respect of things in themselves. Beyond knowledge *that* I am (as appearance), says Kant, we cannot go. My intelligence may frame a concept of self. But the intuition of self which alone would satisfy the condition of cognition (152f.) is impossible, since intelligence cannot by definition be intuited and in any case manifests itself only as conditioned by the inner form of time, which is beyond conceptuality.[4]

It should by now be clear why Schlegel, searching for modernity's representative philosopher, did not select Kant. Kant's project, despite his radicality and systematic approach, still seemed incomplete. By 1794 Kantian transcendental philosophy had already been subjected to several critical analyses, most notably by Friedrich Heinrich Jacobi (1743–1819). Jacobi argued in Humean style that our cognitions of things are in fact mere mental representations, which relate to things in themselves in a way not intelligible to us.[5] This sceptical-fideistic line found its ultimate expression in Jacobi's suggestion that in a transcendental enquiry any chain of conditions ultimately ends in the unconditioned: since this cannot be made an object of cognition, *all* cognition rests at last on something beyond reason, a *salto mortale* of intuitional conviction, or faith.[6] But it was Fichte (1759–1814), fixing on Kant's central yet highly tentative account of subjectivity, who offered a far more radical account of subjectivity and cognition. The 'Wissenschaftslehre' was intended to complete the critique of pure reason.[7] However in one of its most accessible formulations, the *Zweite Einleitung in die Wissenschaftslehre* (1797; *Second introduction to the theory of knowledge*),[8] Fichte holds against Kant that there *is* an intellectual intuition (459). He agrees that such a thing cannot be formulated conceptually and demonstrated in a proof through propositions, still less can its meaning be communicated. But it *can* be experienced, and Fichte's work in this context is full less of argument than of exhortations to the reader to follow his instructions and reproduce the experience in themselves. The experience is of primal self-consciousness (Kant's pure apperception) as sheer activity (463), the activity of those who as it were looking inward try merely to think themselves. This, says Fichte, is an immediate, spontaneous consciousness *that* the subject is active and *what* that activity is. As such, despite its pre-reflexive status, it is characterised by unquestionable necessity. It is the sole fixed reference point of all philosophy (466). On the basis of this ultra-Cartesian account of intellectual intuition Fichte moves to the conceptual level, and deduces the conditions of the possibility of self-consciousness implied by his notion of the subject as pure activity. What we call self-consciousness is in fact an empirical structure of reflection, the mere result of something prior.[9] The empirical subject ('Ich') initially (as it were) thinks itself. Yet this subject is limited in reflection by something not itself, the object ('Nicht-Ich'). It being impossible in reflection to transcend the reciprocal determinations of the series (thinking the thinking of thinking, and so on *ad infinitum*) except in intellectual intuition, the philosopher concludes speculatively that the reciprocal subject–object structure of empirical self-conciousness must be the result of the activity of a postulated absolute subject which contains all reality and which consists in free self-positing, a kind of unlimited emanation of sheer activity ('productive imagination', 215). This so far hardly accounts for empirical reality, the facts of our limited consciousness. But Fichte further deduces that the absolute subject must *itself* freely limit – negate – the potentially infinite centrifugal flow of activity. This generates an equal and opposite centripetal dynamic. The facts of empirical consciousness, then, emerge from something like an a priori narrative. They are the result of a primal division and alienation from the unified, absolute, and free source of being. Empirical experience, in which the subject feels alternately free and yet determined by the object, is the relatively stable result of this infinite–finite interaction. In practical terms, the thing in itself ('Not-I') has been explained away; the relative autonomy of things is accounted for by the limiting activity of the absolute subject necessary to constitute empirical reality. The subject too is accounted for, as the pure freedom of spontaneous activity (which admittedly is only experienced in intellectual intuition). Practical and theoretical domains of philosophy, systematically separated in Kant, are joined at the root, and the ethical task of the subject is to overcome the scission between empirical and absolute freedom made concrete by the resistance of the 'Not-I'. Unsurprisingly, this absolute subjectivism, with its celebration of unconditional freedom as the very essence, origin and end of the human person in the world of contingent necessity, seemed to Fichte and (for a time) Schlegel to have developed philosophy in the revolutionary age to an ultimate point. Goethe's classicist friend and collaborator Friedrich Schiller (1759–1805) called it subjective Spinozism. Schlegel's Romantic friend and collaborator Friedrich von Hardenberg (Novalis; 1772–1801), who like Schlegel recognised the spirit of the age in a philosophical system, nominated Fichte for membership of a fanciful *Directoire* of philosophy in Germany as guardian of the constitution (*NS* II, 529f.).

If Fichte's philosophy seemed authentically to represent the revolutionary realisation of subjective freedom in theoretical and practical spheres, Goethe's *Wilhelm Meisters Lehrjahre* was that work of contemporary literature which dealt most fully with another, correlated dimension of subjective development: self-cultivation. In this, the *Bildungsroman* which established the generic paradigm, a representative young 'Bürger' (middle-class man) struggles to become himself: 'to cultivate myself, just

as I am, that from youth on was dimly my wish and my intention'.[10]
Bildung, the means to that sovereignty of self which Meister's name implies, connotes a good deal more than cultivation of the intellect. That,
in a sense, is precisely what Wilhelm protests against. The 'Bürger' were
politically disenfranchised in rationalistic but still-feudal Germany, their
role in the state defined by management and wealth-production. One
of the foils to Wilhelm, his brother-in-law Werner, thinks double-entry
book-keeping is one of the most beautiful inventions of the human spirit.
Wilhelm wants to transcend this impoverished vision, which circum-
scribes human fulfilment with the work-ethic and abstract cleverness.
But in this he asks something his society cannot yet provide to a man of
his provenance: cultivation in the most comprehensive sense, of his individual person – not only intellect, but the senses, emotions, imagination,
physicality, sociability – of whatever potentialities nature has bestowed on
him, so that he may become fully human, a whole person. There seem to
Wilhelm to be only two avenues through contemporary German society
to this goal: that of the leisured aristocracy, with its privileged, essentially
Baroque ideal of personal cultivation, and that of the *déclassé* world of
the theatre. Both exploit the potential of aesthetic experience to bypass
the equation of class, work and personal limitation. Having taken the
only path open to him, into the Bohemian theatre world where art and
work seem one, Wilhelm is disappointed. Self-realisation on the stage
proves to be a mere veneer covering the familiar exigencies of the world
of profit and loss. Yet he does not renounce the potential for personal
growth disclosed by the experience of art. He learns to internalise the
lessons of art (as a kind of nobility of soul) and to practise a kind of free
utopian renunciation of unlimited self-development, recognising his intrinsic limitation at one level, but overcoming it at another, and working
selflessly in a mutually complementary collective of similarly disposed,
mainly aristocratic individuals at projects intended to improve humanity's practical lot – a typical German reaction to the Revolution, rejecting
its means, retaining its aims.

This is admittedly a muted kind of sovereignty of self. Yet what makes
the novel for Schlegel into another embodiment of the fundamental
tendencies of the revolutionary age is not the rather severe (probably
Kantian) ethic Wilhelm arrives at, but the sense in which not philosophy
but *aesthetic experience* exerts a transformative, emancipatory power over
the self in the world of empirical contingency and limitation. After the
theatre episode, Meister reads a spiritual autobiography, the story of a
'schöne Seele' (beautiful soul). Following a spiritual crisis, moral action

has become second nature for the beautiful soul, to such a degree that her ethical perfection translates into an aesthetic quality: she seems positively to incorporate ethical grace in real life (rather than, for example, on stage). From this reading Wilhelm emerges a changed man, ripe for admission to the collective of utopian renouncers. Aesthetic experience, then, *may* (as in the theatre) lead to a loss of the sense of reality. Rightly understood, however, it is also something without which Wilhelm would not have attained the position he does. This is why, having abandoned the theatre, he comes into his aesthetic inheritance (an art collection) at the close of the novel. Art may not be an end in itself; that way existential disaster lies. But used properly, art can make us into what we ought to be. Fichte's philosophy self-reflectively seemed to draw the sum of all philosophy. Goethe's novel seemed like a work of art which self-reflectively drew the sum of all art – and in some way complemented Fichte. This, evidently, is why Schlegel ranked *Wilhelm Meisters Lehrjahre* alongside Fichte and the French Revolution.

But why *does* Wilhelm never consider philosophy as a means to self-cultivation, when at the end of the philosophical century it had just attained such authoritative stature in the works of Kant and Fichte? And in what way might literature, as Schlegel implies, complement the work of philosophy? To grasp this is to understand why literature and philosophy co-operated and competed around 1800. Goethe for his part had constructed the project of *Bildung* – aesthetic humanism[11] – exemplified by *Wilhelm Meisters Lehrjahre* on the foundation of Schiller's mature aesthetics. There was little dispute between the classical duo. But Schiller's aesthetics are the result of a difference with Kant over the means to realise the moral destiny of the human race at this critical, post-revolutionary juncture in its historical development. Schiller was a declared Kantian, who had above all been impressed by the ethics of the critical philosophy, and in many ways his mature aesthetics (and literary writings) can be seen as an attempt to popularise Kantian morality. *Bildung* or aesthetic education nonetheless emerges from a momentous dispute with the sage of Königsberg.

In two complementary works, the *Grundlegung zur Metaphysik der Sitten* (1785; *Foundation of the metaphysics of morals*) and the *Kritik der praktischen Vernunft* (1787; *Critique of practical reason*),[12] Kant, the destroyer of traditional metaphysics, had nevertheless preserved the trace of metaphysics in his rigoristic ethics. No principle derived from empirical experience, he insists, can suffice for pure practical reason to ground moral action. However abstractly formulated, such principles are bound to be heteronomous: contaminated by personal interest in some outcome (*Grundlegung*, 34, 39f.). The moral principle which determines the will must be a priori, totally unconditioned and autonomous, purely formal, grounded compellingly in the structure of reason itself. This is the categorical imperative (45). In reality, the will must of course act to some end and treat others correspondingly. But since humanity – seen as a rational creature – is an end *in itself* (59ff.), the transcendental principle of practical reason is easily formulated: act in such a way that all persons are treated as ends in themselves. Now from speculative reason's standpoint our autonomy as the principle of ethical causality is a mere idea. It is well founded in reason, but no intuition from the realm of determinate phenomena can be found to fill the concept. Yet in the realm of practical reason this essential freedom *can* in a sense be known, in so far as our moral action in itself *demonstrates* the presence of the supersensual in the sensual world: noumenal freedom within the domain of phenomenal law. This is obviously not empirical knowledge. But it *is* knowledge – of a higher realm of nature, altogether cleansed of the sensual: *intelligible* nature. Moral action, then, *is* the intuition of the idea of practical reason, the only certain knowledge available of the *metaphysical* world, and indeed the only basis for postulates regarding the existence of God, freedom and personal immortality. Fichte of course took the chance to identify this consciousness with intellectual intuition (*Zweite Einleitung*, 472), and this is at the root of his claim to have unified the practical and theoretical philosophies.

The inspiring effect on Schiller and his generation of this *tour de force* of post-revolutionary self-determination, the crowning glory of Kant's project to save metaphysics in modernity and the basis of his utopian political philosophy for the ethical state, is well documented. Even so, the further problem arises as to whether and how the abstract and rigoristic categorical imperative might be translated into everyday practice. Kant had unconvincingly insisted that anyone might grasp his ethics, since they are grounded in common-or-garden rationality (*Grundlegung*, 39n). With this Schiller differed. His pioneering essay, *Über Anmut und Würde* (1793; *On grace and dignity*)[13] criticises the categorical imperative as harsh and dualistic, from the characteristic standpoint of Schiller's anthropological holism. He agrees with Kant's ethical rigorism to the extent that the dictation of the moral law must be free of sensuous contamination, that duty must ignore (for example) any striving for (merely individual) happiness. Nevertheless human nature – despite the power of Kant's transcendental analysis – is a holistic unity, irreducibly composed of intellect and sense.

The categorical imperative, sublime document of ethical destiny as it is, seems in reality less to realise human freedom than to repeat the mistakes of the Revolution, ruthlessly to expose human nature's weakness in order to enslave it, and in particular our corporeality, to pure practical reason (463ff.). Thus it perpetuates the fragmentation of the modern subject.

Kant had in fact already offered an alternative mediation between the non-moral and the moral dispositions. *Aesthetic ideas*, he claimed, might do the job by providing the less sophisticated, sensually determined mind with an *analogy* of ethical cognition. For in aesthetic experience, as Kant describes it in the first part of the *Kritik der Urteilskraft* (1790; *Critique of judgement*),[14] we experience objects in a particular and unique way: not as objects of phenomenal knowledge but as sheer appearances, which precisely in this bear a special relation to the ethical. Aesthetic experience is play: the harmonious play of imagination and conceptuality in the act of reflective judgement (100), which spontaneously seeks the concept for the complex and powerful intuition of an aesthetic work, and derives pleasure from its satisfying purposiveness. Of course no concept is ever found. Purposiveness in aesthetic experience is a purely formal property, which is never expressed in some purpose outside itself, so that the object acquires the semblance of autonomy. Without a concept aesthetic experience is excluded from cognition strictly so defined (221). But judgements on art do claim a kind of objectivity and cognitive value. Aesthetic pleasure is admittedly subjective. However, it inheres in the material form of the work, so that the particular experience is shared by all subjects. To that extent aesthetic judgements rightfully claim general assent according to norms judged by the aesthetic sense or faculty of taste (228). Beauty has a sort of cognitive value too, in that aesthetic experience inspires us (249ff.): the powerful intuitions of art factually transcend understanding and so stretch the mind beyond the domain of experience. Hence Kant terms them aesthetic *ideas*. They are analogous to the empirically impossible representation of ideas proper, concepts of reason which may be well founded in reason but transcend any possible empirical intuition. Aesthetic ideas, then, generated by the genius, have the *potential to train us in moral action*. For the appearance of freedom inevitably appeals to something in the subject which is more than nature. It is not strictly freedom, but it does relate to the supersensual ground of freedom. Furthermore, beauty and ethical experience evince strong emotional and structural parallels. Beauty is immediate, disinterested, universally human, and characteristically harmonises antagonistic opposites (imaginative freedom and conceptual necessity). Ethical experience too is immediate, disinterested (albeit in reason's interest), universally human, and harmonises antagonistic opposites (freedom of the will and rational necessity). In short, beauty can be accounted a *symbol* of the morally good (297). As such, it potentially builds an existential bridge between non-moral and moral dispositions to act: habituates us to bending imagination to reason's purpose (even when acting freely), teaches us to find pleasure in sensuality without falling prey to sensual interest, and facilitates the move from being sensually determined to obeying reason's interest without a behavioural leap.

In *Über Anmut und Würde* Schiller remains anything but opposed to the interest of reason, but he radicalises Kant's tentative aesthetic mediation. If reason's ethical interest is to be served reason must not dominate; sensuality and intellect must work together. For this to happen, however, the subject's moral action in the phenomenal sphere must not merely be aesthetically mediated, but must also *express* itself aesthetically. One who obeys the *Diktat* of the categorical imperative is in theory acting freely, and Kant certainly thought of this as the liberating triumph of supersensuality. In fact, he visibly labours. He shows the compulsion in his body language as the signature of the paradoxical violation of something fundamental to his constitution as a human person. The interest of reason is, says Schiller, better served if nature, in reason's realm, is allowed by reason to *remain* nature – if ethical freedom expresses itself not against, but *through* body language, as *second* nature: beautifully. This *visible* harmony of freedom and sensuality, duty and inclination, is 'Anmut', grace. Its incarnation is of course the beautiful soul (*Anmut und Würde*, 468) whose autobiography Wilhelm Meister read. Its purpose is to enlist the aid of sensuality in reason's project: to further humanity's destiny through the harmonious union of the forces in human nature rather than division or subordination. Schiller's aestheticising approach to the ethical orthodoxy of transcendental philosophy thus defines one chief function of literature in this epoch: under the guise of co-operation to preach the rights of corporeality and person against idealism's abstract concept of subject. In this, Schiller's aesthetic meta-Kantianism is also one of the earliest expressions of the critique of the dialectic of Enlightenment, whereby the systematic application of reason characteristic of Kant in particular and modern culture in general is argued to produce rationality and irrationality, freedom and compulsion, in equal measure.[15]

Schiller's elegy 'Der Tanz' (1796; 'The dance') is a good example of what he means in *Anmut und Würde*. These elegant neo-classical distichs celebrate how, in the dance, music's gentle discipline magically liberates the body from natural constraint – as the clumsy skiff suddenly glides in the stream. But this is not all. In the dance a further, higher principle of social ordering – second nature – seems harmoniously to regulate natural appetite. Where the spontaneous, apparently wilful moves of individual couples into the whirling mass threaten chaos and destruction, in fact the power of musical harmony guarantees that new order and form ensue. The poem is thus revealed as an allegory of the relevance of aesthetic grace to the social problem. Even the natural universe is so governed. The inspiring rhythm of living being and the infinitely complex, yet orderly paths of heavenly bodies through the cosmos are like the dance: examples of a universal principle of self-regulating Nemesis, which reconciles freedom and necessity, chaos and order, body and mind, individual and totality, change and continuity, in the measured aesthetic vision, which is henceforth to be respected in life as much as in art. Schiller systematically propounded this programme in a lengthy series of poems, from 'Die Künstler' (1789; 'The artists') on.

Schiller's most important single work, *Über die ästhetische Erziehung des Menschen* (1795; *On the aesthetic education of humanity*),[16] makes the ambition of this aesthetic programme fully explicit. Here he frankly thematises antagonism in the body politic following the French Revolution. Both the French Revolution and German reforms are crude attempts to impose reason on the 'natural' state. By antagonising rather than working with what is natural in the state they paradoxically repress ethical freedom. Thus the political problem is but a wider expression of modernity's basic ill: the personal fragmentation diagnosed in *Über Anmut und Würde*. The domination of either rationality or sensuality must be undone. But not by philosophy. With the establishment of the moral law, philosophy's task is exhausted (*Ästhetische Erziehung*, 590f.). Instead, the experience of beauty is the necessary condition of humanity (600), the *only* way to make people under the one-sided determination of either sensuality or rationality truly humane (641). This is so, Schiller explains in an exhilarating if hyperbolic reformulation of Kantian aesthetic autonomy, because, uniquely, the apparently self-determining beautiful object actually *does* instantiate freedom in (empirical) appearance, not merely in the way the subject might experience it. To sensualists, the numinous reality of self-determination is revealed in an aptly sensual medium, and creates in them the disposition to moral sovereignty. To ethical rigorists, the cause of sensuality is pleaded with grace. *Only* thus, in the transitional zone where philosophy's writ does not run, is the mediation between sensuality and ethical form possible. Thus art now claims responsibility for realising the ethical and political project of practical philosophy. From this flows a programme of universal aestheticisation of human experience. Schiller demands in answer to Kant and the Revolution and in direct affront to the Platonic tradition[17] nothing less than the aesthetic state.

This, then, is the full reason why Meister does not consult a philosophy manual on his journey to self-cultivation, and why *Wilhelm Meisters Lehrjahre* merit their place in *Athenaeums-Fragment* no. 216. When Meister, with his paradigmatic desire for self-development, passes through art to moral sovereignty, he does not merely encounter the beautiful soul. He also – albeit not without criticism – encounters Schiller's meta-Kantian theory of art's transformative power and programme for restoring the human wholeness *beyond philosophy*. Philosophy may have identified the tendency of the modern age, but, as Schiller said in *Über naive und sentimentalische Dichtung* (1795–6; *On naive and reflective poetry*), modernity's gain is also loss, and that loss can only be recuperated through aesthetic discourse. Art thus also becomes the organ of cultural memory and prophet of the utopian future in bad times (*Ästhetische Erziehung*, 594). Classical antiquity offers the lost ideal of holistic self-fulfilment. Goethe and Schiller become committed classicists, typically in works such as Schiller's 'Die Götter Griechenlands' (1788; 'The gods of Greece') and Goethe's 'Römische Elegien' (1790; 'Roman elegies'), both of which seek to synthesise the reflexivity which is the strength and weakness of modern culture with the naivety and spontaneity of the classical idyll. Thus at the dawn of modernity, as Schlegel saw, literature and philosophy share a path but also begin to diverge. Schiller and Goethe inaugurate the tradition of aesthetic modernism,[18] in which the emergence of the notions of absolute subjective freedom in philosophy and reason's absolute authority in culture call forth an aesthetic discourse criticising rationalistic excess. The new belief in the cognitive and performative power of art and literature led to an explosion of creativity in aesthetic theory and experimental literature.

The authoritative tone of *Athenaeums-Fragment* no. 216 betrays that Friedrich Schlegel and his fellow early German Romantics saw their role as more than acknowledging the achievements of idealism and classicism. Like classical humanism, Romanticism emerges in large part from a literary reception of philosophy as the dominant discourse of the Enlightenment, but here the respective importance of Kant and Fichte shifts. Both Goethe and Schiller had studied Kant intensively.[19] Goethe had in 1794 appointed Fichte to the University of Jena. But most of his copies of Fichte's works remained obstinately uncut.[20] As allusions to Fichtean concepts in the *Ästhetische Erziehung* suggest,[21] Schiller had read more. In the end, however, the classical duo dismissed the 'Wissenschaftslehre' as a hypertrophic version of the common-sense distinction between subject and object. But for the early Romantics Friedrich Schlegel and Friedrich von Hardenberg (Novalis) the thinker of absolute subjective sovereignty was the unquestioned philosophical hero. They used Fichte, who wrote no aesthetics, to found their own programme, called first 'Fichtisiren' (Fichticising) (*NS* II, 524, no. 11) and later 'Romantisiren' (Romanticising) (*NS* II, 545, no. 105). Here the disjunctive Kantian relation of aesthetic experience to philosophical cognition, already blurred by Schiller's promotion of aesthetic experience as the voice of holistic human truth, was much more radically redefined.

The fundamental document of this move are Hardenberg's *Fichte-Studien*, philosophical studies of Fichte over the period 1795–6 (*NS* II, 104–296). These recognise the problem of fragmentation, but focus less on the aspect of holistic human truth than on expansion of self-consciousness from the perspective of the Fichtean absolute. Where Fichte had constantly claimed that what he had to say and the way of saying it were ontologically incommensurable, Hardenberg's *Fichte-Studien* begin and end with problems of writing and representation. As with Fichte, the chief problem of philosophy is the meta-critique of Kant: the thinking of identity in the structure of reflection. However, Hardenberg focuses not only on the abstract form of the problem, but also on a concrete aspect, namely, that reflection on identity must occur in a medium: a representation, a language of some kind. Things (such as 'I' and 'Not-I'), must be named in order to form part of the process of reflection. But the name of the thing is derivative and as such cannot fix its essential being. Where there *is* only voice (things coming into being) there can be no echo (*NS* II, 202). This sceptical and relativistic view of representation does not however make Hardenberg into a Shandyesque linguistic critic of absolute subjectivism. He accepts the Fichtean framework, in that the definition of the subject must flow from its reciprocal opposition to the object, and that logically a prior totality, an all-encompassing 'sphere' of being, must be thought in which this reciprocal definition takes place. That totality is however now recognised to be beyond naming and to transcend the representational structure of reflection altogether. We are left with the recognition that the philosophical absolute, whilst logically necessary, is paradoxically an absence, at best an intuition of lost but yearned-for totality from the standpoint of alienated modern reflection.

Our task, then, if we are to think identity, has become aesthetic: to *construct* totality in language on the basis of that privileged primal intuition. The constructed absolute is technically a fiction. But it is a necessary one, for it alone transcends reflection, makes the absent absolute in some sense present and intelligible in the prosaic everyday. *As* a representation it is however also constitutionally provisional and relative, subject to unending revision. It realises the ideal, but must also be acknowledged as only an experimental attempt. The transcendental self thus loses its fixed Cartesian-Fichtean foundation. Fixed in a deeply ironic relation to being and reality, it becomes a fundamentally unstable construct, oscillating between something and nothing. This genesis of Romanticism in a fusion of absolute idealism and linguistic scepticism accounts for its characteristically paradoxical stance of utopianism (unending perfectibility) and irony.

Romantic writing is the practical consequence of this: philosophico-aesthetic performances which do not so much represent the absolute as enact the palindromic figure of thought given by the process of idealistic construction and ironic retraction. At the end of the *Fichte-Studien* this is formulated gnomically as the need to represent the sensual spiritually and the spiritual sensually (*NS* II, 283, no. 633). The development from 'Fichtisiren' to 'Romantisiren' in Hardenberg's classic formulation of 1797 clarifies the technique. Romanticisation, commonly understood since Heine as escapist manipulation of the banal facts of alienated everyday experience (as moonshine transfigures ashen nightscape), in fact performs a bi-polar destabilisation of textual referentiality. The contents of everyday consciousness – ordinary, common, well-known, finite things – are in Hardenberg's metaphor 'potentialised': endowed with the semblance of high significance, mystery, strangeness, infinity, in short, a relation to the absolute. But there is also a corresponding, equal and opposite move. Our notions of the ideal, the higher, the unknown, the mystical, the infinite, are 'logarithmicised': humoristically reduced in semantic stature by being identified with their banal opposite. All this is intended as a provocation (*NS* II, 282) of the late eighteenth-century philistine subject's latent freedom: the liberation of pure transcendentality from the bounds of phenomenal consciousness on the one hand, combined with a healthy sense of self-irony on the other.

There are far-reaching consequences of this semi-modernist, semi-mystical constructivism. Hardenberg and the Romantics abandon the fundamental orientation of both Kant's and Fichte's (indeed all German School) philosophy towards system. Romantic thought has and can only have the character of a fragment: 'the systemless, systematised' (*NS* II, 289, no. 648). Hardenberg's theory of knowledge is also less ratiocination than intuitive *poiesis*. We know things only by making them in words. The essential activity of intellect, as Hardenberg states elsewhere, consists in transforming otherness into ownness, turning the world into home (*NS* III, 434, no. 857). Human nature (recalling Plato)[22] is in this sense essentially poetic: humanity *is* metaphor. Metaphorical making competes boldly with propositionality as a theory of cognition,[23] and Kant's cautious acknowledgement of subjective sources of cognition is dramatically radicalised: the aprioristic and divinatory fantasy experiments of the poet are a better way of achieving insight into nature than severe natural-scientific methodologies of observation and experiment.

All this makes up what Hardenberg calls 'Poesie', and with it comes a corresponding elevation in status vis-à-vis philosophy. He characteristically attacks in metaphor philosophy's 'jagged peaks of pure reason' (*NS* IV, 321) and especially Fichte's 'awesome spiral of abstractions' (*NS* IV, 230). Rather, he says: 'Poetry is the authentically absolute reality – this is the core of my philosophy. The more poetic, the more true' (*NS* II, 647, no. 473). Echoing Schiller, he declares that philosophy's work is done when its legislation has prepared the world for the influence of ideas, but poetry is the key to philosophy, its task communicatively to realise those ideas. Where Schiller had seen the poet as the only true human being and the age as sick, Hardenberg sees the transcendental poet as the transcendental doctor of the human race. Later, the terms 'Poesie' and 'Philosophie' become a kind of correlated shorthand. 'Philosophie' comes to mean less the continuing pursuit of truth through formalised procedures which endow knowledge claims with authority than the ultimative results already achieved by Kant and Fichte. Whenever Romantic writers use the term 'Poesie', it connotes this implicit critique of philosophy. In the end, poetry becomes for the Romantics a mythical entity. Their texts are not only to realise philosophy's project, but also to incarnate absolute poetry. In this sense poetry becomes a cult, and the cult of poetry comes to embody Germany's post-revolutionary answer to the French religion of reason. The abstract quality of some of these procedures should not mask their political status as a response to the Revolution. 'Poesie', said Friedrich Schlegel, is a republican discourse.

The first literary fruit of this new shift in the terms of dialogue between poetry and philosophy is the Romantic Fragment. Its inventor, Friedrich Schlegel, shared much with Hardenberg. He saw intellectual intuition, with its paradoxical transcendence of reflection, as the categorical imperative (epistemological ideal) of theory (*Athenaeums-Fragment* no. 76; *KFSA* II, 176). He rejected both systematic thought and its opposite (no. 53; *KFSA* II, 173), and argued for the complementarity of philosophy and poetry.[24] Philosophical demonstrations, he said, were conducted in 'militarised' technical language, which merely served to legitimate claims to intellectual territory once seized. Philosophical definitions could at best give hints, at worst say nothing or obscure everything. What mattered was simply to know something and say it. In practice, it was far harder to assert than prove something (no. 82; *KFSA* II, 177). But even an assertion was not final, merely a stepping stone of argument. All this was not philosophy but 'Symphilosophie' or 'Sympoesie': a shared intellectual process of creation, which rejects traditional, monologous thought and invites unending, dialogical exploration.

The Romantic Fragment is this characteristically assertoric yet open-ended form, half discursive thought, half metaphorical divination. Perhaps Schlegel's most brilliant Fragment is one of the smallest, *Athenaeums-Fragment* no. 206. This looks like a sparse theoretical definition of the genre: 'A Fragment must as a miniature work of art be entirely isolated from the surrounding world and perfect in itself, like a hedgehog.' The Fragment, says Schlegel, must model totality: relate to the absolute as autonomous microcosm does to macrocosm. Of course his ending, the simile of the (rolled up) hedgehog, depotentialises the pretentious assertion with an abrupt rhetorical descent from the sublime to the ridiculous: a willed humoristic disproportion between transcendental ambition and textual achievement targeted at Schlegel himself and Romanticism in general. Schlegel called this sort of thing transcendental buffoonery. But the point is that this Fragment, whilst it defines the genre, does not do so as a definition in the abstract 'military' language of (philosophical) aesthetics. It *embodies* the definition of the genre by *enacting* what it says, and so *being* a Fragment: momentarily perfect, finally incomplete. It is not theory but intuition, or rather both theory and intuition, definition and thing. Thus it instantiates Schlegel's ideal of Romantic epistemology: intellectual intuition as 'categorical imperative of theory'.

Of course for the Romantics all texts, irrespective of genre and whether considered by their author to be 'finished' works or not, are intrinsically fragmentary. Received notions of author, work and text are revised so as to give the aesthetic turn of Goethe and Schiller still another, unmistakably hermeneutic twist. Homer's classic texts, as Schlegel discovered through the Göttingen scholar F. A. Wolf, were in fact not finished when written by their named author, but successively modified by later, anonymous critics reflecting on and perfecting the 'originals'. Nor was Goethe's *Meister*, their great modern counterpart, complete. Schlegel's *Über Goethes Meister* (1798; *On Goethe's Meister*) began the process of revising it. Reflective criticism is thus more than just evaluation or interpretation. A critic recreates the original text, once digested, at a higher level, and criticism attains the same dignity as poetry or philosophy proper. The Romantics hardly abandoned Kantian individualistic genius in favour of collective creativity, but for them the notion of authorship is fundamentally relativised and pluralised. Hardenberg offered its paradigmatic formulation: 'The true reader must be the author, expanded' (*NS* II, 470, no. 125).

These early insights helped to refound a scholarly discipline. The hermeneutics of Friedrich Schleiermacher (1776–1834), conceived around 1805–6 and first systematised in 1819, but only published as *Hermeneutik und Kritik* (*Hermeneutics and criticism*) in 1838,[25] develop the germinal ideas of his friends. By profession a Berlin reformed theologian, Schleiermacher had made his name with *Über die Religion. Reden an die Gebildeten unter ihren Verächtern* (1799; *On religion. Addresses to its cultivated despisers*), which sought to make religion appeal to the secular mentality of the educated classes by grounding religious experience (irrespective of particular doctrine) in the familiar, philosophically respectable Romantic concept of totalising intuition. Like Schlegel and Hardenberg Schleiermacher had come to be convinced that thought is not independent of the language in which it is cast. Judgements, then, are not purely logical, but also expressive and interpretative acts embedded in the pre-existent structure of communication. The Kantian abstract schematism of concept and intuition must therefore be complemented by a linguistic schematism which mediates the individual utterance of the author with the totality of the language he and his reader use, and dialectics (Schleiermacher's logic) must be complemented by hermeneutics. In this he not only anticipates the Saussurian categories of (general) 'langue' and (individual) 'parole', but is also the author of the term 'speech act' later popularised by J. L. Austin (*Hermeneutik und Kritik*, 89; cf. 76ff.). A text, then, is an intrinsically individual and historical expression of the universal, to grasp it the purpose of hermeneutics. The deceptively simple formulation of this aim – adequate comprehension of another's text (71) – in fact requires a twofold analysis of text and context. Grammatical analysis covers the externality of the language used. From this standpoint the author is merely the site of a particular utterance, the meaning of which can only be grasped as conditioned by the totality of existing semantic possibilities in the language as a whole. Psychological analysis on the other hand recognises the innovative power of individual creativity (style, 168), and only the interpreter's subjective divination of the intended new sense (169f.) can launch the process of understanding proper. The art of hermeneutics demands the synthesis of both approaches. Schlegel, provocative as ever, had insisted that the critic must understand the author better than the author himself. Schleiermacher's formulation of his (unattainable) hermeneutic ideal – 'to understand a text first just as well and then better than its author' (94) – consciously echoes this.

But of course the main expression of the Romantics' hermeneutic approach was their literary writing, in particular the ultimate expression of 'Poesie': the Romantic novel. Almost all Romantics – Hardenberg, Friedrich Schlegel, Ludwig Tieck, Clemens Brentano, E. T. A. Hoffmann, Joseph von Eichendorff – wrote at least one. The Romantic novel attempts to synthesise all known genres in a constantly evolving would-be absolute mode of discourse. But it was also a mode of hermeneutic criticism, a sympoetical dialogue with a constantly evolving 'classic' text. Palimpsest-like, most Romantic novels respond to the epoch-making 'tendency' of *Wilhelm Meister*. But they also respond to philosophy. Schlegel (thinking of Socrates in Plato's *Apology*)[26] saw philosophy as the true home of irony (*Kritisches Fragment*, no. 42), but this only supported his assertion that (Romantic) novels were the Socratic dialogues of his day (no. 26). Schlegel set no limits to their form or theme. In practice, almost all preach the myth of poetry as meta-philosophy and, transcending both Goethe and Fichte, treat some aspect of the crisis of subjectivity in which a specific limitation of philosophical talk is overcome by aesthetic means. Often allusions to Plato (the representative idealist philosopher of classical antiquity) introduce these arguments. Novels by Hardenberg, Friedrich Hölderlin, Friedrich Schlegel and Clemens Brentano exemplify this.

Hardenberg's *Heinrich von Ofterdingen* (1800–2) was an 'apotheosis of poetry'[27] intended to overcome the ambiguous view of art in *Wilhelm Meisters Lehrjahre*. Unlike Wilhelm, Heinrich is not half but a whole poet, and the story shows how mythic poetry triumphs over prosaic earthly existence. In particular, it transforms the temporal horizon of his consciousness, and in this Hardenberg also takes up a famous Platonic problem. In the *Parmenides*,[28] Plato had analysed a paradox of temporality. In time's linear flow motion and rest cannot be conceived together. Where one is, the other cannot be. Some higher, transitional zone, a quintessentially Platonic privileged vantage point inside but outside of time, must exist to mediate their relation. Plato calls it the 'moment', but also considered it beyond conceptuality. The apotheosis of Heinrich's life story *is* just such a 'moment'.

This works through an original narrative technique. Early on, prompted by an encounter with a wandering poet, Heinrich has an extraordinary dream which represents the birth of poetic consciousness in him. In a (Platonic) cave he bathes in the wellsprings of creation, the *menstruum universale* of the cosmic imagination. Here, mere thinking is creation of self and other. This phase of the dream, then, is a literary figuration of intellectual intuition.[29] From this highest level of ideality he passes to external nature, which strangely resembles the earlier domain. In a third realm, ideal and real are synthesised, and he is captivated by a woman's face in the corolla of a large blue flower. All this signifies what the title of part one of the novel suggests: expectation. The dip in the *menstruum universale* connotes initiation into the poetic nature of absolute reality and his awakening self-understanding as part of *natura naturans*. The move into everyday reality suggests subsequent entrapment in the domain of the 'Not-I'. The last phase suggests that love (the woman's face) unites the two realms. When however in part two expectation becomes fulfilment and the dream events unfold in empirical fact, dream and reality, past and future, merge. The reader's perspective is dislocated into a zone where all three temporal dimensions of Heinrich's life dissolve in the paradoxical continuum of a boundless present, inside yet outside of time's flow, the unity of Heinrich's finite consciousness with the infinite productivity of his origin. This skilfully constructed totalising perspective of immanent transcendence,[30] then, is the Platonic 'moment', Romanticised. It is the first of those renowned epiphanic moments which aim to recover the authentic self in modernist literature.[31]

Friedrich Hölderlin (1776–1843), friend of Schelling and Hegel, and with Hardenberg the most powerful poet-philosopher of the first Romantic generation, had followed a strikingly similar path to his own version of the myth of poetry. He argued in the untitled landmark essay known as *Seyn, Urtheil, Modalität* (1794; *Being, judgement, modality*)[32] that subject and object were ontologically one in intellectual intuition, but that this oneness should not be logically confused with identity. Self-consciousness is only possible through a reflective division of the primal oneness of being, in which 'I' and 'Not-I' are separated. Identity is thus incommensurable with the unity of absolute being and itself entails fragmentation. Absolute identity is pre- or meta-reflexive, in this sense past. As with the Romantics, we can only go forward to it, by other means. The cognitively accentuated experience of beauty, with its characteristic harmonisation of antagonistic opposites (recall the pioneering Kantian definition) becomes for Hölderlin the means to attain unity at a higher level.

His novel *Hyperion oder der Eremit in Griechenland* (1797–9; *Hyperion, or the hermit in Greece*),[33] the story of an idealist striver in contemporary Greece under Russo-Turkish colonisation, exemplifies this figure of thought in an historical scheme. Hyperion suffers from the fragmentation and limitation characteristic of modernity, be it the division in his personality, of Greece from its past and destiny, the individual from the state, or humanity from nature, and the novel tells of his progress towards resolution of these conflicts. His guide in this has the same name as the woman who, in Plato's *Symposium*, teaches Socrates the true meaning and nature of love: Diotima.[34] Love, Eros, is for Socrates' wisest woman not a god but a daemon, a mediating figure between the mortal and immortal realms, whose nature consists not in possession of the good, the true and the beautiful, but in striving for them – proceeding via the vision of beautiful form, deeds and knowledge to the vision of absolute beauty itself. Only this makes life worth living, makes the mortal capable of creating the good, the true and the beautiful, of being loved by the gods, and so of reaching immortality.[35] As he looks back on a life of failed striving, it is Hölderlin's Diotima who offers Hyperion hope. But this Diotima prefers silence to talk. When she speaks, it is in song, indeed her entire being seems to consist in this sense in poetry (*Hyperion*, 660), so that Hyperion's encounter with Diotima is less the Socratic process of progressive philosophical enlightenment through dialogue with a wise woman than the overcoming of division and ascent to the vision of divine beauty through love of beauty personified, a muse. For Hyperion, inspired as he is by the encounter with Diotima, philosophy – as Minerva springs from the mind of Jupiter (685) – is the secondary (Athenian) creation of a totalising poetic vision. It will finally become poetry again (685). The work of understanding is mere division, and even reason must follow the vision of beauty, the differentiated oneness ('das Eine in sich selber unterschiedne') of Heraclitus (685ff.) which alone gives meaning to reason's 'demands' (687). Now seeing this appears to come too late. Diotima and Hyperion have separated: he is carried off in a doomed war of liberation, she by illness. However, Hölderlin's novel is not one of action but of sentimental remembrance. Its point is anamnesis, the re-call and re-presentation of the past, so that the past's meaning *thereby* becomes present, and Hyperion's ascent to higher vision is enacted in the text. Stranded in philistine Germany, Hyperion flees to an oasis of natural beauty and experiences a privileged anamnesis of Diotima in response to his yearning. The recuperated presentness of the vision of beauty in the German cultural desert for a moment unites writer and written, releases his poetic voice, makes the novel possible, and sends him on his poetic mission (759f.).

Hyperion contains a further allusion to the *Symposium* when the hero refers to the (in another sense holistic) androgynous oneness which he and Diotima enjoy, in that their love overcomes sexual difference and limitation and makes each fully human. Friedrich Schlegel's *Lucinde* (1799) radicalises this argument (*KFSA* II, 1–82). Here Julius tells a conventional Meisteresque story of his search for self-fulfilment, which passes through stations of emotional, intellectual and artistic development, each embodied by a woman (or a man), until he finds Lucinde. Thus *Lucinde* preaches a full-blown aesthetic-androgynous utopia. Lucinde is a beautiful, Diotima-like muse for whom life and love are identical and who typically embodies the eighteenth-century gender stereotype of woman as undivided ideal of wholeness and closeness to nature (62). But both Julius and Lucinde are artists who *make* their relationship in the poetic sense (65). She too has received the artistic vocation (traditionally the male privilege), and is Julius' intellectual equal. Thus they pursue the aesthetic-erotic ideal of androgyny through sympoetic exchange.[36] They internalise each other's gender role in aesthetic mimicry. Together they explore the gamut of human experience from richest sensuality to strictest intellectuality. In short: *living* beautiful androgyny is the highest truth. Indeed Julius' and Lucinde's union enacts both life *as* art and, as its brilliantly innovative form demonstrates, the 'moment' of totality (16): Julius' life is cast as a brief narrative; but it is embedded in the centre of an arabesque of non-narrative text-types, so that the beginning and end of his story are dissolved in the timeless embrace of Lucinde's presence.

In a new twist, however, *Godwi, oder das steinerne Bild der Mutter. Ein verwilderter Roman von MARIA* (1800–2; *Godwi, or the stone image of the mother. A novel gone wild, by MARIA*)[37] by Clemens Brentano (1778–1842) dramatises the failure of the Romantic pursuit of the self. At one level a pendant to *Lucinde*, it explores the mystery of Godwi's sexuality as he seeks to realise the androgynous utopia with Molly and Violetta. *Godwi* is, however, most significant at the formal level, where digression and Romantic irony indeed run wild. While part one is cast in traditional epistolary form, part two enacts a loss of authorial control. Maria increasingly thematises his ironic despair of finishing the novel (225), longs for it to be over, kneels before Godwi and begs forgiveness for having written it, promises never to repeat the misdeed, and at last persuades his main fictive character to serve as co-author – the joke being, of course, that all this merely makes the text longer. Ultimately, Godwi (415) tells of Maria's death, carried off by a fatal inflammation of the tongue. But even here *Godwi* does not manage to end. In perhaps the longest unclosed ending ever written, biographical monuments to Maria, broadly hinting at his identity with 'Clemens Brentano' (450) (whose middle name was Maria) proliferate. Here the death of the author is establised long before Foucault declared it. The novel moves from the convention whereby a 'real' author narrates a fictive life to a parodistic position from which the fictive character not only criticises the truth value of fiction, but also narrates the death of the 'real' author, so that fiction, once launched, consumes all. In this excess of non-closure the Romantic self is less recovered than trapped. *Godwi* contains a typically Romantic attack on Fichte's regressive version of self-consciousness in intellectual intuition (234f.) as placing shadow in the stead of substance. But his aestheticist alternative culminates in a regress of its own.

Jean Paul (Johann Paul Friedrich Richter, 1763–1825) typifies how far the commitment to aestheticist truth-finding was prevalent among writers around 1800. He shared the Romantics' metaphysical hunger and ironic humour and the classicists' desire for anthropological wholeness. Yet he allied himself with neither, dismissing the Romantics in particular as poetic nihilists arrogantly proposing and disposing of the world from the bastion of their egotism.[38] His *Bildungsroman Titan* (1800) echoes Brentano's Fichte critique. The Fichtean Schoppe, who cannot distinguish between his self and the world it generates, dies of shock when encountering his double.[39] Philosophically gifted and influenced by Friedrich Heinrich Jacobi's philosophical leap into faith, Jean Paul could never have agreed with Kant either. His major debate with the critical philosophy is crystallised in *Das Kampaner Thal oder über die Unsterblichkeit der Seele* (1797; *The Vale of Campano, or on the immortality of the soul*).[40] Kant's philosophy, he says (alluding to the categorical imperative), daily proves our immortality. But this kind of proof is not enough. Only emotion can change a person; even the philosopher in his abstract world needs emotion. But only poetry can function as philosophy's 'electrical condensor', and amplify the abstractions of philosophy into (emotive) bolts of healing electricity (563f.). The demonstration of this is *Das Kampaner Thal* itself, the poetic rendition of a sentimental journey through a paradisal valley, where newly-wed friends debate as they stroll. The main opponent of 'Jean Paul' is the chaplain, a declared Kantian. He keeps his distance from 'Jean Paul' because writers engage with life. The

philosopher by contrast treats all vital ('kräftig') truths and experiences
as the ant does seeds in his nest: he bites out their living germ so that
they will not grow, and uses them as building material. The main conflict comes over immortality. The Kantian is teased. Kant's ethics had
insisted that the value of virtue lay in the struggle for the good in itself,
not in the happiness which the prospect of immortality might offer as
a reward. In that case, the writer's companion Karlson argues, philosophers ought positively to attack the prospect of immortality. Indeed, if
belief in immortality might make us immoral in this world, what will
experience of it in the next do to us? Worse: if immortality cannot be
demonstrated, why make its indemonstrability a reason for believing in
it? The purpose of this dubious wit is to showcase poetry's alternative.
Metaphysical speculation, they accept, is dead. Yet, like crystals embedded in the glacier, there is something in humanity – virtue, truth, beauty –
which is of, but more than nature (611f.). It is these forces, capable of
creating a higher world in us with no original in nature, which suggest
an inner, higher reality. To this humans belong and for it, as strangers
here, they yearn. Only the feeling for this discloses our immortality. Thus
neither philosophical arguments nor ethical action but an image of immortality, plucked from but transcending nature, dominates at journey's
end: the night ascent in two Montgolfier hot-air balloons in which the
characters stand suspended in the ether between heaven and earth – of
the earth, yet with a view of paradise (624ff.). Literature's task for Jean
Paul is the metaphorical revelation of the infinite in the finite.

Philosophers themselves were not immune to the arguments poets
invented to raise the cognitive and performative dignity of aesthetic experience. The unidentified author of *Das älteste Systemprogramm des deutschen
Idealismus*[41] (1795; *The oldest systematic programme of German idealism*), an early
idealist manifesto, insisted that the highest act of reason was an aesthetic
act and a myth. One of its possible authors, Friedrich Wilhelm Joseph
Schelling (1775–1854), was not only the schoolmate of the other candidates for authorship, Hölderlin and Hegel, but also a close associate
of the early Romantic circle in Jena. A philosophical *Wunderkind* who
at twenty-two held a chair in philosophy at Jena, Schelling had heard
Fichte's lectures, and is certainly in the mainstream of the idealist tradition, but he gives his solution of the identity problem a significantly
different, aesthetic emphasis in the tradition of the *Ältestes Systemprogramm*.
In one of his early writings, *Vom Ich als Princip der Philosophie oder über das
Unbedingte im menschlichen Wissen* (1795; *On the I as principle of philosophy or the
unconditional in human knowledge*),[42] he affirms the Romantic-Hölderlinian

critique of Fichte's intellectual intuition. When we seek to think the unconditional or absolute as the highest point of knowledge, we must accept
that the absolute strictly transcends the relational subject–object structure of thought. But if we can refer to the absolute at all, there must exist
a pre-reflexive intuition of it (57f.), and this intuition, since it cannot belong to the conditioned domain of sensuality (69ff.), must be intellectual
('intellektuale', in Schelling's characteristic spelling). What this means
for philosophy becomes clear in the *System des transcendentalen Idealismus*
(1800; *System of transcendental idealism*).[43] Like Fichte, Schelling deduces a
kind of a priori narrative of the becoming of subject and object, intellect and nature. If the absolute is to know itself as identity, then it must
negate its own, unlimited productivity. Thus is constituted a world torn
by that which binds it together, the contradictory tension of infinite and
finite, ideal and real energies of which every part of its fabric is made.
Relative stability can be conferred on this structure only by thinking it
as endlessly *becoming* (450f.), in that the infinite productivity constantly
creates and then negates its finite, ideal-real product in a series of ever
higher, more ideal levels of evolution, all of which are orientated finally to
overcoming the primal division at a level of ultimate indifference. This,
in contrast to Fichte's sullenly resistant 'Nicht-Ich', is the domain of
positively living, organic nature, of which – again in contrast to Fichte –
the thinking subject is for Schelling a part, and from which, *as* part of
this process, it emerges. Philosophy, then, divides for Schelling in this
phase of his career into two distinct areas, transcendental philosophy
and the speculative physics of *Naturphilosophie*, the one devoted to describing the inner history and end of the evolution of consciousness, the
other the history of nature, each complementing the other in the story it
tells. This division of labour, based on the conception of an autonomous
realm of nature distinct from the transcendental subject, finally alienated
Schelling from Fichte. The *Naturphilosophie* had a pervasive influence on
the Romantic thinking of nature. It is in the transcendental philosophy
that the influence of Romantic aestheticism on Schelling can be seen.
For nature as product of the absolute has, says Schelling from the transcendental philosophical standpoint (675ff.), two cognitive dimensions.
On the one hand, it is unconscious of its tendency. On the other, the
fact that it is what it is in the chain of development exemplifies precisely
that tendency. Natural things thus instantiate both blind mechanism *and*
teleological purposiveness, unconscious and conscious productivity, necessity and freedom; they express the finite and the infinite. But how
is this identity to be known *as such*, how is thinking to know the object

not only as object but *also* as manifestation of absolute identity without falling back into division? Only, Schelling insists, in the mode of aesthetic cognition, which in this pre-empts the completion of philosophy's task. The genius, driven by dark creative forces analogous to those of the absolute, produces by acts which are both conscious and unconscious art which sublates all oppositions in the image of absolute harmony. The infinite, thus finitely expressed, is beauty (688), and art, though an artificial product, reveals in this sense the full truth of the natural process. Art is thus an intuitive mode of knowing which uniquely shows both opposition and knowledge thereof *as* identity, yet without reducing identity to a mere object, and so destroying it. Art in this way represents what philosophy cannot yet, and philosophy (echoing Hölderlin's Hyperion) must in this sense end as it began, in poetry (697).

Schelling's *System des transcendentalen Idealismus* marks the apogee of aestheticist influence over philosophical theories of cognition in our epoch. In its wake came another variant of the demand for extending the legislation of the aesthetic into the cognitive domain: aesthetic natural science. Goethe, whose poetry (e.g. 'Mailied', 1770; 'May song') constantly turns on the harmonisation of subject and nature, had long been a pioneer of this (and consequently an outsider to the natural scientific establishment). Confessedly unphilosophical, he had nonetheless always sought to support his explorations of natural phenomena by appeals to leading philosophers. Thus, having instinctively rejected as abstract and fragmentary the dominant mathematical and analytical methods of Enlightenment scientific research (most famously in his polemic against Newton's colour theory methodology), he sought to support his alternative – holistic intuition of living nature in its simplest, most universal forms, or 'Urphänomene' – by reference to Spinoza. Similarly, he derived his notion of metamorphosis in plants and animals (of which *Bildung* is a variant) from Leibniz's concept of the developmental law (entelechy) inherent in each monad. Later, when the rigorous methodology of Kantian criticism became the foundational discourse of scientific cognition, Goethe struggled through some of the *Kritik der reinen Vernunft* and most of the *Kritik der Urteilskraft*. Their arguments for the autonomy of aesthetic and natural phenomena seemed further to confirm his own convictions, and he certainly derived his notions of polarity and intensification ('Polarität', 'Steigerung') as fundamental natural laws from the antagonistic teleology of Schelling's *Naturphilosophie*. In keeping with ancient tradition (Lucretius) and with his own view, Goethe sometimes also sought to present his scientific findings in aesthetic form. The didactic elegy 'Die Metamorphose der Pflanzen' (1798; 'The metamorphosis of plants') renders the growth of plants in a strict yet graceful narrative of rhythmic becoming, which unfolds simple form (the 'primal plant' or organ) through oppositional change to highest sophistication, and in its flowering closes the ring of life and death, individual and species. But although Schiller had tentatively offered aestheticisation as a means of popularising specialist professional science, and Jean Paul had argued in *Das Kampaner Thal* for the poet's ability to intuit natural truths before the philosopher, Goethe never quite practised truly aesthetic science. In the *Kritik der Urteilskraft* (239) Kant had after all dismissed any thought of aestheticising the sciences: beauty cannot provide authentic cognitions.

It was Hardenberg who first proposed an authentically scientific poetry and the poeticisation of all scientific disciplines. In the field of natural science, his novel *Die Lehrlinge zu Sais* (1798; *The apprentices at Sais*) treats in Schellingian fashion a theme from Schiller's Kantian ballad 'Das verschleierte Bild zu Sais' (1795; 'The veiled statue at Sais'). Far more conservative in this area than Goethe, Schiller turns motifs from Egyptian mystery cults into a warning allegory. The neophyte who transgresses the limits of natural scientific exploration and unveils the statue of Isis, goddess of nature, pays with despair and death. Hardenberg's fragmentary narrative contradicts this. His neophyte is an autobiographical narrator, one of many apprentices seeking truth in a temple which looks more like a mining academy (Hardenberg was a highly qualified and experienced mining engineer). All aspire to a dark intuition which will decode the language of nature tantalisingly hinted at in myriad diverse natural formations. The text of *Die Lehrlinge zu Sais* is the narrator's individual solution. Its key argument, as in Schelling, is the aesthetic character of absolute cognition. In the main scene, the neophyte listens baffled to a many-sided philosophical debate on nature, one participant in which is thought to represent Fichte. When discussion collapses in a confusion of abstract speculations, the implication is that discursive cognition offers no access to nature's highest truth. At the same time, the entry of a poetic youth into the circle of disputants on nature suggests that poetic intuition and representation is the key – he tells a fairy tale involving the unveiling of the statue which successfully unites the finite and the infinite in the self, and seems to describe the shape of the apprentice's life. Typically for early Romanticism, there is no accompanying sense of threat.

The most ambitious expression of this tendency is Hardenberg's aesthetically founded encyclopaedia, the German counterpart to the intellectualistic project of D'Alembert and Diderot. The extensive plans are conserved as *Das allgemeine Brouillon* (1798; *The general notebook*). Its key is another variant on the aesthetic construction of the paradoxically absolute standpoint, from which utopian perspective the specialisation and conflict characteristic of natural sciences might appear to have been unified and harmonised. The final form of the project is unclear. Its basic representational strategy appears to have involved developing analogies between the objective domains, languages and methods of the heterogeneous disciplines (*NS* III, 246, no. 49). As the 'Ich' can only be grasped through the (inadequate) representation of what it is not, so one branch of science necessarily requires explication through another. A network of reciprocating correspondences – this points forward to Baudelaire – can thus be set up (usually involving metaphors), which suggests the inner relatedness of all scientific endeavour. Hardenberg certainly hoped to suggest new cognitive paths,[44] but the main aim would have been the aesthetic restructuring of the vast amount of material in *Das allgemeine Brouillon*.

The aesthetic thinking of nature in the Romantic style was also the element of the most powerful woman poet-philosopher of the epoch, Karoline von Günderrode (1780–1806). A close friend of Clemens and Bettina Brentano, Günderrode – compared with Hypatia[45] by her lover, the cultural anthropologist Friedrich Creuzer – was deeply influenced by the early Romantics' proto-feminist theorisations of androgyny. In *Lucinde*, as we have seen, Friedrich Schlegel showed Lucinde sharing in the historically male activity of philosophising with Julius – a radical step, given the dominant Rousseauist gender anthropology of the age, which belittled woman's natural capacity for abstract thought.[46] In the *Athenaeum* Schlegel published *An Dorothea. Über die Philosophie* (1800; *To Dorothea. On philosophy*), where he elaborated his ideas about women's participation in intellectual life to the model for Lucinde, his wife Dorothea Mendelssohn-Schlegel. This Günderrode extensively excerpted,[47] and she evidently took seriously the admonition to reflect. Between 1802 and 1804 she intensively studied fundamental Romantic and philosophical texts:[48] the *Athenaeums-Fragmente*, *Novalis. Schriften*, Schleiermacher's *Über die Religion*, Fichte's *Die Bestimmung des Menschen* (1800; *The destiny of humankind*), Kiesewetter's *Grundriß einer allgemeinen Logik nach Kantischen Grundsätzen* (1795–6; *Outline of Kantian logic*). In her last two years she was preoccupied by (among others) Schelling's *System des transcendentalen Idealismus*, his *Ideen zu einer Philosophie der Natur* (1797; *Ideas for a philosophy of nature*) and *Erster Entwurf eines Systems der Naturphilosophie* (1799; *First sketch of a system of natural philosophy*), and finally the history of Oriental religion. Günderrode's papers are not documents of creative reception to rival Hardenberg's *Fichte-Studien*. But they are evidence of mastery in the most advanced philosophical and aesthetic concepts of her day. What emerges from this rigorous autodidactic philosophical schooling is a Romantic poet who writes under the genderless pseudonym 'Tian'. Günderrode thus shares the aesthetic consensus, but asserts something the French and Kantian revolutions did not – woman's autonomy in thought and deed – and often seeks to impart a specifically feminine accentuation to her articulations of Romantic (and classic) discourse. Her version of the Don Juan myth is almost unrecognisable. The great womaniser is transfixed by a princess's beauty and transformed into a Romantic lover for whom only one woman will do, and at his tragic end he is comforted only by her recuperated memory. Elsewhere 'Tian' contributes with robust intellectuality to ongoing Romantic controversies. Her most successful work, the drama *Mahomed, der Prophet von Mekka* (1805; *Mohammed, the prophet of Mecca*), is a poetic reflection on the validity of Schleiermacher's irenic central category of religious experience, 'Anschauung des Unendlichen' ('intuition of the infinite'). At issue here is precisely the authenticity of Mohammed's overwhelming yet subjective visionary intuitions, with their claim to unify – if necessary by the sword – all positive religions. He is presented as himself vacillating agonisingly between faith and doubt, and the intrinsic division of the prophet's psyche is satisfyingly externalised as the antiphonic chorus. The fictive autobiography *Geschichte eines Braminen* (1805; *Story of a Brahmin*)[49] adopts the outsider's perspective – not a woman, but a man divided between European and Oriental provenance – to preach a sermon against the commercialised egotism of European culture. On the protagonist's spiritual journey the first alternative to this he encounters, Kantian ethics, is rejected as self-fulfilment at the cost of division (306). Commencing a life of introspection in the Orient, Almar turns to religion as the power which re-connects individual and totality. He rejects Mohammed's use of violence to spread the message and, having considered all other major historical religions, ends with what he calls Brahmanism and equates with the unveiling of the statue at Sais, but which is of course a version of Schellingian *Naturphilosophie*: the intuition of the absolute as the primal, infinite ground of all individuality. From this decentred perspective all creatures exist for their own sake, all represent realisations of the infinite 'Naturgeist' (nature spirit) along a ladder of perfection, which comes to unity with itself in the highest forms of consciousness (312f.).

But perhaps the most euphoric and influential expression of aesthetic natural science was a popular lecture series by Gotthilf Heinrich Schubert (1780–1860) delivered in 1806–7: *Ansichten von der Nachtseite der Naturwissenschaften (Views of the dark side of the natural sciences)*.[50] As the title suggests, Schubert claims to have uncovered an unacknowledged dimension of cognition and its vehicle, a buried tradition of esoteric natural science, which leads to ultimate understanding of nature. Its basis is of course another version of Schellingian *Naturphilosophie*, on which is superimposed a Romantic sentimentalist cultural history of the kind we saw in *Die Lehrlinge zu Sais*. At the origin of history humankind existed not in a primitive state determined by crude material necessity, but in an idyll of naive harmony with the totality of nature. In this phase reflective thought is admittedly undeveloped. However, the ancient mysteries (such as those stored in the archives of the temple at Sais, or the Atlantis legend) embody an immediate intuition of the primal unity of humanity and nature, individual and totality, past and future – tantamount to speaking the language of nature (3–9). From this golden age, humanity has fallen into an interim state of decline – history – characterised by reflective division of subject and nature. But humanity is also progressing to a recuperated union with nature. Evidence for this is the modern discovery of universal forces such as gravity and magnetism, which seem to confirm the esoteric claim of the inner connectedness of individual and totality. The hint of the possibility of recovering Atlantean wisdom leads Schubert to his thesis. The basic form or law of all creation and change is a state of ultimate negativity, in which the individual returns to its creative origin and from which it emerges into a new, higher station in the chain of being (21). Evidence of this, the dark side of the natural sciences, are those unexplained instances where creatures from one station of being seem to sympathise with or anticipate phenomena in the next. Insects seem sympathetically to anticipate plants' needs during pollination, animals natural disasters. The modish phenomenon of animal magnetism (mesmerism, somnambulism) is another typical irruption of one sphere of being into another. The magnetic trance is, says Schubert, nothing less than the anticipation of humanity's higher life – the next, Atlantean station of being – in this. This is so – despite the radical circumvention of reflective thought which is its condition of possibility (362) – because of the apparent vast potentialisation of human cognitive powers in the trance. The magnetised seem miraculously able to examine inner body states, sense the presence of minerals underground, read letters in closed envelopes, predict the future and explore the past, and the like. They can do so, says Schubert, because the circumvention of consciousness releases the inherent sympathy of the higher, physical organs of the body with the vast network of affinities that is the universe, and so makes possible the perceptual expansion. Thus history and natural history coincide, and the golden age is rediscovered. The celebration of clairvoyance in the *Ansichten* is the most remarkable expression of German intellectuals' willed faith in a redemptive intuition bought at the price of the total rejection of conscious thinking, but it is also the beginning of the discovery of the unconscious mind.

The first sign of decay in the utopian aesthetic consensus is the *œuvre* of Heinrich von Kleist (1777–1811), who shares Schubert's sceptical view of thought's cognitive power. At first Kleist stands foursquare in the new humanistic tradition. He rejects the profession of military officer because tyrannical discipline is incompatible with *Bildung*, and embarks in 1799 on an encyclopaedic programme of self-cultivation in the sciences, philosophy and literature. But philosophy soon becomes problematic. Committed originally to Enlightenment optimism and pre-critical teleological thinking, Kleist soon records in letters around 1800–1 a traumatic loss of faith in the certainty of knowledge. This he ascribes to Kantian philosophy.[51] Kant had founded the certainty of empirical knowledge in the a priori legislative capacity of the subject, but only in so far as it was applied to phenomena under conditions which excluded the possibility of knowing things in themselves or grasping any teleological purpose of 'nature' (except as a merely regulative principle of judgement). If the evidence of the letters is to be credited, Kleist interprets this gain of empirical certainty at the price of metaphysical certainty as leading to radical scepticism. In what may be an allusion to the schematism of judgement, he argues that if all people viewed the world through green lenses, this constitution of their minds would make it impossible to tell if things were objectively green or if greenness were not simply a property of the subject's way of seeing. That being so, not only is there no metaphysical certainty, there is no certainty of empirical knowledge either. If this analogy is meant as an allusion to Kant, then Kleist does not fully recognise how the Kantian categories function to create intersubjective certainty. It is moreover notable that Kleist names only Kant as his benchmark philosopher, ignoring the later solutions of Jacobi, Fichte, Schelling and others.[52] Kleist is nonetheless thrown by this into existential crisis, rejects philosophy and natural science, and turns to literature. Like Schubert he rejects thinking as a source of truth. As with Schiller, Hölderlin, Hardenberg and Schlegel, the critique of philosophy motivates his poetic vocation.

What he does with literature is another matter. Where his contemporaries never doubted the (variously defined) cognitive or performative power of aesthetic intuition as an alternative to philosophy, Kleist's scepticism is so deeply founded that he places no alternative faith in the aesthetic. He flirts with Schubertian magnetism. In the popular drama *Das Käthchen von Heilbronn* (1810; *Käthchen of Heilbronn*) and the Prussian tragedy *Der Prinz von Homburg* (1811; *The Prince of Homburg*) both Käthchen and the Prince experience magnetic revelations. Alas these cause rather than resolve conflict. Elsewhere, Kleist's literary writings are without exception truth-seeking experiments which explore the limits of both thought *and* literature. An example of the former is the comedy *Amphitryon* (1806). Of this classical motif Kleist makes an agonising comedy of the identity of indiscernible subjects. Amphitryon, having triumphed in battle, sends his servant Sosias to Thebes with the good news. Unfortunately that very night Jupiter has taken advantage of the general's absence, magically assumed his shape, and pleasured his wife Alkmene. Sosias too loses his identity as Mercury takes on Sosias's form. From this a comedy unfolds which constantly threatens tragedy as human cognitive powers (and their emotional consequences) are tested to the limit. The problem is that Jupiter and Mercury are true doubles, indiscernible from their originals, so that not only Alkmene, but even the originals doubt their sense of selfhood, which seems to derive not from autonomous self-definition but from heteronomous determination – the power of the gods. Conversely and paradoxically, even the god's identity is threatened. Alkmene needs a finite image to venerate the otherwise abstract Jupiter, and Jupiter fully unveiled (the allusion to Schiller and Hardenberg is deliberate) would destroy her. But since Jupiter has assumed her husband's form, the god ironically also becomes indiscernible – except through the exercise of arbitrary power.

The great alternative of the age, aesthetic discourse, is given equally short shrift. Grace, the foundational concept of Schiller's epoch-making Kant critique, is cruelly deconstructed in a late essay, *Über das Marionettentheater* (1810, *On the puppet-theatre*). Schiller had aestheticised Kant's rigoristic ethics in *Über Anmut und Würde* by his argument that only grace can harmonise rationality with corporeality and so square the circle of human fulfilment and ethical perfection. Kleist's fictive dialogue counters with a claim that the ultimate expression of grace is paradoxically unattainable by humans. More graceful by far are the soulless, yet gravity-defying puppets dancing in the marketplace (Kleist perhaps has 'Der Tanz' in mind), or the instinctive yet unerring parrying movements of the bear as he duels with a swordsman. Thus the problem is not the body, but humanity's definitive feature: consciousness. Consciousness is not only incapable of founding identity with certainty. It also militates fundamentally against the institution of aesthetic grace. Once a beautiful youth recognises himself in the mirror of reflective thought, his aesthetic potential for mind–body harmony is lost. Only an infinite consciousness, in which the dualism of the opposition is overcome, promises restitution – in an intuition of the absolute, perhaps. But Kleist offers no prospect of this. His novella *Das Erdbeben in Chili* (1807; *The earthquake in Chile*) puts the fully politicised version of aesthetic education from the *Ästhetische Erziehung* to an equally deconstructive literary test. The French Revolution figures as the natural disaster. After its purging of the corrupt and hierarchical order a rural idyll spontaneously emerges which unmistakably represents the realised aesthetic state. When immediately thereafter the practices of the former regime are re-instituted and the aesthetic state destroyed, Kleist's verdict on Schiller is clear. That state cannot last either, given the fundamental insecurity of things. Kleist may well have derived this last notion from his friend Adam Müller's philosophical *Lehre vom Gegensatze* (1805; *Theory of opposition*),[53] which argued that successive states of thought and things are equally prompted by moments of negation. These generate ever-changing series of oppositional states, without however ever moving through a truly dialectical synthesis in the manner of Schelling – or Hegel. But Kleist doubtless relished expressing this view in the literary language invented by Schiller.

Kleist apart, the fundamental tendencies of the early part of the epoch observed by Friedrich Schlegel were breaking up. When Napoleon crushed the Prussian army at the battle of Jena-Auerstädt in 1806 and the old Germany was occupied and then abolished by the imperialist heir of the Revolution, the optimism and cosmopolitanism characteristic of both literary and philosophical strands of development in Germany modulated into something more conservative and nationalistic. In philosophy, one expression of this is an intensified focus on society or nation rather than the individual. Fichte's *Reden an die deutsche Nation* (1806; *Addresses to the German nation*) transposed the ethical mission of the sovereign ego into the historical and cultural mission of the sovereign German nation. In literature, Schiller's *Die Jungfrau von Orleans* (1800; *The maid of Orleans*) had against the background of the Wars of Coalition put the tragedy of Jeanne d'Arc at the service of national regeneration, as the heroine's moral conflict becomes an inspiring legend of missionary self-sacrifice in the interest of a divided nation. Schiller's earlier solution to the political problem – aesthetic education proper – is represented here in the court of the ineffectual and irrelevant poet-king Réné. This early appropriation of aesthetic humanism to propaganda was enthusiastically taken up by writers of the following generation during the epoch of the wars of liberation, 1806–15, and need concern us here no further.

These popularising developments with their strident compensatory affirmations of collective identity are however mirrored at a deeper level by a more radical tendency to undermine the earlier generation's confident theses in literature and philosophy. The later Romantic E. T. A. Hoffmann (1776–1822) probably heard Kant's lectures at university in his native Königsberg, and knew Schelling's *Naturphilosophie*. But like all Romantics he engaged primarily as a poet with the received problems of 'Philosophie' and 'Poesie'. Decisively influenced by Karl Philipp Moritz's empirical psychology of the 1780s, Hoffmann became fascinated by the speculative Romantic psychology of Schubert, Johann Christian Reil and Carl Alexander Ferdinand Kluge, which investigated abnormal and psychopathological states of mind. In this tradition, Hoffmann's *œuvre* radically questions the capacity for sovereignty of self-consciousness and seeks to validate unorthodox modes of cognition. Hoffmann particularly admired Schubert's *Symbolik des Traumes* (1814; *The symbolism of dream*).[54] This development of Schubert's theory in a sense renewed pre-modern dream theory. Most dreams, says Schubert, are significant. The significant ones represent a privileged state of intuitive insight directly related to the magnetic trance. Like the trance, like poetry and indeed nature itself, they are unconscious products of absolute creativity, of the 'hidden poet' in us (*Symbolik*, 3), which impose themselves on the conscious mind and possess the prophetic power of the primal language. Frequently they comment ironically or morally on events in the subject's prosaic waking life, rather like conscience (which Hardenberg called the divine part of our being). But in our post-lapsarian state the primal language has undergone the confusion of Babel. The spiritual tendency of dreams can be mistaken and perverted into demonic temptation. Thus even at this, the highest stratum of its intuitive power, the subject is constitutionally divided – torn between temptation and the voice of conscience. Indeed, the perversion of the poetic inner voice can become so powerful that it takes on the concrete form of something already seen to good effect in Jean Paul and Kleist: the *Doppelgänger* (66). This freshly destabilised version of the Romantic subject, torn between higher self and evil double, is taken up by Hoffmann in his first novel, the fictive autobiography *Die Elixiere des Teufels* (1814–15; *The devil's elixirs*), in order to comment on the Romantic tradition. As we have seen, the project to recover the transcendental self had made autobiographical forms, from Hardenberg's *Die Lehrlinge zu Sais* on, into one of the favourite Classic-Romantic genres. *Die Elixiere des Teufels* ostensibly continues this tradition. The monk Medardus, torn in his Schubertian way between spiritual and sensual tendencies, is at the end of his adventurous life asked by the abbot to write his autobiography for psychotherapeutic purposes. Having done so, Medardus should be able to grasp his life's form and meaning and thus – like Hardenberg's apprentice – hover in sovereign self-understanding above his contradictions. In fact, the text dramatises its own failure. At a critical moment of moral conflict catalysed by drinking a dubious elixir, Medardus' Schubertian *Doppelgänger*, the ruthless sensualist Viktorin, is born. Unconscious forces within him compel him to take on Viktorin's role. Thereafter he oscillates unpredictably and heart-rendingly between both roles. Various forms of self-analysis – before the authorities of the law, the church, and the new institution of (Reilian) clinical psychotherapy – all fail to heal the intrinsic duplicity of Medardus' person. So, unfortunately, does the aesthetic autobiography. Sometimes the *Doppelgänger* seems a real and concrete individual, sometimes a mere projection, sometimes he seems to have died, yet again he re-surfaces, so that Viktorin's status as fact or fiction remains agonisingly ambiguous. Worse, this figure from the past colonises the identity of Medardus as he writes in the present. This dislocated perspective is shared by the reader. *Die Elixiere des Teufels*, then, is not merely a literary version of Schubert's theory. It is also a deconstructive commentary *in* the Romantic tradition *on* the Romantic tradition. Both pillars of authority on which that tradition stands are undermined: the recuperable autonomy of the subject and of the text as means to that. *Die Elixiere des Teufels* also features a puppet play – from Kleist to Büchner always the signal for an attack on the aesthetic humanist tradition. But this time the target is not Schillerian grace. In the puppet-play of David and Goliath,[55] presented by the novel's raisonneur, the artist-fool Belcampo-Schönfeld, Goliath figures with a disproportionate giant head as the representative of consciousness, moral guardian and censor of the animal in us – with predictable results. Nor does Hoffmann spare *Naturphilosophie* or magnetism. *Die Bergwerke zu Falun* (1814; *The mines at Falun*) exploits another Schubertian motif. In his *Ansichten* (215f.) Schubert told how (thanks to vitriolated water in the shaft) a young miner's body was recovered perfectly preserved many decades after his disappearance – to the shock of his aged wife. Of this Hoffmann makes a response to the Classic-Romantic Isis myth. The young miner Elis's disappearance is motivated by the desire to encounter the divine queen of nature, who has conquered his young wife in his affections. The discovery of his petrified body – preserved for eternity, yet lifeless – mockingly deconstructs Hardenberg's understanding of the Isis myth. Hoffmann's *Magnetiseur* (1814; *The mesmerist*) exposes the magnetic rapport as merely an exploitive power-relationship between the mesmerist and his suggestible victim.

With Schubert, Kleist and Hoffmann, the high esteem of philosophers and poets for aesthetic intuition as a panacea for the sovereign yet divided Kantian subject passes its high point. Against this background, Georg Wilhelm Friedrich Hegel (1770–1831), schoolfriend of Schelling and Hölderlin, and Fichte's successor as Professor of Philosophy at Berlin University in 1815, draws the sum of the epochal tendencies in both philosophy and art. His synthesis is deeply critical of the spirit of the age, and it set the terms of dialogue for the rest of the nineteenth century. He shares many idealist and Romantic convictions. Indeed, in proposing subjectivity as the primal and ultimate reality, he is more radical even than Kant and the Romantics. In a work often regarded as the introduction to his mature philosophy, the *Phänomenologie des Geistes* (1807; *Phenomenology of spirit*),[56] Hegel argues that subjectivity is identical with being or living substance (23). But this overarching subjectivity cannot be adequately grasped in its most general or abstract form, in some such formulation as 'the absolute'. Such an assertion is at best a beginning. To be adequately grasped, the abstract concept must be understood as result, fully and concretely realised. Hegel thus (like Schelling) focuses on the process of becoming from abstract to concrete – here called phenomenology – whereby the absolute unfolds itself by negation to full self-knowledge in and through the particular concrete domains of reality – nature, history, the state, art, religion and philosophy. But the way this is achieved exposes a gulf between Hegel and Romanticism. If the Romantic commitment to intuitionism is about anything, it is about overcoming division and the consciousness of division. Yet Romanticism falls short of this, the definitive modern aspiration. For intuition, its chosen mode of exhibiting the mediation of the absolute, in fact merely perpetuates the dualism it seeks to overcome. In a well-known passage (where Hegel probably has Schellingian *Naturphilosophie* or Hardenberg's aesthetic encyclopaedism in mind), he notes caustically that merely to confront the absolute idea (true in itself, he does not doubt) with empirical material with which it might be claimed to be identical, so that all is indifferent in the absolute, amounts to empty formalism. This is not systematically mediated self-realisation of abstract concept and particularised reality so much as capricious divinations ('Einfälle') (21) and empty depth (17). Famously deconstructing Hardenberg's central poetic metaphor for the dark insight of intuition, Hegel concludes that this, so far as philosophy is concerned, is the night in which all cows are black (22). His stark alternative is to redefine the cognitive potential and ontological status of thought. To exclude reflection from truth as they (and in a sense Kant) did is to mistake the nature of reason (25). A formulation such as the absolute may be true *in* itself ('an sich'), but is not yet fully mediated with its otherness, the sense in which the absolute *in* its otherness (being, particularised difference, reality) is also *for* itself ('für sich'). Subjectivity rethought is thus nothing less than the dialectical movement of reflective thought through this negation to the *negation of the negation* and full self-consciousness *in and for itself*. This becoming – when fully thought through – is spirit, truly systematic self-knowledge, philosophy. Hegel's epistemology thus contrasts strongly not only with Romantic intuitionism but also with Kant. Kant had concluded that the ultimate reality of things in themselves was by definition inaccessible to our faculty of thought, structured as it is by the categories. Hegel points out that Kant often transgresses his own set epistemological boundaries: he seems to recognise some cognitive dignity in aesthetic ideas; and his claim that we cannot know things in themselves paradoxically implies some kind of knowledge of them. For Hegel, thought properly understood is the essence of intelligible being, and thinking things through contradiction to reconciliation is itself the disclosure of truth. There is no domain transcending thought.

This uncompromising advocacy of self-transparent thought as the sole adequate vehicle of the pursuit of truth leads to a characteristic re-evaluation of aesthetic cognition in Hegel's mature philosophy, which (by contrast to the *Phänomenologie*) works out the realisation of the idea in world history. Nature and the state are objective realisations of the idea. But the self-knowledge of spirit must go beyond these particular realisations and reflect the absolute as such, free, as Hegel says in his *Vorlesungen über die Ästhetik* (1820–9; *Lectures on aesthetics*),[57] of the straitening confines of existence (XIII, 128–39). Hegel sees three vehicles of this, in ascending order of sophistication – art, religion and philosophy. In all of them we experience not relative, but higher, substantial truth, in which all contradictions are harmonised (XIII, 137f.), including, for example, that of spirit and nature. The way in which this epistemological hierarchy is established follows the pattern of the dialectic and the critique of modes of cognition. They are distinguished only by form. Art presents knowledge of the absolute harmony and unity of spirit in an individual, sensual and objective form, for intuition and feeling: the absolute idea, no less, in an adequate sensual manifestation as a unity of form and content. In this, Hegel seems for a moment to adopt the Romantic position. He is however merely registering the temper of the Romantic age, only to transcend it at once. For art is not the highest mode of self-consciousness for spirit. Its sensual mode of representing the absolute is art's own limit. Spirit needs to know itself in a form adequate to its own inwardness, and rejects the externality of art. And this is the case in Hegel's epoch, when art has already achieved its maximum. In religion the absolute is known in the more adequate, subjective and inward mode. But religion too has its limit. Religious consciousness is characteristically emotionalised and devotional, lacking in clarity. And this, of course, is the work of the highest mode of spirit's self-knowledge, philosophy, which unifies thought, as the highest form of objectivity, with religion's subjectivity.

Hegel thus recognises the dominance of Romanticism in his own epoch of post-Goethean modernity, but only in order to condemn it. In terms of art history, he distinguishes three modes of aesthetic expression within the basic definition: the symbolic, the classical, and the Romantic. The most primitive, the symbolic, is dominated by an undeveloped – abstract – notion of the idea, which is held to be representable (Hegel is thinking of Oriental cultures) by any natural creature. This leads to an inevitable aesthetic tension between the symbol and the idea. In classical art, the idea has attained full understanding as concrete spirit or true inwardness, for which the only adequate expression (Hegel is thinking of Greece and Goethe) is the human form. In classical art, by contrast with the symbolic, the idea is not embodied *as* the sensual reality of the human form; human form represents sensually the spiritual objectivity of the idea. In this sense classical art is the fragile aesthetic ideal. Romantic art, as always in Hegel, represents an unharmonious and passing synthesis of self-knowledge. As characteristically inward, spirit at this level by definition cannot be adequately expressed in art. Romantic art recognises this. Intrinsically divided, it embodies the tension between true inwardness and *any* sensual representation, and – pointing to religion – rejects the latter. This is meant to suggest that not only Romantic art, but *all* art will pass away (at least in this function), and it leads Hegel to a fierce critique of Romanticism (in the work of Friedrich Schlegel) which for decades determined its prestige. Romanticism is egocentricity, intuitionism and frivolous irony. Fichte he presents as propounding the ability of the self to create a disposable reality by an act of will. The Romantic artist is the aesthetic analogue of this, a genius creating his own aesthetic disposable world which is lacking in fundamental earnestness and open to ironic destruction at any moment. As with the Schelling critique of the *Phänomenologie*, then, the Romantic aesthetic subject stops half-way, cannot go beyond negativity to full mediation with the real, and remains trapped in the prison of the self whilst yearning helplessly to transcend it. The expression of the idea as irony thus dominates Romantic art. This is neither Schlegel's well-intentioned transcendental buffoonery nor the truly comic, but a grotesque caricature of comedy, in which even what is valuable in the aesthetic representation is wilfully destroyed by irony, valued as a principle for its own sake. This is mirrored by Hegel's interpretations of Romantic literature. Drama, for example, is for Hegel the genre capable of showing beauty – the overcoming of conflict – in its most profound development (XIII, 267). Kleist is thus attacked for the lasting consciousness of division in his dramas.[58] Unsurprisingly, Hegel condemns the Romantic fashion for 'magnetic' characters. This is the symptom of intrinsic division. Kleist's Käthchen and Prince of Homburg prefer the trance to clear thinking (XIV, 201f.). They have no true character, being inhabited by a force which is yet other to them, and thus fall prey to dark powers. In true art, by contrast, there should be nothing dark, true characters should always be at rest in themselves, and such literature is the vapid, frivolous and empty product of a sickness of mind. But the ironic character, constantly turning into its opposite, is the Romantic ideal (XIII, 314f.). And precisely this is the problem of E. T. A. Hoffmann (XIII, 289, 315).

Hegel's judgements are in general admirably informed, apt and perspicuous. Nonetheless it should be clear that Hegel's insistently harmonistic standpoint makes him blind to Romantic literature's powerful disclosure of the existential pathology and suffering of the divided modern person and of the pre- or unconscious strata whence they emerge; Romantic irony is not as empty of content as Hegel suggests. Moreover history appears to disagree with Hegel's judgement on the end of art, which has so far usurped religion's position in modern culture and thus confirmed the Romantic rather than the Hegelian view of cultural history.[59] Far from dying, the tradition of self-consciously reflexive, experimental art inaugurated by Romanticism has established itself as the basic form of modernist literature in our search for meaning, recognisably extending through the traditional canon of micro-epochs to the present. And Hegel's philosophical standpoint, his fundamental concept of self-transparent, self-present thought, the crux of his challenge to the

Schellingian and early Romantic philosophies of identity, has also failed
to establish a consensus in modern philosophy. Philosophers in the French
semiological tradition deny the capacity of thought to be self-present in
the system of differential signifiers.[60] Those in the Wittgensteinian tradition deny the possibility of a universal meta-language such as Hegelian
philosophical discourse.[61] Even those in the Hegelian-Marxian tradition
deny the capacity of philosophical dialectic to express the contradictions of modern industrialised culture.[62] Most recently, those standing
between the continental and analytic traditions of philosophy reassert
the late Schellingian critique of Hegel – that the bare facts of existence
cannot be brought as such before thought, but require intuitive presentation – as the inauguration of the existential tradition and a revalidation
of self-ironising Romantic discourse.[63] Thus the Romantic tradition in
both art and philosophy has – so far – outlived Hegel.

Goethe's *Faust* (1808–32), in a sense, is the prime instance of this. Faust
is the ultimate divided Romantic hero, who instantiates in literature
precisely the figure of thought set out by Hegel in the preface of the
Phänomenologie. Emblematically imprisoned in his narrow, high-ceilinged
Gothic study, he rejects metaphysics but yearns to re-establish the connection between his person and the life of the universe. Until now, the
university has been the vehicle of that ambition. But its characteristically abstract form of scholarship is no match for his inner desire. Experimental physics will not raise the veil of nature. He has exhausted
the knowledge inventory of all four contemporary faculties (theology,
medicine, law, and alas philosophy too). Faust's turn to an alternative
form of knowledge both esoteric and intuitionist thus mirrors the trend
of the age. Yet Goethe presents this with critical distance. The sign of the
macrocosm, with its intoxicating spectacle of living, interwoven totality
and individuality, promises all, but remains mere spectacle – doubtless
a verdict on the vulgar Romantic tradition. And Faust's project is diminished still further through his subsequent rejection by the lower, but
no less transcendent 'Erdgeist' (spirit of the earth). Reduced to the typically modern state of an absurd acceptance of existence without meaning (except that which he himself can bestow), Faust finally receives in
Mephistopheles not so much a devil as a principle of negation. What
follows, then, is the epic dramatisation of the modern subject's search
for meaning in the age for which the absolute is present only as negation.
Faust continues to value the spontaneity and immediacy of intuitive experience. But he equates that neither with poetry (HA III, 59; lines 1788ff.)
nor with absolute knowledge (HA III, 149; line 4727). One particular

interest of the work is to set that drama in a moral framework – this is the point of the devil's presence in a post-Christian work. But another is its representativeness. This is why Faust seeks to encompass in his person (in both parts of the drama) nothing less than the sum of human experience. In this ambition, *Faust*, for all its anti-Romantic tendencies, is something like the counterpart to Hegelian philosophy in aesthetic form.

Thus if the domestic tragedy of Gretchen in part one of the drama represents the first opening of Faust's divided and desiccated psyche to the transforming (if not yet redemptive) power of love, part two vastly widens the tragic compass. Gretchen turns out (for the moment) merely to have prefigured the true object of Faust's Romantic yearning: Helena, ideal of classical beauty. Goethe uses Faust's romance with Helena, whom he first conjures as an aesthetic illusion but then really encounters, as a structure through which to reflect poetically on the deepest tendencies of the age and indeed of occidental cultural history – perhaps the highest fulfilment of the literary side of Schlegel's dictum of 1798. These include republican and monarchic forms of government: the site of the encounter with Helen, centre of part two, is the banks of the upper Peneios, scene of the battle between imperial Caesar and republican Pompey. But they also include reflections on the dominant contemporary theories of the genesis of life on earth (Vulcanism and Neptunism in the persons of Anaxagoras and Thales), and even a harsh, aesthetically founded critique of the introduction of paper money to fund war (an allusion to the trend-setting *assignats* of the French Revolution). There is another swipe at Fichteanism. The theme invested with most significance is, however, the great cultural division of the epoch: the confrontation of classicism and Romanticism, antiquity and modernity, in Helena and Faust. But the fate of their child, Euphorion, gives Goethe's verdict. Based on Byron, Euphorion is the very incarnation of poetry, love and freedom (including political freedom). But Icarus-like he kills himself, through impatience. Helena's fate as *femme fatale* is confirmed. As the combination of beauty and happiness proves too unstable, she chooses to return to the realm of the shades – memory. Faust continues as he must to struggle, and the drama now incorporates great themes – the technological mastery of nature and colonialism – which concern modernity to this day. Yet tragic resignation, programmed into it by the negativity of the pact with the devil, haunts the rest of the text. Faust's modernistic assent to life involves the acceptance of existential restlessness, whereby fulfilment – the intuition of the beautiful moment – would also entail death. When Faust appears for a moment to be satisfied in contemplation of his deeds, Mephistopheles closes the trap, but he is confuted by a re-deemer God on a point of interpretation. But even this is not the end for Faust, who, it is suggested, will now progress to higher spheres of being under Gretchen's tutelage. Even after Helena, then, he remains a fragment, possessed by the memory of wholeness, unendingly in pursuit of perfection.

NOTES

1 Friedrich Schlegel, *Athenaeums-Fragment* no. 216, in *KFSA* II, 198f.

2 See Jürgen Habermas, *Strukturwandel der Öffentlichkeit. Untersuchungen zu einer Kategorie der bürgerlichen Gesellschaft* (Frankfurt am Main: Suhrkamp, 1991) (first edition 1962).

3 On subjectivity in modern German philosophy and modern culture see Julian Roberts, *The logic of reflection. German philosophy in the twentieth century* (New Haven and London: Yale University Press, 1992) and Charles Taylor, *Sources of the self. The making of modern identity* (Cambridge: Cambridge University Press, 1989).

4 See Manfred Frank, '"Intellektuale Anschauung". Drei Stellungnah-men zu einem Deutungsversuch von Selbstbewußtsein: Kant, Fichte, Hölderlin/Novalis', in Ernst Behler and Jochen Hörisch (eds.), *Die Aktualität der Frühromantik* (Paderborn, Munich, Vienna, Zürich: Schöningh, 1987), pp. 96–126, esp. pp. 96ff.; Andrew Bowie, *Aesthetics and subjectivity. From Kant to Nietzsche* (Manchester: Manchester University Press, 1990), p. 20.

5 See Friedrich Heinrich Jacobi, *David Hume über den Glauben, oder Idealismus und Realismus. Ein Gespräch* (1787), in *Werke*, 7 vols. (Leipzig: Fleischer 1812–25), vol. II, pp. 3–288, esp. pp. 143ff.; compare his *Ueber den transcendentalen Idealismus*, vol. II, pp. 305f.

6 See Jacobi's contribution to the *Pantheismusstreit* (pantheism controversy), in *Werke*, vol. IV/2, supplement 7, pp. 125–67. Jacobi's ringing phrase *salto mortale* is found earlier in his version of the controversy with Lessing, vol. IV/1, p. 59.

7 See J. G. Fichte, *Zweite Einleitung in die Wissenschaftslehre, für Leser, die schon ein philosophisches System haben*, in *Werke*, ed. I. H. Fichte, 8 vols. (Berlin: de Gruyter, 1971), vol. I, pp. 451–518, here esp. pp. 469–88.

8 See note seven.

9 This is based on Fichte's *Grundlage der gesammten Wissenschaftslehre, als Hand-schrift für seine Zuhörer* (1794), in *Werke*, vol. I, pp. 83–328, esp. pp. 91ff.

10 '[M]ich selbst, ganz wie ich da bin, auszubilden, das war dunkel von Jugend auf mein Wunsch und meine Absicht' (HA VII, 290).

11 See Nicholas Saul, 'Aesthetic humanism. German literature 1790–1830', in Helen Watanabe-O'Kelly (ed.), *The Cambridge history of German literature* (Cambridge: Cambridge University Press, 1997), pp. 202–71.

12 In *Werkausgabe*, vol. VII, pp. 7–102 and pp. 103–302.

13 In Friedrich Schiller, *Sämtliche Werke*, ed. Gerhard Fricke and Herbert G. Göpfert, 5 vols., 6th edn (Munich: Hanser, 1980), vol. V, pp. 433–88.

14 In *Werkausgabe*, vol. X, pp. 73–301.

15 See Theodor Adorno and Max Horkheimer, *Dialektik der Aufklärung* (Frankfurt am Main: Fischer, 1979) (first edition, 1947). Also Hartmut Böhme and Gernot Böhme, *Das Andere der Vernunft. Zur Entdeckung von Rationalitätsstrukturen am Beispiel Kants* (Frankfurt am Main: Suhrkamp, 1985) and Nicholas Saul (ed.), *The body in German literature around 1800*, Special number, *German Life & Letters* 52:2 (1999), 'Introduction', pp. 115ff.

16 Schiller, *Werke*, vol. V, pp. 570–669.

17 In Plato's *Republic* of course poets had been banished from the polis.

18 See Silvio Vietta, *Die ästhetische Moderne. Eine problemgeschichtliche Darstellung der deutschsprachigen Literatur von Hölderlin bis Thomas Bernhard* (Stuttgart: Metzler, 1992), esp. pp. 21–33.

19 On Goethe see Géza von Molnár, *Goethes Kantstudien* (Weimar: Hermann Böhlaus Nachfolger, 1993) and 'Goethe and critical philosophy: The *Wissenschaftslehre* as supplement to his Kant-Studies', in Clifford A. Bernd, Ingeborg Henderson and Winder M. McConnell (eds.), *Romanticism and beyond. A Festschrift for John F. Fetzer* (New York: Peter Lang, 1996), pp. 57–77.

20 Molnár, *Goethes Kantstudien*, p. 19.

21 See for example the footnote in the sixth letter (Schiller, *Werke*, vol. V, p. 577) and the reference to the 'Selbsttätigkeit' (self-activity) of reason (642).

22 Recall Socrates' view of human nature's basic creativity in the *Symposium* (205c), in *The collected dialogues of Plato including the letters*, eds. Edith Hamilton and Huntingdon Cairns (Princeton, NJ: Princeton University Press, 1961), p. 557.

23 See Manfred Frank, *Einführung in die frühromantische Ästhetik* (Frankfurt am Main: Suhrkamp, 1989), pp. 7–24, esp. pp. 16ff.; also Andrew Bowie, *From Romanticism to Critical Theory. The philosophy of German literary theory* (London and New York: Routledge, 1997), esp. pp. 65–89, 272ff.

24 See *Kritisches Fragment* no. 115 (*KFSA* II, 161); 'Über die Philosophie. An Dorothea' (*KFSA* VIII, 52); *Ideen-Fragment* no. 48 (*KFSA* II, 261); *Ideen-Fragment* no. 108 (*KFSA* II, 267).

25 The best edition is *F.D.E. Schleiermacher: Hermeneutik und Kritik. Mit einem Anhang sprachphilosophischer Texte Schleiermachers*, ed. and introduced by Manfred Frank (Frankfurt am Main: Suhrkamp, 1977).

26 See for example Socrates' paradoxical assertion that his wisdom consists in knowing what he does not know, in *The defence of Socrates*, 20d–21e, *Collected dialogues*, pp. 3–26, esp. pp. 7f.

27 Letter to Ludwig Tieck, 23 February 1800, *NS* IV, 322.

28 See *Parmenides*, 156a–157b, *Collected dialogues*, pp. 920–56, esp. pp. 947f.

29 See Géza von Molnár, *Romantic vision, ethical context. Novalis and artistic autonomy* (Minneapolis: University of Minnesota Press, 1987), p. 108.

30 The term is from Herbert Uerlings, *Friedrich von Hardenberg, genannt Novalis. Werk und Forschung* (Stuttgart: Metzler, 1991), p. 14.

31 See Theodor Ziolkowski, 'James Joyces Epiphanie und die Überwindung der empirischen Welt in der modernen deutschen Prosa', *Deutsche Vierteljahresschrift* 35 (1961), 594–616. On the *Parmenides* in the context of Kierkegaard see Julian Roberts, *German philosophy. An introduction* (Oxford: Polity Press, 1988), p. 199. The Parmenidean moment is central to Walter Benjamin's aesthetics of modernism. See his 'Über den Begriff der Geschichte', in *Gesammelte Schriften*, ed. T. W. Adorno, Gerschom Scholem, Rolf Tiedemann and Hermann Schweppenhauser, vol. I/2 (Frankfurt am Main: Suhrkamp, 1974), pp. 691–704, esp. p. 695; also, for the concept of 'Jetztzeit', pp. 701 ff. The tradition is continued in Adorno, *Ästhetische Theorie*, ed. Gretel Adorno and Rolf Tiedemann (Frankfurt am Main: Suhrkamp, 1970), p. 52, and Karl Heinz Bohrer, *Ästhetik der Plötzlichkeit. Zum Augenblick des ästhetischen Scheins* (Frankfurt am Main: Suhrkamp, 1981), pp. 7 ff., 180 ff.

32 In Friedrich Hölderlin, *Sämtliche Werke und Briefe*, ed. Michael Knaupp, 3 vols. (Munich and Vienna: Hanser, 1992–3), vol. II, pp. 49f.

33 In *Sämtliche Werke*, vol. I, pp. 609–760.

34 See *The collected dialogues of Plato*, pp. 526–74, esp. pp. 553–63.

35 *The collected dialogues of Plato*, pp. 562f. (211a–212c).

36 Lucinde, as critics have pointed out, never has the chance to realise *her* androgyny.

37 In Clemens Brentano, *Werke*, eds. Wolfgang Frühwald, Bernhard Gajek, and Friedhelm Kemp, 2nd edn, 4 vols. (Munich: Hanser, 1973–8) (1st edn, 1963–8), vol. II, pp. 7–458.

38 Jean Paul, *Vorschule der Ästhetik* (§2), in *Werke*, ed. Norbert Miller, 6 vols. (Munich: Hanser, 1959–63), vol. V, pp. 7–456, esp. pp. 31 ff. (§2).

39 In *Werke*, vol. III, pp. 11–830, esp. pp. 766f., 800. Compare the *Clavis Fichtiana*, in *Werke*, vol. III, pp. 1013–56.

40 In *Werke*, vol. IV, pp. 563–626.

41 Either Hegel, Schelling or Hölderlin. See Franz Rosenzweig, '*Das älteste Systemprogramm des deutschen Idealismus* Ein handschriftlicher Fund', *Sitzungsberichte der Heidelberger Akademie der Wissenschaften*, Philosophisch-historische Klasse (1917), 5. Abhandlung. An English translation is appended to Andrew Bowie, *Aesthetics and subjectivity*, pp. 255ff. More recently, Henry Harris, *Hegel's development* (Oxford: Clarendon, 1972–88), vol. I, offers strong arguments for Hegel's authorship.

42 In *Schriften*, ed. Manfred Frank, 6 vols. (Frankfurt am Main: Suhrkamp, 1985), vol. I, pp. 39–134.

43 In Schelling, *Schriften*, vol. I, pp. 395–702.

44 Hardenberg to Friedrich Schlegel, 7 November 1798, *NS* IV, 263.

45 In Karoline von Günderrode, *Sämtliche Werke und ausgewählte Studien*, ed. Walther Morgenthaler, Karin Obermaier and Marianne Graf, 3 vols. (Basle and Frankfurt am Main: Stroemfeld, 1990–1), vol. III, p. 344.

46 See Jean-Jacques Rousseau, *Émile ou de l'éducation* (Paris: Garnier Flammarion, 1966), pp. 465ff.
47 Günderrode, *Sämtliche Werke*, vol. II, pp. 278–81.
48 See Günderrode, *Sämtliche Werke*, vol. II, pp. 273–417.
49 Günderrode, *Sämtliche Werke*, vol. I, pp. 303–14.
50 Dresden: Arnold, 1808.
51 See Heinrich von Kleist, *Sämtliche Werke*, ed. Helmut Sembdner, 2 vols. (Munich: Hanser, 1993) (first edn 1952), vol. II, pp. 634, 636f.
52 Although Fichte's *Bestimmung des Menschen* (Berlin: Voss, 1800), pp. 91ff., also offers a strikingly similar argument and image. See Ernst Cassirer, *Heinrich von Kleist und die Kantische Philosophie* (Berlin: Bruno Cassirer, 1919).
53 See Adam Müller, *Kritische, ästhetische und philosophische Schriften*, ed. Walter Schroeder and Werner Siebert, 2 vols. (Berlin and Neuwied: Luchterhand, 1976), vol. II, pp. 195–248, esp. pp. 201ff., 215ff.
54 Bamberg: C. F. Kunz.
55 *Die Elixiere des Teufels*, in E. T. A. Hoffmann, *Werke*, ed. Walter Müller-Seidel, 4 vols. (Darmstadt: Wissenschaftliche Buchgesellschaft, 1984), vol. II pp. 248ff.; compare pp. 217f.
56 In G. W. F. Hegel, *Werke*, ed. Eva Moldenhauer and Karl Markus Michel, 20 vols. (Frankfurt am Main: Suhrkamp, 1970), vol. III.
57 Hegel, *Werke*, vols. XIII–XV.
58 In the *Philosophie des Rechts*; Hegel, *Werke*, vol. VII, p. 267.
59 For an alternative view, see Stephen Houlgate, *Freedom, truth and history. An introduction to Hegel's philosophy* (London and New York: Routledge, 1991), pp. 168–75.
60 See Jacques Derrida, *Marges de la philosophie* (Paris: Minuit, 1972).
61 See Jean-François Lyotard, *La condition postmoderne* (Paris: Minuit, 1979).
62 See Adorno's *Ästhetische Theorie*.
63 See Andrew Bowie, *Schelling and modern European philosophy. An introduction* (London: Routledge, 1993).

CHAPTER THREE

Two realisms: German literature and philosophy 1830–1890

John Walker

The two most important facts about German literary realism in its European context are its difference and its difficulty of definition. One of the most important reasons for both is the way German literary realism in the nineteenth century is closely linked to, yet never identical with, a philosophical discourse about what 'reality' means. Both the link and the difference between literary and philosophical discourse are sharply focused in one of German realism's earliest and most canonical texts, Georg Büchner's *Lenz* of 1835.

Büchner's *Novelle* is a narrative of the mental illness of the poet Lenz. In the middle of the story, however, is a dialogue concerned with the relationship between art and reality. In this dialogue, the *Kunstgespräch*,[1] Lenz debates with the visitor Kaufmann the relationship between artistic creation and reality itself. Büchner's narrator, using an overtly philosophical vocabulary, describes the time as the beginning of the 'idealistic' period in German literature, and Lenz's position is defined in radical opposition to that movement. The philosophical question marks implicit in the use of the term 'idealistische Periode' are underscored by Lenz's response. Lenz objects to the view that the task of art is aesthetic transfiguration ('Verklärung') of reality. But he objects equally to the idea that the object of literature is to reproduce reality itself. Lenz's response (which includes no semantic opposite to Kaufmann's 'idealistisch') cannot be equated with any naive doctrine of realism, philosophical or literary. What Lenz really denies here is not philosophical idealism but *dualism*: the notion of a division between the truth of human experience and a higher truth of art. Life, ugly or beautiful, is for Lenz the touchstone of literary as well as humane truth. The philosophical idiom which enables him to say this is that of German idealism, especially its affirmation that the intellectual, ethical and aesthetic modes of truth are ultimately one and underwritten by the real presence of God. But the philosophical standpoint of absolute idealism, clearly apparent in Lenz's definition of the task of the artist in relation to a theology of divine creation, is negated by what happens to Büchner's character Lenz, for whom inward vision and outward experience are divorced to the point of schizophrenic breakdown. Moreover, they become divorced chiefly *because* Lenz tries actually to see and to experience the world in the terms which absolute idealism suggests. Gradually new narrative perspectives – some compatible with philosophical idealism, some opposed – force Büchner's readers to confront the *differences* between literary and philosophical articulations of reality, and so ask what 'reality' is and means.

Büchner's *Lenz*, untypical in many respects of the literature of its time, does typify a major difference between German and European realism in the nineteenth century. Nineteenth-century German realism often lacks that philosophical incuriosity about the idea of reality which characterises literary realism elsewhere in Europe.[2] German realism is insistently concerned with the question of what inner human reality means and how it should be represented in art. It relates that question to the situation of the artist in modernity and the tension between aesthetic and philosophical articulations of human subjectivity. Indeed, in some of its expressions it anticipates that heightened concern with linguistic and aesthetic representation which is a central feature of European modernism. German realism, in short, characteristically lacks the emphatically mimetic quality of mainstream European realism.[3] This difference of German realism is the most important source of its relevance to philosophy. German philosophy in the nineteenth century is overwhelmingly idealist and strongly emphasises the importance of aesthetic experience. For German thinkers in the idealist tradition from Hegel to Nietzsche aesthetic experience communicates truth, or even replaces cognitive truth, in ways directly relevant to philosophy. In nineteenth-century Germany idealist philosophical aesthetics coexist with, and often decisively inform, literary realism.

The literary and philosophical uniqueness of nineteenth-century German realism reflects the social and cultural distinctiveness of Germany in the same period. Just as Germany was industrialised and urbanised much later than the rest of western Europe, remaining a politically fragmented semi-feudal state with a largely agrarian economy until the second half of the nineteenth century, so German literature can seem to have retained forms which celebrate psychological inwardness and poetic creation above the claims of social realism. It is not surprising, therefore, that many critics have linked the two differing paths and read the key texts of German realism as the reflection of a retarded economic development which prevented the emergence of a modern political and social domain. It is but a short step from such an analysis to the view that nineteenth-century German literature is not an engagement with, but a retreat from modernity: what Terry Eagleton calls an ideology of the aesthetic which neither challenges nor reflects, but rather evades the reality of modern experience.[4]

I want to present an alternative view of German realism by looking at the differences as well as the parallels between German literary and philosophical history from 1830 to 1890. Realism as a literary category cannot, at this point in German literary history, directly be translated into its philosophical counterpart, even if it is decisively influenced by the philosophical discourse of the same period. There are two realisms in nineteenth-century Germany: one defined by philosophical aesthetics, the other by imaginative literature. The two realisms coexist but never fully coincide. German philosophy in the nineteenth century continues into the age of European realism that emphasis on the autonomy of the aesthetic, and the general cultural and ethical relevance of art, which is one of the most important legacies of Weimar Classicism. In so doing, German philosophical aesthetics sometimes suggest that the truth revealed by art is more significant than that which can be observed in the actual social, economic and historical world. In nineteenth-century German literature, on the other hand, a philosophically informed idea of the autonomy of aesthetic communication is also the source of a powerful social critique. German literary realism is especially concerned with the way cultural and symbolic discourses can underpin or conceal actual social power. It can therefore expose with particular clarity not just the differences, but also the links between the aesthetic and the socio-political articulation of reality.

This chapter will be concerned with the relationship between these two kinds of realism: the one philosophically, the other imaginatively defined. That relationship is one of tension as well as influence. For the philosophical framework often conflicts rather than converges with the literary form. Realism in the German-speaking world not only reflects a different (and sometimes 'pre-modern') kind of social reality, but also questions the coherence of that reality in some remarkably modern ways. This critical potential is highlighted by the difference between literary and philosophical discourse in nineteenth-century Germany.

THE AFTERMATH OF IDEALISM, 1830–1848

The philosophical context: art as critique and art as redemption

German classical and Romantic literature was crucially informed by the idea of the autonomy of the aesthetic. For the Romantics no less than Goethe and Schiller, art offers a form of immediate experience which is not available to philosophy and which, precisely because of its immediacy, has a general social and political relevance. This belief is fundamentally challenged, although essential elements of it are sustained, by the literature of German realism between 1830 and 1890. In this section I want to explore the philosophical background to that challenge in the aftermath of German idealism, in the period between 1830 and 1848 known as the *Vormärz*.

In broad terms these decades witness two kinds of reaction against idealist aesthetics. The first, associated with the reception of Hegel by the radical cultural critics of *Das junge Deutschland* (Young Germany) and writers like Büchner, Heine and Gutzkow, I will call art as *critique*: the idea that literature is equipped and required to intervene in the political life of Germany under the Restoration. The second, associated chiefly with the work of thinkers like Friedrich Schlegel, Schelling and Schopenhauer and writers like Grillparzer and Stifter, I will call art as *redemption*: the idea that art can redeem reality (the religious echo is deliberate) by its aesthetic transfiguration. Both movements share some common features: the idea that art must now fulfil part of the cultural role formerly played by religion; a radicalisation of the idea of aesthetic autonomy inherited from German idealism, combined with a critique of that idea in relation to the social context in which it is applied; and a philosophical aesthetic which is not identical with the literary practices it inspires, indeed which may suggest a polarity between philosophical discourse about literature and literature itself.

The key mode of philosophy, cultural criticism and philosophical aesthetics in Central Europe around 1830 was Hegel's philosophical idealism. The elements in Hegel's thought most relevant to the literary practice of the 1830s and 1840s in Germany are his thesis of the 'end of art' in modernity and the analysis of the end of Romanticism which supports it. Both must be understood in terms of the relationship between philosophy and aesthetic experience in Hegel's thought as a whole.

For Hegel, art is linked to philosophy because both are modes of absolute Spirit, which is the ultimate truth. But the cognitive status of art is inferior to that of philosophy, and it is necessarily cancelled out and overcome ('aufgehoben') when philosophy concerns itself with aesthetic experience. For Hegel, a fully philosophical – fully reflective – understanding of aesthetic experience, whilst necessary to its truth, makes specifically *aesthetic* experience impossible.

This is the source of Hegel's famous and paradoxical thesis of the 'end of art' in his *Vorlesungen über die Ästhetik* (1831; *Lectures on aesthetics*).[5] The very conditions which make modern philosophy necessary also mean that art cannot do justice to the truth of modern experience. Hegel argues that modern society (that following the French Revolution) is characterised by a reflective self-consciousness which can only be satisfied by the insight which philosophy provides. Art, necessarily tied to a sensuous medium, can only fully reflect the truth of a society in which the connection between culture and self-consciousness is still partially immediate or given. The cognitive status of art and its connection to history as a mode of absolute Spirit mean that the true object of modern art can only be the reality of modern experience. But the nature of that experience means that it cannot adequately be embodied in art. Modern art therefore becomes a mode of consciousness in which form is necessarily alienated from substance. At the same time, the conditions of modern society make something other than a conceptual – that is, philosophical – representation of reality urgently necessary. Because modernity means the *sundering* of subjectivity from every organic bond, the reconciliation with reality (146f.) which art once promised is needed more than ever. The condition of modernity is precisely that existential homelessness which philosophy, by conceptual knowledge, offers to overcome. Thus the logical priority which Hegel gives to philosophy over art is not confirmed, indeed it is challenged, by the logic of historical experience which Hegel's own thought suggests.

Hegel's philosophy of art, therefore, has a critical role in the structure of his thought. It suggests a conflict between his philosophical account of art and any literary practice which that account might actually inform. Hegel's aesthetic draws our attention not only to the difference, but also to the relationship between art and the general experience of the culture and society which art interprets: a relationship, not an identity. The identity between history and its intellectual articulation which Hegel's broader system suggests is thoroughly undermined by his philosophy of art. For Hegel suggests that the relationship of subjectivity to society which modern art must reflect will be one of tension and negation: exactly that unrest and pain (141–2) which Hegel describes as the fate of humanity unreconciled to the objective condition of modern life. Modern art, in other words, entails both cognitive dissonance and social and cultural critique.

Hegel expresses his thesis of the 'end of art' in historical terms as the dissolution of the *Romantic* form of art ('Die Auflösung der romantischen Kunstform'[6]), which he in turn defines as the art of the whole post-medieval age. Romanticism, for Hegel, itself presupposes a loss of connection between aesthetic subjectivity and the objective content given by human ethical life in any age (228). The true concern of Romantic art is always the inner life of the soul; external subject matter and outward form are important only if (and because) they have the capacity to make that inner life manifest. What is new about the post-Romantic age, Hegel argues, is that it has lost even that capacity. This leads to a radical ambivalence in Hegel's account of modern literature. He offers a suggestive account of the way modern literary forms, especially the realist novel, can articulate key features of modern experience: the contingency of social life, the dissociation of the public from the private, and the displacement of ideal values from the outward, cultural into the inner, psychological domain. But Hegel's critical insight into modern culture is in constant tension with his thesis that the truth of modern experience cannot adequately be rendered by art at all. Thus he argues, in terms which will influence German theoreticians of realism throughout the century, that modern social reality is intrinsically 'prosaic' (219), because it no longer reflects the inner life of the soul. The modern social sphere, Hegel suggests, must appear to art as the sphere of the trivial and the 'novelistic' ('das Romanhafte', 215). The *Bildungsroman*, for example, is now exhausted as a form because its only possible content is the integration – unworthy, Hegel suggests, of any serious literary treatment – of the individual into the framework of modern society. Hegel's arguments about the inadequacies of the realist novel as a representation of modern experience thus run counter to some of the most influential theorists of realism. In *Die Theorie des Romans* (1920; *The theory of the novel*),[7] for example, Georg Lukács argues that the alienation of modern subjectivity from any culturally embodied source of meaning finds its fullest expression in the realist novel. That is so because the novel can represent better than any other form the totality of modern society (70ff.). That the modern subject can never be fully reconciled with such a society – indeed that he or she is 'transcendentally homeless' (41) in the modern world – is adequately represented in the realist novel, which reflects the totality by its plurality of perspectives and constant play of irony. For Hegel, on the other hand, these characteristics of modernity mean that the totality of modern society cannot adequately be represented in art at all. Only philosophy, for Hegel, can grasp the modern world as a whole, because only philosophy can do justice to the reflective self-consciousness by which modernity is defined. Tragedy ('Tragödie'), for Hegel, is therefore also incompatible with modernity. Classical tragedy, he argues, was concerned with the clash of substantial ethical claims, both private and social in scope, in the moral life of the individual. But modern tragedy or 'Trauerspiel' can only be concerned with the collision of subjective purposes with outward social circumstances, the problem of means and ends; and this, Hegel claims, is incompatible with the ethical seriousness which tragedy demands.[8] The key modes of modern art, therefore, will be irony and comedy. Despite this, Hegel considers drama, not the novel, to be the most appropriate literary form for modernity. For drama is about autonomy, not mimesis: it is the genre least dependent either on a written text or on reference to a really existing social world, and so most suited to the expression of modern subjectivity.[9]

Hegel's analysis of the end of Romanticism implies that any specifically modern literary mode – especially any 'realism' which concerns itself seriously with the significance of modern society – is doomed to failure. Yet the arguments which lead to that verdict, when read critically, suggest a major weakness in Hegel's thought which is however a major source of its relevance to the literature of nineteenth-century Germany. The link Hegel makes between the idea of the end of art and the end of Romanticism prompts us (as it prompted the generation after Hegel's death in 1831) to ask questions about what can happen after Romanticism. Why should modernity be incompatible with the ethical and spiritual function of art? What might a German literary realism, informed by Hegel's philosophical legacy and yet affirming and embodying the autonomy of literary communication, look like? Why (the question will be especially relevant to the great German novelists of the late century) should the characteristically modern concern with subjectivity and irony be incompatible with the emphasis on the totality of social and cultural life which defines the realist novel? These are not Hegel's questions. But the conceptual idiom of Hegel's thought was so powerful, and so relevant to the cultural situation of Germany in the 1830s and 1840s, that they are asked by the literary generation after Hegel in essentially Hegelian terms. That is, in terms of a discourse which is philosophically idealist but historically and culturally realist: one which enables its exponents to ask probing questions about the social and political conditions, and the social and political relevance, of literary production.

The dominant mode of German intellectual life in the 1830s and 1840s is neither philosophy nor literary criticism, but a form of cultural criticism or 'Kritik'[10] which connects both philosophy and literature to the general life of the age. The aspect of Hegel's thought most relevant to the idea of 'Kritik' is his philosophical theology and its doctrine of objective Spirit: the idea that the purpose of God is worked out in human historical development, of which the Christian Incarnation is the apex but not the exclusive mode. The term 'Kritik' also suggests the method of historical criticism in theology, exemplified by the work of David Friedrich Strauss, who in *Das Leben Jesu* (1835; *The life of Jesus*) examined the earliest documents of Christianity in their historical context and sought to reinterpret Christian belief in anthropological and implicitly secular terms. But in the 1830s and 1840s it is the *link* between this kind of critique and the criticism of both literature and society which is most culturally relevant. In those decades, left Hegelians like Bruno Bauer, Max Stirner and Arnold Ruge insist that Hegel's philosophical reinterpretation of Christianity really does explain the content of Christian belief in anthropological terms. The reasons for the persistence of religious belief must therefore be sought in the real experience of human life, especially the social and political conditions under which religion continues to exist. The gap between objective truth and religious representation is to be explained in terms of the alienation of that experience itself. Ludwig Feuerbach, the most influential writer of this school, argues in *Das Wesen des Christentums* (1844; *The essence of Christianity*) that religion articulates the social essence or species-being ('Gattungswesen') of humanity which the individual, separated in his or her limited being, projects as an infinite power beyond the human world. Common to all these writers is a critical and often highly ironic use of theological vocabulary: a discourse in which the distance between the language of theology and its real historical application energises a political critique.[11] At the same time the left Hegelians introduce into Germany much of the secular thought of France. Thus the scientific socialism of Saint-Simon, with its notions of sexual equality and the link between technological development and social change, and the positivism and philosophical atheism of Auguste Comte enter German intellectual life at a time when Hegelian theological dialectic is equally influential. The mixture will prove explosive.

In the mid 1840s post-Hegelian cultural criticism is decisively transformed and given a direct political relevance by the work of Karl Marx.

In his *Deutsche Ideologie* (1844; *The German ideology*),[12] Marx argues that 'Kritik' alone can never be an adequate critique of society. 'Kritik', if it is thorough enough, might expose the link between ideal consciousness and real conditions and the function of the former as a legitimation of the latter. 'Kritik' might also urge its philosophical and theological adherents to make society at large conscious of the link and to use that consciousness as a vehicle of political change. But it can never, Marx argues, enable such change, because it lacks any adequate idea of the real relationship between consciousness and social experience. For Marx, that relationship is expressed by the concept of *ideology*. For Marx, ideology means not just the way real conditions are reflected in consciousness, but the way that reflection is produced by the dynamic of the conditions themselves. The dynamic of the basis of human society, the sphere of labour and material production, also dictates the dynamic of its ideological superstructure. The enlightenment of consciousness cannot therefore lead to the transformation of being. To pretend otherwise (as Marx in the *Deutsche Ideologie* accuses the left Hegelians of doing) is to fight phrases, not realities (20).

Yet the concept of ideology which Marx develops in the *Deutsche Ideologie*, and the idea of economic determinism on which it is based, are nothing like as crude as its later use in his *Manifest der kommunistischen Partei* (1848; *The manifesto of the Communist Party*) suggests. Marx differs from his Hegelian predecessors in drawing attention to the primacy of economic life over the ideological forms by which that life is reflected. But he also offers a much more subtle and persuasive explanation of the persistence of ideology itself. The distorted reflection of reality in ideology, Marx argues in one of his most famous metaphors, is as real a consequence of the distortion of relationships in human society as the inversion of images on the retina is of the structure of the eye (20). It follows that ideology cannot be overcome by any form of intellectual critique, but only by the transformation of the social reality from which ideology derives. How then is the revolutionary consciousness necessary for the transformation to be created, if ideology also functions as a legitimation of the condition which it pretends to describe? The focus of his argument is the public domain which links consciousness and practice together. He thus argues that revolutions are no more automatically produced by impersonal economic forces than they are the consequence of an ideal dissatisfaction. The political and social act which they require cannot be dissociated from the innumerable egoistic deeds which make it happen (362).

Marx's argument creates, although it does not fill, a space for a new kind of 'Kritik': a discourse which ironically highlights both the link and the distance between political action and the critique of ideology. It also points to one of the key themes of Marx's early work: the mismatch between the development of political history and that of intellectual history which (he argues) defines German cultural life. That German thought has outpaced German politics is, for Marx, as definitive of German politics as it is of German thought. Marx's insight into the dialectical relationship between consciousness and practice – not his programmatic statements about the primacy of one over the other – is what makes his work relevant to the general literary culture of his age. That insight suggests a literary, not a philosophical irony: one which is embodied in cultural images, because it understands how cultural symbolism is rooted in material life and can therefore be a powerful vehicle of political change.

In the 1830s and 1840s *Das junge Deutschland* is deeply influenced by the left Hegelian idiom, especially the idea that literature and philosophy reflect, and are in turn embodied in, the real course of human history. But *Das junge Deutschland* radically challenges the priority which Hegel gives to philosophy as better equipped to express that relationship. Writers like Karl Gutzkow, Heinrich Laube and Ludwig Börne argue that the political and social marginalisation of art which as Hegel's later idealism implies neither reflects nor addresses the condition of Germany in their time. For in that age it is *philosophy* in the Hegelian mode, with its promise of the secular realisation of a theological hope, which is most negated by actual historical experience. For the writers of *Das junge Deutschland*, therefore, art must become autonomous precisely because of that prosaic character of modernity which, as Hegel and his followers have shown, makes the continuation of art in the Romantic mode impossible. For the radical post-Hegelian generation, art becomes autonomous because it occupies the gap between the philosophical discourse of absolute idealism and the real cultural context to which that discourse is applied. In so doing, art also begins to occupy the space previously held by religion.[13] Aesthetic symbolism, like the religious faith it increasingly supplants, seeks to mediate between the arguments of the philosophers and the cultural traditions of the people. But, for the radical literary heirs of Hegel, the point of that mediation is to manifest difference, not identity: to reveal the distance between the Christian and Romantic symbols of German culture and the repressive political reality which those symbols endorse.

One of the sources of German realism, then, is 'Kritik': a discourse profoundly aware of the difference as well as the connection between reality and its symbolic representation. In the same cultural context another strand emerges in philosophical aesthetics which will become increasingly influential on German realism as the century progresses: the idea of art as *redemption*.

The link between art and redemption, philosophical aesthetics and Christianity, is particularly explicit in the work of Friedrich Schelling (1775–1854). With the disillusionment of the post-Hegelian generation, Schelling's arguments about the autonomy of art as a vehicle of human subjectivity gain renewed currency. In his last great philosophical work, *Die Philosophie der Offenbarung* (1843; *The philosophy of revelation*),[14] Schelling revisits his earlier aesthetic mythology in the light of Hegel's speculative theology. He addresses what he sees as the key problem of his age: how to reconcile with actual historical experience the speculative synthesis which German idealism, especially the work of Hegel, has produced. The obvious contradiction between that synthesis and the condition of Germany in the 1840s has provoked a powerful reaction against philosophy in German life (92). This conflict is focused on the social and cultural meaning of Christianity. Hegelian idealism has identified the scope of Christianity with the whole of secular experience, and yet undermined belief in any contingent historical embodiment of religious truth (121f.). Schelling describes his philosophy as a positive one, which must supersede as well as presuppose Hegel's negative dialectic (151f.). He also calls it a philosophy of reality. By this he means two things. First, philosophy must accept the reflective truth which Hegel's negative dialectic has disclosed: reason and revelation cannot be opposed (148). But, unlike abstract idealism, the new positive philosophy must reconnect reflective truth to the experience – social and political as well as religious and philosophical – of the post-Hegelian age. There must therefore be a new Christian theology, rooted in a new mythology which articulates Christian truth in symbolism accessible to the people (250ff.).

The work of Friedrich Schlegel (1772–1829), equally influential on the post-Romantic generation, is less explicitly Christian but still theologically informed. For Schlegel, the aesthetic mode of truth is both the product and the expression of the religious mode of truth, which it sustains by witnessing to transcendence in modernity. In his *Philosophie der Geschichte* (1828; *Philosophy of history*) and *Philosophie des Lebens* (1828; *Philosophy of life*) Schlegel argues that the only true modern heir to religion is aesthetic symbolism, a secular mythology which links art to the intellectual and political life of a people and so fulfils an organic role denied to conceptual knowledge. Schlegel asserts that the end of religion as an autonomous mode of truth also entails the end of art. But Schlegel's disciples, unlike those of Hegel, emphasise not the actual difference, but the potential convergence between art, now the cultural bearer of the truth of religion, and the ethical life of the human community which religion once sustained. In the aesthetics of Schelling and Schlegel lies one of the roots of the idea of symbolic or poetic realism, which will be particularly influential in German narrative fiction later in the century.

The philosophy of Arthur Schopenhauer (1788–1860) differs radically from that of Schelling and Schlegel because, although it gives cardinal importance to art, it abjures any form of religious, especially Christian, assent. For Schopenhauer, indebted more to Kant than to Hegel, aesthetic truth is fundamentally and irrevocably different from any conceptual mode. The central thesis of his *Die Welt als Wille und Vorstellung* (*The world as will and representation*), first published in 1818 but most influential three decades later, is that the primary reality of all experience is the will. Because the will always construes the world as the object of its desire, the intelligence which is the will's prisoner is epistemologically self-centred, seeing the world only as the mental object or 'Vorstellung' of its particular and limited perspective. For Schopenhauer, liberation can come only from a non-conceptual insight which pacifies the will and so releases its subject from the emotional and intellectual bondage which desire always entails. Art, for Schopenhauer, is a means of such insight. Schopenhauer is thus neither a Romantic nor a philosophical realist. The purpose of art is neither to represent a reality external to the subject, nor to express the subject's inner life, but to create an autonomous reality which transforms the self by a truth which is always beyond the grasp of the mind. Tragedy is for Schopenhauer the highest form of drama, and drama (because of its embodied immediacy) the highest form of representational art. Its purpose is to liberate the self from the principle of individuation by the transforming experience of suffering. Given his philosophical assumptions, it is not surprising that Schopenhauer is concerned primarily with the non-verbal and symbolic arts, especially music (he has nothing of note to say about the novel).

Literary texts

One of the most important features of German literary realism is the way it departs from and sometimes undermines the philosophical discourses of critique and redemption which inform it. It does so not just because the philosophical idiom of the age is overwhelmingly idealist, but also (and more importantly) because the role of art which that idealism suggests can never philosophically be fulfilled or indeed adequately defined. The philosophical frameworks are necessarily relativised as soon as they are applied to the reality of human society in their time. For both modes are defined by an understanding of social experience in negative, not positive terms: one which sees society in terms of a transcendental meaning which it potentially could, but actually does not, embody. That shared understanding means that critique and redemption are not simply opposites, but dialectical partners which interact in the stuff of literary texts.

A prime example of that interaction is the work of the most influential German writer of the age, Heinrich Heine (1797–1856). The major philosophical influence on Heine's work is certainly Hegel, whose cultural influence he analyses in his essay *Zur Geschichte der Religion und Philosophie in Deutschland* (1834; *On the history of religion and philosophy in Germany*) and elsewhere. But for Heine, unlike Hegel, the irony and subjectivity of Romanticism mean not the dissociation but the closest possible connection of aesthetic and social truth. In his essay *Die romantische Schule* (1832; *The Romantic school*) Heine argues that Romanticism is the key German literary mode because Romantic symbolism, and Romantic alienation, represent the actual condition of German political life. Literary Romanticism, especially when linked to Catholicism and the idealisation of the German medieval past, is politically a profoundly conservative force. But at the same time Romantic imagery and irony, because they embody the alienation of the German literary class from the political public domain, are of the greatest political import. For Heine, the reasons for the end of Romantic art lie in the *positive* relevance to literary creation of the modern demand for political and social democracy and the humane application of knowledge. It is the positivity of these demands which give to Romantic irony its cultural relevance and critical power.

This paradox energises Heine's greatest work, *Deutschland. Ein Wintermärchen* (1844; *Germany. A winter's tale*), a satirical epic which describes a trip across Germany to Hamburg which Heine made from his Parisian exile in 1843. In this text, Heine is concerned to expose what Marx in the same year called 'die deutsche Ideologie': an ideology of philosophical idealism and ethical inwardness which prevents the realisation of German political freedom. The point of Heine's poetic irony is neither to criticise the German ideology nor to reflect it, but to address and transform his readers' consciousness with poetic images which have an autonomous cultural life. The poem consists of a series of tableaux depicting real locations like Cologne Cathedral and the Teutoburg Forest, pregnant with the cultural memories of Germany which, at the time Heine is writing, are enlisted in the service of Romantic reaction. Heine's ironic realism deconstructs the official meaning of each locale. Cologne Cathedral, for example, the home of reactionary Catholicism and the symbol of Germany's medieval past, becomes the site of anti-Semitic pogroms and the tomb of the Prussian, Austrian and Russian emperors, whose skeletons he imagines smashed by the *Doppelgänger* who translates his thoughts into action.

For Heine, the metamorphosis of German Romanticism into political critique does not mean the end of art as such, but the end of the politically quiescent and yet highly politicised idea of aesthetic autonomy which is the political deficit of Weimar Classicism. His definition of the purpose of art in the post-Romantic age in these terms typifies one of the strands in the making of German realism. Yet there is no single literary form in Germany which can be designated the natural exponent of the realist mode; the bourgeois novel, in particular, does not fulfil this function here.

The key modes of early German realism are not the novel, but the drama and the *Novelle*. Dramatic realism is above all a realism of discourse: one which reflects the social objectivity of language. Drama is thus especially suited to reflect the life of an age in which there is a critical gap between social experience and its cultural – that is, primarily, its linguistic – representation. All the major dramatists of the age – Büchner, Grabbe, Hebbel, Grillparzer, and the Viennese comic dramatists Nestroy and Raimund – have this dual focus. Some, like Hebbel, explicitly articulate a philosophy of history which they link with questionable success to the dramatic depiction of actual historical events. Others, like Christian Grabbe (1801–36) in *Napoleon oder die Hundert Tage* (1830; *Napoleon or the hundred days*), use a discontinuous dramatic technique to portray the same historical events from several different social and linguistic perspectives. Sometimes, as in Grabbe's *Scherz, Satire, Ironie und tiefere Bedeutung* (1827; *Jokes, satire, irony and deeper meaning*) or (more light-heartedly) in Johann Nestroy's (1801–62) *Der Zerrissene* (1844; *The agonised one*), the distance between a philosophically saturated cultural discourse and actual social experience leads to satire or the comedy of dialogue.

The capacity of drama to thematise the tension between social experience and its linguistic representation is exemplified by the work of the greatest dramatist of the age, Georg Büchner (1813–37). In his plays a non-mimetic literary form and a philosophical perspective which owes more to idealism than to realism become the source of a dramatic historical realism which anticipates modern drama.

Büchner's major historical tragedy *Dantons Tod* (1835; *Danton's death*) deals with political and personal conflict among the leaders of the French Revolution against a backcloth of political terror (the action is set in 1793 under Robespierre's Jacobin dictatorship) and mass revolution. The core of the drama is the political problem of means and ends, which Hegel had declared could not be successfully treated in modern tragedy. Büchner's play proves Hegel wrong. Its two key characters, Danton and Robespierre, represent two radically different views of political action. For Robespierre, leader of the Committee of Public Safety, historico-political reality follows mechanical laws as surely as material nature. The task of the revolutionary, therefore, is to exploit such laws, whatever their human cost, in the interests of progress. For Danton, his opponent, the object of the Revolution is to realise human autonomy as Kant had understood it: to enable each human being to fulfil their nature, by treating all human beings as ends in themselves, never as means to an external end.

Danton is executed because, unlike Robespierre, he is unable or unwilling to manipulate events, especially the power of public opinion, in favour of his own interests. This apparently mechanistic dynamic, as well as Büchner's famous comment that, in studying the Revolution, he was overwhelmed by the 'horrible fatalism of history' ('den gräßlichen Fatalismus der Geschichte')[15] has led some critics to see the play as an exposition of Hegelianism understood as historical determinism, in which Danton dies because he is unable to understand the dialectic of history. Nothing could be further from the truth. The realism of the play derives neither from the chain of historical events with which it deals, nor from discourse about those events, but from the dramatically embodied interaction between the two. Throughout the play Robespierre is associated with a form of pseudo-scientific historical materialism, Danton with a Schopenhauerian pessimism which abjures action and is plagued by existential boredom ('Langeweile') and doubt. But this conflict of discourses only becomes a dramatic conflict because of the political context in which it occurs. Danton's apparent nihilism is the shadow side of his profoundly humane idealism. Animated by an idea of human fulfilment which, like its antecedent in German idealism, emphasises the difference between human and material nature, he is unable to continue to participate in a programme which (in Rousseau's words) forces people to be free. The long philosophical dialogues in the Conciergerie are as much a part of the play's realism as the crowd scenes and political speeches. These dialogues, in which aesthetic imagery and metaphor of extraordinary power are generated without any real referent in the objective situation of the participants, exactly capture that consciousness in excess of the facts which Schopenhauer describes as the fate of the will engaged in self-destructive action. But their dramatic force derives not from the ideas they contain, but from the way they objectify a vision of human liberation which cannot, in the given circumstances, be politically realised.

Büchner's realism is focused in socio-psychological terms by his semi-documentary *Woyzeck* (1836). This play, concerned with the real case of a soldier executed for murdering his lover despite clinical evidence of insanity, uses dramatic realism to question even more radically what 'reality' means, especially the idea of reality which leads to Woyzeck's conviction. In a key scene a doctor examines Woyzeck and discovers mental aberration. But the doctor, who combines materialist science with Hegelian moralism, is himself profoundly aberrant in his identification of human and mechanical nature. For him the world, like the body, is a machine to be controlled by a detached, objective mind. Woyzeck is said to be alienated because his imagination (he hears voices) is as real to him as the alienated human world he inhabits, yet he is also deemed free and responsible. Hence this philosophy has human and dramatic consequences, and Büchner exposes the inability of both scientific and philosophical discourse and contemporary society to represent *human* reality: a reality which (like the aesthetic vision of his character Lenz) is the locus of creative energy rather than the object of mechanical laws. Büchner's literary realism has therefore no direct philosophical equivalent. He sometimes uses a philosophical idiom in his plays to ask questions about the idea of reality which the society of his day requires in order to survive in its existing form. But the relevance of the philosophical discourse is defined by literary form.

The link between literary form and a philosophy of history is more explicit in the work of Friedrich Hebbel (1813–63). In his preface to *Maria Magdalena* (1844) he counters Hegel's objection that modern tragedy can reveal only the contingency of modern life, by arguing that the real object of modern drama is not the conflict between the middle and the upper class (which Hebbel, following Hegel, qualifies as accidental), but rather necessary conflicts within both society and the inner life of the individual. For Hebbel, tragedy implies a necessity which is ontological and historical, not just social or psychological in kind.[16] Tragedy articulates especially the experience of transitional periods in human history, one of which he identifies as his own. Tragedy therefore has both a metaphysical and an ethical function. One of its purposes is to articulate the meaning of the emergence of the modern age, in which the ethical order is no longer given by tradition but must consciously be appropriated by the citizens of the modern state.

Hebbel thus employs conservative Hegelian categories to announce a programme for modern tragedy which, Hegel's own argument suggests, will be difficult if not impossible. What happens in his dramas themselves? His best-known work, *Maria Magdalena*, is a tragedy set in a petit-bourgeois milieu. Its motif – the seduction, pregnancy and abandonment of a woman of the respectable working class – differs from the frequent treatment of a similar theme in bourgeois tragedy because the conflict between father and daughter is not caused by the daughter's relationship with a suitor from a higher social class. Rather, the focus of the drama is the effect of the daughter's situation on her family's position *within* their own class. The power of the play derives from the way it depicts the *internalisation* of social norms and the conflict that process engenders. The 'tragic' choice which Maria is forced to make – to commit suicide or to force her father to do so when he discovers her pregnancy – is not a conflict of two socially embodied ethical powers in the Hegelian sense. It is a collision between two equally irrational imperatives, both of which can issue only in the social or physical destruction of the agent. The play is thus an example of social realism less because it shows a complex and meaningful interaction between psychological and social life, than because it shows a world in which the two are immediately and unconsciously fused. It is Hebbel's rendering of this *narrowness*, a world in which modernity can only be negatively imagined, not positively experienced, which is the key to the play's success. *Maria Magdalena* is thus a powerful (and remarkably modern) example of social realism in spite of, not because of, Hebbel's philosophical scheme.

Hebbel's other major plays, concerned with historical rather than contemporary themes, manifest a similar contradiction, which is however hardly ever resolved with dramatic integrity. *Judith* (1842) deals both with a historical situation (the conflict between the Jewish people and their pagan ruler Holofernes) and a personal conflict (the sexual frustration of a virgin widow and her desire for revenge after she has been violated). Judith's prior motive for killing Holofernes is that he is the general of the army which is besieging the Jewish city, but the personal motive that takes over at the moment of killing is anger because she has allowed him to sleep with her as a prelude to the murder. Hence the political and the personal dramas do not mesh; one kind of necessity does not connect with the other. Hebbel's attempt, in his theoretical essay *Mein Wort über das Drama* (1843; *A word on drama*), to justify his procedure by appealing to an idea of historical necessity shows only the impossibility of staging his metaphysical scheme. This failure becomes manifest (and its ideological implications obvious) in *Agnes Bernauer* (1852), in which a politically motivated execution is described as a sacrifice to necessity and at the same time given an implausible dramatic motivation by an equally improbable sexual plot.

The Austrian dramatist Franz Grillparzer (1791–1872) differs radically from his German contemporaries in rejecting the idea that any philosophy of history can effectively be represented on the stage. For Grillparzer drama and philosophy are polar opposites. Although philosophically informed, indeed the author of an aphoristic aesthetic tract which takes issue with the heritage of German idealism,[17] Grillparzer insists that the immediacy of the stage must take precedence over philosophical reflection. In particular, he rejects the idealist aesthetics of Hegel. His plays thus emphasise less the theoretical expression of ideas than the contingency and immediacy of action; gesture, costume and setting are important, and dialogue is used more to reveal misunderstanding and self-deception – the gap between thought and action – than to expound a vision of the world. But this 'anti-philosophy' of the stage conceals a vision of Grillparzer's own. In his history plays *König Ottokars Glück und Ende* (1825; *King Ottokar, his rise and fall*), *Libussa* (1845) and *Ein Bruderzwist in Habsburg* (1848; *A Habsburg brothers' quarrel*), all of which deal with the fate of the multi-ethnic Habsburg empire, Grillparzer challenges both historicism and idealism. For Grillparzer, human history is informed neither by a transcendental design nor by the rational intentions of humankind. It is a theatre of contingency.

Dramatic realism, the key form of early German realism, is a realism of discourse: one which thematises the gap, even the contradiction, between social experience and its ideological interpretation. That contradiction was also the central concern of the German novel between 1830 and 1848. In the 1830s and 1840s the bourgeois realist novel is replaced in Germany by the social novel or *Sozialroman*, a hybrid form as much philosophical as it is social in emphasis. In this form the idea of society is constructed by a discourse which owes more to cultural criticism and the philosophy of history than it does to the immediate observation of social life. It is thus vitiated by the absence of that bourgeois public realm which, elsewhere in Europe, accompanied the development of social realism. One of the most famous *Sozialromane* of the age, *Die Epigonen* (1836; *The epigones*) by Karl Immermann (1796–1840), thematises the cultural despair of the generation which came to maturity in the epoch of liberal German nationalism before 1815, and can find no outlet for its ideals under the Restoration. The modernisation and incipient industrialisation of German society are suggested, but never fully explored, by the decision of the protagonist Hermann to withdraw from society into the artificial idyll of an agrarian community. In the novel *Wally die Zweiflerin* (1835; *Wally the sceptic*) by Karl Gutzkow (1811–78), ideological (often theological), psychological and sexual elements are combined. The heroine is an aristocratic and cultivated woman, habituée of the salons of a court city, who is forced into an arranged marriage with the Sardinian ambassador to a petty German state. She eventually commits suicide, not because of her love life but because of religious doubts, prompted by reading her lover's testament of faith based on the works of leading critical theologians (a radical theological treatise forms a major part of the novel and was the chief reason for its censorship by the authorities). This extraordinary work closely links two key motifs of social criticism in the literature of *Das junge Deutschland*: religious scepticism and sexual emancipation. Because an entirely secularised Christian theology is the ideology of the political establishment, philosophical or theological critique replaces engagement with society in explicitly social terms. Society, in other words, is approached in literature via the *ideologies* which sustain it. But this apparent deficit has some surprising consequences. The feminist novel and the theme of sexual oppression, in which the link between ideology and exploitation is especially apparent, play a much greater role in early German realism than they do elsewhere in Europe at the same time.[18]

The other major form of the German novel in the 1830s and 1840s – the historical novel – may be seen as a different response to the same cultural nexus. The German historical novel suffers initially from the same kind of cultural deficit which inhibits the growth of German social realism: the failure of a modern polity to emerge organically from the course of German history. In Germany Romanticism lives on in historicism: the idea that the key to understanding (or even changing) the German present lies in the German past. The German historical novel is thus only obliquely a realist form. Historical fact sits uneasily with historicist ideology. In the historical novels of Ludwig Tieck

(1773–1853), for example, religious or dynastic conflicts are treated as surrogates for problems of political responsibility and historical change. Willibald Alexis (Theodor Häring; 1798–1871), the most influential German practitioner of the historical novel before 1848, stands out because of his consciousness of the difficulties of the genre and the sophistication of the techniques he uses to overcome them. For Alexis, the advantage of the historical novel is that it treats historical events which live on in the traditions of the people. But he doubts whether there is a living connection between those traditions and the present experience. The historical novel must be about more than myths and heroes; its point is precisely to *create* an imaginative link between past and present, which draws its power from the realism which the treatment of historical material provides. His two-part novel *Hans Jürgen und Hans Jochem* (1846–8) attempts this with a treatment of the political history of the Reformation, in which Protestant theology and the dynamics of social change are linked in a way which reflects both the political and cultural contradictions of Germany before 1848.

The *Novelle* is distinguished from other kinds of prose fiction by the compression of its form and the intensity of symbolic representation which that achieves. Where the realist novel renders an extensive world of social experience, made credible by the way it stands for the wider world outside the text, the *Novelle* characteristically offers us a narrow world, often of a single person or small group, which relates to the broader society via symbols which express both psychological and cultural life. Features such as these, as well as the conservative political allegiances of some of its practitioners like Adalbert Stifter and Eduard Mörike, have often led literary historians to see the *Novelle* as the major form of *Biedermeier*: the conservative cultural, religious and literary reaction against Romanticism which strongly influenced German provincial life under the Restoration. This can easily obscure the capacity of the *Novelle* for a remarkably modern form of realism. This may be illustrated by a text from a writer often regarded as the epitome of *Biedermeier* conservatism: Grillparzer's *Der arme Spielmann* (1847; *The poor minstrel*). Grillparzer's central character Jakob, like Büchner's Lenz, is an artist whose vision of experience puts him out of gear with any possible field of successful action. This scion of a patrician Viennese family, disinherited and disappointed in love, ekes out a precarious living by playing a violin on public holidays. But the real focus of the story lies in the different attitudes to reality (and to art) which the relationship between narrator and character implies. The narrator (the first 'Ich' of the story) goes to the outskirts of Vienna on a summer Sunday to observe a popular festival and discovers Jakob. In a parody of Hegelian moralism (which recalls Grillparzer's own aphorisms and diaries) he remarks approvingly on the moral, even religious uplift which conscious membership of a human group can bring. This attitude – moral patronage and formal detachment – Grillparzer's narrator brings to bear on everything and everyone, Jakob included. He aptly describes it as an inordinate anthropological desire ('anthropologischer Heißhunger')[19] which the very difference of the old musician has provoked. That difference consists not just in his eccentricity and social marginality but also in his devotion to that high culture (he plays – badly – classical scores which he can hardly decipher) which the narrator has consciously deserted on his anthropological expedition. Jakob's life is redeemed by music, a process which the surface narrative describes as sexual sublimation but which, the structure of the story suggests, is both real and true. For Jakob too, when playing or listening, experiences that liberation which Büchner's Lenz enjoys when he contemplates the masterpieces of Dutch realist painting: redemptive self-loss in the real presence of beauty – here in non-representational art. Grillparzer's wordy narrator, however, wants to see and to represent everything about the object of his curious hunger. And he does, except for the one thing that matters most: the irreducibility of his character's being to the object of a psychologically detached and verbally explicit realism. Grillparzer and Büchner, despite their differences, both practise a particular kind of realism. Both explore the realm of aesthetic symbolism. For Grillparzer no less than for Büchner that realm is both an indictment and a redemption of the realm of common experience.

This double energy – at once aesthetic and ethical, redemptive and critical – is characteristic of early German realism and the major source of its relevance to the philosophical discourse of its age. Early German realism, like the philosophical aftermath of German idealism, articulates both the difference and the connection between aesthetic and socio-historical truth. But it defines both the difference and the relevance in a way very different from German philosophy. German realism is therefore most philosophically relevant when it shows and embodies the difference between literary and philosophical communication. That relevance becomes increasingly clear as a mature German realism, engaging with and yet still creatively different from the main European tradition, emerges after 1848.

THE REALISM OF TRANSFIGURATION, 1848–1871

In the two decades after 1848 German literary realism develops its own form of the realist novel. In the second half of the nineteenth century no less than the first, however, there is no direct correlation between German literary realism and any philosophical equivalent. On the contrary, the link established in the aftermath of German idealism between literary realism and an implicitly idealist philosophical ontology is sustained in the heyday of the German realist novel. In mid-century, however, the historicist strand in Hegelian idealism becomes increasingly detached from its theological and metaphysical roots and gives way to an ontology of immanence, for which truth is to be found in the organic totality of social and cultural life. Ontological immanence becomes linked to aesthetic presence. In the wake of the abortive liberal revolution of 1848, perceptions of the general cultural relevance of literature also begin to change. The literature of the *Vormärz* had sustained into the post-Romantic age a belief common to both German Romanticism and German philosophical idealism: the idea that literature can enable political enlightenment and social change, because it can communicate with the wider culture in ways denied to other modes of discourse, especially philosophy. In the years after 1848 the cultural and social relevance of this idea changes decisively. The role of art comes to be seen as more the transfiguration than the transformation of reality. With the emergence of poetic realism, German philosophical aesthetics posits art as the constructor of a parallel reality which is of greater human significance than the world of common experience but nevertheless discloses the essential truth of that world. The links between this view of art and political resignation are clear. But after 1848 no less than before, the practice of German literary realism never simply coincides with, indeed it often undermines, the idea of realism which German philosophical aesthetics propounds.

Philosophical context

The most important intellectual movement of mid-nineteenth-century Germany is historicism. Hegel's view of history gives way, under the influence of both positivist scholarship and a more secularised form of Protestant theology, to a concern with the real dynamics of historical change and the actual connection of human knowledge to the social and cultural life of an age. This movement has two major sources: first, the rise of positive historiography, typified by the work of Johann Gustav

Droysen (1808–84), whose *Vorlesungen über Encylopädie und Methodologie der Geschichte* (1858; *Lectures on the methodology of the study of history*) inaugurate a new age of historical scholarship. For Droysen, causality and context, not purpose, become the key categories of historical understanding. In the work of Leopold von Ranke (1795–1886), on the other hand, an emphasis on the historicity of truth remains entirely compatible with philosophical idealism. For Ranke, history is the objective reality of the Spirit ('das Real-Geistige'). This conception differs from Hegel's idea of history as objective Spirit in that for Ranke neither philosophy nor scholarship can discern any objective law of historical progress. Cultural formations, because they are expressions of the human Spirit and not subject to mechanical laws, can be understood neither inductively nor deductively, but only by an act of empathetic insight. The task of the historian is to *imagine* how things really were. Ranke thus allows more than Droysen for a link between the historical and the aesthetic mode of truth. For Jacob Burkhardt (1818–97), a specialist in Renaissance civilisation, the key to understanding history is human culture in its intellectual and artistic expression. Art is not only autonomous but represents a second and higher reality on earth which transcends and redeems the empirical course of history.

The two strands – positivist and idealist – in nineteenth-century German historicism might seem at first sight to be opposed. Yet they have much in common which relates to the general cultural situation of the age. Both, although linked to actual historical scholarship, are emphatically *philosophies* of history. Both insist, as Hegel had done, on the link between human historical *consciousness* and history itself. Droysen's positivism no less than Ranke's and Burkhardt's idealism give to the productive imagination of the historian a key role in historical understanding. In philosophical terms, therefore, both strands have more in common with epistemological idealism than with realism. History, for both, is a human science. Its theses cannot be tested against a reality categorically separate from the interpreting mind. History thus remains closely linked to hermeneutics; its method owes as much to the interpretation of cultural documents as it does to the analysis of social facts.

The political and philosophical ambivalence of historicism (and the potential convergence of its idealist and positivist strands) is made clear by its application to the study of contemporary German society. The most thoroughly secular strand in German historicist thought is that influenced by the French philosopher Auguste Comte (1797–1857). In his *Cours de philosophie positive* (1857; *Lectures on positive philosophy*) Comte argues that humanity progresses from a mythical, through a metaphysical, and into a positive (i.e. the modern) age, in which natural science provides the model for the organisation of both knowledge and society. Most striking in the German reception of Comte after 1848, however, is the almost total eclipse of his empiricist method by the determinist philosophy of history which his metaphysical system implies. The emergence of German sociology in the mid-nineteenth century is decisively influenced by a view of society as an organic whole which can be grasped only through the modes of its cultural as well as its political representation. The conservative historian and political theorist Heinrich von Treitschke (1834–96) argues in his book *Die Gesellschaftswissenschaft* (1858; *The science of society*) that the very indissociability of private and social life which characterises modernity means that the science of society is inseparable from the political science of the state. The economic and civil life of a people can be grasped only via the political form of its organisation, which is equally the source of its cultural and ethical coherence.

Treitschke illustrates a characteristic of German intellectual life which is directly relevant to the particular character of German realism: an emphasis on the way modern society is politically and culturally *represented*, which shifts the definition of the political towards that of the cultural domain. It is in this context that we should understand the coexistence with positivist historicism of its apparent opposite: the aesthetic cultural pessimism which finds its fullest expression in the philosophy of Schopenhauer and the music dramas and cultural criticism of Richard Wagner (1813–83). In his manifestos *Die Kunst und die Revolution* (1849; *Art and revolution*) and *Das Kunstwerk der Zukunft* (1849; *The work of art of the future*), Wagner gives to art a directly political function. In both psychological and metaphysical terms he argues that the result of the suppression of nature by culture has produced a tension which can only be released by revolutionary change. For Wagner, the impending social revolution is a result of both the demands of the proletariat for political and cultural recognition and the instinctual forces which have been suppressed by the process of civilisation itself.[20] Art, for Wagner, is entirely antithetical to any form of discursive knowledge. Its role is to celebrate the surrender of knowledge ('Wissenschaft') to the instinctual energy of life ('Leben').[21] The function of art is to harness this energy and to give it a cultural and ethical purpose. The social revolution has created the strong human being; art must now create the beautiful one. In operas like *Tannhäuser*, *Parsifal* and *Tristan und Isolde* Wagner expresses an idealised and ideologically charged vision of the German past, in which Christian symbolism is fused with the mythology of medieval Germany in historical fables, often with thinly disguised anti-Semitic overtones. With his concept of the *Gesamtkunstwerk* or integrated work of art, Wagner seeks to combine several artistic forms – music, poetry and sumptuous stage décor – to form historical epics which will transcend the limitations of the historical novel and historical drama, and so create a new popular German mythology in which the German present will be organically and symbolically connected to the German past.

Wagner's profoundly irrationalist political and aesthetic programme is an extreme example of the potential convergence of the two most powerful streams in nineteenth-century German culture: historicism, with its idea of historical determinism, and aestheticism, with its idea of the autonomy of art. Both surface outside the historical context and without the historical reflectivity which accompanied their initial emergence. But precisely this historical displacement is one of the most important reasons for their relevance to the development of German literary realism after 1848. That relevance is made clear by some of the most influential literary and aesthetic definitions of realism in the age. Theodor Vischer (1807–87) argues in his *Ästhetik oder die Wissenschaft des Schönen* (1847–58; *Aesthetics, or the science of beauty*) that modern economic rationality is the enemy of art. Echoing Hegel's thesis of the prosaic character of modernity, Vischer argues that the beautiful forms are not modern, and the modern ones not beautiful ('Die schönen Formen sind nicht zeitgemäss, und die zeitgemässen nicht schön').[22] But, unlike Hegel, Vischer does not derive from this any thesis of the 'end of art'. Rather, he argues that the task of art is to aestheticise the present: to reconcile modern subjectivity with an objective cultural life. Vischer uses the term realist art ('die realistische Kunst') to describe this aesthetic programme. In what sense is his position realist? Clearly not a philosophical one. For Vischer, art creates a second objective reality which aesthetically embodies the truth of actual experience. His literary realism, in other words, is predicated on ontological idealism. He gives to the novel – the central form of modern realism – only limited recognition. Unlike Hegel, Vischer argues that the *Bildungsroman* is the form most adequate to modern experience. But this is so only because of its ability to transfigure that experience: its social dimension is defined by the conjunction of the truth of life with the beautiful illusion fostered by classical humanism.

Otto Ludwig (1813–65), who coined the term poetic realism ('poetischer Realismus') in 1858,[23] makes the link between the ideas of realism and aesthetic autonomy especially close. Poetic realism is the product of a specifically aesthetic imagination which creates the autonomous, complete and ordered world of a work of art: a world which reveals the meaning of the actual world of experience. Poetic realism, he argues, stands halfway between naturalism and idealism. The former simply reflects the contingency of experience; the latter reduces it to an ideal intellectual unity. Poetic realism acknowledges in reality only as much contingency as it can organise into an aesthetically satisfying whole. It is therefore especially relevant to the compressed and highly organised form of the *Novelle*.

Theories of this kind acknowledge the relevance of modernity to literature only to argue that modern reality can and should be transfigured by literary form. Just as the political thought of the age argues that the loss of an organic past can be mitigated by an ethically informed study of the present, so its aestheticians seem to suggest that literature can reconcile its readers to modernity by sustaining a life of aesthetic inwardness. The age of poetic realism continues to witness a creative tension between literary and philosophical representations of reality. Poetic realism is a literary form which powerfully illuminates the way modern society is reflected, interpreted and transfigured in the minds of its members. But such a form need not reduce the truth of modern society to the discourses which represent it. It can transfigure the real not just by making us see reality through an aesthetic perspective, but also by making us aware of the distance between our actual social experience and the perspectives through which we are made to see it. The following section explores how that realism works in some representative texts.

Literary texts

Between 1848 and 1871 German literature, first in Switzerland and then in Germany itself, produces its own version of the classic form of European realism: the realist novel. At the same time the *Novelle*, a genre specifically associated with poetic realism, becomes a major form throughout the German-speaking world. Drama, however, is almost entirely eclipsed during this period by prose. By contrast, the historical novel in this period is much more important than it was before 1848. The link between the historical novel and the *Gegenwartsroman* (novel of contemporary society), already present before 1848 in the work of writers like Gutzkow, becomes more explicit. One of the most famous examples of the genre is Wilhelm Raabe's (1831–1910) *Chronik der Sperlingsgasse* (1856;

Chronicle of Sparrow Lane), which recounts the history of the first half of the nineteenth century from the standpoint of a private scholar living alone in Berlin. Raabe's text includes a complex treatment of the problem of literary and historical representation and so anticipates a major emphasis of his mature realist fiction. The period after 1848 also sees an upsurge of interest in the historical novel proper, which begins to free itself from its Romantic roots and to become a vehicle for the critique and analysis of the present as much as the past. Willibald Alexis's *Ruhe ist die erste Bürgerpflicht* (1852; *Quiet is the citizen's first duty*) and its continuation *Isegrimm* (1854) treat the political upheavals of Prussia during the Napoleonic wars whilst focusing on problems of ethical and political choice – order or freedom, patriotic duty or social solidarity, loyalty to the state or conscience – which reflect the political and cultural situation of Germany after 1848.

The realist novel in the German-speaking world between 1848 and 1871 takes several different forms, some of which tend towards a critical social realism and some more towards the poetic transfiguration of experience which the philosophical aesthetics of the time propound. The distance as well as the relationship between the two poles is illuminated by a comparison of two of the best-known German realist novels of the age: *Soll und Haben* (1855; *Debit and credit*) by Gustav Freytag (1816–95), and Raabe's *Der Hungerpastor* (1864; *The hunger pastor*). Both of these novels are *Bildungsromane*, and both are concerned with the relationship between the inner aesthetic life and the outward life of society. Both thematise the act of literary representation itself, and both link the ideas of literary and social representation. Yet the critical force of realism is very different in each case. *Soll und Haben*, which chronicles the entry into professional life of the merchant's apprentice Anton Wohlfart of Breslau, is only superficially concerned with the dynamics of economic life. Its real concern is with the self-consciousness of the emerging bourgeois class. The ethos of the old-fashioned warehouse business where Anton serves his apprenticeship is opposed to that of the aristocracy who cannot retain their inherited wealth in an age of capitalist speculation, but more sharply contrasted with that of Anton's Jewish fellow apprentice and eventual competitor Veitel Itzig. In the course of the improbable plot the aristocratic von Rothsattel family, into which Anton initially wants to marry, is ruined by Jewish intrigue. Anton partially rescues Baron von Rothsattel from what is seen as Jewish ruthlessness but is rejected as his future son-in-law because of his bourgeois origin. He eventually marries the sister of his erstwhile mentor in Breslau.

This text, the first of many German novels of trade with an anti-Semitic subtext, is remarkable less for what it says than for what it passes over in silence. The epigraph to the novel suggests (and its plot is supposed to show) that free economic activity is the key to the strength and stability of the state.[24] The position of the nobility, eventually forced to speculate on the market with their wealth, is shown as untenable in the modern age and indeed dependent on the skill and intelligence of the *Bürgertum* for its survival. But the bourgeois hero Anton is celebrated above all for a bogus renunciation: his *appearing* not to live according to the logic of the system which his work supports. He thus passively accepts, but does not actively identify with, the speculative capitalism which ruins the nobility and from which he attempts to rescue them. The real logic of capitalism is embodied (and apparently condemned) in Itzig. Anton becomes a successful businessman whilst adopting the ideology of aesthetically coloured inwardness which legitimates the dying feudal class; that class, however, can survive only by participating in the system that ideology denies. The nobility is defeated in economic reality, the *Bürgertum* in ideological appearance. But ideological appearance (as greater German realists will show) is in this society what *politically* legitimates the *Bürgertum* itself. Despite its economic success that class is politically represented in the German *Reich*, as Treitschke had argued it should be, as an estate: a social group defined according to the political categories of the pre-modern age, not as the class of individual entrepreneurs on which its economic activity depends. In Freytag's novel the contradiction is celebrated, not analysed; the 'prosaic' character of modernity is both confirmed and yet apparently denied. *Soll und Haben* thus fulfils exactly Friedrich Vischer's programme of an ideal realism: it reconciles the 'truth of life' with a 'beautiful illusion', whilst sustaining the belief that modern forms are never really beautiful, nor beautiful ones really modern.

The plot of Raabe's *Der Hungerpastor*[25] offers a remarkable parallel. The Gentile Hans Unwirsch and the Jew Moses Freudenstein graduate from the *Gymnasium* and enter university at the same time. An idealistic Protestant is contrasted with a clever and philosophically educated Jew who emigrates to Paris and attempts to seduce Franziska Götz, the daughter of the patrician family to which Hans acts a tutor. Hans eventually rescues Franziska, they marry and finally settle down to the life of a pastor and his wife in a Mecklenburg village. The racial and ideological subtext is clear. What differentiates Raabe's novel from Freytag's is the way it treats the representation of social experience itself. Crucial to its meaning is the idea of hunger. On its first page the narrator announces that his intention is to treat of hunger, what it means, what it desires and what it can do. The personification of this force, which is described in Schopenhauerian terms as both a destroyer and a preserver, is linked at once to the book's historical realism and to the problem of literary representation. His book, the narrator ironically declares in a parody of Hegelese, offers a modest narrative in three parts taken from the 'great process of emerging, being and decaying – of the infinite becoming, which we call the development of the world' (5f.). The book is dedicated to 'the holy power of true hunger'. In effect *Hunger* is a metaphor for human desire of every kind – material, sexual, spiritual. The theme of 'hunger' and its representation underlies the novel's depiction of society. Superficially there is a crude opposition between ideal Christian and materialistic Jewish desire. More interesting is the way the novel seems to equate the representation of desire with the representation of society itself. Both leading characters are indirectly involved with *representing* the force which drives them. Freudenstein writes a thesis on 'The material as a moment of the divine' ('die Materie als Moment des Göttlichen', 133). The ironic echo of Hegelian historicism minus the conscience is clear, not least because its author is transparently more concerned with promoting his interest in the real, not the ideal world. At much greater length the novel treats Hans's desire to write his autobiography, which he plans to call a book on hunger. His difficulty in doing so is described in the language of idealist aesthetics. Hans's problem is his excessive subjectivity, which will not allow him to capture reality in any objectively real aesthetic form. He must therefore write a book which distorts reality or no book at all.

Like Schopenhauer's cosmic will, Raabe's *Hunger* is necessarily at odds with *Vorstellung* (representation). Schopenhauer, of course, was chiefly concerned with the non-representational art of music and only peripherally interested in literature. But Raabe's novel is a work of social realism centrally concerned with the problem of representation in a sense remarkably similar to that which Schopenhauer's argument defines. More relevant than the novel's superficial typology of Christian inwardness and Jewish materialist dialectic is the way it shows how any representation of hunger – which stands for the real dynamic of social desire – is impossible on the terms which aesthetic idealism defines. In other words, it shows how the problem of literary representation is also the problem of human subjectivity in modernity, one which cannot be resolved by the ideal recuperation which aesthetic inwardness offers. As the century progresses, the link between social and aesthetic representation, which is also the link between social and poetic realism, will become an increasingly important theme of German realism.[26]

At mid-century, the link is most fully apparent not in Germany but in Switzerland, in the work of Gottfried Keller (1819–90). Keller, imbued with the Swiss tradition of secular republicanism, portrays a society which in its political and cultural optimism differs significantly from that of Germany after 1848. It differs also in the link it establishes between an emphatically *poetic* realism and social critique. For Keller, poetic realism means giving form to the humane impulse already implicit in the dialectic of social and cultural life in his time.[27] The earliest and most influential novel of bourgeois realism in the German language is Keller's *Der grüne Heinrich* (1854–5; *Green Henry*). This shares with Dickens and Balzac the depiction of an epic totality of the objects of social and cultural life. But it differs in its central concern with the problem of representation. In the course of a journey from Switzerland into the *Reich* and back the novel's artist-hero, Heinrich Lee, moves from emotional self-deception into mature emotional and sexual life; from the subjectivity of a purely aesthetic consciousness to participation in public life; and from subjective psychological idealism into an objective social realism, symbolised by his study of natural science and his acquaintance with the materialist philosophy of Feuerbach. But Heinrich's personal history cannot be reduced to a simple progression from the aesthetic to the ethical. His choice is not an either/or between an aesthetic and an ethical perspective on experience, for both perspectives inform the many choices which his development entails. Thus his growing disappointment in love and awareness of his own sexual self-deception are paralleled by the abandonment of his project, when studying in Munich, of an entirely subjectivist and non-representational art. The aesthetic and personal journey of Keller's Heinrich is in the opposite direction to that of Raabe's Hans: from aesthetic inwardness to real participation in the social world. A key moment is his participation in a carnival in his native village which re-enacts the story of the Swiss national hero Wilhelm Tell. This transfiguring representation of one of the founding myths of Switzerland reveals a social truth pertaining as much to the present as to the past: in the performance Heinrich's Rousseauian vision of Swiss democracy gives way to the insight that society must be energised by interests, not ideas. The political state and economic society must be connected, indeed one must represent the other. By contrast, a second pageant described in the novel – the civic performance of Hans

Sachs's *Meistersinger* in Munich, in which the organic community of the Middle Ages is celebrated with the city workers represented in guilds and medieval costume – rings both aesthetically and socially hollow (the episode parodies the cultural and political pretensions of Wagner's *Gesamtkunstwerk*). The idea of an organic link between art, culture and economy which the Munich festival (like much contemporary German social thought) celebrates is negated by the actual position of Heinrich and his associates, self-deceived aesthetes both mentally and materially separated from the wider life of German society. In Keller's novel a range of different articulations of social experience – economic, aesthetic, political, philosophical – interact in a way which makes it impossible to discern where the private ends and the social begins. The historicist social science of Treitschke tends to reconcile the difference by describing both in terms of the political superstructure of the state. By contrast, Keller's realism affirms the plurality as well as the interconnection of the modes in which society can be experienced and understood, and the relevance to all this of aesthetic representation.

The work of the Austrian writer Adalbert Stifter (1805–68) represents the opposite end of the spectrum of poetic realism. If Keller's realism focuses on the social relevance of aesthetic representation, Stifter's emphasises aesthetic transfiguration itself. Indeed, in much of his narrative prose Stifter is more concerned to transfigure than to represent experience: to construct an autonomous aesthetic order which will redeem actuality. In 'Die Kunst und das Göttliche' (1867; 'Art and the divine'), Stifter argues that the task of art is to reveal the divine which is manifested in Being. In so doing art communicates a heightened form of reality: what Stifter calls reality in its most real form, 'die wirklichste Wirklichkeit'.[28] This untranslatable phrase signals an idea present in German realism since Büchner: art as an evocation of reality as divine revelation. For Stifter, however, revelation is less an energy than a state: a condition in which ontological, ethical and aesthetic truth are one. In Stifter, the convergence of literary realism with an idealist philosophical ontology is complete. The highest form of realism is idealism, which shows that reality is a revelation of God. This programme inevitably involves a shift in focus away from the social and onto the natural or the historical world, and so an apparent integration of the contingency of experience into an aesthetic order. Yet this process reveals a psychic, indeed even a social truth in spite of itself. That truth, precisely because it is unspoken, tells us much about the limits as well as the achievement of poetic realism. Stifter wrote two major novels: a *Bildungsroman*, *Der Nachsommer* (1857;

Indian summer), and an historical novel, *Witiko* (1865–7). It is in Stifter's *Novellen*, however, narrower in focus but much more varied in theme, that the originality and modernity of his realism are most apparent.

In his collection *Bunte Steine* (1852; *Coloured stones*), Stifter counters the charges of provincialism, narrowness and psychological and social naivety frequently levelled against the *Novelle*. Art, Stifter argues in his preface, has an ethical function and so is second only to religion in the ontological order. His focus on apparently small and insignificant themes, taken from the life of the common people, reflects both an ethic and an aesthetic of proportion ('Maß'). For Stifter there is a gentle law ('sanftes Gesetz') behind both human and natural phenomena. Truth is not revealed by the dramatic, the contingent or the unusual, but by the order implicit in ordinary things. The task of art is to disclose that real order – in sometimes surprising ways. Stifter here links poetic realism to Goethean humanism, which he seeks to transmit following 1848.

In 'Turmalin' ('Tourmaline'), for example, a pensioner living alone with his retarded daughter in a Viennese apartment turns out to have been living the consequences of a profound mental disturbance. The story also thematises the problem of artistic representation and its human costs. On the fringes of the world of art, Stifter's pensioner is obsessed by the public realm which the modern city represents. Indeed, publicity has replaced beauty and even truth in his experience. His walls are totally obscured by paintings and drawings of famous men, and his furniture fitted with rollers so that he can see them from any angle. In the end (the internal narrative reveals) Stifter's pensioner is destroyed by the solipsistic subjectivity of his mode of being. After his best friend has eloped with his wife, he retires to a basement flat where his daughter, kept in a state of physical and mental incarceration, is required by her father to imagine and to narrate the story of his death and burial, and her mother's guilt and subsequent suicide. For Stifter's pensioner an alienated devotion to 'art' is the negation of individuation in both self and another. This tightly constructed story thus combines a moral message with a thoroughly modern kind of reflection about the nature of human selfhood and its links to artistic imagination, representation and madness.

By contrast, Keller's *Novellen* share with his novels an emphasis on social and economic experience and a sceptical and often satirical treatment of Swiss life. *Romeo und Julia auf dem Dorfe* (1856; *A village Romeo and Juliet*) has two sources: the Shakespearean fable, transposed into Switzerland and onto a dispute between two peasant families over land, and a real occurrence widely reported in the German-speaking press: the suicide of two teenage lovers, children of warring parents, near Leipzig in 1848. At the beginning of the story Keller signals his intention to exploit the symbolic resonance of the traditional story for a more effective treatment of the contemporary event.[29] Keller uses all the techniques of poetic realism to explore sexuality, cruelty, blindness and prejudice in the suffocating environment of the Swiss provinces. The story both constructs an alternative reality, typified by the lovers' sexual idyll on a hay-barge passing through the town and emphasised by a profusion of poetic images, and deconstructs it by showing how the Rousseauian idyll must necessarily end in death. The lovers are caught in a double bind. In this society they are denied both marriage (because of family honour) and elopement (because of social censure). They can therefore only fulfil themselves before, or even because, they die. The alternative reality which Keller's realism creates is thus the instrument of a potent social critique.

Poetic realism can seem to offer an ideal aesthetic order in retreat from the emergence of modernity in the German-speaking world. Yet German realism after 1848 continues to be a potentially critical form which addresses questions of social and cultural legitimacy via the symbolic construction of social meaning. Most importantly, one central feature of early German realism is sustained by poetic realism and will be equally relevant to German realism after 1871: the literary practice of poetic realism is not identical with and may indeed undermine its parallel philosophical discourse. The poetic transfiguration of experience can help us to see reality as a significant whole. But it can also enable us to see reality critically, by making us conscious of the way reality is represented in both literature and society. The problem of representation will become the central concern of German realism after 1871.

THE REALISM OF REPRESENTATION: 1871–1890

The idea of representation, both aesthetic and social, is central to both literature and philosophy in Germany between 1871 and 1890. In this period the problem of the aesthetic representation of experience becomes one of the central concerns of German philosophy. The idealist emphasis on the autonomy of the aesthetic reappears as the belief that art can reveal reality, indeed even justify it, in a way wholly different from that of cognitive knowledge. Art comes to be seen, most influentially by David Friedrich Strauss in *Der alte und der neue Glaube* (1872; *The old faith and the new faith*), not just as the cultural heir to religion, but as an aesthetic replacement for religious faith. At the same time, rapid urbanisation and industrialisation under the *Kaiserreich* present a serious challenge to the idealist belief in the primacy of art as a mode of cultural communication. Philosophical aestheticism affirms the value of art for art's sake, whilst the empirical study of society makes the cultural marginalisation of the artist increasingly apparent. A form of literary realism now emerges in Germany which is distinguished from its European counterparts by its concern with the symbolic representation of human society. The literary and philosophical discourses are of course related. Yet the creative tension between philosophical and literary discourse which characterised the beginnings of German realism is intensified, and acquires a general cultural relevance, as that realism attains its mature form.

Philosophical context

The disjunctive relationship of the two discourses is exemplified by Friedrich Nietzsche (1844–1900), the greatest German philosopher and cultural critic of late nineteenth-century Germany, whose thought gives to the aesthetic a cultural and cognitive primacy it had not enjoyed since the age of German idealism. Nietzsche's thought aestheticises philosophy itself. For him philosophy cannot discover or communicate any objective truth, because its logical categories, and abstract nouns like 'truth', 'causality' and 'substance' which represent them, are fictions which project the psychological drives of the subject onto a supposedly objective world of experience. 'Truth', for Nietzsche, is but a 'mobile army of metaphors'.[30] The illusory character of philosophical argument derives from taking metaphor for truth. But all self-reflective or critical knowledge – including Nietzsche's own, which perceives and seeks to articulate this – is likewise subject to the illusion wrought by language. Nietzsche's own dialectic cannot therefore be a vehicle of *truth*. It must be a logically decentred, ironic mode of discourse: a pragmatic power-play with illusion in which rhetoric is essential to philosophy and the boundaries between philosophy and literature become blurred. The most famous example of this kind of writing is Nietzsche's quasi-narrative, quasi-philosophical fable *Also sprach Zarathustra* (1885; *Thus spake Zarathustra*).

The primacy of the aesthetic in Nietzsche's thought has a second and equally important source. Nietzsche contends that the reality of Being cannot be grasped as truth, but only as the expression of a will to power. For Nietzsche as for Schopenhauer there is an unbridgeable difference between the world as will and the world as representation or *Vorstellung*. There is therefore no conceptual link between the ultimate character of experience and *any* mode in which we represent that experience to ourselves. But we can be conscious of, and creatively affirm, the life of the will in an aesthetic mode. Nietzsche shares with Schopenhauer an emphasis on the role of art, especially music, in this reconciliation. But he differs radically from Schopenhauer in his understanding of its source and purpose. For Nietzsche, the subjective will unites itself to the world not by denying, but by affirming itself. The source of this reconciliation is not insight into a real world of essences behind the world of appearances, but affirmation of the world *as* appearance in the mode of aesthetic illusion. For the world of appearances is the only world there is; 'truth' exists only as perspective. The aesthetic representation of the world, therefore, can neither represent nor disclose truth; but it can change our experience from a life-destroying into a life-enhancing illusion.

In his *Umwertung aller Werte* (1887; *Transvaluation of all values*)[31] Nietzsche sharply contrasts his own form of aesthetic pessimism ('Künstlerpessimismus') with the moral or religious kind ('moralisch-religiöser Pessimismus') (II, 773). He describes his own position as a pessimism of strength and even as a form of theodicy (II, 685): an aesthetically inspired affirmation of the world on the basis of a thoroughgoing philosophical nihilism. In *Die Geburt der Tragödie* (1872; *The birth of tragedy*) Nietzsche had argued that the most adequate form of this affirmation is tragedy, which links aesthetic form (the Apolline) to the anarchic energy of the will (the Dionysian), and so enables us to experience that energy but never to know, to understand or to control it. Nietzsche's thought thus propounds an idea of aesthetic autonomy far more radical than the German idealist tradition envisaged. For Nietzsche, art is not just a privileged mode of truth relevant to cognitive knowledge. Art *replaces* cognition as the only meaningful mediation between human subjectivity and the world. Yet Nietzsche's epistemology, if such it can be called, is thoroughly idealist. It denies not just the thing-in-itself but any idea of experience as the coherent *object* of the mind. In *Umwertung aller Werte* Nietzsche argues that what we call being is what produces an effect on our own subjectivity (II, 615). What we call knowledge is the way we represent experience: the way we transform all experience into the world we know (II, 617). The expression 'it is' can be reduced to 'it means'; and meaning is defined by the will to power, not truth.

The absolutism with which Nietzsche espouses this position has profound consequences. Culturally as well as philosophically Nietzsche's thought presents the paradox of an absolutely self-reflective critique which issues in a positive affirmation of actual experience. Much of his cultural criticism depends on genealogy: the historical or psychological demonstration of the origins of particular beliefs. In his *Zur Genealogie der Moral* (1887; *The genealogy of morals*), for example, Nietzsche argues that the liberal Enlightenment of modern Europe has its roots in Christianity, and that Christianity itself derives from a 'slave revolt of morality' prompted by a spirit of resentment against the life-affirming Dionysian culture of the ancient world. But the logic of Nietzsche's epistemology means that genealogical critique can yield no relevant insight into the truth or falsehood of any belief. Nietzsche's own critical knowledge is, and knows itself to be, the product of the very cultural tradition whose hidden logic it claims to describe. He therefore describes himself as the proud inheritor of the two cultural influences his philosophy most powerfully attacks: Christianity and the culture of Romantic inwardness which he sees as its product.

This self-negating mode is intrinsic to Nietzsche's thought as a whole. It is the product of a dialectic which can always see through, but never see beyond, the world of cultural and aesthetic symbols by which we represent experience to ourselves. Nietzsche's thought is as much the expression as the critique of the culture of his time in which, he tells us, inward consciousness and outward experience have been separated by the mechanism of society.[32] His philosophy reflects but cannot transcend this schizophrenic condition. Because it is essentially perspectivist – that is, both subjective and idealist – Nietzsche's philosophical representation of reality cannot truly engage with the social and historical world. Nietzsche is no true psychological realist because his critique constantly implies, but never truly acknowledges, the relevance of the social and cultural context in which all psychological and sociological judgements inhere. It is hardly surprising, therefore, that Nietzsche comments on Flaubert and the realist novel of France in dismissive terms which suggest that the novel can no more communicate an objective social or psychological truth than philosophy can a metaphysical one (*Umwertung*, II, 461). Nietzsche's thought illuminates the literature of its age less because of its influence than because of its structure: because it articulates in philosophical terms the consciousness of its age, which is also articulated in the very different mode of narrative realism. For Nietzsche's major philosophical concern – the way experience is represented – is also one of the key literary concerns of Theodor Fontane and other realist writers.

Apart from Nietzsche, the dominant philosophical influence in Germany between 1871 and 1890 is *Lebensphilosophie* (vitalism), of which the most significant proponent is Wilhelm Dilthey (1833–1911).

Lebensphilosophie seeks especially to provide an epistemological basis for the human sciences or *Geisteswissenschaften*. In his most important work, *Einleitung in die Geisteswissenschaften* (1883; *Introduction to the human sciences*), Dilthey argues against historicism that the objective teleology of history cannot be rationally discerned. Historical explanation in the normal sense is thus concerned only with the *phenomena* of history, not its ultimate purpose. The category Dilthey uses to designate that ultimate reality is life ('Leben'). For Dilthey, there is a living reality behind all human history and cultural experience which is the key to its meaning. Like the Kantian thing-in-itself, Dilthey's 'Leben' cannot conceptually be known. But, unlike the thing-in-itself, 'Leben' can be intuitively and yet adequately experienced ('erlebt') in the cultural experiences ('Erlebnisse') which disclose its meaning. The method of the cultural and historical sciences must therefore be radically different from that of natural science. Their object is to make possible an act of imaginative understanding which cannot be rationally grounded and has more in common with aesthetic appreciation than causal explanation. The truth of 'Leben' – also the truth of history and culture – can be experienced but never fully understood. And because the truth of 'Leben' is understood as the truth of reality ('Wirklichkeit'), reality itself becomes an unstable and problematic idea, implicit but never fully revealed in the world of actual phenomena. The thought of Dilthey thus brings to a head a tendency latent in mid-century German historicism: a concern with human society which concludes that social reality can never be conceptually or critically known as a whole. Indeed, Dilthey argues in 1875 against Auguste Comte that the complexity of modern society cannot be understood by a positivist social science, but only by an empathetic understanding of the vast objective system of human ethical and cultural life.[33]

The second most important intellectual influence in Germany under the *Kaiserreich* was scientific materialism, closely allied to a philosophy of social determinism and Darwinism, which was popularised in Germany in the last decades of the nineteenth century by thinkers like Ernst Haeckel (1834–1919) and Ludwig Büchner (1824–99). This philosophical movement, unlike *Lebensphilosophie* and Nietzschean metaphysics, was closely paralleled by a literary form: naturalism. This double movement, despite its emphasis on natural science, has more in common with *Lebensphilosophie* and Nietzsche's negative metaphysics than is immediately apparent.

German naturalism no less than German realism is a form concerned with the ways human experience is interpreted and therefore represented. Many of its key manifestos define the task of art as the exploration of the human meaning of modernity: the world produced by the application of natural scientific knowledge. Wolfgang Kirchbach, for example, in an essay entitled *Was kann die Dichtung für die moderne Welt noch bedeuten?* (1888; *The meaning of literature for the modern world*)[34] takes Darwinism in its broadest application as the defining intellectual movement of the modern age. The theory of evolution, he argues, has destroyed the basis for the anthropocentric world-view which underpinned classical humanism. Evolution is not a theory. It is a truth, because it empirically describes the place of man in the natural process (110). But it is precisely for this reason that Darwinism (like all science) leaves the question of meaning open; and it is with this question that literature (112) must be concerned. Evolutionary biology need not lead to mechanistic materialism. The former is a fact, the latter a value. In an allusion to Nietzschean and Wagnerian aestheticism, Kirchbach argues that the popularity of the non-conceptual art of music in Germany is a consequence of the failure of German writers to interpret the relevance of modern knowledge to literary creation. Modern scientific knowledge differs from classical philosophy because it has formed not just the intellectual but also the real human world – the world of 'railways, telephones . . . and the science of war' – and it is the task of modern literature to develop a poetic consciousness adequate to that world (111ff.).

German naturalism continues to reflect the concern, central to German intellectual life since the age of German idealism, with the capacity of art to reflect reality in ways inaccessible to discursive knowledge. But the naturalists differ from their idealist predecessors by defining the difference of aesthetic experience in relation to natural science, not philosophy. Literary naturalism is certainly influenced by scientific materialism; but it is entirely incompatible with any philosophically naive realism. On the contrary, it involves a distancing of both artist and audience from reality which anticipates many of the techniques of modernism. German naturalism, no less than the metaphysical nihilism of Nietzsche or the aesthetically charged idealism of Dilthey, raises insistently the question of what our experience of reality in modernity means and *therefore* of how it should be represented in art. It is on that question that my concluding discussion of German literature from the 1870s to the 1890s will focus.

Literary texts

German philosophy between 1871 and 1890 brings to full expression two tendencies inherent in German thought since the age of German idealism: a reflectivity which constantly relates the idea of reality to the structure of human subjectivity, and an emphasis on aesthetic representation as a privileged mode of truth. At the same time, German literary realism at the end of the nineteenth century offers an independent and often highly critical view of the social, cultural and even political context from which that philosophical emphasis springs. The link between the two is most apparent in the evolution of the German realist novel.

In the later work of Wilhelm Raabe, the traditional themes and formal devices of the *Bildungsroman* tradition are linked to a critique of the ideology of aesthetic inwardness and an increased concern with the problem of narrative representation itself. Raabe's last work, *Die Akten des Vogelsangs* (1895; *The archives of Vogelsang*), for example, is concerned with an 'anti-hero' who seeks an alternative reality outside society; that reality, however, can be constructed only on the terms which society defines. A provincial official, Karl Krumhardt, receives a letter informing him of the death of his boyhood friend Velten. Unlike Krumhardt, who has established a successful bourgeois existence, Velten had been unsuccessful in love and had never settled down (the letter is from his childhood sweetheart Helene, since married to another). Having followed Helene to America, Velten returned to the German province of his childhood, now changed beyond all recognition, to wind up his affairs and eventually to die. He ended his days in complete solitude apart from occasional visits from his childhood friend. News of Velten's death prompts Krumhardt into trying to understand and to write about his life.

Despite superficial similarities, this text radically undermines the valorisation of aesthetic inwardness which so characterises the German fiction of the mid-nineteenth century. For Velten's inwardness is also his otherness. It is defined by ideas familiar in German culture since the early nineteenth century, notably 'Gemütlichkeit' (emotional warmth), and yet is incompatible with any successful mode of being in the society in which he has to live. When Velten returns from America after his mother's death he has no wish, despite his considerable means, to take any part in the life of the community. All he can do is to burn his inherited furniture and to speak of 'Gemütlichkeit' – in truth his only real value – in the third person and as a cultural peculiarity of the Germany he has left. Velten's alienation is reflected in the narrative technique.

Framework narration is not, as often in the *Novelle*, used to introduce distance or ambiguity into a situation. Rather, it reflects the inability of the fictional narrator to understand and therefore represent the radical otherness of his friend's mode of being. He cannot talk to his friend, whose key statements are quotations from German literature about the condition of spiritual alienation itself. Velten's irony about 'Gemütlichkeit' is not redemptive, because it is not part of a shared narrative perspective in which 'Gemütlichkeit', like other attitudes to experience, might take its place. Rather it is a desperate attempt to compensate for the absence of any shared perspective at all: a condition of illusion which is anything but beautiful.

The most important figure in the development of German realism after 1871 is the novelist Theodor Fontane (1819–98), who decisively developed the psychological emphasis of nineteenth-century German realism. He too is concerned with the way social reality is represented in the inner psychological life. But he is distinguished by his analysis of the social meaning of that representation: the link between the public and the private representation of experience. In his essay *Unsere lyrische und epische Poesie seit 1848* (1853; *Our lyric and epic poetry since 1848*)[35] Fontane had argued that realism is about what is true ('das Wahre') as much as what is real ('das Wirkliche', 242). The distinction is crucial. Realism is not about the photographic reproduction of reality; indeed it presupposes an element of transfiguration ('Verklärung') or refinement ('Läuterung', 241). But the purpose of that process is to reveal the tendencies which lie hidden in actual experience.

This programme is in effect a critique of the social construction of reality, especially that ideology of inwardness which combines an ideal rejection with a practical endorsement of social norms. This is exemplified by *Effi Briest* (1896),[36] which deals with the seduction, adultery and social exclusion of an upper-class girl married at eighteen to a man twice her age. In a key scene, Innstetten, Effi's husband, has learnt of her adultery and is debating with his friend Wüllersdorf his obligation to fight a duel with her seducer Crampas six and a half years after the event. He declares himself to be free of any feeling of hatred or desire for revenge and says that he loves his wife. Yet he claims to be subject to a compulsion which has both social and personal force.

So powerful is 'that tyrannising social something' ('jenes uns tyrannisierende Gesellschafts-Etwas') (236) that it unconsciously compels Innstetten to the very action – the disclosure of his marital disgrace to his friend – which objectively sanctions his inner conviction that there is only one way to act. He really believes he must defend his honour because he has unconsciously chosen to destroy its social appearance, by telling another person of his social shame. That the 'social something' compelling him to act exists only in appearance he is thoroughly aware. He calls it idolatry ('Götzendienst') and not the true judgement of God ('Gottesgericht') or conscience. But, he says, we must submit to the idol as long as it is socially valid ('Wir müssen uns ihm unterwerfen, solange der Götze gilt') (237f.). The system is indeed one of illusion, but the illusion is real: real because it is internalised in the social consciousness of its adherents, and *therefore* in their acts. For Innstetten, as for the society he represents, the idea of moral truth is replaced by what Nietzsche called the problem of credibility. What matters to him is not what determines his acts, or even ultimately what they are, but how they appear to others. But Fontane's literary hero, unlike Nietzsche's philosophical one, can never be satisfied with illusion. For he possesses no real standpoint outside the social system which might reveal that system for what it is. The tyrannical social something of which Innstetten speaks, like Dilthey's vast system of social norms, determines his actions even if he cannot understand it. Yet for Fontane's character the system has lost its ethical warrant. He thus serves an idol empty of meaning whilst conscious of that very emptiness.

The year after the publication of *Effi Briest* the sociologist Emile Durkheim argued in his essay *Du suicide* (1897; *On suicide*) that modern society, even in its most intimate aspects, can be understood only as a system of social *facts* which are real independently of those who observe or experience them.[37] However, the very objectivity and reification of social norms can itself be understood only in relation to the social consciousness for which such norms are binding. That is true especially of a society, like that of late nineteenth-century Germany, in which the development of social consciousness only belatedly and indirectly reflects rapid and traumatic changes in the world of social facts: a society in which, as Ferdinand Tönnies argued in his seminal work *Gemeinschaft und Gesellschaft* (1887; *Community and society*), the values and symbolic practices of an organic, pre-industrial community are in constant tension with the atomisation of social life which the process of modernisation entails. The power of Fontane's realism is that it shows us this more powerfully than philosophy or sociology can do. It is the adequate literary reflection of the Prussian *Kaiserreich*, in which consciousness is divided from social reality because of the very nature of that reality. In late nineteenth-century Germany, a rapidly modernising industrial society retains the cultural forms – the social importance given to the code of military honour, the awarding of military or aristocratic titles to successful businessmen – which belong to a pre-modern age. This is indeed (as Nietzsche says) a society in which inner life and outward experience have been separated by the social mechanism. But Fontane's literary realism, unlike Nietzsche's philosophical dialectic, is capable of showing us the meaning of that divorce in actual experience.

With the achievement of a mature narrative realism after 1871 the kind of historical novel common earlier in the century, with its post-Romantic and historicist tone and its subject matter taken from the distant past, is largely eclipsed in German literature. The historical novels of the Swiss writer Conrad Ferdinand Meyer (1825–98), for example, like *Die Versuchung des Pescara* (1887; *The temptation of Pescara*) and *Die Hochzeit des Mönch* (1883–4; *The marriage of the monk*) with their medieval and Renaissance themes, are of largely historical interest today.

The German literary movement most directly concerned with social milieu, and which most directly addresses the advent of an industrial proletariat under the *Kaiserreich*, is naturalism. The key form of German naturalism, however, is not prose but drama. With the advent of naturalism, the German theatre regains something of the significance as a cultural and social forum it had enjoyed in the aftermath of German idealism. At the end of the nineteenth century it is not with idealist rhetoric or philosophical history but with the conditions of modern industrial society that German drama is chiefly concerned. Yet naturalism, despite its preoccupation with social milieu, is also a drama of discourse, in which the social objectivity of language is a central theme.

In the case of Gerhart Hauptmann (1862–1946), the most significant German naturalist playwright, the link between a realism of representation and social realism is especially close. All his major plays are marked by an almost photographic rendering of social milieu. Most innovative is Hauptmann's use of the 'Sekundenstil' dialogue technique, which seeks to reproduce the exact quality of human speech under the pressure of emotion from one second to the next. This technique, which closely links verbal expression to bodily gesture and nervous state, owes much to the materialist biology and psychology of the age, in which human behaviour is described (and, for some, explained) in physiological and therefore determinist terms. Similarly, Hauptmann's concern with heredity and environment was influenced by Darwin and French positivist historians like Hippolyte Taine (1828–93). Yet in each of Hauptmann's major plays there is a tension between the outward course of events, often suggestive of social and psychological determinism, and the ways to interpret and represent those events.

Die Weber (1892; *The weavers*) deals with a strike and uprising of the Silesian weavers of 1844. The play focuses on the threat posed to the handloom weavers by mechanisation, and so on the moral and material conflict caused by modernisation in an industrial community. The central opposition is between the younger generation (the agitator Jäger), with a radically secular interpretation of events and eager for political change; and the older generation (the old weaver Hilse), imbued with an ethic of pietistic inwardness and so, despite their suffering, unwilling outwardly to rebel. The tension between these two positions is dramatically focused by the public reading of the revolutionary weavers' song by the strike leaders, and its effect on the workers. The song bitterly attacks the idea that any appeal to ideal values can mitigate the weavers' plight. Pity is only a beautiful feeling. But the way the workers respond to the song is determined as much by their culturally inherited consciousness of themselves – which leads them, for example, to perceive an analogy between its lines and verses of the Bible – as it is by the material facts of their condition. The drama shows that consciousness expresses milieu. But the relationship between consciousness and milieu, however close, is not deterministic. The play exhibits not a closed, but a radically open structure. It is therefore naturalistic in two different but related senses. First, it depicts human experience as part of a structure of natural causality. Second, it draws attention to the difference between human and material nature: that creative tension between 'Wahrheit' and 'Wirklichkeit' which is also the energy of German realism.

This double perspective is evident in several of Hauptmann's great plays. *Vor Sonnenaufgang* (1889; *Before the dawn*) deals both with hereditary alcoholism and mental disease in a family of Silesian farmers, and with the discourse of social Darwinism and eugenics. The core of the plot is the relationship between Helene, daughter of an alcoholic and brutal father, and the doctrinaire social scientist and reformer Alfred Loth, whom she hopes to marry and so escape from her situation. Loth returns her love but then rejects her on discovering her genetic inheritance; she commits suicide in despair. The success of the play can be understood only in the context of the close links, in late nineteenth-century Germany, between the philosophy of social Darwinism and movements for social reform. Explanations of both physical and mental disease in terms of heredity, and therefore eugenics, were widely believed to be scientifically true. Hence the philosophy which Loth personifies could plausibly be held by Hauptmann's audience to explain the events of the play. But in human terms it leads to tragedy, engendered by the blindness of its exponent to the human consequences of his beliefs, and therefore his acts. 'Wirklichkeit' and 'Wahrheit', reality and its interpretation, are once again shown to be different. Yet the sphere of interpretation is also shown to be central to human reality itself, and therefore to tragic drama.[38]

For the naturalists, no less than the great German realists, the sphere of interpretation is also the sphere of the literary representation of experience. In *Papa Hamlet* (1889; *Father Hamlet*), the best-known work of Arno Holz and Johannes Schlaf, the problematic link between the two spheres is explicitly thematised. This narrative text deals with the squalid circumstances in a Berlin tenement of an unemployed actor, Niels Thienwebel, who eventually murders his child in a drunken rage. Dialogue in the story oscillates between 'Sekundenstil' in Berlin dialect, which reflects the semi-obscene monologues of a drunken father, and snatches of quotations from Shakespeare's *Hamlet*, in which Thienwebel once acted the leading role. In true naturalist fashion the switch from one register to another is often shown to be provoked by sensory stimuli, but the two registers also reflect two equally potent levels of Thienwebel's being. Like Büchner's Lenz, Holz and Schlaf's Thienwebel lives both on a level of material causation (manifest in mental illness) and on a level of aesthetic illusion, which represents a 'Wirklichkeit' or experience of reality as potent as his material surroundings. Holz and Schlaf's story no less than Büchner's *Novelle* shows a character who is both radically determined by circumstance and yet free in his capacity for aesthetic representation. In both cases that capacity exceeds, but does not liberate them from, their actual condition. In both cases the achievement of literary form is to make us conscious of both the difference and the connection between the two levels of being.

Naturalism, then, like classical realism, is about the representation, interpretation and critique of social reality. It articulates a social truth which could not be expressed otherwise, especially not by the philosophical and scientific idioms which it takes up and views through the critical perspective of literary form. Naturalism no less than realism insists, in radical contrast to both the idealist philosophy and the materialist social science of its age, on the human significance of the duality of fact and value: that being can never be reduced, even if it is always connected, to meaning.

The relationship of literature to philosophy in Germany between 1830 and 1890 is one of creative and relevant difference. Reading the literature of German realism in philosophical context is valuable especially because it highlights the cognitive dissonance which literature embodies. To be sure, the German philosophy of the age itself insistently argues that aesthetic truth can be cognitively relevant, indeed that philosophy has an intrinsic deficiency which only art can supply. But the place which nineteenth-century German philosophy gives to art, especially literature, is never the same as the one which German realism autonomously claims. German literature therefore tells us as much about German philosophy between 1830 and 1890 as the converse. In particular, it shows us the philosophical as well as the social relevance of the autonomy of the aesthetic. It shows us why and how literary realism resists interpretation on terms other than its own; and how that resistance can enable a powerful cultural and social critique.

German realism no less than classicism and Romanticism is philosophically informed. But in the realist age the link between philosophical aesthetics and literary practice is both looser and more dialectical than before. German literary realism offers a powerful corrective to the tendency, certainly latent in idealist philosophical aesthetics, for aesthetic autonomy to turn into an ideology of the aesthetic, in which a mechanistic public domain is legitimated by an apparently autonomous, because really disengaged, aesthetic mode of communication.[39] German philosophical aesthetics between 1830 and 1890 is epistemologically idealist and emphasises the non-representational and non-verbal arts. German literary realism is centrally concerned with the means, in both literature and life, by which human experience is interpreted and therefore represented. It achieves exactly that form – the novel as an explanation of the self-consciousness of modernity – which Hegel declares to be impossible and Nietzsche and Schopenhauer ignore. Through its thematisation of the multiple and conflicting *discourses* of modernity, the German realist novel exemplifies rather than departs from what Bakhtin identifies as the key capacity of the novel as a genre: the ability to show a dialogic relationship between different and conflicting ways in which social reality is experienced and described.[40] German realism is therefore a critical mode, because it exposes not only the link, but also the difference between the real dynamics of human society and the symbols by which we represent and interpret them.

German literary realism is above all a literature of real presence which is most adequately understood when read immediately as a text, not as mediated by a theoretical context. But it is precisely that capacity for immediacy which makes it so relevant to its philosophical context.

Nineteenth-century German realism is distinct from its European counterparts because (in some of its forms) it is concerned with a society in which modernity is only imperfectly developed. But it is also
distinct because (in most of its forms) it anticipates many of the features of European modernism itself. In particular, it manifests a reflectivity about linguistic and symbolic representation which exceeds that
of classical European realism. If 'language-consciousness' (J. P. Stern)[41]
and self-consciousness about 'the fact of realism, its writing, the activity of its production' (Stephen Heath)[42] point beyond realism towards
modernism, then nineteenth-century German realism is certainly a precursor of modernism. To be sure, that literary anticipation is matched by
a philosophical one in which, in the aesthetics of German idealism and its
heirs, many of the insights of postmodern 'language-consciousness' are
foreshadowed by a philosophical tradition which is conscious of much
more than language. But the literary vision of German realism shows
us something unique and important about modernity. It shows us how
reflectivity and critique work most powerfully when they are not divorced from the immediacy which literature embodies. It shows us how
a critique of modernity can be rooted in the *experience* of modernity: that
unfinished project to which literature remains an indispensable guide.

NOTES

1 See Georg Büchner, *Sämtliche Werke und Briefe*, ed. Werner Lehmann, 2 vols.
   (Hamburg: Christian Wegner, 1967), vol. I, pp. 86–9.
2 This view of European realism as a whole is persuasively argued in J. P.
   Stern, *On realism* (London: Routledge and Kegan Paul, 1973), pp. 28ff. My
   indebtedness to the late Professor Stern will be apparent throughout this
   essay.
3 See Erich Auerbach, *Mimesis: dargestellte Wirklichkeit in der abendländischen
   Literatur* (Bern: Francke, 1946), pp. 457ff.
4 See Terry Eagleton, *The ideology of the aesthetic* (Oxford: Basil Blackwell,
   1990).
5 See G. W. F. Hegel, *Sämtliche Werke*, Jubiläumsausgabe, ed. Hermann Glockner, 20 vols. (Stuttgart: Friedrich Frommann, 1964), vol. XII, pp. 30f.
6 'Die Auflösung der romantischen Kunstform', in *Sämtliche Werke*, vol. XIII,
   pp. 217–40.
7 Georg Lukács, *The theory of the novel: a historico-philosophical essay on the forms of
   great epic literature* (London: Merlin Press, 1971) pp. 70ff.
8 *Werke*, vol. XIV, pp. 562ff. Hegel uses the term 'moderne Tragödie' to refer
   to post-medieval tragedy and the term 'romantisches Trauerspiel' to refer
   to the Romantic tragedy of his own day. Both, for Hegel, are distinguished

by their emphasis on subjective character and motive and loss of substantial ethical content.

9 'Die Auflösung', *Werke*, vol. XIII, p. 233.

10 For a contemporary exposition of this term see Heinrich Laube, 'Die neue Kritik', in Jost Hermand (ed.), *Das Junge Deutschland: Texte und Dokumente*, (Stuttgart: Philipp Reclam, 1966), pp. 102–7.

11 See Jost Hermand (ed.), *Der deutsche Vormärz: Texte und Dokumente* (Stuttgart: Philipp Reclam, 1967), pp. 70–3, 173–6.

12 Karl Marx and Friedrich Engels, *Werke*, ed. Institut für Marxismus–Leninismus beim ZK der SED, 42 vols. (Berlin: Dietz, 1960–1983), vol. III, pp. 9–521.

13 See Heinrich Laube, 'Ludwig Tieck' and Johannes Scherr, 'Jung-Deutsche', in Hermand (ed.), *Das Junge Deutschland*, pp. 44–50, 349–52.

14 F. W. J. Schelling, *Philosophie der Offenbarung 1841–42*, ed. Manfred Frank (Frankfurt am Main: Suhrkamp, 1993). The work was first published in 1843, based on a course of lectures Schelling delivered at Berlin in the winter of 1841–2.

15 See Büchner's letter to Minna Jaeglé, 10 March 1834, in Büchner, *Werke*, vol. II, p. 425.

16 Friedrich Hebbel, *Werke*, ed. Gerhard Fricke, 5 vols. (Munich: Carl Hanser, 1963–7), vol. I, p. 326.

17 Franz Grillparzer, 'Zur Kunstlehre', in *Sämtliche Werke*, eds. Peter Frank and Karl Pörnbacher, 4 vols. (Munich: Carl Hanser, 1964), vol. III, pp. 213–39.

18 For a fuller account of the feminist novel in nineteenth-century Germany, see Gail Finney, 'Revolution, resignation, realism 1830–1890', in Helen Watanabe-O'Kelly (ed.), *The Cambridge history of German literature* (Cambridge: Cambridge University Press, 1997), pp. 272–326, esp. 279–87.

19 Grillparzer, *Werke*, vol. III, p. 150.

20 Richard Wagner, *Ausgewählte Schriften und Briefe*, ed. Alfred Lorenz, 2 vols. (Berlin: Bernhard Hahnefeld, 1938), vol. I, p. 177.

21 Wagner, *Ausgewählte Schriften*, vol. I, p. 201.

22 Friedrich Theodor Vischer, *Ästhetik oder die Wissenschaft des Schönen*, ed. Robert Vischer, reprint of 2nd edn (Munich, 1922–3), 6 vols. (Hildesheim: Olms, 1996), vol. III, pp. 97ff.

23 Otto Ludwig, *Shakespeare-Studien*, ed. M. Heydrich (Leipzig, 1872), pp. 264ff.

24 Gustav Freytag, *Soll und Haben*, 2 vols., 23rd edn (Leipzig: Hirzel, 1888), vol. I, title page: 'Der Roman soll das deutsche Volk da suchen, wo es in seiner Tüchtigkeit zu finden ist, nämlich bei seiner Arbeit' ('The novel must seek the German people in the sphere of their greatest capacity, namely their work') (Julian Schmidt).

25 Wilhelm Raabe, *Sämtliche Werke*, ed. Karl Hoppe, 20 vols. (Freiburg im Breisgau and Braunschweig: Hermann Klemm, 1951–), vol. VI.

26 I am indebted here to Robert C. Holub's discussion of Freytag and Raabe in *Reflections of realism: paradox, norm and ideology in nineteenth-century German prose* (Detroit: Wayne State University Press, 1991), pp. 174–201.

27 See Keller's letter to Hermann Hettner, 26 June 1854, in Gottfried Keller, *Gesammelte Briefe*, ed. Carl Helbling, 4 vols. (Bern: Benteli, 1950), vol. I, p. 400.
28 Adalbert Stifter, *Gesammelte Werke*, ed. K. Steffen (Basel and Stuttgart, 1972), pp. 381 f.
29 Gottfried Keller, *Sämtliche Werke*, ed. Jonas Fränkel, 22 vols. (Zürich and Munich: Eugen Rentsch, 1926–49), vol. VII/1, p. 84; cf. 'Die Romantik und die Gegenwart', in *Sämtliche Werke*, vol. XXII, pp. 311–16.
30 *Über Wahrheit und Lüge im aussermoralischen Sinne* (*On truth and lie in the extra-moral sense*), in Friedrich Nietzsche, *Sämtliche Werke*, eds. Colli and Montinari, 8 vols. (Berlin and New York: Walter de Gruyter, 1972), vol. I, pp. 880–1.
31 Nietzsche, *Umwertung aller Werte*, ed. Friedrich Würzbach (Munich: Carl Hanser, 1969). This is the best modern edition of this text, based on Nietzsche's *Nachlass* and published after his death.
32 *Vom Nutzen und Nachteil der Historie für das Leben* (*On the use and abuse of history for life*), in *Sämtliche Werke*, vol. III/1, p. 325.
33 See Wilhelm Dilthey, *Gesammelte Schriften*, ed. Georg Misch (Stuttgart, 1958), vol. V, p. 73.
34 Wolfgang Kirchbach, 'Was kann die Dichtung für die moderne Welt noch bedeuten?', in Erich Ruprecht (ed.), *Literarische Manifeste des Naturalismus 1880–1892* (Stuttgart: J. B. Metzler, 1962), vol. I, pp. 109–17.
35 In Theodor Fontane, *Sämtliche Werke*, ed. Walter Keitel, 20 vols. (Munich: Carl Hanser, 1969), vol. III, pp. 236–60.
36 Fontane, *Werke*, vol. I, pp. 7–296.
37 Emile Durkheim, *Suicide: A study in sociology*, trans. John A. Spaulding and George Simpson, ed. George Simpson (London: Routledge and Kegan Paul, 1968), pp. 37–8.
38 Compare Ritchie Robertson's discussion of this play, chapter four, p. 160.
39 For a powerful exposition of this view of nineteenth-century German aesthetics, see Eagleton, *Ideology of the aesthetic*, especially pp. 153–72, 234–61.
40 See M. M. Bakhtin, *The dialogic imagination: four essays*, ed. Michael Holquist, trans. Caryl Emerson and Michael Holquist (Austin: University of Texas Press, 1996), pp. 264ff.
41 Stern, *On realism*, p. 159.
42 Stephen Heath, 'Realism, modernism and language-consciousness', in Martin Swales and Nicholas Boyle (eds.), *Realism in European literature: essays in honour of J. P. Stern* (Cambridge: Cambridge University Press, 1986), p. 112.

CHAPTER FOUR

Modernism and the self 1890–1924

Ritchie Robertson

German and Austrian modernism produced such a rich body of writing that any account must be drastically selective. I shall focus mainly on the generation of conservative modernists, Thomas Mann (1875–1955), Rainer Maria Rilke (1875–1926) and Hugo von Hofmannsthal (1874–1929), who adapted traditional forms for new purposes and explored continuities between past and present. They will be flanked by Theodor Fontane (1819–98), who confronted modernity in his novels of the 1890s, by the somewhat older naturalist writers, and also by the younger generation, including Franz Kafka (1883–1924) and Georg Trakl (1887–1914), who can be seen as early expressionists. Their work reached a peak of achievement in the early 1920s: in 1921 Hofmannsthal published his comedy *Der Schwierige* (*The difficult man*); in 1922 Kafka wrote *Das Schloß* (*The castle*) and Rilke completed the *Duineser Elegien* (*Duino elegies*); and in 1924 Thomas Mann published *Der Zauberberg* (*The magic mountain*).

If we ask how the conservative modernists drew on philosophy, we encounter a problem. The achievements of academic philosophy largely passed them by. The major movement in German philosophy, the neo-Kantianism based at Marburg and Heidelberg, received little attention from literary figures; only in the 1920s did neo-Kantian ideas filter into the wider cultural sphere through the work of Ernst Cassirer (1874–1945) on myth and Hans Vaihinger (1852–1933) on fictions. The founder of modern mathematical logic, Gottlob Frege (1848–1925), was an obscure professor at Jena, ignored even by the few philosophers qualified to appreciate his work. The originator of phenomenology, Edmund Husserl (1859–1938), made himself inaccessible to a lay public by his technical vocabulary, though as we shall see he did try to explain his work to Hofmannsthal. Instead, we shall find that the philosophy they absorbed, as ordinary educated people seeking to understand their lives, was that of earlier generations. Above all, theirs was the age of Nietzsche. Nietzsche died in 1900, having collapsed into hopeless insanity in January 1889. Just when he could no longer appreciate it, he suddenly received recognition throughout Europe for his timely, cogent attacks on inherited pieties. A still greater time-lag marked the reception of Schopenhauer (1788–1860). Though first published in 1819, his *Die Welt als Wille und Vorstellung* (*The world as will and idea*) found few readers till mid-century. By the 1890s, many of Schopenhauer's and Nietzsche's ideas meshed with a body of thought, bearing the authority of natural science, whose key word, 'life' ('Leben'), gave it the name 'Lebensphilosophie'. Darwin and his German populariser Haeckel helped to shape the thinking of a generation. When new ideas did gain acceptance, as happened gradually with the leading concepts of psychoanalysis, they often did so by seeming to fit into such familiar paradigms. Thus Schopenhauer's Will, Haeckel's conception of animate matter, and the Freudian unconscious, all matched the turn-of-the-century model of life as powerful unconscious striving. To relate philosophy and literature, we must ask which works were actually read, and how they were read. This means descending from the peaks of academic philosophy to such influential works of popular philosophy as Haeckel's *Die Welträtsel* (1899; *The riddles of the universe*), Wilhelm Bölsche's *Das Liebesleben in der Natur* (1898–1903; *Love-life in nature*), and Houston Stewart Chamberlain's *Die Grundlagen des neunzehnten Jahrhunderts* (1899; *The foundations of the nineteenth century*).

Even when philosophy is thus broadly defined, its relation to literature is not straightforward. The modernists professed little expert knowledge of philosophy. Rilke claimed to have read no philosophy except 'a few pages of Schopenhauer'.[1] Kafka, we are assured by his friend Max Brod (1884–1968), had no head for abstract philosophy and thought mainly in images.[2] We should not wholly accept such disclaimers. When Brod first met Kafka, they spent an evening arguing about the relative merits of Nietzsche and Schopenhauer. Rilke read widely in biology and 'Lebensphilosophie'; guided by the biologist Jakob von Uexküll (1864–1944), he even struggled through the first fifty pages of Kant's *Kritik der reinen Vernunft* (*Critique of pure reason*).[3] Thomas Mann and Hofmannsthal knew Schopenhauer and Nietzsche. But if we ask *how* they read, we find that they might, like Thomas Mann, gather a broad general sense of their authors' ideas, or, like Kafka, attend to striking images, or, like the young Hofmannsthal, absorb the mood rather than the content of the books that attracted them.

Even in plausible cases of intellectual influence, we find pitfalls. The reflective letter of 24 August 1893 where Fontane tells his daughter: 'Schopenhauer is quite right: "the best thing we have is compassion"'

might suggest that Fontane's tolerance has a philosophical under-
pinning.[4] But Fontane has not grasped Schopenhauer's doctrine of compassion as the sole means of freeing oneself from a world doomed to
suffering; he considers compassion only in the familiar sense, as a social
virtue.[5] When Mann's Tonio Kröger talks about 'the blonde and blue-
eyed people', we may think of Nietzsche's famous passage comparing
exponents of master morality to 'the splendid blonde beast, roaming
lustfully after prey and victory' (N II, 786); Mann himself suggested the
link many years later (M XI, 110).[6] But if the allusion really existed in 1903,
it could only have been humorous – Hans Hansen as blonde beast! – and
it seems unlikely that the word 'blonde' would have sufficed to recall a
specific passage in Nietzsche. It would rather have evoked a whole body
of contemporary quasi-racial assumptions, typified by Fontane's Kantor
Jahnke (in *Effi Briest*, 1895), whose Nordic enthusiasms include a liking
for fair-haired, blue-eyed people because they are 'purely Germanic'
(F IV, 217).

The intellectual historian does need to consider questions of influence
and reception, but also to be realistic about how that reception occurred.
We should imagine authors as excitedly absorbing, reshaping and creatively distorting their sources. These sources are found not only on the
peaks of philosophy, but also among the foothills. To understand their
reception, we need to examine, as Werner Michler has done in his recent study of Darwinism and literature, the intellectual and imaginative
models which conceptual thinkers shared with creative writers.[7]

In exploring these interconnections, I want to use as a guide the concept of the self. Charles Taylor has shown how much investigation of
this concept can illuminate the history of philosophy and literature.
Without directly following Taylor's scheme, I will try to show how the
German literature of this period stages a debate among several philosophical conceptions of the self. Behind them, historically, stands the self
of rationalism. Rationalism sets a purely intellectual reason, emotionally
disengaged from its surroundings, against the diversity of the empirical world. This conception of the self, further radicalised, appears in
the *Essay concerning human understanding* (1690) by the empiricist John Locke
(1632–1704), for whom the mind has 'a power to suspend the execution
of any of its desires; and . . . is at liberty to consider the objects of them,
examine them on all sides, and weigh them with others'.[8] This rational
self, sharply divided from the emotional, desiring, embodied person, is
called by Taylor the 'punctual self': the self, conceived as a point without

extension, and critically disengaged from experience. Empiricism, however, turns the tables on the rational self by questioning its empirical existence. This is the conclusion reached by David Hume (1711–76) in his *Treatise of human nature* (1739): 'For my part, when I enter most intimately into what I call *myself*, I always stumble on some particular perception or other, of heat or cold, light or shade, love or hatred, pain or pleasure. I never can catch *myself* at any time without a perception, and never can observe anything but the perception.'9 In what follows I will call the modern version of this ambiguous subjectivity the 'minimal self'. Kant sought to escape from Hume's aporia by the idealist construction of a noumenal self which exercises authority over the actual, phenomenal self. But the relation between these two remained problematic: the theoretical omnipotence of the noumenal self contrasted uneasily with the phenomenal self's subjection to natural forces and impulses. Fichte (1762–1814) sought to reconnect consciousness with empirical reality by conceiving the self not as primarily a *knowing* subject but as an *active* subject. Far from helplessly watching a world it cannot control, the Fichtean self follows a 'Trieb zu absoluter, unabhängiger Selbstthätigkeit' ('an urge to absolute, independent self-activity') by imposing its will on the world.10 I shall call this conception of the self as will 'the embattled self'.

As subsequent thinkers, especially Schopenhauer and Nietzsche, develop the concept of the will, it escapes from the control of the self and becomes an impersonal, autonomous force by which the self is helplessly driven along. Given the prestige of biological science in the later nineteenth century, such an impersonal force could readily be equated with the laws of evolution, with various vital principles and life-forces, and with the unconscious revealed by psychologists from the Romantics to Freud and Jung. Such forces could, but need not, seem frighteningly alien. For one could imagine oneself as a part of these forces, immersed or rooted in them by one's innermost being, one's very self. After all, as Nietzsche proclaimed through his Zarathustra, the intellect, and the so-called soul or spirit, formed only a tiny part of the self: 'Aber der Erwachte, der Wissende sagt: Leib bin ich ganz und gar, und nichts außerdem; und Seele ist nur ein Wort für ein Etwas am Leibe' (N II, 300; 'But he who is awake and knowledgeable says: I am wholly body and nothing else; and soul is only a word for a part of the body'). The self as reconceived by vitalism, mysticism, or psychoanalytic self-understanding will be called 'the unconscious self'.

But Nietzsche's statement points to ways in which the unconscious could be made conscious, not through psychoanalysis, but through the recovery of bodily experience, and therefore I shall examine, not so much intellectual constructions, but literary recreations of what I shall call 'the embodied self'. The embodied self, inhabiting and enjoying the physical world, is also the social self, and hence my account will end with ways of reconceiving the existence of the self in what Taylor calls 'moral space': not society as studied by the sociologist (though the rise of sociology is an important feature of this period) but the 'webs of interlocution', the multiple relationships with others, which are essential to humanity.[11]

The self exists within a framework of shared meanings and shared values. In this period, many people contemplated escaping from such frameworks. One escape was into scientific detachment, in which the self examines a universe from which human meanings and values have been excluded. Another escape was proposed by Nietzsche: the strong person, represented by his literary prophet Zarathustra and anticipating the 'Übermensch' (variously translated as Superman, Overman or Overperson), should discard current values, create his own, and impose them on others by force of will. The latter conception will concern us when we examine the embattled self. I turn now to the former: to the impersonal universe conceived by positivist science.

SCIENTIFIC NATURALISM

Any conception of the self had to find its place in the bleak universe presented by materialist science. The Christian world order of earlier centuries felt unimaginably remote, thanks to the Enlightenment's aggressive challenging of theism and to the historical researches into the Bible pursued from Hermann Samuel Reimarus (1694–1768) to David Friedrich Strauss (1808–74) and beyond. But science had not just dispelled belief in God. It had also undermined any absolute ideal. 'Wherever the spirit is now working rigorously, powerfully, and without fakery, it has wholly discarded the ideal', said Nietzsche; 'the popular term for this abstinence is "atheism"' (N II, 897).

Hence the rational universe of Hegel seemed just as remote as the Christian universe. His dictum 'What is rational is real, and what is real is rational' was incompatible with modern science. In contrast to the 'Naturphilosophie' of Romanticism, which postulated an indwelling world soul behind appearances, positivist science achieved its successes by concentrating on empirical data and explaining them solely with reference to physical and chemical forces. In philosophy, likewise, Nietzsche insisted that metaphysics – the belief in any non-empirical principle, such as Plato's ideas or the Kantian noumenon – was obsolete.

The notion that anything existed besides the material universe survived only as a wistful longing. Wolfgang Riedel has argued that the Romantics, seeking to re-establish Christian faith on a post-Enlightenment, emotional basis with the 'feeling of absolute dependence' formulated by F. D. E. Schleiermacher (1768–1834), in fact surrendered the rational content of theology so thoroughly that later in the century David Friedrich Strauss, in *Der alte und der neue Glaube* (1872; *The old faith and the new faith*), could call it a matter of indifference whether one's faith were in God or in the physical universe.[12] Strauss's complacent doctrine of progress, attacked by Nietzsche in the first of his *Unzeitgemäße Betrachtungen* (1873; *Untimely meditations*), was close to the liberal Protestantism of Albrecht Ritschl (1822–89), who thought that man's moral and cultural progress would gradually realise the kingdom of God on earth.

To many observers, Christianity wilfully ignored the undeniable findings and the growing prestige of natural science. The nineteenth century was a heroic age of science, when it was still possible for a towering figure like the physicist and physiologist Hermann von Helmholtz (1821–94) to command several scientific fields, while wealthy amateurs like Charles Darwin could still make original contributions. The drawback of positivist science, however, was that its working method – the reduction of phenomena to what could be reproduced, predicted and quantified – itself became the world-picture that it purported to reveal: a universe governed by blind forces and mathematical laws. Again, Nietzsche drew the consequences most radically. Man was no longer the measure of all things, but simply a natural being, with no more claims to a higher destiny than ants or earwigs had (N I, 1046). Nietzsche declared it his mission to translate man back into nature:

über die vielen eitlen und schwärmerischen Deutungen und Nebensinne Herr werden, welche bisher über den ewigen Grundtext *homo natura* gekritzelt und gemalt wurden; machen, daß der Mensch fürderhin vor dem Menschen steht, wie er heute schon, hart geworden in der Zucht der Wissenschaft, vor der *anderen* steht. (N II, 696)

to master the many vain and enthusiastic interpretations and connotations that have hitherto been scribbled and painted over that everlasting text *homo natura*; to ensure that henceforth man can confront man in the same way that, hardened by the discipline of science, he confronts the *other* nature.

Freud (1856–1939) similarly recounted the history of modern science as three blows to man's naive self-esteem. Copernicus had shown that the earth was not at the centre of the universe; Darwin, that man was not at the apex of creation; and Freudian psychoanalysis, that the ego ('das Ich') 'is not even master in its own house' (*SE* XVI, 285).[13]

Nietzsche, however, went further than Freud was to do by questioning scientific positivism itself. He argued that the will to truth was the only moral imperative that had survived its Christian origins; that this compulsion had disclosed a comfortless universe, and was now turning against itself by revealing that truth was unattainable. What counted as 'truth' was merely a set of ideas that had adaptive value in the evolutionary process but guaranteed no insight into the real nature of things. As early as 1872 Nietzsche summed up human history as the story of clever animals who lived on a dying planet, invented knowledge ('Erkenntnis'), learnt at the last moment that all their knowledge was worthless, and cursed their existence as they died (N III, 270–1).

Materialism could, however, be combined with other conceptions which made the universe, if not more homely, at least more intelligible. The idea of natural forces seemed to have been prefigured by Schopenhauer's theory of the will as the reality, the Kantian 'Ding an sich', concealed behind the world as we represent it. The will has no purpose, any more than the force of gravity has a purpose. It is a blind force which is most apparent in sexual desire and which condemns people to suffering, either from frustration or from satiety. The only escape from suffering, Schopenhauer maintained, was to renounce the will by silencing desire in a manner that he found prefigured in Buddhism and Hinduism. Although Schopenhauer's will might sound dangerously metaphysical, it could be assimilated to the concepts of natural science because it is not something transcendent, wholly different from phenomena; it *is* the phenomena, but seen from inside rather than outside.

In all these conceptions, the self was helpless before a universe that was imagined either as an all-powerful machine or as a relentless force. There were philosophical attempts to reconcile the self with the scientific universe. Thus Rudolph Hermann Lotze (1817–81) sought to overcome the mind–body problem – the absolute disjunction defined by Descartes between matter (*res extensa*) and mind (*res cogitans*) – by arguing that both were versions of the same thing. Since atoms were indivisible, as was mental reality according to Descartes, they must be spiritual as well as material, and so the world could be conceived as unified by its spiritual nature. These ideas appealed to naturalist writers who turned to science, such as Bölsche and the Hart brothers. Instead of the dead universe implied by physics, they imagined themselves inhabiting an animated universe where even molecules had sensations and consciousness. 'We must believe in the sentient molecule', declared Julius Hart (1859–1930).[14]

Around 1900 these beliefs were widely current under the name 'monism'. Their leading propagator was Ernst Haeckel (1834–1919), who considered himself to be placing Spinoza's conception of the world as 'deus sive natura' (God or Nature) on a scientific basis. According to Haeckel's most popular work, the universe is completely filled with substance ('Stoff'). The spaces between atoms are filled by ether, or imponderable matter, whose existence explains how action at a distance is possible. Everything is material, but matter is animated, and every biological cell contains a soul, which Haeckel calls 'psychoplasm' or soul-substance; this cell-soul, however, is not a distinct spiritual entity, but a very rudimentary form of consciousness. Consciousness is a biological function which extends from the simple power of sensation and movement shared even by cells up to the reasoning capacities of humanity. Thus humanity is naturally at home in a world full of low-level spiritual activity, linked to the unconscious activity of nature. Haeckel proclaims a monistic religion, aesthetics and ethics. To monistic religion, there is no need for special places of worship, for the whole universe is a sacred place. Monism has changed our aesthetic standards by opening our eyes to the beauties of large-scale and microscopic nature. Monistic ethics (borrowed from Herbert Spencer, 1820–1903) rest on the equivalence of egoism and altruism: social duties are merely social instincts. Man was no longer a dual being, split between his spiritual and material or his intellectual and animal natures, but a unitary being, matching the monistic cosmos around him.

Those who were not attracted by the cult of the sentient molecule could still find refuge from the indifferent universe of modern science by invoking the concept of 'life'. Like 'reason' in the Enlightenment, 'life' now seemed a fundamental concept which could stop any argument and beyond which there was no appeal. Its authority extended beyond biology to philosophy, where it formed the central concept of 'Lebensphilosophie', the school of thought associated especially with Wilhelm Dilthey (1833–1911) and Georg Simmel (1858–1918).

Dilthey shared the positivist and Nietzschean disbelief in metaphysics. His starting-point, 'life', was not remote and abstract; it was

immediate and concrete, and known best in moments of intense experience ('Erlebnis'). On this concept Dilthey based a critical theory which
gave a supreme place to 'Erlebnislyrik', the poetry, typified by the lyrics
of the young Goethe, in which moments of heightened experience were
preserved and transmitted to readers. But he also established principles of
interpretation that were constitutive for the humanities. While the natural sciences demanded detachment, the humanities, said Dilthey, started
from involvement in life. For example, the lyric poet always starts, not
from an idea, but from a situation. But he does not stay there. He develops
the situation imaginatively to bring out its general features as experienced
in a living context, not by a specific individual, but by an ideal lyric self.[15]
Similarly, the historian should not start from an idea. He should not, like
Hegel, try to understand history as the expression of a universal principle.
He involves himself in the actions of individual historical figures, understands them on the basis of his and their shared humanity, and arrives at
generalisations. Hence the study of history – and by extension of all human affairs – consists in a circulation of experience, understanding, and
generalisation. Thus, after Nietzschean scepticism, a hermeneutic theory
based on 'Lebensphilosophie' restored the possibility of knowledge.

  More generally, the slogan 'life' was popular because, in contrast to the
physicists' reliance on mathematical abstraction, it seemed to promise direct contact with reality. Truth lay in experiences of intense, sensual, even
ecstatic contact with nature. In his much-read work of popular science
and philosophy, *Das Liebesleben in der Natur*, Wilhelm Bölsche (1861–1939)
offered a world-view based on universal Eros. Like Schopenhauer and
Freud, Bölsche sees life as governed by a 'Trieb', a drive; but instead of
will or libido, it is love. This universal force is illustrated by the mass cop-
ulation of millions of herrings off the Norwegian coast. Man is one with
nature: the theory of evolution demonstrates our basic unity with the
rest of organic life. Such primordial coupling, Bölsche declares, is the ultimate source even of our cultural conception of motherhood, illustrated
by Raphael's Madonna. 'And you are linked with all these beings that
aeons ago were you and yet not you, through the prodigious world-force
of love, of procreation, of eternal generation and change.'[16] In calling
love the universal force that binds created life together, Bölsche updates
Lucretius and also Dante.[17] The demise of Christianity will be com-
pensated for by an awareness of the love pulsating through the organic
universe. Even the dissolution of the individual in death may be a form
of love, symbolised by self-loss in orgasm. Bölsche occasionally envisages
a kind of neo-pagan future when those parts of the body now dismissed

by 'fig-leaf fanaticism' as indecent will be publicly displayed, celebrated, even worshipped as sacred.[18]

Such notions drew on the conception of ecstatic Dionysiac unity evoked by Nietzsche in *Die Geburt der Tragödie* (1872; *The birth of tragedy*). In this powerful but fanciful work, which cost him his scholarly reputation, Nietzsche proposed the ancient Greeks as models for the present, but to do so he had to represent them in anachronistic terms. His Athenians attended tragedies, which Nietzsche assimilated to Wagnerian music dramas, and received a proto-Schopenhauerian message about the misery of life and the illusory character of individuation. Greek tragic theatre was a religious occasion. The truth about life, normally unbearable, was uttered by the chorus, and the spectators felt momentarily released from individuation into the unity promoted by the cult of Dionysus: 'Despite fear and pity we are happy and alive, not as individuals, but as the one living entity with whose procreative pleasure we are fused' (N I, 93).

For many writers the cult of 'life' could be a substitute for religion. Lou Andreas-Salomé (1861–1937) wrote a poem entitled 'Lebensgebet' ('Prayer to life') which Nietzsche set to music, beginning:

> Gewiß, so liebt ein Freund den Freund,
> Wie ich Dich liebe, Rätselleben –
> Ob ich in Dir gejauchzt, geweint,
> Ob Du mir Glück, ob Schmerz gegeben.[19]

> Certainly, a friend loves a friend
> as I love you, enigmatic life –
> no matter whether I rejoiced or wept in you,
> whether you gave me happiness or pain.

We note how a personal relation to God has been transferred to an enigmatic abstraction; how the writer, whether ecstatic or suffering, still feels herself to be comfortingly enclosed *within* life.

'Lebensphilosophie' was not only comforting, however. The unity of all life implied the removal of any distinction between man and animals. 'Along with the natural scientists I deny that there is any moral world order,' wrote Leopold von Sacher-Masoch (1836–95); 'for me, man is not the image of God, but only the most intelligent and therefore the cruellest of the beasts.'[20] Haeckel maintained that the most primitive humans, such as the Veddahs of Ceylon, were closer to animals than to a Goethe or a Darwin. Nietzsche insists on man's animality. Kafka takes up this theme especially in his collection of stories *Ein Landarzt* (1919; *A country doctor*) by blurring the difference between men and animals.

If man was an animal, society must be a jungle. Popular Darwinism represented life as a naked struggle for survival. The political theory known as Social Darwinism advocated ruthless competition which would benefit the race by eliminating the weak. Its milder exponents worried, as Darwin had done, about these consequences of evolution, but others found additional support in Nietzsche. Regarding modern civilisation as a herd of domestic animals made sick by Judaeo-Christian morality, Nietzsche denounced compassion as the greatest threat to those few surviving healthy individuals who could in future reshape humanity like sculptors and operate upon it like surgeons (N II, 1168–9). His most ruthless disciple, Alexander Tille (1866–1912), who advocated the killing of cripples and dismissed Christian ethics as an illusion of the weak, synthesised these ideas in his book *Von Darwin bis Nietzsche* (1895; *From Darwin to Nietzsche*).

When tested by the literary imagination, scientism contends with compassion. In *Vor Sonnenaufgang* (1889; *Before the dawn*), Gerhart Hauptmann (1862–1946) brings a Darwinian sociologist, Alfred Loth, into a family of morally and medically degenerate nouveau-riche farmers, lets him fall in love with the apparently healthy daughter who is desperate to escape her milieu, and then has him abandon her on discovering that any children they had would suffer from hereditary alcoholism.[21] As the physician and cultural critic Max Nordau (1849–1923) noted in his polemic *Entartung* (1892; *Degeneration*), Hauptmann's science is as implausible as that of his dramatic precursor Ibsen (cf. Osvald's 'softening of the brain' in *Ghosts*). Loth typifies the shortcomings of a merely theoretical or scientistic approach to human problems.

Naturalist writers, despite their professed scientism, in fact demand our compassion for social suffering. The unemployable craftsman in *Meister Timpe* (1888; *The master craftsman Timpe*), by Max Kretzer (1854–1941), and the Berlin proletarians in *Die Familie Selicke* (1890; *The Selicke family*) by Arno Holz (1863–1929) and Johannes Schlaf (1862–1941) tug at our heart-strings. Rilke initially sympathised with Nietzsche's doctrine in the story *Der Apostel* (1893; *The apostle*), with its sermon against 'poisonous' Christian love, but soon afterwards urged sympathy for the nameless urban poor in the third part of his *Stunden-Buch* (1905; *Book of hours*). A more complex attitude towards what Nietzsche called the 'Schlechtweggekommene' ('those who have come off badly') is found in the early Thomas Mann. Tonio Kröger regrets that his readers are 'people who always fall down', i.e. born losers for whom poetry is compensation, 'a gentle revenge on life' (M VIII, 303). In 'Der Weg zum Friedhof' ('The road to the cemetery') the unfortunate Lobgott Piepsam, who despite his pietist forename has lost all his family and taken to the bottle, is on his way to visit his relatives' graves when he is knocked down by 'Life', personified as a healthy young cyclist.

Although German naturalists produced no large-scale sociological study of modern life matching Zola's Rougon-Macquart series, they firmly connected the problems of modernity to the transformation of life by urbanisation. Their hesitating analysis was developed by Georg Simmel in *Die Philosophie des Geldes* (1900; *The philosophy of money*), a powerful analysis of how the money economy, by rendering life more abstract, both impoverishes and empowers the individual. In the money economy, the individual is dependent on an immense number of other people, but they are important to him only as functions, not as personalities. Since the modern self exists at the centre of a huge variety of functions, roles, relationships, this dependence can be paradoxically transformed into freedom. Instead of merely being non-dependent, like a hermit, modern urban man can be truly independent: all his social relations are mediated through money, so that while he needs the services of countless people, he is not compelled to rely on any particular one of them. For those with a less complex understanding of modern urban life, it was tempting to retreat into nature as a more congenial setting for the self. A typical example, praised in its day as a modern counterpart to the Song of Solomon, is Johannes Schlaf's prose-poem *Frühling* (1896; *Spring*), written during the author's recovery from a nervous breakdown. Its rhythmic prose and dithyrambic verse derive from Walt Whitman and Nietzsche's Zarathustra. From enjoying the spring sun, the speaker enters into other consciousnesses – those of an old man, a child, a beetle – and finally anticipates death as the dissolution of his personal identity into the monistic unity that already surrounds him.[22]

Frank Wedekind (1864–1918) used nature similarly but more flexibly in *Frühlings Erwachen* (1891; *Spring awakening*). The young Wedekind knew the pessimistic thought of Schopenhauer and Eduard von Hartmann, but in his play he treats critically the world of human institutions (the family, the school, prisons) and connects his adolescent protagonists with nature. We see them in woods, in gardens, in a hayloft, and beside the river (symbolising the stream of life) that runs through the play; their powerful, joyous, but sometimes sado-masochistic sexuality contends with adult attempts to repress it through miseducation, hypocrisy, punishment and abortion. The born loser, Moritz, commits suicide; the predestined survivor, Melchior (significantly said to be a strong swimmer), passes into the care of a Masked Man who embodies life.

THE MINIMAL SELF

The self might confront a bleak, inhuman universe. Or it might be absorbed into the surging life-force. In either case, what was the self? Had it any substance, depth, complexity, resilience?

In the 1890s, both the Berlin Naturalists and the Vienna Impressionists tended to envisage the self as an extensionless point, a perspectival standpoint, or a mere fiction. In the innovatory fiction of naturalism, such as Arno Holz's *Ein Tod* (1889; *A death*) and *Der erste Schultag* (1889; *The first day at school*), the characters behave with deterministic predictability, but the narrative perspective offered to the reader registers all events with equal attention – the groans of a dying man, the conversation of his unnoticing companions, the humming of a trapped bluebottle as a sadistic schoolteacher beats a child to death. The characters are automata; the reader is the mere camera-like eye that observes them.

Impressionism, as a form of writing that concentrated on conveying sensations by accumulating adjectives, found its theorist in the Viennese critic Hermann Bahr (1863–1934). In 1890 Bahr urged his contemporaries to move beyond naturalism by attending not only to external reality but also to how it was apprehended by the nerves:

Die alte Psychologie findet immer nur den letzten Effekt der Gefühle, welchen Ausdruck ihnen am Ende das Bewußtsein formelt und das Gedächtnis behält. Die neue wird ihre ersten Elemente suchen, die Anfänge in den Finsternissen der Seele, bevor sie noch am klaren Tag herausschlagen.[23]

The old psychology finds only the ultimate effect of feelings, the expression finally formulated by consciousness and retained by memory. The new psychology will seek their initial elements, their beginnings in the darkness of the soul, before they emerge into the clear light of day.

But in thus continuing empirical inquiry, Bahr found, as Hume had done, that its object vanished. Hume ended by defining the self as 'nothing but a bundle or collection of different impressions, which succeed each other with an inconceivable rapidity, and are in a perpetual flux and movement.'[24]

Bahr found these ideas developed by Ernst Mach (1838–1916), who, like Helmholtz, belonged to the nineteenth-century tradition of polymathic scientists. While holding a chair of physics at Prague, his interests led him to the psychology and philosophy of perception. He retained the conviction, which he claimed to have derived at an early age from Kant's *Prolegomena zu einer jeden künftigen Metaphysik* (1783; *Prolegomena to any future metaphysics*), that the contents of consciousness could not be reliably connected with external reality. In *Die Analyse der Empfindungen* (1886; *The analysis of sensations*) Mach maintained that consciousness consisted of sensations, and that the self which received these sensations was simply a complex of feelings, moods and memories, attached to a body. By changing only gradually, this complex gives the illusion of permanence; but in fact there is no permanent, substantial self underlying the flux of sensations. 'The self is past saving' ('Das *Ich* ist unrettbar'), Mach proclaimed.[25] There cannot, then, be any personal immortality; but neither is there any firm boundary separating one person's consciousness from another's, nor any real continuity between my present self and my past selves. The illusion of continuity comes from the chain of memories connecting my present to my past.

Having read the second (1900) edition of Mach's book, Bahr synthesised it with other philosophical ideas. The notion that reality is flux goes back to the pre-Socratic philosopher Heraclitus and his maxim 'All things flow'. Nietzsche took up this idea in his exposition of the pre-Socratics. And it seemed easily compatible with Haeckel's monism, for which reality was a single continuum, neither material nor mental. Nietzsche was equally sceptical about the self, arguing that the 'Ich' was a mere fiction required by grammar: the sentence 'ich denke' ('I think') requires the assumption of an 'Ich' as grammatical subject; but that does not mean that the self has any real existence (N II, 615–16). From all these components Bahr concocted a philosophy of impressionism:

Alle Trennungen sind hier aufgehoben, das Physikalische und das Psychologische rinnt zusammen, Element und Empfindung sind eins, das Ich löst sich auf und alles ist nur eine ewige Flut, die hier zu stocken scheint, dort eiliger fließt, alles ist nur Bewegung von Farben, Tönen, Wärmen, Drücken, Räumen und Zeiten, die auf der anderen Seite, bei uns hierüben, als Stimmungen, Gefühle und Willen erscheinen.[26]

All divisions are here erased, the physical and the psychological fuse, element and sensation are one, the self dissolves, and everything is a mere everlasting flux that seems to pause in one place and flow more rapidly in another; everything is mere movement of colours, sounds, temperatures, pressures, spaces and times, which appear on the other side, to us, as moods, emotions and will.

Even before Bahr discovered Mach, his Viennese contemporaries were thinking along similar lines. Hofmannsthal's notebooks of 1894 consider the self as discontinuous and find continuity only in the physical bond between the individual and his ancestors. These ideas find poetic expression in 'Terzinen: Über Vergänglichkeit' ('On transience, in terza rima'), while 'Manche freilich...' ('Many, indeed...') expresses a cautious monism:

> Viele Geschicke weben neben dem meinen,
> Durcheinander spielt sie alle das Dasein,
> Und mein Teil ist mehr als dieses Lebens
> Schlanke Flamme oder schmale Leier,
>
> (H I, 26)
>
> Many destinies are woven alongside mine,
> all are intertwined by existence,
> and my part is more than this life's
> slender flame or narrow lyre.

Yet there is no firm evidence that the young Hofmannsthal knew Mach's work.[27] Arthur Schnitzler (1862–1931) similarly explores the discontinuities of the self in *Anatol* and other early works. Yet he read Mach only in 1904.[28] If their conceptions of the self have a single source, besides the monism derived from Haeckel and Nietzsche, then it is Walter Pater's 'Conclusion' to *The renaissance* (1873), avidly read by Hofmannsthal. Having quoted Heraclitus, Pater (1839–94) describes how, on reflection, experience dissolves into 'a group of impressions – colour, odour, texture', which are 'unstable, flickering, inconsistent'. 'Every one of those impressions', Pater concludes, 'is the impression of the individual in his isolation, each mind keeping as a solitary prisoner its own dream of a world.'[29] This image of the self as prison reappears in Hofmannsthal's fictional dialogue on dramatic and novelistic characterisation (1902) where Balzac is made to say: 'There are no experiences save the experience of one's own being' (H VII, 486).

The illusion of the self was sustained, as Pater remarked, by language. The theory of the discontinuous self needed a new theory of language, and this was provided by the journalist and novelist Fritz Mauthner (1849–1923) in his *Beiträge zur Kritik der Sprache* (1901–2; *Contributions to the critique of language*). Mauthner was steeped in the scepticism of Nietzsche, though he did not know the argument that so-called truths are merely dead metaphors, propounded in Nietzsche's essay 'Über Wahrheit und Lüge im außermoralischen Sinne' ('On truth and lies in a non-moral sense'), which was published only posthumously in 1903. Mauthner takes empiricism and nominalism to an extreme by arguing that language does not exist as an abstraction but only as a social practice, an activity among people. Language does not express independently existing thought, nor does it conform to any rules of logic or grammar. Thought, logic and grammar exist only within language, just as there is no abstract 'blueness' independent of blue things. Language is vague, elusive, ambiguous. Most conversation consists in misunderstanding: the word 'tree', for example, has different associations for everyone who uses it. Language cannot be a vehicle of knowledge. Not only poetic language, but also everyday, scientific and philosophical language are metaphorical, presenting 'images of images of images'.[30] The history of language is a continual search for new metaphors to replace those that have been worn out; though outside poetry their metaphorical character is soon forgotten. Most language use is mere meaningless chatter. Moral and philosophical terms ('virtue', 'immortality', 'idea', 'category') are empty; their use is mere insolence. Modern science is just another mythology composed of abstractions. Nothing can be known except the unreliability of language. The only valid use of language is poetic, because poetry seeks only to arouse emotions and stimulate moods.

Not surprisingly, Mauthner's theory appealed especially to poets. Its philosophical weakness is the self-contradiction of extreme scepticism: for if non-poetic language is meaningless, then so are Mauthner's arguments for the meaninglessness of language. But Mauthner seemed to confirm the special character of poetic language. 'People are tired of hearing talk', wrote Hofmannsthal in 1895. 'They have a deep loathing for words, for words have placed themselves in front of things. Hearsay has swallowed the world' (H VIII, 479). Rilke in 1897 contrasted the poet's word with the word as everyday currency (R IV, 54). And Stefan George (1868–1933), inspired by contact with the French Symbolists, devised not only a new poetic diction but his own orthography and typography. This much-discussed 'crisis of language' ('Sprachkrise') did not, as is often claimed, concern the inadequacy of language as such. After all, language can only be adequate or inadequate in relation to a specific purpose. It concerned the renewal of poetic language to express nuances of emotion and sensation. And that in turn, as I shall argue later in this chapter, demanded a richer and more plausible conception of the self than the punctual theory of impressionism.

Literature often challenges philosophy by asking how its claims would look if one tried to live by them. Accordingly, Hofmannsthal and

Schnitzler oppose the disintegrative implications of impressionist psychology by stressing memory, continuity and responsibility. The impressionist adventurer in Hofmannsthal's first play, *Gestern* (1891; *Yesterday*), on learning that his wife has been unfaithful to him, finds he cannot shrug off his betrayal as merely the experience of a previous self. Continuity is undeniable, and it implies morality. The aesthete who lives from moment to moment, from lover to lover, betrays others without satisfying his own emotional needs, as Claudio demonstrates in Hofmannsthal's *Der Tor und der Tod* (1893; *The fool and death*). Schnitzler treats the aesthetic adventurer humorously in his cycle of one-acters, *Anatol* (1893), ironically in *Liebelei* (1895; *Dalliance*), and satirically in *Leutnant Gustl* (1900), an early experiment in stream-of-consciousness narration, where Gustl's naive associative thinking, even when contemplating suicide, convinces the reader of his shallowness.

Both Hofmannsthal and Schnitzler endow memory with ethical significance. In Hofmannsthal's *Elektra* (1903), the heroine refuses to forget her father's murder, even at the risk of self-destructive obsession. In Schnitzler's novel *Der Weg ins Freie* (1908; *The road to the open*), Georg von Wergenthin survives emotionally harrowing experiences, while his Jewish counterpart Heinrich Bermann risks being trapped in meditation on the past. Both writers are examining a moral problem originally explored by Nietzsche. Loyalty to the past is an attractive quality, as Nietzsche admits in his essay on the uses and abuses of history; but health requires one to forget one's experiences and move on to new ones, just as one needs to digest one's food (N II, 799). In literature, it becomes clear that to live only in the present is to deny one's responsibilities, but fixation on the past is deadly.

THE EMBATTLED SELF

We have seen how Fichte resolved Humean and Kantian doubts about the self by arguing that the self could reconnect itself to the world through resolute action. The ethics of activity with which Fichte inspired Berlin students in 1807 also seemed appropriate to the new Germany established by Bismarck's 'Realpolitik'. Appropriately, Fichte appears as an invigorating lecturer in Fontane's first novel, *Vor dem Sturm* (1878; *Before the storm*).

Later philosophies also explore the will, but with different emphases. Schopenhauer's impersonal will, present in human desires and in natural forces, was reinterpreted by Nietzsche, who rejected Schopenhauerian pessimism, as will to power. Organic beings were not motivated by any purpose; such arguments belonged to an obsolete teleological outlook. Instead, they were animated by a will to power that invented purposes for itself as it went along. And this will to power was the key, not just to organic activity, but to all energy of whatever kind. The universal principle that Dante found in love, 'the force that moves the sun and the other stars', is for Nietzsche power-hunger. Yet Nietzsche also attacks the error of explaining perceptible events by hypothetical and invisible causes, and includes the will among the latter (N II, 973). His claim that everything is animated by the will to power seems impossible to reconcile with his campaign against belief in non-empirical, metaphysical entities.

During the Nietzsche vogue at the turn of the century, however, such contradictions could pass unnoticed. Nietzsche's concept of the will helped him to construct the image of the 'Übermensch', foretold by his prophet Zarathustra, who will create new values. When he mentions antecedents like Cesare Borgia or Napoleon, he encourages us to imagine the 'Übermensch' as a heroic dictator, a supremely embattled figure, who will sweep away the democratic tyranny of modern herd-animals.

A salutary comment on such fantasies is a somewhat neglected short story by Thomas Mann, 'Beim Propheten' (1904; 'At the prophet's'), which presents the embattled self humorously, but with undertones of distaste and warning. The 'prophet' is based on Ludwig Derleth (1870–1948), a Munich poet of cosmic pretensions, whose poems Mann had heard read by a disciple. The narrator ascribes the prophecies to 'the self, despairingly enthroned' ('das verzweifelt thronende Ich', M VIII, 362). When the prophet's diatribes are read out, the narrator remarks: 'A feverish and frightfully irritated self arose in lonely megalomania, threatening the world with a torrent of violent words' (M VIII, 368). The shrill tirades and empty threats of this prophetic self are clearly overcompensating for its exclusion from ordinary life.

The embattled self, evoked by Nietzsche or mocked by Mann, is of course gendered as male. Schopenhauer had laid the groundwork for this conception in his 'Metaphysik der Geschlechtsliebe' (1851; 'Metaphysics of sexual love'), where he described the sexual urge as the principal expression of the will to live. The individual's desire was as illusory as individuality itself. It was merely the vehicle for the determination of the species to survive (S III, 588). The overriding good of the species accounts for the apparent incongruity of many sexual partnerships, and for men's frequent inclination to promiscuity contrasted with women's monogamy. Thus Schopenhauer sees conflict built into the relation between the sexes. His misogyny, most bitterly expressed in his essay 'Über die Weiber' (1851; 'On women'), pleased many readers. Hence Schopenhauer's philosophy of sexual love found a twofold response. Many were grateful to him for giving a central element of human experience a corresponding place in his philosophy. But his treatment of women tended to emphasise conflict between the sexes and to portray man as intellectually superior and woman as principally the instrument of the will to live.

The male embattled self could be imagined not only as an individual but as typifying the race. The adoptive German Houston Stewart Chamberlain (1855–1927), in his *Grundlagen des 19. Jahrhunderts*, portrayed the 'Germanic' race in similarly heroic terms, but with an ambivalence that increased his book's appeal. For while the triumphant Germanic race could take credit for all the achievements of civilisation, it was now under threat from the swirling 'racial chaos' of mulattos, mestizos and mongrels that was threatening to submerge the modern world. Similar fantasies dominate the extraordinary psychotic autobiography by the judge Daniel Schreber (1842–1911), *Denkwürdigkeiten meiner Nervenkrankheit* (1903; *Memoirs of my nervous illness*).

Nietzsche's conception of embattled masculinity also includes an account of femininity as cunning, pliable, anxious to yield to a man who imperiously takes what is offered (N II, 237). Ironically, Nietzsche himself was attracted to intelligent, challenging women like Lou Andreas-Salomé, and supported the admission of women to Swiss universities. But his literary fantasies suited readers who were alarmed by the growing women's movement. Some writers thought the intellect or spirit was gendered as male, as in Stefan George's poem from *Der Stern des Bundes* (1914; *The star of the covenant*) beginning:

> Die weltzeit die wir kennen schuf der geist
> Der immer mann ist: ehrt das weib im stoffe,
> Er ist kein mindres heiligtum.[31]

> Our epoch was created by the Spirit
> Which is forever Man. Honour womankind in Matter,
> It is no less in sanctity.

Just as George here aligns masculinity with the spirit and femininity with the material world, so Otto Weininger (1880–1903) in his scandalous doctoral thesis, *Geschlecht und Charakter* (1903; *Sex and character*), created an influential image of the gendered and embattled male self. After ridiculing Hume's dissolution of the self into a bundle of ideas, Weininger reestablishes, on logical and ethical grounds which he considers ultimately identical, the Kantian conception of the noumenal, autonomous self. Every significant ('bedeutend') person must affirm the self ('das Ich'), and discovers his individuality in a conversion-like event called the 'Ich-Ereignis'. Acknowledging no higher authority than its innate sense of duty, this self is solitary: 'Man is *alone* in the universe, in immense, everlasting solitude.'[32] But the supreme self, that of the genius, escapes from isolation because his self is infinite and universal, a microcosm of the universe. This ideal is male. Within Weininger's basically bisexual psychology, beings in whom the M component predominates are masculine, those with dominant W are feminine. The latter lack a Kantian intelligible self. While the male wants to produce intellectual offspring, the female wants to reproduce her kind. Hence sensual love is a trap for the genius. Woman, in the two basic types Weininger distinguishes – mother or whore – seeks to drag him down.

If, as Darwinism already suggested, the essence of life was conflict, then it was appropriate that the most unyielding conflict should be waged between man and woman, with the intellectual man threatened by the unreasoning, instinct-driven female. This conception, already present in Strindberg's marital dramas, reappears in many naturalist and expressionist works. In Hauptmann's *Bahnwärter Thiel* (1888; *Linesman Thiel*), the protagonist's split sexuality draws him first to a delicate, sensitive woman, then, after her death, to a rawly physical woman who controls him by satisfying his powerful libido. A similar conflict is presented allegorically in the early expressionist drama by Oskar Kokoschka (1886–1980), *Mörder Hoffnung der Frauen* (1908; *Murderer hope of women*), where man, the ascetic bearer of the spirit, escapes from erotic slavery by destroying the sexualised civilisation embodied by the woman.

It was, however, possible for male writers to reverse the signs and celebrate this very conception of femininity. Hence the response to Weininger by Karl Kraus (1874–1936): 'An admirer of women assents with enthusiasm to your arguments for despising women.'[33] For the sensual woman could seem the last repository of affection, spontaneity, nature, instinct, in a world given over to the intellectual analysis and technological 'progress' which, in Kraus's view, were put to shame by the sinking of the *Titanic*. The intellectual man would perish without the sensual woman: 'The sensuality of woman is the primal spring at which man's intellectuality finds renewal.'[34] But the embattled male self also risked destroying this female source of life, and such a fatal conflict was dramatised by a writer Kraus greatly admired, Frank Wedekind, in his *Lulu* plays.

Originally planned as a single 'monster tragedy', Wedekind's dramatic portrayal of Lulu became two separate but linked dramas with mythic titles, *Erdgeist* (1895; *Earth Spirit*) and *Die Büchse der Pandora* (1904; *Pandora's box*). Lulu, an orphan kept by a male protector, Schön, is based on such nineteenth-century *grandes horizontales* as Liane de Pougy and Cora Pearl, but also on archetypes like Eve, Helen of Troy and Pandora. 'Earth Spirit' implies both the uncontrollable, elemental being conjured in Goethe's *Faust I* and the 'evil spirit of earth' invoked in Schiller's *Wallenstein*. Hence Lulu is ambivalent: a gifted dancer, she seems like 'the embodiment of life's happiness', but being also amoral and unfeeling, she causes the death of each of her husbands. Yet any criticism of Lulu rebounds on the society which treats artistic genius as a saleable commodity, passes a woman from one man to another, tolerates the double standard by which Schön proposes to keep Lulu as his erotic mistress while marrying a pure girl, and finally gives Lulu the choice between two forms of prostitution – in a Cairo brothel or on the London streets. Wedekind shows a society polarised between the rational calculation of the white-slave trader Casti-Piani and the physical humanity of the ultimately helpless Lulu. The dealer in women's bodies is the most drastic, caricatural, and repellent version of the embattled male self.

In other ways, too, the embattled self seeks to command nature. Marshall Berman has identified the developer, the agent of technical modernisation, as a quintessentially modern figure, and has traced his genealogy from Goethe's Faust (with the unrealised project for reclaiming land from the sea) down to modern city planners.[35] We can include in his family tree such figures as Melville's Ahab and Storm's Hauke Haien, who impose their will on nature by hunting the whale and building dykes. Mann's Thomas Buddenbrook attempts such ruthlessness when he breaks with the probity (or just caution) of his family and buys the Pöppenrade harvest while it is still in the ear. This risky speculation is for him a means of proving his (masculine) strength. When the harvest is destroyed by hail, however, nature symbolically avenges man's transgression of the boundary between cultivation and exploitation.

Nature and modern civilisation are perhaps most sharply contrasted in a story which, by presenting this antithesis with textbook clarity, has recently gained much attention, *Die Ermordung einer Butterblume* (1910; *The murder of a buttercup*) by Alfred Döblin (1878–1957).[36] The businessman Michael Fischer, with his jerky movements, his black suit, and his habit of bullying his apprentices, becomes obsessed with a buttercup which he calls 'Ellen', thereby projecting onto it the repressed feminine side of his own nature; eventually he decapitates it, only to be overcome with guilt and rush out to his destruction in a dark forest. A funnier caricature of a detestable bourgeois is Theobald Maske in the play *Die Hose* (1911; *The knickers*) by Carl Sternheim (1878–1942). For the calculating and aptly named Maske, respectability is the 'Tarnkappe', the Wagnerian helmet of invisibility, behind which he pursues his desires, and even his bi-weekly adultery, where his physical nature finds satisfaction, is subjected to the deadening routine which props up his life.

The embattled self is solitary, not only in lacking relations with other people, but sometimes also in being dissociated from the shared values that make social life possible. The embattled self can reject prior moral norms and frameworks, as Thomas Buddenbrook does in his commercial speculation, and as Nietzsche's 'Übermensch' will do on a grand scale. We find a disconcertingly Nietzschean moment in Fontane's last novel, *Der Stechlin* (1898), when Dubslav von Stechlin and Pastor Lorenzen discuss heroism. To illustrate his conception of modern, individual heroism by contrast with the 'herd courage' of merely obedient soldiers, Lorenzen recounts how a Polar explorer, Lieutenant Greeley, found that one of the party was secretly stealing provisions and putting all their lives at risk, so shot the thief from behind and thus saved the others' lives. Against Dubslav's misgivings, Lorenzen insists that it was admirable of Greeley to perform a deed which 'contradicts all divine commandments, all law and all honour'; Greeley might have observed traditional moral sanctions and faced his death if he alone had been involved, but he was a leader, and therefore obliged to perform 'a terrible Something' (F v, 344). Despite the unfamiliar context, we can recognise a familiar motif from German literature, that of the necessary crime, performed by embattled selves in Büchner's *Dantons Tod* (1835; *Danton's death*) and Hebbel's *Agnes Bernauer* (1852), and celebrated by Nietzsche in *Die Geburt der Tragödie* in the person of Prometheus. But one might wonder whether such crimes are as necessary as their perpetrators claim. In Lorenzen's story, Greeley does not remonstrate with the thief; he simply kills him.

Although the embattled self may transgress moral boundaries, it feels most comfortable within established institutional frameworks, which

provide an alternative to self-examination. The embattled self identifies with a historical process, a nation or an organisation. Thus Thomas
Buddenbrook identifies with the family firm and allows his own inner life
to wither. Aschenbach in *Der Tod in Venedig* (1912; *Death in Venice*) serves the
Prussian state by his writing, as his ancestors served it through administration or soldiering; he rejects self-analysis, turns his back on moral
ambiguity, denies the link between understanding and compassion, and
adopts the motto of Frederick the Great – 'Endure' ('Durchhalten').
He gains national popularity with a series of sternly moralising novels,
only to discover unsuspected depths of inadmissible erotic passion within
himself.

In identifying with an institution and a historical process, the self avoids
interpreting its own life as a narrative. The history of the institution replaces the biography of the self. Thus Innstetten in Fontane's *Effi Briest*
(1895) has a career rather than a biography; Thomas Buddenbrook identifies with the family firm; in Aschenbach, the public figure has almost
smothered the private self; and Josef K. in Kafka's *Der Prozeß* (1914; *The
trial*) considers himself first and foremost the deputy manager of a bank.
The institutional self is incapable of change and growth. It is cut off from
its past and its future.

The self capable of change, by contrast, goes through a series of stages
which are not sharply discrete. Thus childhood should ideally survive
as the capacity of play which is part of friendship (as opposed to mere
consociation for some practical purpose) and of erotic companionship (as
opposed to the mere satisfaction of physical desire). Fontane's Innstetten
turns his daughter into a priggish automaton. Thomas Buddenbrook
has a hostile relationship with his son Hanno, vainly seeking in him
compensation for his own failures. Josef K. dislikes children and drives
them away; his humour takes the form only of sour amusement at other
people's disabilities (like the paralysed muscle in the face of one of his
subordinates); he associates with other professional men for the sake
of networking and supporting one another's self-esteem; and his sexual
relations are exploitative.

Faced with a crisis, the embattled self remains stuck in a frozen heroic
posture. It substitutes stoic endurance for change and growth. Forced
into introspection by the prospect of a duel, Innstetten discovers an
internalised and irresistible 'social something' ('Gesellschafts-Etwas').
Later, isolated and unhappy after rejecting his wife, he can only take the
advice given by his colleague Wüllersdorf: 'To stand in the breach and endure until you are killed, that's the best thing' (F IV, 288) – inhuman advice

recalling Aschenbach's 'Endure'. Josef K.'s fictional life moves in a circle. By his thirty-first birthday he seems no closer to the self-knowledge which the Court invited him to seek by arresting him on his thirtieth. His last chance comes when the Chaplain summons him by name from the pulpit. There could hardly be a clearer indication that K. himself, the person not the functionary, is being called to account. But the hints contained in the parable of the doorkeeper are lost on K. In the parable, the doorkeeper typifies the man whose freedom is restricted by his place within an institution. The Man from the Country is the free man, able to enter the Law if he so decides. Yet, intimidated by authority, he refrains from challenging it and spends the rest of his life outside the door which, as he learns in his dying moments, was intended specifically for him to enter.

Not only should one's life retain the past: it should also anticipate the future. The only certain fact about my future is that I shall die; and as I grow older I need to incorporate this fact into my consciousness, to prepare myself for death, so that my death shall not be a meaningless, brute, external intervention in my life but the consummation of my life as a meaningful process. Thus the death of Dubslav in *Der Stechlin* occurs amid a social setting of servants and neighbours. Dubslav endures the process wearily but stoically, reflecting: 'The "self" is nothing – one must absorb that idea. An eternal law is taking its course, that's all, and its course, even when called "death", must not frighten us' (F v, 372). And after his death, the snowdrops brought by the girl who is said to be his illegitimate child carry a faint hint of resurrection.

To the embattled self, however, death is the ultimate threat. For in persisting in a frozen heroic posture, the self is really refusing to live in order not to die. The death of Thomas Buddenbrook is unexpected, undignified, degrading. Returning from a painful visit to the dentist, he collapses in the street, and has his face and clothes sullied by the winter slush. Mann's language is detached and clinical, as it is later when describing Hanno's death from typhus. It is as though the language and assumptions of scientific positivism defined the whole horizon of human experience; its language may be used ironically, but no other language is available.

After Thomas's death the word goes round that 'Senator Buddenbrook has died of a tooth', and the disparity between the event and its occasion brings home to us that for years now Thomas has not been living. He has been soldiering on, married to an unloving wife and committed to a career he knows is trivial, sustained by sheer will-power. The one moment of relief comes when he takes a volume of Schopenhauer

off the shelf and reads the chapter on 'Death and its relation to the inde-
structibility of our essential being'. Though what Mann actually reports
is a strange amalgam of Schopenhauer and Nietzsche, the prospect of
absorption into the primal unity temporarily consoles Thomas for the
increasingly evident futility of his life. It has been argued that the whole
of *Buddenbrooks* is patterned on Schopenhauer; but attention to Mann's
actual reading reveals that he encountered Schopenhauer only at a late
stage in the composition of the novel.[37] If Mann the novelist did make
use of Schopenhauer, it was much later, when composing the *Joseph*
tetralogy and *Felix Krull*, in which the individual is represented as a mere
temporary mask for an impersonal, archetypal identity.[38]

Thomas's death is a symbolic punishment for his attempt to disregard
the fact that he would die. For, as Schopenhauer maintained in his essay
'Über das metaphysische Bedürfais des Menschen' (1851; 'On man's metaphysical need'), man is distinguished from other animals by his reason,
and hence by his ability to confront death consciously. One can put
the matter more starkly with the help of some eloquent pages by Martin
Heidegger (1889–1976) on death: I know that I will die; but I can only too
easily blur this awareness by taking refuge in the impersonal, inauthentic
identity of what Heidegger calls 'das Man', and by uttering such truisms
as 'man stirbt' (roughly, 'we've all got to go some time'). This inauthentic
life is not the same as fear of death. How can one not be afraid to die?
But, says Heidegger, the inauthentic person has not the courage to be
afraid of death ('Das Man läßt den Mut zur Angst vor dem Tode nicht
aufkommen').[39] Heidegger gives an illustration of this situation from
literature with Tolstoy's *The death of Ivan Ilyich*. But we can find it also in
German presentations of the embattled but deeply vulnerable self.

THE UNCONSCIOUS SELF

Among conceptions of the self in this period, those associated with
Freudian psychoanalysis[40] deserve a central place. For, although psychoanalysis has not gained the secure scientific standing that Freud hoped
for, it has decisively shaped twentieth-century Western notions of humanity. In psychoanalysis, a bewildering number of intellectual currents
converge, and though it is often difficult to trace particular affinities
in detail, psychoanalysis forms the route through which many assumptions of late nineteenth-century German culture have been transmitted
to the wider world. I shall indicate briefly some ways in which Freud's

central concepts are related to the philosophical ideas we have been examining.

In doing so, a paradox in Freud's work must be pointed out. He considered himself a positivistic scientist. Through his teacher Ernst von Brücke (1819–92) he had acquired Helmholtz's ambition to explain organisms entirely by physical and chemical forces. At the same time, he had a powerful imagination and overweening ambitions. His work draws on an insight into human character worthy of the great moralists and on an immersion in literature from the Greeks to his contemporaries. This helps to explain why Freudianism now finds most sympathetic readers in the humanities.

Psychoanalysis was intended, above all, as a means of exploring the unconscious. At first Freud used the term to denote mental contents which had been hidden from the conscious self by repression. Later, however, he talked of the unconscious as a mental domain with its own laws, where nothing is forgotten, time does not pass, and logical contradictions are tolerated. The principal contents of the unconscious are urges or drives ('Triebe'), a term Strachey translated as 'instincts' in the *Standard edition*. Freud first used the term when speaking of the sexual drive in *Drei Abhandlungen zur Sexualtheorie* (1905; *Three essays on the theory of sexuality*). Drives are biological in origin, but Freud locates them on the border of the physical and the mental. They may be understood as psychological equivalents of bodily instincts. In Freud's later work, drives develop from scientific hypotheses into mythical forces. In 1932 he declared: 'Instincts are mythical entities, magnificent in their indefiniteness' (*SE* XXII, 95).

Freud himself acknowledged Schopenhauer as a forerunner. In 1917 he paid tribute to 'the great thinker Schopenhauer, whose unconscious "Will" is equivalent to the mental instincts of psycho-analysis' (*SE* XVII, 143–4). When he later postulated a conflict between the libido and the death-drive (which seeks to reduce the expenditure of energy and thus aims at the final stasis of death), he remarked that he was entering the harbour of Schopenhauer's philosophy (*SE* XVIII, 50). Thus Freud re-established a connection with the Romantic philosophy of nature which nineteenth-century positivism had sought to discard. For Schopenhauer's blind will was reformulated as the unconscious by Eduard von Hartmann (1842–1906), author of *Philosophie des Unbewußten* (1869; *Philosophy of the unconscious*), whose work forms a bridge between Romantic 'Naturphilosophie' and psychoanalytic theory. Thomas Mann was right, therefore, in calling Freud 'a true son of the century of Schopenhauer

and Ibsen' and in recognising Freud's theory of the unconscious as
a translation of Schopenhauer's metaphysics into psychological terms
(M XI, 484, 487).

These powerful and mostly unconscious instincts constantly threaten
Freud's 'self' ('das Ich'; the 'ego' in the *Standard Edition*). Freud compares
the self to 'a man on horseback, who has to hold in check the superior
strength of the horse' (*SE* XIX, 25). Here we recognise an ancient image,
used by Plato in the *Phaedrus*, of reason as the charioteer guiding two
horses. Schopenhauer varies the metaphor by making the self an uneasy
horseman:

Denn was, für ein unbändiges Roß, Zügel und Gebiß ist, das ist für den Willen
im Menschen der Intellekt: an diesem Zügel muß er gelenkt werden, mit-
telst Belehrung, Ermahnung, Bildung u.s.w.; da er an sich selbst ein so wilder
ungestümer Drang ist, wie die Kraft, die im herabstürzenden Wasserfall erscheint, – ja, wie wir wissen, im tiefsten Grunde, identisch mit dieser. (S III, 238)

For the intellect is for the will in man that which reins and bit are for a head-
strong horse: it must be guided by these reins, through instruction, admonition,
education, etc.; since it is in itself a wild, tempestuous urge, like the force that
is manifest in the plunging waterfall – indeed, as we know, basically identical
with it.

Freud's enfeebled self, no longer master in its own house, can
strengthen itself by memory. Philip Rieff, one of Freud's most thoughtful
interpreters, remarks: 'By deepening it [memory] to include the unconscious, he made memory more of a clue to the human condition than it
had been since Plato's theory of anamnesis.'[41] Freud and his early associate Josef Breuer (1842–1925) discovered that hysterical patients could
be cured of their afflictions by remembering the event that had initiated their hysteria. Hysterics suffered mainly from reminiscences, which
had to be restored in order to free them from the past. The psychoanalytic method, or 'talking cure', consisted in allowing the patient to
recover memories, often insignificant in themselves, from which a narrative could be constructed that would make explicit their unconscious
motives. Their earlier history, especially that of childhood, turned out to
supply the template on which their present relationships were based. An
analogy suggests itself with the ethical importance of memory in the work
of Schnitzler and Hofmannsthal. Memory unifies the self, freeing it from
helpless confinement in the present, giving it a meaningful connection
with its past.

At the same time, psychoanalysis acknowledges the enormous power of the past. And psychoanalytic inquiry reveals a striking similarity with the analytic structure of naturalist drama. Typically, an outsider – Werle in *The wild duck*, Loth in *Vor Sonnenaufgang* – enters a family circle and gradually unearths shameful secrets from the family's past. As corruption and weakness in the Ekdal family, alcoholism and sexual transgression among the Krauses, are disclosed, the family idyll is revealed as a battleground of powerful wills, and the inquiries of the outsider precipitate the catastrophe. The study of the Bauer family in one of Freud's case histories, *Bruchstück einer Hysterie-Analyse* (1905; *Fragment of an analysis of a case of hysteria*), has often been compared to a carefully plotted piece of prose fiction.[42]

In the powerful will that Freud acknowledged as the driving force behind his inquiries, we can recognise the will to power that Nietzsche discerned at work even, or especially, in apparently 'pure' research. Although scholarly research might mean renouncing material rewards, it could give the satisfaction of exercising the will to power on oneself. Freud's psychoanalysis was an inquiry as well as a therapy. It was free from moral judgements. It rejected all comforting illusions about human goodness or freedom. Freud's pessimism becomes most overt in his late works, especially *Das Unbehagen in der Kultur* (1930; *Civilisation and its discontents*). Here civilisation is depicted as a tragic process. To control his drives and be able to live with his fellow humans, man creates an agency within himself, the super-ego or conscience, that places him under a discipline more severe than any merely external constraint would be. The most highly civilised people have the most active consciences and are therefore the most unhappy. Freud's essay provides the grim satisfaction of understanding this state of affairs. He sees no way of changing it. Such teeth-gritting honesty can be motivated only by a Nietzschean intellectual will to power. Similarly, the determined honesty that runs through Schnitzler's writings, including his diaries and autobiography, did not improve his conduct, as he repeatedly notes: 'that I have never tried to deceive myself about the nature of my feelings or about the character of the people close to me has saved me neither from suffering wrong nor from doing wrong.'[43]

Here we recognise the embattled self as scientific and psychological inquirer. The truth it uncovers in Freud's work is even harsher. From *Die Traumdeutung* (1900; *The interpretation of dreams*) onwards, Freud maintains that the route to adulthood leads through the Oedipus complex of hatred for one's father and desire for one's mother. To become a man – that is, to become like one's father – every man must oppose and overcome his father, paying in guilt the price of maturity. In other words, the self must transgress the moral framework of his upbringing in order to attain adulthood. One may wonder whether the 'Oedipus complex' is a self-aggrandising masculine myth, a generalisation from Freud's personal myth of the hero.[44] Freud, however, retains the idea and extends it into human prehistory in *Totem und Tabu* (1911; *Totem and taboo*), arguing that all civilisation is founded on the killing of the primal father, 'this memorable and criminal deed, which was the beginning of so many things – of social organisation, of moral restrictions and of religion' (*SE* XIII, 142). Thus the long-standing German cultural motif of the necessary crime is made an essential element of human history and of individual development. The transgression of frameworks is no longer reserved for the solitary hero or the Nietzschean 'Übermensch'. It is made democratically available as a stage in the life of every man.

Since Freud develops the concept of the embattled self, he goes less far than many contemporaries in exploring the unconscious self. For Freud the unconscious is to be controlled, tamed, brought under the scrutiny of the conscious self: 'Wo Es war, soll Ich werden' ('Where id was, there ego shall be' (*SE* XXII, 80). Unlike such heretics as Jung, Freud was reluctant to consider the unconscious as a valuable reservoir of power or wisdom. This reluctance is particularly apparent in his treatment of dreams. In interpreting dreams as multiply coded imaginary fulfilments of unacknowledged, normally erotic desires, Freud was extending the territory claimed by positivist science and opposing earlier, especially Romantic notions that dreams might convey truths from the unconscious or from outside the self. Such notions, Freud thinks, are mere survivals of religious illusion: 'The high esteem in which dream-life is held by some schools of philosophy (by the followers of Schelling, for instance) is clearly an echo of the divine nature of dreams which was undisputed in antiquity' (*SE* IV, 5). Thus *Die Traumdeutung* may be seen as part of Freud's lifelong campaign against religion.

The literary use of dreams found more support from Schopenhauer and Nietzsche. Schopenhauer explains the suspension of time and space in dreams and prophetic clairvoyance as possible within Kantian idealism, since 'the objective world is a mere phenomenon of the brain' (S V, 263). Freud, unable to accept this explanation, draws on Schopenhauer to exemplify the theory that in dreams time, space and causality are suspended, but ascribes their suspension to the peculiar laws of the unconscious. Nietzsche suggests that dreams give us access to primitive modes of thought, maintaining that the faulty logic in dreams is a survival of the bad reasoning used by primitive man: 'the dream brings us back to remote states of human culture and supplies us with a means of understanding them better' (N I, 455). These arguments licensed novelists to give their dreaming heroes access to the prehistory of mankind. Thus in the novel *Der Tod Georgs* (1900; *The death of Georg*) by Richard Beer-Hofmann (1866–1945) the protagonist dreams about the ceremonies at the temple of Hierapolis in Syria, which culminate in a sexual orgy, and in *Der Tod in Venedig* Aschenbach's intensely vivid dream conjures up a Dionysiac procession and a sexual orgy from archaic Greece. In *Der Zauberberg* Hans Castorp, lost in the snow, has a vision of the ancient Mediterranean and then of hideous rites in a temple. He concludes: 'The great soul, of which you are a particle, must sometimes dream through you, in your manner, about dreams that it always secretly dreams of – its youth, its hope, its happiness and peace, and its blood-sacrifice' (M III, 684).

This fascination with dream-life as the place where the individual unconscious stores ancestral residues goes hand in hand with the renewed interest in mysticism at the turn of the century. Past mystical writers were read with enthusiasm. Wilhelm Bölsche republished the mystical aphorisms of Angelus Silesius; Martin Buber (1878–1965) compiled an anthology of mystical testimonies from around the world; Kafka read Meister Eckhart; Hofmannsthal quoted from the Persian Sufi mystic Jalal al-Din Rumi (H VIII, 344). However, the term mysticism was used loosely to signify any kind of preternatural experience. Its popularity indicates dissatisfaction with the narrow conception of reality held by positivistic science, rather than any authentic return to the mysticism of earlier centuries.

Traditionally, mystical experience has been understood in Christianity and Islam as the union of the soul with God through the divine love. It is an emotional but also a cognitive experience. In it, the self retains its integrity even though everything inessential in it is dissolved by contact with the divine. And the experience, though brief, leaves the self strengthened in inner peace, charity and humility. Modern mysticism, however, corresponds to post-Schleiermacher interpretations of Christianity in emptying out the cognitive content and trying to fill the gap with emotion. Thus Buber, inspired by Nietzsche's account of Dionysiac intoxication in *Die Geburt der Tragödie*, claims that the essence of mysticism is the feeling of ecstasy. This is not cognition ('Erkenntnis') but an experience ('Erlebnis'). To suppose that it is an experience of God is mere projection.[45] Having absorbed 'Lebensphilosophie', Buber was applying its concept of 'Erlebnis' to mysticism. One may reply, however, that mystical experience without cognition is like feeling enthusiastic without enthusiasm about anything in particular: however intense the experience, it risks being isolated from the rest of one's life and lacking any meaning. Moreover, Buber implausibly assumes that all mysticism is of the same kind, ignoring crucial differences in the religious traditions of humanity.

Although modern mysticism is sometimes a watered-down derivative of earlier theistic mysticism, it can often be assigned to one of two other types of mysticism, as distinguished by R. C. Zaehner.[46] There is, first, the experience in which the phenomenal world is recognised as unreal by contrast with the soul, which realises that it is one with the Absolute. This experience is recorded and explored in the great Hindu texts containing the dictum 'tat tvam asi', 'that art thou', which the amateur Indologist Schopenhauer transmitted to a wide readership. Second, there is the experience in which one feels oneself to be one with the phenomenal world. Here the phenomenal world is recognised as real, and as not distinct from the self. This is not pantheism, since God is not invoked; it is rather, as Zaehner says, panenhenism or 'one-and-all-ism'. Mystical doctrines inspired by monism fit this type. They claim that the self can experience union with the totality of things, of life, or the infinite. Karl Joël (1864–1934) in his much-read *Seele und Welt* (1912; *Soul and world*) describes mystical experience by contrast to the transient sensual world as a feeling in ourselves of the boundless stream of life, a community with near and far, and a oneness with all being – as if infinite life were within.[47] Such an experience seems to be evoked in the quasi-mystical moments in *Buddenbrooks* when the presence of the sea suggests the loss of normal boundaries, as when Hanno spends his holidays at the seaside: 'a mild narcosis ['Betäubung'], in which consciousness of time and space and everything limited was blissfully swallowed up' (M I, 632). Another version occurs in Hofmannsthal's famous Chandos Letter, in which the imaginary English nobleman describes how his depression is interrupted only by moments of illumination in which an ordinary object – a harrow, a watering-can, a dog lying in the sun – seems filled with 'a surging flood of higher life' (H x, 467). In 1913 Rilke recorded a strange experience in the garden of Duino Castle in which he felt he had reached 'the other side of nature': all the objects around him 'seemed more distant and somehow more true', and a periwinkle flower seemed full of inexhaustible meaning (R IV, 667, 668).

These special moments in which trivial objects become transfigured were called by James Joyce 'epiphanies', a useful term adopted by modern critics.[48]

Some of these experiences seem vulnerable to reductive analysis. Freud explained the 'oceanic feeling', which his friend Romain Rolland claimed as the basis of religion, by interpreting it as a regression to early childhood: the condition of an infant at the breast, unable to distinguish his own ego from the external sensations flowing in upon him (*SE* XXI, 66–7). Mann's 'narcosis', symbolised by the ocean, invites this explanation. Hofmannsthal's Lord Chandos, however, seems as authentic a mystic as Proust. His epiphanies amid mundane life resemble the commonplace experiences in Proust – tasting the madeleine, treading on uneven paving-stones, glimpsing the twin steeples of Martinville – which escape from the order of time and provide the narrator not only with preternatural happiness but with the hidden order of his life.

However, one can distinguish other ideas and phenomena which were less plausibly claimed to be mystical. For example, mysticism was adduced to supply the cognitive deficiencies of positivist science. While positivism presupposed a punctual self, set apart from the world and able to represent the world adequately in language, Mauthner's critique argued that any linguistic representation of the world was a mere fiction, for reality, a flux of impressions and sensations, eluded any attempt to define it through language. Hence Gustav Landauer (1870–1919) maintained in *Skepsis und Mystik* (1901; *Scepticism and mysticism*) that we could be at one with the world, not through intellectual constructs, but through mystical contemplation. Robert Musil (1880–1942) in his early novel *Die Verwirrungen des Zöglings Törleß* (1906; *The confusions of the pupil Törless*) explored the intellectual enigma posed by imaginary numbers like the square root of minus one – logical fictions on which the apparently objective structure of mathematics is based.

Other writers claim a mystical sense of unity with the human group (often called 'the race') to which they belong. Thus Chamberlain sought 'race' by looking 'into the depths of the soul'.[49] Aware that 'race' was a dubious concept, he tried to protect it against critical scrutiny by making it a matter of immediate and intuitive awareness. Buber, after his studies of mysticism, told Zionist audiences that their Jewishness consisted in a profound, mystical union with all previous generations, located in the blood, and the mystical search for unity was part of the Jewish psyche, shown especially in messianism and its reduced version, socialism. Here 'mysticism' is being used to give an irrational authority to political ideologies.

If traditional mysticism strengthens and integrates the self, we may see its negative counterpart in the dissolution of the self that can occur on the verge of insanity. William James (1842–1910) maintains that 'in delusional insanity, paranoia, as they sometimes call it, we may have a *diabolical* mysticism, a sort of religious mysticism turned upside down'.[50] This provides an approach to those modernist poets who have experimented with drugs to heighten their consciousness and whose poetry expresses their psychic conflicts within a religious context, signalled by blasphemy and despair rather than faith. The obvious examples are Baudelaire, Rimbaud and their Austrian devotee Georg Trakl. Trakl's short life, with his drug addiction and his possible incestuous relationship with his sister, and his opaque, haunting poetry have invited the attention of psychoanalysts. The most persuasive study, *Das Gedicht als Sühne* (1985) by Günther Kleefeld, argues that the emotional frigidity of Trakl's mother gave him a basic attitude of insecurity and mistrust towards the world. Such a child will be unable to work through and overcome its destructive urges and paranoid terrors. Unable to grow out of primary narcissism, it remains fixated on this phase, and may later seek to regain the 'oceanic feeling' of maternal absorption through drugs; Trakl was taking drugs by the age of fifteen. Trakl's ideal self, the 'beautiful angel' evoked in a letter, was too remote to save him from guilt and terror.[51] In his poetry, images from religion are often linked with sex and sadism. Sexual murder is a recurring theme, represented by the demonic figure of Bluebeard. When the ideal self, like Kaspar Hauser, (St) Sebastian, or the 'gentle orphan' of 'De Profundis', is exposed to violence, the poems hint that the violence stems from another part of the self: the 'Ich', an outcast associated with darkness, silence and cold metal. In 'De Profundis' this 'Ich' is punished by being abandoned like the corpse of his victim. Thus the poem also suggests the ultimate identity of murderer and victim as two aspects of the self, linked in a sado-masochistic fantasy. As in all forms of addiction, the self finds its aspirations towards purity foiled by the stronger, appetitive will that keeps it imprisoned in its nightmarish nether world. The unattainable unity of the self is often imagined as androgyny; the redemptive figure of the 'she-youth' ('Jünglingin') would both acknowledge and transcend the incestuous urges that gave rise to it.

Another form of dispersal of the self can be found in the prose and poetry of Georg Heym (1887–1912), who also admired Rimbaud.

His powerful short story *Der Irre* (1911; *The madman*) explores dissociation by entering into the mind of a sex-murderer who, while throttling his victim, has fantasies of dream-like freedom, riding through the ocean on a fish. Heym's poetic self is both weak and strong. It lacks boundaries, projecting itself into the world, yet it consists of violent destructive energy. His poetry is largely impersonal. In its dehumanised cityscapes, people appear only as corpuscles flowing helplessly through the city's blood-stream, or as a mass waiting to be crushed. The city and its natural and supernatural surroundings are full of furies. Destructive energy is channelled into the Flying Dutchman, riotous demons or a barbaric war-god, and controlled only by the strangely rigid iambic pentameter that Heym predominantly employs. The poetry enacts the dissociation with which Heym empathised so compellingly in his fiction.

All the currents discussed here converge in the work of Hofmannsthal, whose most daring exploration of psychic fragmentation and mystical experience occurs in his unfinished novel *Andreas oder die Vereinigten* (1932; *Andreas, or the unified ones*). Hofmannsthal began it in 1907 and wrote the longest surviving portion in 1912. The psychology of the hero, an immature, sexually troubled 22-year-old, sent by his parents on an educational journey from Vienna to Venice in 1778, comes partly from the account given by William James of the melancholy 'sick soul', often a divided character who seeks unification. Andreas encounters a pious and a playful woman; from Hofmannsthal's notes, it appears that they are one and the same person, a case of multiple personality, based on his reading of Morton Prince's real-life case-history, *The dissociation of a personality* (1906). Prince tells how his Boston patient Miss Beauchamp, a sedate and self-controlled young woman, was tormented by a separate self, the lively 'Sally', who would play such tricks as getting drunk so that Miss Beauchamp should have a hangover. In Hofmannsthal's novel, the playful, erotically active Mariquita is an unacknowledged portion of the personality of the serious Maria, whose emotional life has been damaged by a brutal husband. The two are connected by a little dog which symbolises the inarticulate physical basis of their shared humanity. Had the novel been continued, Andreas would have had such strange experiences as getting into bed with Mariquita and later waking up to see Maria rushing away. He would eventually have restored her to unity, and in doing so have unified his own divided personality.

Much of the narrative is told retrospectively through Andreas's memories, which guarantee the ultimate integrity of the self. One strand of his personality, the desire for purification through love, is projected onto the farm-girl Romana whom he met on his journey; but an opposed, sadistic strand is externalised in his evil servant Gotthilff. His sense of being implicated in Gotthilff's crimes leads to a despondent feeling of identification with a dog that Gotthilff has poisoned, and later to a triumphant identification with a hovering eagle. James remarks that the divided self may be unified through mystical experience.[52] Andreas's two mystical experiences suggest a manic-depressive character. His guilty identification with the dead dog belongs to the depressive stage. His identification with the eagle makes him feel that his self is expanded, that he surveys the world, as in many recorded experiences of nature mysticism. A further implication is that, in identifying with a bird of prey, Andreas accepts the evil impulse within himself as part of the amoral totality of life. These two experiences, however, show that he is still unstable, veering between depression and mania; genuine unification will come only through the encounter with another person. Like Trakl's poetry, Hofmannsthal's psychological study, extraordinary in its vivid immediacy and economical lyricism, points beyond psychology to spiritual extremes of good and evil.

THE BODY AND THE SENSES

Among the various versions of the self that we have been considering, the embattled self stands aloof from the world, but the minimal self and the unconscious self both offer new ways of conceiving the relation between the self and the world. If my self is just one particle in the universal flux, or if it is an outcropping from my unconscious, then I am already in the world, though my place there may be apparent only to mystical insight.

But there is a much more obvious way in which I am in the world: through my body and my senses. My body is not simply a vessel in which my self travels through the world. As Nietzsche's Zarathustra says, I am my body: 'Behind your thoughts and feelings, my brother, stands a mighty ruler, an unknown sage, called the self [*Selbst*]. He dwells in your body, he is your body' (N II, 300). In Hofmannsthal's 'Gespräch über Gedichte' (1903; 'Dialogue on poetry'), our emotions are said to be so intimately linked to our sensations that our real existence is to be sought outside us, in the surrounding world. 'A certain movement with which you jump down from a high carriage; a sultry, starless summer night; the smell of damp stones in a hallway; the feeling of icy water splashing over your hands from a well: your entire inner possession is attached to a couple of thousand earthly things like that . . . If we want to find ourselves, we must not descend into our interiors; it is outside that we are to be found, outside' (H x, 497). For Hofmannsthal and many contemporaries, impressionism, with its focus on sensations, led to the recovery of bodily experience.

Impressionism means learning to see. *Wie ich es sehe* (1896; *How I see it*) by Peter Altenberg (pseudonym of Richard Engländer, 1859–1919) contains seemingly casual verbal sketches (later renamed 'studies' in another metaphor from painting) which evoke the visual world of Vienna through the seasons. In Rilke's novel *Die Aufzeichnungen des Malte Laurids Brigge* (1910), the protagonist is 'learning to see'. His efforts are driven by an existential need: initially reacting with horror and disgust to the squalor of modern Paris, he disciplines his feelings by describing urban scenes in painterly terms. Here Rilke was inspired by Cézanne, whom he admired for endowing ordinary objects with a higher reality. Writing to his wife in October 1907 about the Cézanne exhibition in the Salle d'Automne, Rilke praises 'this thick padded blue of his, his red and his shadowless green and the reddish swarm of his wine bottles', and stresses what commonplace objects he paints: 'the apples are all cooking apples, and the wine bottles belong in round shapeless old coat pockets.'[53]

But Rilke's appreciation of the world around our bodies does not rely only on sight. He and his contemporaries also attend to those undervalued senses of taste and smell which German classical aesthetics excluded from consideration altogether. Consider this sentence from Beer-Hofmann: 'A lighted window shimmered through the twigs of the tall lime-trees in the garden, and from the dark masses of the mountains the wind brought the scent of new-mown hay'.[54] Beginning with sight, the sentence moves on to make objects visually indistinct and give all the more prominence to scent ('Duft'). Richard von Schaukal (1874–1942) observes flowers 'in the earthy scent of soil' ('im erdgen Bodenduft').[55] Trakl writes: 'the scent of resedas wanders through the sick window' ('Resedenduft durchs kranke Fenster irrt').[56] In Hofmannsthal's enigmatic 'Lebenslied' ('Song of life'), the affirmation of life is expressed through the grand gesture of pouring costly ointment over animals.[57]

The sense of smell has been particularly problematic for aesthetics. As the sense which is more highly developed in animals than ourselves, it has often seemed an undignified reminder of our animal nature. Smell is also an element in sexual experience, as Rilke reminds us in 'Persisches Heliotrop' ('Persian heliotrope'), where the flowers please the beloved by pervading the stillness with a scent of vanilla and cinnamon. At the end of Musil's *Törleß* we are told that Törless 'examined the faintly perfumed smell that rose from his mother's waist';[58] the word 'smell' ('Geruch') instead of 'scent' ('Duft') conveys the boy's awareness of his mother's body and her sexuality. In Kafka, smell acquires metaphysical overtones. Waiting in the courtyard for the Castle official Klamm, K. climbs into Klamm's coach and sniffs his cognac, which gives off a 'sweet and flattering' aroma; but when he tastes it, it changes 'from something that was hardly more than the bearer of sweet scent ['Träger süßen Duftes'] into a drink fit only for coachmen'.[59] This passage has been read, perhaps rightly, as a sign of Kafka's Manichaean leanings: spiritual things can only be degraded by assuming material form.[60]

If my relation to the world is essentially through my body, then it may be felt most intensely in sexual contact with another body. Nietzsche's account of Dionysiac ecstasy includes unbridled sexuality. But while Nietzsche calls such orgiastic experience a 'witches' brew' (N I, 27), later writers affirmed it with fewer reservations. In a poem by Ernst Stadler (1883–1914) the lyric self, addressing a woman, assimilates sex to natural processes of death and renewal, with woman as the fruitful earth:

> In deine Erde
> > will ich meine irre Glut vergraben und
> Sehnsüchtig blühend
> > über deinem Leibe auferstehn.[61]

> In your earth
> I will bury my frenzied ardour and
> yearningly blossoming
> be reborn over your body.

Stadler's word 'auferstehn' illustrates the contemporary desire to claim religious dignity for sex, or to reduce religious events to sexual processes. Hauptmann in *Der Ketzer von Soana* (1918; *The heretic of Soana*) tells how a young priest discovers in erotic contact with a peasant girl a new understanding of his own religion, an overwhelming sympathy with all creation, and a possible synthesis with pagan phallus-worship. In Rilke's notorious phallic poems of 1915, an erection becomes 'the god's image', a woman's lap becomes 'the counter-Heaven' ('Gegen-Himmel', R II, 136). In *Der Brief des jungen Arbeiters* (1922; *Letter from the young workman*) Rilke attacks Christianity for devaluing earthly life and particularly sex; and in a contemporaneous letter he wishes that sexual sensations could be placed 'under the protection of a phallic deity, who will perhaps need to be the *first* when a crowd of gods again bursts in upon humanity, after such long absence'.[62]

The emphasis on the phallus confirms that Stadler, Rilke and Hauptmann were mainly concerned with male sexuality. Female sexuality, however, found a gifted spokeswoman in Else Lasker-Schüler (1869–1945). Tenderness coexists with physical passion and sensuous richness in poems like 'Mein Liebeslied' (1910; 'My love-song'):

> Auf deinen Wangen liegen
> Goldene Tauben.
>
> Aber dein Herz ist ein Wirbelwind,
> Dein Blut rauscht, wie mein Blut –
>
> Süß
> An Himbeersträuchern vorbei.[63]
>
> On your cheeks lie
> golden doves.
>
> But your heart is a tornado,
> your blood surges, like my blood –
>
> sweetly
> past raspberry-bushes.

Lasker-Schüler's love poetry grows in emotional complexity, however, when it acknowledges the childish fear of loneliness and the adult fear of death that underlie her search for love. Thus the love poem 'Versöhnung' ('Reconciliation') includes the line: 'If we cuddle each other, we won't die' ('Wenn wir uns herzen, sterben wir nicht').[64]

Lasker-Schüler also typifies modernist writers by exploring complex gender identities. Like Trakl, she has a private myth of androgyny, represented by the sexually ambiguous figure of Tino of Baghdad. Subtle notions of sex and gender were being explored by psychologists and by practitioners of the new discipline of sexology. Both Freud and Weininger proposed that human beings were essentially bisexual. Freud argues that each male or female bears traces of the anatomy of the opposite sex, suggesting that 'an originally bisexual physical disposition has, in the course of evolution, become modified into a unisexual one, leaving behind only a few traces of the sex that has become atrophied' (*SE* VII, 141). He

suggests that before puberty, the manifestations of libido are of a masculine character in both girls and boys, and that a feminine sexual identity
is acquired only after puberty. Although Freud's readiness to interpret
femininity as a subdivision of masculinity seems remarkable, such arguments did help to question the strict division between 'male' and 'female'
and open up a space for more ambiguous gender identities.

During this period male homosexuality finds expression in literature. It
appears boldly in Wedekind's *Frühlings Erwachen* and Mann's *Tod in Venedig*,
and covertly in the male–male relationships depicted elsewhere in Mann
(*Tonio Kröger*), in Kafka (the relationship between Karl Rossmann and the
Stoker in the first chapter of *Der Verschollene* (1911–14; *Missing without trace*),
in Hofmannsthal (Pierre and Jaffier in *Das gerettete Venedig* (1904; *Venice
preserved*); Andreas and Gotthilff in *Andreas*), in the violence and sodomy
practised by the schoolboys in Musil's *Törleß*, and later in Brecht's *Baal*
(1918).

The most daring representation of female homosexuality is the Gräfin
Geschwitz, Lulu's devoted and self-sacrificing adorer, in Wedekind's *Die
Büchse der Pandora*. Wedekind described her as the principal tragic fig-
ure of the play, though also as enduring the curse of unnaturalness.
Women writers, even those whose feminism had been stimulated by
reading Nietzsche, were more cautious in their portrayal of lesbianism.
Gabriele Reuter (1859–1941), who visited the insane Nietzsche in 1895,
portrayed emotional attachment to another woman in her novel *Aus guter
Familie* (1895; *From a good family*), but only as a transient phase, while the
Nietzsche-inspired lesbian Elisabeth Dauthendey (1854–1943) suggested
in her essays *Vom neuen Weibe und seiner Liebe. Ein Buch für reife Geister* (1900;
On the new woman and her love. A book for mature spirits) that such attachments
should not be degraded by physical contact.

THE LANGUAGE OF THE SENSES

To find words for the experience of the embodied self amid a world of
sensuously fascinating objects, writers had to escape from an inherited
language heavy with literary reminiscences and find a new, economical language. Hofmannsthal's Lord Chandos eloquently expresses
his yearning to learn 'a language in which the mute things speak to me'
(H VII, 472).

The renewal of poetic language was the achievement especially of
Hofmannsthal and Rilke. Though rich in poetic echoes, Hofmannsthal's
early poetry also admits bodily experience by its use of inconspicuous,

'unpoetic' words like 'schwer', 'leicht', 'dumpf' ('heavy', 'light', 'dull') to
express states of the body, as in 'Manche freilich . . .':

> Manche liegen immer mit schweren Gliedern
> Bei den Wurzeln des verworrenen Lebens
>
> (H 1, 26)
>
> Many lie forever with heavy limbs
> at the roots of tangled life.

Here the slow, dragging verse-movement corresponds to the paralysing
'heaviness' in the limbs; what might seem an abstruse allegory featuring
a tree of life is brought home directly to our senses. Rilke, on the other
hand, concentrated on conveying the specific and separate existence of
objects, as Cézanne did in painting and Rodin in sculpture. 'The thing
is distinct', he wrote to Lou Andreas-Salomé, 'the art-thing ['das Kunst-
Ding'] must be yet more distinct; . . . the model *seems*, the art-thing *is*.'[65]
But of course the heightened reality that Rilke wanted to disclose in
objects is something conferred on them by the act of perception, and
Rilke's so called 'thing-poems' ('Dinggedichte') in fact convey how they
are perceived and how, far from being discrete objects, they are rendered
meaningful by human associations. Thus 'Der Ball' ('The ball') performs
the anthropocentric gesture of personifying its object in order to focus our
attention both on the ball itself and on the visual and tactile sensations
with which we experience it:

> Du Runder, der das Warme aus zwei Händen
> im Fliegen, oben, fortgiebt, sorglos wie
> sein Eigenes; . . .   (K 1, 583)
>
> You round thing, that passes on the warmth from two hands
> in your flight, aloft, as carelessly as though it were
> your own; . . .

It has been argued that this poetic recreation of objects and the process
of perception corresponds to the phenomenological inquiries being
undertaken at the same time by Husserl.[66] And it is an intriguing fact
that Hofmannsthal met Husserl in 1906 and soon afterwards received
from him a letter explaining the phenomenological method:

Sie fordert eine von der 'natürlichen' wesentlich abweichende Stellungnahme
zu aller Objectivität, die nahe verwandt ist derjenigen Stellung u. Haltung, in
die uns Ihre Kunst als eine *rein ästhetische* hinsichtlich der dargestellten Objekte
und der ganzen Umwelt versetzt. Die Anschauung eines *rein* ästhetischen

Kunstwerkes vollzieht sich in strenger Ausschaltung jeder existenzialen Stellungnahme des Intellects und jeder Stellungnahme des Gefühls u. Willens, die solch eine existenziale Stellungnahme voraussetzt.[67]

It requires an attitude to all objective entities that differs entirely from the 'natural' one. Such an attitude is closely related to the stance and position in which your art, as a purely aesthetic activity, places us vis-à-vis the objects represented and the entire surrounding world. The contemplation of a purely aesthetic work of art occurs to the strict exclusion of any existential attitude of the intellect and any attitude of the feeling and the will which presupposes such an existential attitude.

Husserl's phenomenological reduction consists in bracketing out the actual existence of objects and focusing solely on what is present to consciousness. This *epochè* or 'Wesensschau' is supposed to elucidate the structure of consciousness by concentrating on essences. He claims that its artificially narrow focus resembles that of aesthetic contemplation.

There is something like phenomenological reduction when Hofmannsthal and Rilke focus, for example, on colours in themselves, as Hofmannsthal does in the *Briefe des Zurückgekehrten* (1907; *Letters from a homecomer*) and Rilke in the poem 'Blaue Hortensie' ('Blue hortensia'). They differ from Husserl, however, in that they reproduce those subjective perceptions that Husserl wanted to escape from because of their incompleteness; they do not seek a further essence behind the object perceived. If they analyse experience into its phenomenal constituents, they do so in order to put it together again. Moreover, Husserl, a devout Lutheran, betrays his Protestant asceticism in his severely Kantian view of art: he believes that art invites disinterested contemplation. Just this asceticism, however, was devastatingly analysed by Nietzsche in the third essay of *Zur Genealogie der Moral*. There Nietzsche juxtaposes Kant's famous principle with Stendhal's definition of beauty as 'une promesse de bonheur', a promise of happiness (N II, 845–6). The aesthetic which Hofmannsthal and Rilke are actually practising is Stendhalian rather than Kantian. In abstracting from empirical reality, their aim is to enrich the self by restoring more fully the pleasurable, sensuous experience of the world.

In the masterpieces of high modernism we find a recurrent narrative appropriate to the embodied self. For the self, as it becomes conscious of its embodied condition, realises also that its body is constantly aging and decaying, and that it must die. The world around it, however satisfying, is transient, and it too is transient. But rather than moving people to reject the world, like Schopenhauer, this moral *anagnorisis* is the starting-point for personal humility, for a civilised and forbearing relation to others, and for an appreciation of the goods of this world that is sharpened by their transience.

The great works of the early 1920s all brood on death. In the Berghof sanatorium to which Thomas Mann takes the ordinary, unreflective protagonist of *Der Zauberberg*, death is an omnipresent secret. The patients know, but do not admit, that many of them will never be cured. As custodian of the Berghof gramophone, Hans Castorp comes to understand that Romantic music, even so innocuous a piece as Schubert's 'Lindenbaum' ('Lime-tree'), expresses a morbid longing for death. Kafka's snow-covered landscape, with its preternaturally long winter nights and its population of villagers in abject awe of Castle officials, suggests a strange limbo between life and death. Rilke's *Duineser Elegien*, above all, are a sustained meditation on how in the midst of life we are in death. The opening Elegy dwells on our precarious attachment to the world and on the fate of those who have died young and whose presence we can still sense; it intimates that the experience of the dead, as they gradually detach themselves from life, is not utterly different from that of the living, who cannot feel fully at home in the world. Rilke touches grimly on the death of children; he presents city acrobats achieving brief triumphs before the imaginary milliner 'Madame Lamort'; and he contrasts human life, bounded and constrained by the prospect of death, with the assurance of animals who do not live in time and do not know that they will die.

The confrontation with death is presented in two ways: as an unusual experience that makes one revise one's life; or in an elaborate allegorical manner. For Hans Castorp, the crucial episode is his visit to the X-ray laboratory where he is allowed to see the interior of his own hand and feels that he is looking into his own grave, with the future processes of decomposition already marked out. For the first time in his life, Hans realises that he will die (M III, 306). The crucial experience for Hofmannsthal's Hans Karl turns out to have been a symbolic death, when he was briefly buried alive by an explosion in the war and had a vision of the pattern of his life, including the woman destined to be his wife. His intimacy with death enables him to continue life through marriage. And despite his humorously inept demeanour, it gives him a depth of character that attracts his future wife Helene and contrasts decisively with the purposeful shallowness of his embattled rival, the German Neuhoff, who harangues Helene about the power of his will.

Allegory appears in the 'Schnee' chapter of *Der Zauberberg*, where Hans, lost in the snow, has a vision of athletic 'Children of the Sun' and of a temple where hags are devouring a golden-haired child. The strange associations of these images distract one from the simple antithesis of life and death which they are apparently intended to embody. However, the episode has a formal neatness in relativising both the vapid humanism of Settembrini, who calls death a 'sacred condition of life' (M III, 280), and the gloomy dogmatism of the Jesuit Naphta. Rilke similarly resorts to allegory after the gradual affirmation of earthly, embodied existence. The Tenth Elegy shows us an imagined landscape of death and suffering, modelled on Egypt and full of whimsical personifications; but it is perhaps more persuasive when it expresses the affirmation of earthly life in the images of downward-pointing catkins and spring rain falling on dark soil. The images point, not upwards towards an unbelievable transcendence, but downwards towards the familiar natural world. Rilke's acceptance of death makes possible a Nietzschean affirmation of life. Addressing the earth in the spirit of Zarathustra's injunction, 'Remain true to the earth!', Rilke concludes: 'You were always right, and your holy invention / Is familiar death' (R II, 229).

The lyric self of the *Elegien*, however, is solitary. To see how the awareness of death affects the movement of the self in moral space, we need to look at Kafka and Hofmannsthal. *Das Schloß* is almost a social novel: the outsider K. seeks to find a footing within the village community by marriage to Frieda, but their relationship founders on the self-centredness of K.'s embattled self and on his obsession with the Castle. Only after Frieda, in a poignant scene, has ended their relationship, does K. lose his pugnacity in the death-like sleep that overtakes him in the presence of a Castle official. In Hofmannsthal's major works, conversely, confrontation with death – Andreas's mystical identification with the dead dog, Hans Karl's burial in the war – precedes a successful object-choice, and that in turn makes possible what Hofmannsthal called the 'allomatic process' in which two selves mutually transform each other in a lasting relationship. In his self-analytical jottings *Ad me ipsum* (1916) Hofmannsthal wrote: 'Attachment to the world through the attachment of two individuals' (H X, 607). Such attachment is represented in his fables and comedies of marriage: the highly symbolic *Frau ohne Schatten* (*Woman without a shadow*, completed 1915), *Der Schwierige* (1919; *The difficult man*) and *Arabella* (1928). Divided selves, such as Andreas and Hans Karl, are unified through the combination of projection and recognition (symbolised by mirrors) in which they choose a partner. By doing so they avoid the passivity of the

minimal self and the false heroics of the embattled self and are admitted
to the wider world of society.

NOTES

1 Letter to Hermann Pongs, 21 October 1924, quoted in August Stahl,
  ' "ein paar Seiten Schopenhauer" – Überlegungen zu Rilkes Schopenhauer-
  Lektüre und deren Folgen', *Schopenhauer-Jahrbuch* 69 (1988), 569–82; 70 (1989),
  174–88 (p. 572).
2 Brod, *Über Franz Kafka* (Frankfurt: Fischer, 1966), p. 268.
3 See Malte Herwig, 'The unwitting muse: Jakob von Uexküll's theory
  of Umwelt and twentieth-century literature', *Semiotica* 134 (2001), 553–
  92.
4 Theodor Fontane, *Briefe*, ed. Otto Drude and Helmuth Nuernberger, 4 vols.
  (Munich: Hanser, 1976–82) vol. IV, p. 284.
5 Contrast Walter Müller-Seidel, *Theodor Fontane: Soziale Romankunst in Deutschland* (Stuttgart: Metzler, 1975), pp. 83–4, 104, with Dieter Borchmeyer,
  'Fontane, Thomas Mann und das "Dreigestirn" Schopenhauer–Wagner–
  Nietzsche', in Eckhard Heftrich et al. (eds.), *Theodor Fontane und Thomas Mann*
  (Frankfurt: Klostermann, 1998), pp. 217–48.
6 T. J. Reed, 'Nietzsche's animals: idea, image and influence', in Malcolm
  Pasley (ed.), *Nietzsche: imagery and thought* (London: Methuen, 1978), pp. 159–
  219 (p. 180).
7 *Darwinismus und Literatur. Naturwissenschaftliche und literarische Intelligenz in
  Österreich, 1859–1914* (Vienna, Cologne and Weimar: Böhlau, 1999),
  pp. 14–17.
8 Quoted in Charles Taylor, *Sources of the self: the making of the modern identity*
  (Cambridge: Cambridge University Press, 1989), p. 770.
9 David Hume, *A treatise of human nature*, ed. L. A. Selby-Bigge and P. H.
  Nidditch (Oxford: Oxford University Press, 1978), p. 252.
10 Johann Gottlieb Fichte, *Die Bestimmung des Menschen* (1800), in *Sämmtliche Werke*,
   ed. J. H. Fichte (Berlin: Veit und Comp., 1845), vol. II, pp. 167–319 (p. 249).
11 Taylor, *Sources of the self*, p. 36.
12 Wolfgang Riedel, *Homo natura. Literarische Anthropologie um 1900* (Berlin and
   New York: de Gruyter, 1996), pp. 53–60.
13 Freud took this scheme from Haeckel: see Lucille B. Ritvo, *Darwin's influence
   on Freud* (New Haven and London: Yale University Press, 1990), pp. 22–30.
14 Quoted in Riedel, *Homo natura*, p. 108.
15 Wilhelm Dilthey, *Der Aufbau der geschichtlichen Welt in den Geisteswissenschaften*
   (Leipzig: Teubner, 1927), p. 132.
16 Wilhelm Bölsche, *Das Liebesleben in der Natur*, 3 vols. (Leipzig: Diederichs,
   1903), vol. I, p. 6.
17 Cf. Dante, *Paradiso*, XXVII, 112–14. On Lucretius and other predecessors, see
   Riedel, *Homo natura*, p. 256.
18 Bölsche, *Liebesleben*, vol. II, pp. 267–8.

19 Andreas-Salomé, *Lebensrückblick*, ed. Ernst Pfeiffer (Zürich: Niehans; Wiesbaden: Insel, 1951), p. 47

20 Quoted in Michler, *Darwinismus und Literatur*, pp. 119–20.

21 Compare John Walker's comments in chapter three, pp. 144f.

22 Schlaf, *Frühling* (Leipzig: Verlag Kreisende Ringe, 1896), p. 84.

23 Hermann Bahr, 'Die neue Psychologie' (1890), in *Zur Überwindung des Naturalismus: Theoretische Schriften 1887–1904*, ed. Gotthart Wunberg (Stuttgart, Berlin, Cologne and Mainz: Kohlhammer, 1968), p. 57.

24 Hume, *Treatise*, p. 252.

25 Ernst Mach, *Die Analyse der Empfindungen und das Verhältniss des Physischen zum Psychischen*, 2nd edn (Jena: Gustav Fischer, 1900), p. 17.

26 Hermann Bahr, 'Impressionismus' (1904), in *Zur Überwindung des Naturalismus*, p. 197.

27 Links are sought in vain by Gotthart Wunberg, *Der frühe Hofmannsthal. Schizophrenie als dichterische Struktur* (Stuttgart, Berlin, Cologne and Mainz: Kohlhammer, 1965), pp. 30–3.

28 Arthur Schnitzler, *Tagebuch 1903–1908*, ed. Peter Michael Braunwarth et al. (Vienna: Verlag der Österreichischen Akademie der Wissenschaften, 1990), p. 89 (28, 29 Sept. 1904).

29 *The works of Walter Pater*, 10 vols. (London: Macmillan, 1910), vol. I, p. 235.

30 Fritz Mauthner, *Beiträge zur Kritik der Sprache*, 3 vols. (Stuttgart: Cotta, 1901–2), vol. I, p. 122.

31 Stefan George, *Werke*, 2 vols. (Düsseldorf and Munich: Küpper, 1958), vol. I, p. 387.

32 Otto Weininger, *Geschlecht und Charakter* (Munich: Matthes & Seitz, 1980), p. 210.

33 Quoted in Edward Timms, *Karl Kraus, apocalyptic satirist* (New Haven and London: Yale University Press, 1986), p. 89.

34 Karl Kraus, *Schriften*, ed. Christian Wagenknecht, 20 vols. (Frankfurt: Suhrkamp, 1989–94), vol. VIII, p. 13.

35 Marshall Berman, *All that is solid melts into air: the experience of modernity* (New York: Simon & Schuster, 1982).

36 Most recently by Richard Murphy, *Theorizing the avant-garde: modernism, expressionism, and the problem of postmodernity* (Cambridge: Cambridge University Press, 1999), pp. 114–41.

37 Contrast Erich Heller, *The ironic German: Thomas Mann* (London: Secker & Warburg, 1958), p. 30, with T. J. Reed, *Thomas Mann: the uses of tradition* (Oxford: Clarendon Press, 1974), p. 82.

38 See Helmut Koopmann, 'Thomas Mann und Schopenhauer', in Peter Pütz (ed.), *Thomas Mann und die Tradition* (Frankfurt: Athenäum, 1971), pp. 180–200.

39 Martin Heidegger, *Sein und Zeit* (1927) (Tübingen: Niemeyer, 1993), p. 254.

40 Compare Russell Berman's remarks on Freud in chapter five, pp. 229ff.

41 Philip Rieff, *Freud: The mind of the moralist*, 3rd edn (Chicago: University of Chicago Press, 1979), p. 41.

42 See Dorrit Cohn, 'Freud's case histories and the question of fictionality', in Joseph H. Smith and Humphrey Morris (eds.), *Telling facts: history and narration in psychoanalysis* (Baltimore and London: Johns Hopkins University Press, 1992).

43 Arthur Schnitzler, *Jugend in Wien*, ed. Therese Nickl and Heinrich Schnitzler (Vienna: Molden, 1968), p. 83.

44 See Frank J. Sulloway, *Freud, biologist of the mind: beyond the psychoanalytic legend*, 2nd edn (Cambridge, MA, and London: Harvard University Press, 1992), pp. 476–80.

45 Martin Buber, 'Einleitung: Ekstase und Bekenntnis', in *Ekstatische Konfessionen* (Berlin: Schocken, n.d. [1909]), p. 13.

46 See R. C. Zaehner, *Mysticism sacred and profane* (Oxford: Clarendon Press, 1957), pp. 28–9.

47 Quoted in Riedel, *Homo natura*, p. 96.

48 Theodore Ziolkowski, 'James Joyces Epiphanie und die Überwindung der empirischen Welt in der modernen deutschen Prosa', *Deutsche Vierteljahresschrift* 35 (1961), 594–616; further discussed by Manfred Engel, *Rainer Maria Rilkes "Duineser Elegien" und die moderne deutsche Lyrik* (Stuttgart: Metzler, 1986), pp. 58–9.

49 Chamberlain, *Die Grundlagen des neunzehnten Jahrhunderts* (Munich: Bruckmann, 1899), p. 503.

50 William James, *The varieties of religious experience* (1902) (London and Glasgow: Collins, 1960), p. 410.

51 See letter of 24 October 1912 in Trakl, *Dichtungen und Briefe*, ed. Walther Killy and Hans Szklenar, 2 vols., 2nd edn (Salzburg: Otto Müller, 1987), vol. I, p. 491.

52 James, *Varieties*, p. 180.

53 Rilke, letter to Clara Rilke, 7 October 1907, in *Briefe*, ed. Karl Altheim, 2 vols. (Wiesbaden: Insel, 1950), vol. I, pp. 184–5.

54 Richard Beer-Hofmann, *Der Tod Georgs*, in *Gesammelte Werke* (Frankfurt: Fischer, 1963), p. 524.

55 Quoted in Dominik Pietzcker, *Richard von Schaukal: Ein österreichischer Dichter der Jahrhundertwende* (Würzburg: Königshausen & Neumann, 1997), p. 63.

56 'In der Heimat', in Trakl, *Dichtungen and Briefe*, vol. I, p. 60.

57 For the source of this image, see Richard Exner, *Hugo von Hofmannsthals "Lebenslied"* (Heidelberg: Winter, 1964), pp. 84–5.

58 Robert Musil, *Gesammelte Werke*, ed. Adolf Frisé, 9 vols. (Reinbek: Rowohlt, 1978), vol. VI, p. 140.

59 Franz Kafka, *Das Schloß*, ed. Malcolm Pasley (Frankfurt: Fischer, 1982), Textband, p. 164.

60 Erich Heller, 'The world of Franz Kafka', in *The disinherited mind: essays in modern German literature and thought* (Cambridge: Bowes & Bowes, 1952), pp. 157–81 (p. 178).

61 Ernst Stadler, 'In diesen Nächten', in *Dichtungen*, ed. Karl Ludwig Schneider, 2 vols. (Hamburg: Ellermann, 1954), vol. I, p. 143.

62 Rilke, letter of 23 March 1922, in *Briefe*, vol. II, p. 349.

63 Else Lasker-Schüler, *Gedichte*, ed. Karl Jürgen Skrodzki, 2 vols. (Frankfurt: Jüdischer Verlag, 1996), vol. i, p. 119.

64 Ibid., p. 166.

65 Rilke, letter of 8 August 1903, in *Briefe*, vol. i, p. 55.

66 Contrast Käte Hamburger, 'Die phänomenologische Struktur der Dichtung Rilkes', in her *Philosophie der Dichter* (Stuttgart, Berlin, Cologne and Mainz: Kohlhammer, 1966), pp. 179–275, with Wolfgang G. Müller, 'Rilke, Husserl und die Dinglyrik der Moderne', in Manfred Engel and Dieter Lamping (eds.), *Rilke und die Weltliteratur* (Düsseldorf and Zürich: Artemis & Winkler, 1999), pp. 214–35. Compare Russell Berman's remarks on Husserl in chapter five, pp. 232f.

67 Husserl, letter of 21 January 1907, quoted in Rudolf Hirsch, *Beiträge zum Verständnis Hugo von Hofmannsthals* (Frankfurt: Fischer, 1995), pp. 275–6.

The subjects of community: aspiration, memory, resistance 1918–1945

Russell A. Berman

The cultural transformations associated with the collapse of the Wilhelmine empire in 1918 affected German literature and philosophy in quite distinct ways. Formal philosophy, lodged in the universities, was among the most conservative institutions in German society and one that underwent little change, despite the social upheaval, while creative literature grappled with profoundly transformative and avant-garde dynamics. Consequently it is not surprising to find literary discourse in the Weimar Republic more supple and imaginative than philosophical writing, and it is above all in literature, in the critical statements by authors (rather than by professional philosophers), and in the judgements of literary critics that one finds an ongoing working-through of the fundamental problems of the day.

Nineteenth-century poetic realism had measured the shapes of the objective world, both society and nature, and thereby rethought the category of totality inherited from classical philosophy. Turn-of-the-century modernism directed its attention to the inner world of the subject, its anxieties and aspirations, and the limits of its capacity to perceive the world around it. Yet notwithstanding a sense of a growing estrangement between subject and object, Wilhelmine culture was able to maintain a superficially cohesive landscape of meaning, no matter how fraught with neo-Kantian dualities: the simultaneity and co-existence of an isolated individuality and its reified, natural-scientific environment. The assault on this conventional organisation of meaning, inherent in the reception of the literary works of Ibsen and Dostoevsky, as well as in the writings of Nietzsche and Freud, remained marginal until the enormous catastrophe that separates two epochs: the First World War; and it is in the literature of the war, rather than in contemporary philosophy, that the gravity of the cultural consequences became apparent.

Thus the young Bertolt Brecht, still a 'Gymnasium' (grammar school) student but already a published journalist, provoked a scandal with an

essay he wrote for his Latin class in 1916 which included the assertion:
'The saying that it is sweet and proper to die for one's fatherland can
be seen only as crass propaganda.' The attack on the famous lines of
Horace *dulce et decorum est pro patria mori* was not merely a denunciation of
militarism; nor was it solely adolescent protest. More broadly, Brecht denounces established culture as propaganda and trickery when measured
from the ultimate standpoint of an existential awareness of death – a
perspective that calls into question all the nineteenth-century ideas and
ideals, which lose credibility in the face of the carnage of war. From the
standpoint of catastrophe, established culture is nothing more than a lie,
a 'Lebenslüge'.

A decade later, Brecht's schoolboy anti-canonism metamorphosed
into one of the grand poems of the *Hauspostille* (1927; *Manual of piety*),
again a scandal of blasphemy and anti-militarism, the 'Legende vom
toten Soldaten' ('Legend of the dead soldier'). A series of quatrains in a
simple rhyming pattern, fully consonant with Brecht's stylistic populism,
the ballad recounts the gruesome and surreal story of a soldier who dies
on the battlefield but who is exhumed, declared still fit for service, and
marched off to battle once again. A doctor lends his medical authority,
a priest provides the incense, a patriotic civilian marches along, and the
women cheer the parade. All of society is caught up in the celebration,
organised around the figure of the dead soldier, whose death is masked
by the frolic:

> So viele tanzten und johlten um ihn
> Daß ihn keiner sah.
> Man konnte ihn einzig von oben noch sehn
> Und da sind nur Sterne da.
>
> Around him so many danced and howled
> That none could him espy.
> You could only see him from above
> Where only stars looked down from the sky.[1]

The truth of the carnival is nothing but the repression of the knowledge of
death in the imperial vanity fair. The poem calls into question the viability
of the shared ideals: the doctor's science, the priest's religion, the civilian's
patriotism, and so on. It unmasks the cultural world of the nineteenth
century as little more than self-deception, but this truth, the revelation
of social falsehood, is also solely visible from above, from the heavens,
where there are only stars: only heaven knows the truth. The image
leaves the character of circumambient nature suspended ambiguously

between two alternatives: nature is either a disenchanted cosmos from which the gods have departed (for only stars are looking down) or the imagery suggests a recovered metaphysics, some ultimate meaning that could relativise ideological secularism. In that case, the stars stand in for a genuine life which an anamnestic literature, a literature that can overcome repression, might recall. In the meantime the poem marks the cyclical fate of the soldier, from a heroic death in the first strophe to another heroic death in the last. The philosophical alternative to this eternal return of the dead would be a qualitatively different knowledge. What would a thoroughly different way of living entail? The competing discourses of the era provide alternative answers: vitalist experience, existentialist being, Marxist practice.

The literature of the period 1918–1945 confronted Wilhelmine idealism with questions of an ultimate existential order. Simultaneously the stance of triumphant natural science, that had characterised much of the previous century and especially its methodological positivism, was challenged by a growing discontent with reason. Yet above all, the erstwhile concerns with the vicissitudes of the individual gave way to an urgent interest in the constitution of community as the location of a possibly full and meaningful life: an alternative to the death, no matter how heroic, that conventional culture demanded of the individual in the trenches.

An awareness of the tragic tensions within established culture pervaded the thought of Max Weber, whose writings on method and on social and economic history became foundational for twentieth-century social science. As early as 1901 in his seminal *Die protestantische Ethik und der Geist des Kapitalismus* (*The Protestant ethic and the spirit of capitalism*) he described the paradoxical connection between material progress and spiritual decay, the withering of personality and the specifically modern experience of being trapped in an 'iron cage' ('stahlhartes Gehäuse') of professionalism.[2] In his writings on religion, he described how modern culture loses a single organising centre as it devolves into separate value spheres with competing and sometimes incompatible desiderata or ideals. Weber suggests that conflict is inescapable, and an ultimate harmony impossible. He describes an underlying tension between objective structure and subjective meaning, two quite distinct levels of analysis, but each indispensable for the understanding of social phenomena, including aesthetic culture. In order to achieve a modicum of stability, any social structure has to be able to command the belief of its participants, it must have a legitimacy, yet Weber, as a theorist of modernisation, distinguishes among various modes of legitimacy: traditional,

legal, charismatic. The tragic fate of post-traditional modernity is that
the effort to establish a rational legal order leads to bureaucracy, and
the only alternative to that ossification is the irrational force of exoge-
nous creativity: charisma or, as Weber puts it sceptically, 'new prophets'
('neue Propheten').[3]

Acutely aware of the internal inadequacies and limits of modern society, Weber nevertheless became its stalwart defender against the growing
anti-rationalism of the younger generation during the First World War,
and his clarion call for the defence of the structures of scientific rationality resounded in his famous address 'Wissenschaft als Beruf' ('Science as
a vocation'), delivered at the University of Munich in 1918. His argument
depends on a tension between the external condition of science, i.e. the
organisation of the university, and the internal calling of the scholar.
Beginning with the former, Weber describes the nature of the modern university, its increasingly bureaucratic or 'state-socialist' character,
which he contrasts with traditional university life. The new university
takes on more of the features of the modern industrial enterprise, and it
shares the same organisational deficiencies. Side by side with processes of
rationalisation, it is coloured both by a process of selection which favours
mediocrity and by the irrational role of chance.

Yet Weber's main concern involves explaining the importance of a firm
subjective commitment to science, the ethos of the scholar. He mounts
an extended argument against rising anti-rationalist currents among the
students, for which science *qua* scholarship appears narrow and calculating, lacking the heroic grandeur of a genuine life. Thus, in an initial
strategy, he insists that even scholarship at its most rational requires irrational moments of inspiration or imagination. The established culture
which the young generation denounces as routinised and technical in
fact relies on exactly that creativity which its critics claim it lacks. Weber
thus attempts to undermine his neo-Romantic opponents' insistence on
the distinction between a sterile scientific rationality and creative irrationalism. However, the main argument asserts that a serious devotion
to one's calling as a scholar leads to a greater authenticity than do irrational appeals to the force of personality or the priority of 'experience'
over reason. Rushing prematurely towards a claim for deep meaning
without the hard work of pursuing the internal logic of a project is, for
Weber, a fruitless shortcut or mere demagoguery. Against this cult of
immediacy he posits a Protestant ethic of consistent and rational effort,
which applies not only to science but to art as well, two parallel structures
of objective culture. The notion of the artist rigorously devoted to the

disciplined pursuit of art found its clearest expression five years earlier in the figure of Gustav von Aschenbach in Thomas Mann's *Der Tod in Venedig* (1913; *Death in Venice*).

In the Munich address, Weber defended the realm of established culture as rationally legitimate – be it as art or as science – against calls for an irrationalist immediacy which he regarded as somehow linked to the bad popularity of the 'crowd phenomenon' ('massenhaft auftretende Erscheinung').[4] The irrationalist searches for an easy answer to the unanswerable questions of meaning in the modern world; hence Weber's accusation of triviality. The genuine scientist cannot provide ultimate meaning, just as the genuine artist in the modern age cannot provide the comprehensive totalities of significance which other cultural epochs might have allowed. Just as Marx had once suggested that Achilles becomes impossible in the age of gunpowder and bullets,[5] Weber now underscores how a public, monumental art becomes impossible in the wake of a rationalisation that has banished immanent meaning from the world, and fragmented a once unified experience into a multiplicity of particularist value spheres. There is, Weber posits, a parallelism between art and religion: each is the potential carrier of irrational values, but in our disenchanted world, which has lost the immanence of meaning, a crude assertion of value by *fiat* leads only to the degraded belief structures of sects or monumental aesthetic 'monstrosities' (he means the official statues of Wilhelmine culture, but this is surely an anticipation of Nazi art as well). Genuine art takes on a quite different character: *pianissimo*, hermetic and small. Weber means the poetry of Stefan George, who associated his symbolist verse with a decided withdrawal from the public and a refusal of communicative meaning.

Weber's diagnosis of modern culture is complex because it accepts and even admires the process of rationalisation while also recognising its consequences in terms of a deep-seated erosion of structures of meaning: due to specialisation, there is little opportunity to grasp the totality of being; due to professional routines, the individual ceases to engage the full quality of lived experience; due to bureaucratisation processes, creativity is impeded. Hence the ambivalent attitude towards irrationality. Sceptical of regressive tendencies, Weber nevertheless recognises that the revitalisation of an enervated culture can only proceed from the irrational wellspring of the charismatic 'new prophets'. Many aspects of Weber's analysis reappear in the work of Georg Lukács, first in the neo-Hegelian *Theorie des Romans* (1916; *Theory of the novel*) and then in the reworking of Marxism in *Geschichte und Klassenbewußtsein* (1923; *History and class consciousness*); the critique of rationalisation eventually became a central component of neo-Marxism and Critical Theory.

In the context of modern fragmentation, according to Weber, genuine literature necessarily retreats from its public mission into a self-enclosed autonomy. It lays no claim to found communities, since community is precluded by the objective alienation of the era. The autonomy aesthetics of the period around 1800 had a more hopeful agenda of aesthetic education, which Schiller, for example, viewed as a path preferable to Jacobin politics. In contrast, Weber's argument regarding the aesthetic is marked by resignation and retreat, even though he still engaged vigorously in the political sphere. It is his insistence on the absolute incompatibility of the aesthetic and the political that marks him as a defender of the separation between the institutions of art and the institutions of the state. In the language of the period, this corresponded to the aestheticist distinction between life and art, which Peter Bürger has described as the fundamental structure of the nineteenth-century bourgeois organisation of culture.[6] It was, after all, this Wilhelmine world that could locate politics in the sprawling government buildings in Berlin while sequestering culture on the 'Museum island'.

Despite Weber's demand that literature retreat from the public sphere and resign itself to its autonomous status, contemporary literary debates explored more aggressive programmes. Might art provide a more vigorous alternative to rationalised modernity? Might literature chart an emancipatory course so that the individual could be 'freed from the cold skeleton hands of rational orders, just as completely as from the banality of everyday routine?'[7] This problem persists through the literary imagination of the subsequent decades in the effort to articulate a poetic that might transcend Weber's resigned autonomy in order to achieve a community with a vibrant public culture. The work of art became a vehicle for the expression of discontents with modernity. However, whether aesthetic form could ever effectively overcome Weber's *pianissimo* is another matter.

In the context of the war and its aftermath, Oswald Spengler developed a comparable verdict in his *Der Untergang des Abendlandes* (1918/1922; *Decline of the West*),[8] a wide-ranging survey of civilisation oriented toward a morphology of world history. Cultural phenomena, of which the West is but one example, are treated as expressions of underlying laws of history. This historicising relativisation of the present echoed contemporary cultural pessimism. Spengler locates an alternative to this decline in a vitalist and therefore irrational power: history as a supra-personal tribunal of judgement (p. 1194). Just as for Weber, the end of the

Wilhelmine empire led Spengler to summative civilisational-historical judgements, and both come to identify the role of irrationality in history. However, while Weber incorporates irrationality into a framework of rational modernity, Spengler points to the emergence of a fundamentally new regime beyond the rule of reason.

Expressionist aesthetics represented a counter-programme to hegemonic rationality, and its literature represents an incandescent alternative to the routinisation of modernity. As a term, 'expressionism' referred at first to painting and the visual arts, and was only later applied by Kurt Hiller to the poetry of the young generation during the second decade of the century. It suggests that the substance of the world is imbued with an internal spiritual essence, pre-conceptual, passionate and extraordinary, which the work of art brings to the fore. This expressivity stands in opposition to the tendency of the modern age to emphasise those merely external characteristics which lend themselves to accurate measurement but which are devoid of spiritual substance. In contrast to impressionism, which depended on natural-scientific claims regarding the sensations of light on the retina, but equally in contrast to naturalism with its scientific and deterministic predispositions, expressionism dismisses such external phenomena as inconsequential; genuine significance lies at the spiritual core.

Expressionist painting and sculpture in particular, but literature at times as well (cf. Gottfried Benn's *Ithaka*) translated this critique of modernity into a primitivist celebration of non-modern peoples (leading to a complex entwinement in the contemporary discourses of colonialism). Societies outside of the European sphere of influence, especially traditional African and South Pacific cultures, were judged to be closer to the essence of human experience. This same valorisation of a human essence could invert into vigorous appeals to human solidarity in the context of the end of the First World War and the German revolution of 1918–19. Yet the very abstraction of such idealism frequently robbed it of any convincing specificity; its capacity to refer so quickly to everything suggested an inability to refer to anything in depth. This dialectic of expressionism corresponds to the utopianism of the late teens and early twenties, an explosion of enthusiasm that quickly dissipated.

The philosophical substance of literary expressionism is summed up in Kurt Pinthus's introduction to his seminal anthology of expressionist poetry, *Menschheitsdämmerung* (1919; *Dawn of humanity*). Indeed it commences with a reflection on its genre. It is not an 'anthology', associated with the epistemology of conventional positivist scholarship, which groups authors of the same time or poems with the same theme. Instead Pinthus chooses an alternative designation, 'collection' (*Sammlung*), implying not only the editorial labour of collecting separate texts but also the cultural and spiritual project of achieving the focused concentration of 'collection'. Thus the volume goes beyond displaying selected poems of a group of authors; instead it acts out the essential impetus of the literature. The goal of expressionist literature is 'collection', understood as a spiritual alternative to the superficial objectifications and fragmentations of modernity.[9]

Pinthus issues a call to escape the vacuity of the present in order to reach a deeper, more authentic temporality and the vibrant chaos of a lived totality, one which escapes neat classification and in which poetry claims to recover a true humanity. This leap into authenticity requires an extensive cultural criticism that proceeds from a rejection of determinism, of science and of technology, all associated with convention and decline. In their place, Pinthus proposes an essentialist ethics, dependent on humanity's capacity to save itself. The rejection of external objectivities corresponds to an emphatic subjectivism with an activist nuance, an advocated unity of subject and object quite different from their estrangement in neo-Kantianism or Weber's insistence on separate value spheres. Expressionism thereby paves the way for the politicisation of literature, in the sense that the concern with the structure of public life (rather than a solely internalised sensibility and the character of the epistemological subject) takes on ever greater urgency. Furthermore, this urgency explains the expressionist tone, the insistent, sometimes overwrought and imposing resonance, which Pinthus describes in a way that contrasts explicitly with Weber's preference for hermetic symbolism and its *pianissimo*:

wenn diese Dichter in ausschweifender Weitschweifigkeit, in unmäßigem Fortissimo psalmodieren, stöhnen, klagen, schreien, fluchen, rufen, hymnen – so geschieht es niemals aus Hochmut, sondern aus Not und Demut. Denn nicht sklavisches Kriechen, untätiges Warten ist Demut; sondern es ist Demut, wenn einer hintritt und öffentlich aussagt, bekennt und fordert vor Gott und den Menschen, und seine Waffen sind nur sein Herz, sein Geist und seine Stimme.[10]

When these poets groan, mourn, scream, curse, call and sing hymns in expansive digressions and immeasurable *fortissimo* – this is never a matter of pride but of urgency and humility. For obsequious crawling or indolent waiting are not humility. Rather humility is when one goes and publicly witnesses, confesses, and demands before God and man, and one's only weapons are one's heart, spirit and voice.

Metaphors of war and revolution pervade expressionist writings, indicating a fundamentally adversarial stance: this is a critical literature that challenges established form. *Menschheitsdämmerung* includes titles that repeatedly convey this posture; several invoke 'Aufbruch' ('breaking camp'), notably one by Ernst Stadler. In long hymnic lines reminiscent of Hölderlin, the poem stages the prospect of battle, a sudden awakening, that allows for the intensity of absolute experience: 'our eyes would drink full and glowing of world and sun'.[11] This is the 'experience' towards which the rationalist Weber directed so much caution, and Stadler's poem, for all its brilliance, confirms his concerns. Thus the putative singularity of the experience is undermined by a temporality of repetition that structures the poem, while the substance of the conflict remains worrisomely undefined: the grounds for the battle are evidently not even worth mentioning. More irksome is the fact that the poem concedes that the utopia of authenticity is equally available in a moment of peace – 'It was sweet to while and lose oneself / To strip the body of reality as from rusty armour'[12] – rendering the celebration of battle perplexingly arbitrary. If human essence is available in peace, why seek it in war? This unclarity inherent in the expressionist project explains the wide divergence of political directions which expressionist authors later took, from left to right. The result was the so-called 'expressionism debate' of the 1930s, a set of charged and often polemical exchanges over the implications of expressionism in the context of National Socialism and communism.

The attempt to emancipate an essential humanity from the constraints of a routinised existence defines the expressionist stage as well, for example in Georg Kaiser's *Von morgens bis mitternachts* (1912; *From morning to midnight*), first performed in 1917. A bank teller's encounter with a mysterious woman incites him to leave his conventional family and his stultifying job; he absconds with sixty thousand Marks, searching for ultimate experience. Borrowing from Strindberg, Kaiser structures his route as a passage through several stations, compounded by specific Christological references: his death in the final scene is glossed as *ecce homo*. Yet the search fails, as authenticity proves repeatedly elusive. The teller traces a path from one allegory of death at the outset of his journey, to another at the end (not unlike Brecht's soldier's path), underscoring the pointlessness of the efforts. 'Why do I descend? Why did I take the path? Where shall I still go? . . . From morning to midnight I am running in circles.'[13] While expressionism could develop in political directions (e.g. in the dramas of Ernst Toller) or into religion (as in the religious philosophy of Karl Barth, Martin Buber or Rudolf Otto), the key texts demonstrate the limits of a project obsessed with broad generalisations. Notwithstanding its own rejection of the excessive conceptualism of the nineteenth century, expressionism participated in even greater abstraction, and its heroic pursuit of authenticity frequently remained imprecise, contributing to the decline of the movement by the early twenties. Nevertheless expressionist literature set a standard for the presentation of philosophical problems inherited from the Wilhelmine era: the urgency of rethinking the relationship of the subject to community, and the critique of positivist science.

For all of its radical rhetoric, expressionism accepted the institutional landscape of the Wilhelmine era. Expressionist painting competed to enter the galleries, and expressionist theatre struggled to displace naturalism on the stage. The fundamental structure of cultural institutions went unchallenged, a recognition of the profound separation of art from the practical concerns of everyday life. This conventional distinction, inherited from the Classic-Romantic era, faced vociferous critics in the avant-garde movements of the period around 1920, most notably in Dada. Originating in Zürich in Hugo Ball's *Café Voltaire*, where it attracted an international clientele in the neutral city during the war, the Dada movement spread to Germany. It took a particularly political turn in Berlin through the influence of Richard Huelsenbeck, whose 'Dadaist manifesto' commences with an aggressive attack on expressionism, accused of creative complacency and, implicitly, complicity with the established order. All the expressionist talk of spirituality is treated as little more than a strategy for commercial success. For the Dadaists, expressionism remains deeply rooted in Wilhelmine structures of subjectivity, a cult of interiority, and this is precisely why it remains loyal to the objective structures of imperial social life. No matter how it might amplify its idealism, as idealism it fails to escape the problems of neo-Kantianism. In contrast, Dada invokes a nihilistic rejection of these cultural structures with an eclecticism that can combine appeals to primitivist magic with aggressive juxtapositions of aesthetic form and everyday life. At its philosophical core, Dada replaced the humanistic idealism of expressionism with anarchistic attempts at an anti-logocentrism, a thoroughgoing rejection of the order of logic and language.

The signature aesthetic form of Dada was the sound-poem, performed in the Zürich cabaret and consisting of sequences of sound and neologisms, with no syntax and, particularly, no semantic value. The distance from expressionism is particularly salient, since the point of the Dadaist protest is not to find some imaginary authentic meaning, a putatively legitimate alternative to corrupt convention, but rather to undermine meaning altogether. The cultural criticism that had been germinating since the late 1890s takes a radical turn in Dada, since the subversion of meaning is implicitly linked to a revulsion against social structure (although this political link tends to become more pronounced during the later years of the movement). Thus the alternative to the scientific rationality of the positivist age is not sought in an affective irrationalism but in a much more profound anti-rationalism that would undercut all semantic coherence. The specific rejection of communicative language in the sound-poems builds on the linguistic scepticism that had grown, especially in Vienna, in the writings of Hugo von Hofmannsthal, Karl Kraus and Ludwig Wittgenstein: Dada's demolition of standard language represents an effort to purge quotidian speech of the corruption to which it had allegedly succumbed in the era of commercialised journalism.

Dada pursues a similar approach to the institution of art, which surrenders its separate and sacrosanct status. Its birth in a context of popular performance, the cabaret of Zürich, already blurs the line between entertainment and art, and the specifically provocative stance that Dadaist performers would assume vis-à-vis the audience led to important innovations. Dada challenged the tenets of autonomy aesthetics, winning for itself the sometimes contested designation of anti-art or anti-aesthetic. It would however be more appropriate to consider the Dadaist aesthetic as a corrective to an objectified formal structure still evident in expressionism, while remaining quite indebted to notions of the incommensurable or apotropaic substance of art. Far from constituting an anti-art, Dada's polemic pushed art away from conventional morphology and therefore towards ever greater autonomy. Consequently Dadaists claimed that any material or medium would be appropriate for art, from conventional oil paint to a counter-intuitive choice such as railroad tracks, as long as an underlying principle of aestheticisation is observed. Instead of constitutive categories of classical Western aesthetics such as subjectivity or mimesis, Dada conveyed an urgency to transform life into art. This avant-garde strategy of appealing to post-conventional artistic values ultimately heightened the expectations of art by modernising them.

The most direct consequence of the Dadaist expansion of the range of artistic activity was the montage, the introduction of heterogeneous materials, particularly everyday materials, within a single work, with the intention of irritating the recipient schooled in conventional taste and thereby eliciting a reaction of shock or provocation, key elements of the Dada performance. At times the provocation could be defined in abrasively political terms, as in the photomontage work of John Heartfield or Hannah Höch. The frequent mixture of visual imagery and literary text, for example in Kurt Tucholsky's 1929 volume *Deutschland Deutschland über alles* (with Heartfield montages), alone indicates a challenge to a logocentric regime of representation. However, whether that challenge entailed an enriched aesthetic or merely a political provocation, or, finally, a regressive concession to the taste dictated by an increasingly non-literary popular culture, can only be adjudicated in terms of individual works. The larger, epochal question involves evaluating the impact of the Dadaist attack on the institution of art: either as the source of an expanded sensibility that would ultimately generate the innovative modern art of the twentieth century or – in its rejection of subjectivity, its levelling of high and low registers, and its dismissal of semantic values – as a precursor of the postmodern agenda. The complexity of Dada's philosophical legacy is surely that both lineages can be traced across the century.

While Dada's revolt against logocentrism tilted towards an anarcho-communism (always mitigated by a vibrant individualism and anti-conformism), a similar protest against rationalising modernity took place within the broad range of writers vaguely grouped as part of a 'conservative revolution' during the Weimar years. Despite a shared antipathy towards what was perceived as the mechanical legacy of the Enlightenment and the democratic political forms imposed on Germany through the Versailles Treaty, it is impossible to ascertain a unified or systematic programme; the conservative revolutionaries are even less a coherent group than the expressionist poets. Nevertheless, drawing on a Nietzschean legacy (hence the cultural-critical antagonism to the present of the Weimar Republic), the conservative camp postulated a heroic stance in defence of an embattled tradition, whether this heroism was projected onto the writer, the nation or the soldier. The underlying commonality is therefore an emphatically agonistic account of existence grounded in the group's self-understanding as an uncompromisingly adversarial voice against the levelling trajectory of social modernisation.

The influence of the poet Stefan George and the intellectuals close to him represented a prominent source of this conservative aesthetic thought. The most prominent spokesmen for the Georgean legacy was Friedrich Gundolf, professor of literature in Heidelberg and the author of numerous volumes with extensive influence on the intellectual life of the

Weimar years. The self-conscious cultivation of language in George's symbolism, a poetic highly influenced by Mallarmé, was transformed by Gundolf into an insistence that language provides the fundamental source of life and cultural organisation. A Heideggerian thinking *avant la lettre* is quite apparent in Gundolf's account of George himself, whose role he casts above all in terms of a resuscitation of language, since the revolution in poetic language is the precondition for an appropriate reform of cultural life: 'Language and poetry are the most prominent signs of a general condition that stretches from everyday life to religion.' Yet the institutions of civic life – the state, the economy, the press, the theatre – have all become reified within a degraded mass culture. The only hope for renewal lies in the quality of authentic language, the absolute opposite of the 'things' to which life has been reduced. Thus Gundolf continues:

Sprache und Dichtung sind uns hier nur die faßlichsten Zeichen eines Gesamtzustandes der von den Alltagsverrichtungen bis zur Religion reicht . . . Die Sprache ist das innerste Bollwerk des Geistes in einer Welt der Dinge, sie ist die letzte Zuflucht des Gottes im Menschen, wenn es keine durchseelte Kirche, keine öffentliche Magie und kein Geheimnis mehr gibt.[14]

Language and poetry for us here are merely the most comprehensible signs of a state of totality which stretches from everyday business to religion . . . Language is the innermost bulwark of the spirit in a world of things; it is the last resort of God in man, when there is no inspired Church, no public magic, no secrets any more.

For Gundolf, poetic language has the same status *pneuma* had for Weber: in the fallen world, only a new spirit can lead to an authentic revivification. This aesthetic politics anticipates both Heidegger's treatment of the work of art as an originating source of culture, and Adorno's insistent expectation that the autonomous work of art could represent the vehicle with which reified modernity might be criticised and transformed. This is not merely a matter of literature anticipating philosophy but, more so, aesthetic language becoming the vehicle for the redemptive aspirations which philosophy can articulate only clumsily. Yet while Heidegger and Adorno would focus on the vicissitudes of the work of art in culture, i.e. the work itself or the aesthetic object, Gundolf's George cult maintains an element that would later disappear: the emphatic focus on the subjectivity of the individual poet, the human spirit of creation as it is sedimented into the objects of culture. Thus Gundolf is not interested merely in George's poetry, that collection of texts, but rather in the heroic personality itself,

Stefan George, whom Gundolf would cast as a leader, a *Führer* – a term which would become susceptible to enormous politicisation in the National Socialist period, in ways far from Gundolf's intention. For the essence of leadership is the capacity to imbue form with spiritual substance, and it is the study of that spirit which is the proper occupation of the humanities, the *Geisteswissenschaften*, the sciences of the spirit. Hence Gundolf's vociferous rejection of studying cultural objects or 'things' in positivist isolation, since the point is the inherent spirit, not their reified appearance. In a different stylistic register, Pinthus made much the same argument regarding the distinction between anthology and collection.

The insistence on the spiritual core of culture, and therefore on the creativity of individuals, implies a rejection of natural scientific approaches, of dissections of the presumably organic work and its integrity. For Gundolf, the whole is greater than the sum of the parts, while scientific analysis only examines the fractions. Moreover the inherently analytic tendency of modern intellectual life is seen as subverting the authority of spiritual achievement through a programme of cynical denigration. This destruction of the auratic sway of art, Gundolf suggests, only contributes to an exacerbation of the cultural malaise, as he remarked pointedly in a letter of 1926 to Karl Vossler:

Ehrfurcht ist heute, eben heute auch für die Wissenschaft und um der Wahrheit willen so nötig wie Kritik und sie ist viel bedrohter. Wer sie willentlich oder unwillentlich schwächen hilft, schadet sogar der Erkenntnis ... In der Zerstörung der Andacht sehe ich heute eine weit grössere Gefahr, als in der Verkümmerung der, freilich mehr gepriesenen als geübten Kritik.[15]

Today, and especially today, for the sake of scholarship and truth, reverence is as necessary as criticism, and it is more endangered. Whoever helps to weaken it, intentionally or not, damages knowledge ... I see a much greater danger in the destruction of reverence than in the decline of criticism, which is of course praised more often than practised.

On one level, Gundolf operates with the binary opposition of criticism and contemplation ('Betrachten', perhaps better rendered as 'appreciation'), in which case his mapping of the potential reception of the work of art stands in an antipodal relationship to the programme for the critical and activist audience inherent in Brechtian poetics and Benjamin's theory of the contemporary work of art. Gundolf's model of reverential reception is precisely the passivity which the left modernists would attempt to correct. On the other hand, Gundolf is successful at translating the furore of Nietzschean cultural criticism into an analysis of the inadequate reception of art in modernity, a devalued capacity for the aesthetic, and the recognition that a fundamentally anti-aesthetic posture may be an integral component of a conformist society. Robbed of both historical consciousness and an understanding of the potential for individual heroism, modernity appears to the cultural conservative as a site of impoverishment, rather than emancipation.

Elsewhere in the conservative revolution, this same heroism was projected onto the nation and the landscape, for example in the writings of Ernst Bertram. The rejection of nineteenth-century teleological history could lead to a rearticulation of meaning in terms of space and spatiality. For Bertram and others, this space became national, at times racial, but always somehow embattled. Moreover, just as Gundolf could blur the lines between scholarship and literature, science and art, Bertram would explore the border between literary expression and music, claiming a particular musicality as the core of the German experience. Whatever cultural historical materials might be mobilised in defence of the claim that music represents a particularly salient aspect of German cultural achievement, Bertram suggests that Germany, thanks to this musicality, has the advantage of a diminished logocentricity. The core of its culture is less logical, conceptual and philosophical, more musical, poetic and emotional.

Thus in a speech in 1924 on Klopstock, the eighteenth-century poet, Bertram multiplies the musical bias in German cultural history several times:

Die rechten Bildner und Erzieher des deutschen Wesens und Wortes sind immer noch Musikanten gewesen. Ein Schulmeister muss singen können, sonst sehe ich ihn nicht an, hatte Luther aus tiefstem Volkstum heraus gesagt. Auch Klopstock hat teil an dem kostbarsten und unvergänglichsten Schatz unsres Volkes; auch er ist ein Musiker und Musikant gewesen, wie, in welcher Art immer, alle seelenführenden Deutschen von Walter von der Vogelweide bis zu Nietzsche. Wohl stimmen wir, mit einem leichten Flor von Selbstbescheidung als Bewahrer des Wortes, wohl stimmen wir zu, wenn gerade Nietzsche, der letzte vollendete große Bildner unseres Wortes, selbst sagt, die deutschen Musiker hätten es immer besser gemacht als die deutschen Dichter: Bach besser als Klopstock, Beethoven besser als Schiller, Mozart besser als Wieland, Wagner besser als Kleist. Aber in der Sphäre des Wortes haben sich wenige so aller Möglichkeiten der Musik bemeistert, wie unser zweiter großer Sänger des *Messias*, dem der Meister des ersten *Messias*, Händel (sieben Jahre vor Klopstocks *Messias*anfang steht sein *Oratorium*), immer ein verehrtes Bild geblieben ist in seinem heroischen Pietismus.[16]

The real shapers and educators of German culture and language have always been musicians. A schoolmaster must be able to sing, otherwise I won't give him the time of day, Luther once said in full accordance with popular sentiment. Klopstock too took part in this most valuable and eternal treasure of our nation, he too was a musician and performer, in the same way as all leading poets have been from Walter von der Vogelweide to Nietzsche. We, as guardians of the word, must humbly agree with Nietzsche himself, our last great wordsmith, who said that German musicians had always done better than German poets: Bach better than Klopstock, Beethoven better than Schiller, Mozart better than Wieland, Wagner better than Kleist. But in the sphere of the word, few have mastered all the musical possibilities as well as our second bard of the Messiah, who revered the master of the first *Messiah* Handel (his *Oratorio* was completed seven years before the start of Klopstock's epic) with his heroic pietism.

The priority of the affective musical community implies the marginalisation of the public sphere as a forum for rational debate; in other words, the privileging of music maps onto a conservative political agenda. For Settembrini, the liberal pedagogue in Thomas Mann's *Der Zauberberg* (1924; *The magic mountain*), music is consequently described as 'politically suspect' ('politisch verdächtig').[17] In addition, the subordination of verbal culture to musical expression resonates curiously with the Dadaist insistence on rhythm and sound (Bertram too insists on the priority of rhythm),[18] but of course cultural conservatism links this musicality to a quite different political and cultural-historical programme than did Dadaist anarchism. Nevertheless it is not without significance that the literary culture of the Weimar Republic was flanked by movements which were quite sceptical of the quality of everyday language and which imagined a deeper, non-communicative authenticity. This neo-Romantic and, particularly, Schopenhauerian perspective explains why the novel of the German experience of the era, Mann's *Doktor Faustus* (1947), is the fictional biography of a composer, just as it sheds light on the fact that Adorno's most comprehensive aesthetic writings pertain to music.

Ernst Jünger adapts many of these conservative tropes but removes them from the domain of art, conventionally understood; instead the battlefield and the heroism of the front soldier provide his model for authentic experience. Yet it is no particular individual soldier with whom Jünger is concerned: neither the individual subject nor even the national subject are of central significance. Jünger's war accounts are by and large uncannily decoupled from any specific German patriotism. Instead he insists that a core experience of war is constitutive to our being. The result is an invocation of a 'new man', emerging from the trenches, stripped of the frills of nineteenth-century subjectivity, lacking in subjective depth, and therefore all the more steeled for participation in an accelerated world of conflict:

Das ist der neue Mensch, der Sturmpionier, die Auslese Mitteleuropas. Eine ganz neue Rasse, klug, stark und Willens voll. Was hier im Kampfe als Erscheinung sich offenbart, wird morgen die Achse sein, um die das Leben schneller und schneller schwirrt . . . Neue Formen wollen mit Blut erfüllt werden, und die Macht will gepacket werden mit harter Faust. Der Krieg ist eine große Schule, und der neue Mensch wird von unserem Schlage sein.[19]

This is the new man, the storm pioneer, the elite of Central Europe. A brand new race, smart, strong, and full of will. What appears here in battle as revelation will be tomorrow's axis around which life will swirl faster and faster . . . New forms want to be filled with blood, and power must be grabbed with a hard fist. The war is a grand school, and the new man will be cut like us.

The expressionist new man, who combined affective depth and the potential appeal to human solidarity, has become something quite different. The erstwhile hypersubjectivity, still dependent on Wilhelmine neo-Kantianism, is stripped of any interiority or belief structures, let alone any utopian thinking. Jünger's battlefield existentialism anticipates the philosophy of anti-humanism which emerged from Heidegger's fundamental ontology, as well as the anti-subjectivism of much twentieth-century thought. Instead of positing authentic experience as a context in which to retrieve a possible subjectivity from a degraded world, Jünger effectively solves the problem of the subject by suppressing it: human existence is cast instead as a perpetual struggle, from primitive jungles full of terror to the modern battlefield. Far from being treated as a catastrophe, war is embraced as the fundamental situation of social being, the underlying truth that had been hidden by the obfuscation of Enlightenment liberalism. Reminiscent perhaps of the expressionist mood of *Aufbruch*, Jünger's account lacks any of the poets' utopian aspirations. His celebration of war is purely post-metaphysical, devoid of any aspiration of transcendence. Hence also a repeated dismissiveness of the institutionalised culture, including the aesthetic culture, of the bourgeois world. His rejection of establishment aesthetics makes him resemble at times a mirror image of the leftist critics of aesthetic institutions, Benjamin and Brecht. However, Jünger rejects the optimism of progressivist teleology as delusional hope, and in its place he posits a world of stark conflict and battle.

During the war, Thomas Mann shared many of the cultural conservative predispositions, including a dismissive attitude towards Enlightenment notions of progress and an explicit hostility to the modalities of mass democracy which he identified with the 'West', Germany's wartime opponents England, France and the United States. In his *Betrachtungen eines Unpolitischen* (1918; *Considerations of an unpolitical man*) he celebrated the specifically undemocratic aspects of the German cultural legacy, as expressed notably in the works of Schopenhauer, Wagner, and Nietzsche. Germany's opponents framed their fight explicitly as a battle against *Kultur*, while Germany justified the war in its defence. For Mann, the bourgeois democracy of the West undermined the possibility of genuine art and heroic individualism, leading instead to a politicised mass culture. In many ways a polemic directed against his brother, Heinrich, Mann's *Betrachtungen* won him the reputation as a key conservative and anti-democratic thinker, on the eve of the collapse of the *Kaiserreich*.

Yet four years later his address *Von deutscher Republik* (1922; *On the German republic*), delivered in Berlin, is a foundational text of Weimar democracy and an eloquent redefinition of German Romanticism in specifically progressive terms. Mann expends considerable energy trying to underscore the continuity, rather than the rupture, between his two positions. As political philosophy, however, the address is particularly noteworthy in its use of aesthetics. Indeed, far from casting the aesthetic as an absolute alternative to the political (in the tradition of conventional autonomy aesthetics), Mann operates with art as the specific medium with which to explore the opportunity for a democratic polis. Instead of the separated value spheres of politics and art which structured the argument in 1918, Mann works towards an account that culminates in a synthesis, a sublation of opposites, including politics and art, as the specific essence of a 'German republic'.

Mann proceeds from the assumption that his conservative audience would regard the notion of a 'German republic' as oxymoronic; had he not earlier argued that a republic or a democratic regime (the two designations are interchangeable in this context) would be inimical to German *Kultur*? His challenge therefore is to demonstrate how a specific mode of republicanism might indeed be compatible with German traditions, and he solves this problem through a turn to the aesthetic dimension. Aesthetics take on the task of providing representation for the nation, yet nationalism – Mann's second argumentative move – necessarily maintains a cosmopolitan dimension. Hence his reference to naturalism's dependency on Russian and Scandinavian sources, as well as to Naturalism's antipode, the symbolist Stefan George, whose emphatic Germanness was nourished by his formative reading of French poetry. Against the conservative nationalists who would define German identity as exclusive and suspicious of the foreign, Mann insists that the most successful German identity always integrates a cosmopolitan horizon. This in turn explains the central rhetorical device of the essay. In order to demonstrate the compatibility of German identity with what otherwise appears to be the foreign principle of democracy, Mann explores, through a series of quotations and commentaries on them, the points of agreement between the German Romantic Novalis (Friedrich von Hardenberg) and Walt Whitman, cast as the bard of American democracy. Again, the aesthetic dimension has become the location for the representation of a political agenda.

According to Mann, the imperial system imposed a deep separation between the political and the cultural spheres. Excluded from government, the nation as a whole, and its cultural intellectuals in particular, withdrew into aesthetic autonomy, leaving the affairs of state in the hands of the dynastic leadership, no matter how its incompetence made the nation cringe. The republic, in contrast, becomes the 'unity of state and nation', in so far as the dualities of the old regime have been overcome, replaced by a community defined in terms of syntheses which, for Mann, have a specifically German national character:

Deutsch aber, oder allgemein germanisch, ist jedenfalls der Instinkt eines staatsbildenden Individualismus, die Idee der Gemeinschaft bei Anerkennung der Menschheit in jedem ihrer Einzelglieder, die Idee der Humanität, die wir innerlich menschlich und staatlich, aristokratisch und sozial zugleich nannten und die von der politischen Mystik des Slawentums gleich weit entfernt ist wie vom anarchischen Radikal-Individualismus eines gewissen Westens: die Vereinigung von Freiheit und Gleichheit, die 'echte Harmonie', mit einem Worte: die Republik.[20]

The instinct for a political individualism is German or, more generally, Germanic: the idea of community as well as the recognition of the humanity of each of its members. It is the idea of humanity that we recognise as inherently human and political, aristocratic and social at the same time, and which is equally distant from Slavic political mysticism as it is from the radical individualism of a certain West. It is the combination of freedom and equality, a true harmony, in other words: the republic.

The 'radical individualism' of the West implies the anarchy of the capitalist marketplace and its degradation of cultural substance; Slavic 'political mysticism' points to Dostoevksy and Bolshevism. Precisely as a republic, Germany avoids both extremes and represents an alternative, simultaneously aesthetic and political, allowing both for individualism and for community while preventing either principle from becoming exclusive. The political form of the 'republic' therefore corresponds to the cultural project of 'humanity' (or humanism: 'Humanität').

At the conclusion of the address, Mann suggests a gender-political, homoerotic substance to the republic, combining a celebration of masculine camaraderie with an otherwise conservative cultural pessimism. Both Novalis and Whitman are shown to maintain a fascination with death and decline, which would undercut any superficial historical optimism. Yet Mann underscores a distinction between their decadence and the more consistent pessimism associated with Nietzsche; hence the death instinct remains constitutive for but not exclusively determining of the culture of the German republic. It is part of humanity, but only part of it:

Zwischen ästhetizistischer Vereinzelung und würdelosem Untergange des Individualismus im Allgemeinen; zwischen Mystik und Ethik, Innerlichkeit und Staatlichkeit; zwischen todverbundener Verneinung des Ethischen, Bürgerlichen, des Wertes und einer nichts als wasserklar-ethischen Vernunftphilisterei ist [die Humanität] die deutsche Mitte, das Schön-Menschliche, wovon unsere Besten träumten.[21]

Between aestheticist isolation and an undignified disappearance of the individual in the general; between mysticism and ethics; between interiority and politics; between a morbid rejection of all that is ethical, proper, valuable and a simplistic philistinism of reason, [humanity] is the German middle, the beauty of humanity, of which our best thinkers dreamed.

The antinomies sublated in the republic also structure central aspects of one of the grand novels of ideas of the period, Mann's *Zauberberg*. Drawing on the tradition of the *Bildungsroman*, it recounts the story of the education of Hans Castorp, a young engineer from Hamburg, who travels to an Alpine spa to visit a convalescent cousin. His initial plans for a short stay stretch into a seven-year sojourn, for much of which he is torn to and fro between competing mentors: the reactionary Jesuit Naphta, who preaches a doctrine of conservative revolution, and the Enlightenment rhetorician Settembrini, who mouths all the correct liberal aspirations but drowns them in his own never-ending stream of verbiage. This ideological competition between Naphta's historical pessimism and Settembrini's faith in a grand narrative of progress is echoed in the formal structure of the novel. For, on the one hand, it surely does trace an individual development, young Castorp's spiritual growth to maturity, and thereby endorses the very possibility of education and improvement; on the other hand, its temporal structure is replete with Wagnerian leitmotifs, a signature of Mann's fiction, suggesting a perpetual repetition rather than developmental progress. Linear and cyclical accounts of temporality coexist in an uneasy tension throughout the novel, which takes time itself as one of its predominant subjects.

Mann's cultural philosophy culminates in the famous 'Snow' chapter. Caught in a sudden blizzard, Castorp finds shelter under the roof of a mountain hut, but quickly loses himself in a daydream. At first he is delighted by the vision of a Mediterranean scene of brilliant nature and beautiful humanity, but behind this classical civilisation, hidden in a temple, he discovers a horrible secret of ugliness and human sacrifice. At this intellectual climax of the novel, the dialectic of two competing principles comes to the fore, illuminating the whole pedagogical enterprise. Castorp has taken Settembrini at his word, ventured out into nature and away from the moribund decadence of the sanatorium, but he has also ventured into the unknown, tempting death, in a way the rationalist would surely not countenance. Yet it is through this foolhardy adventure, in which he has risked all, that he gains the insight of the dream: the point is not that culture is a mere veneer beneath which a genuine truth of horror lurks – that would lend an ultimate superiority to the force of death. Instead there is a balance; civilisation and culture are celebrated as achievements despite death, even though their glory can never fully banish the forces of destruction. The dialectic vision describes Settembrini and Naphta as opposites dependent on each other. Progress and reaction, life and death are inseparable from one another, rather than alternatives between which one must choose. The novel endorses the democratic project of progress and Enlightenment (Settembrini's mission) but only to the extent that it reserves room for the irrationality of existence (of which Naphta was the polemical advocate).

Mann presents an aesthetic justification of democracy in order to demonstrate how democracy might, counter-intuitively, be compatible with conservative German culture. It was however in the circles of the radical left that the interaction of democracy and culture was explored most rigorously and consistently. During the Wilhelmine period, Marxism had spread through the burgeoning German working-class movement and the leading political grouping associated with it, the Social Democratic Party. Despite rhetorical appeals to revolutionary sentiments, the Marxism of that period entailed a strictly economic description of capitalism and a firm faith in the evolutionary laws of history, both of which tenets differed little from standard nineteenth-century thought. However, in the wake of the Russian Revolution in 1917 and the abdication of the Kaiser in 1918, a new political terrain emerged with numerous political parties on the left, advocating sharply divergent programmatic, ideological and philosophical stances. The syndicalist 'council communist' movement that swept through Germany in 1918–19 left an indelibly activist mark on German radicalism which continued to thrive as an important undercurrent even after the stabilisation of the primacy of the two statist parties on the left, the Social Democrats and the Communists. Meanwhile the coincidence of the political revolution and the vitality of new, *soi-disant* 'revolutionary' artistic movements (expressionism, Dada, and other avant-garde groupings) led to a discursive overlap: aesthetic theory became political theory and vice versa. Although earlier Marxism consisted primarily of debates on economics and political institutions and was only marginally concerned with cultural matters (cf. the literary-historical writings of Franz Mehring), Marxist philosophy in the Weimar period and during the exile years after Hitler's accession to power became centrally concerned with matters of literature and aesthetics.

Bertolt Brecht was the most prominent literary Marxist, both in his extensive 'theoretical' writings and in his literary works. Starting from a fundamentally anti-establishment adversariality that drew considerable strength from his literary sensibility (as evidenced in the early poetry, discussed at the outset of this chapter), Brecht came to Marxism in the course of the twenties, relying on his tutor, the theoretician of Council Communism, Karl Korsch. Despite frequent references to economic matters (normally in the imputation of particular 'interests'), Brecht effectively transforms Marxism from a fundamentally social-scientific description of capitalist exchange mechanisms with a deterministic world-view into a theorised ethics of practice, i.e. a description of social being based on the tenet that humans both undergo change and incite transformations of their environment. Despite significant differences, this philosophical (as opposed to economistic) Marxism had its corollaries in Lukács's neo-Hegelian *Geschichte und Klassenbewußtsein* as well as in the early writings of Herbert Marcuse, informed by the influence of his teacher, Martin Heidegger. In all three cases, the reformulation of the Marxist project along broad philosophical lines represented a recovery of the philosophical tenor of the early Marx's own project, which included a level of conceptual reflection that had largely disappeared into the studies of capitalist economy in the second half of the nineteenth century.

Brecht advocated a literature and, more broadly, a thinking that is 'eingreifend', a term which can be translated as 'engaged', in the sense of 'engaged literature' but which should be rendered more properly as interventionist. It defines thinking as an intervention into social relations which therefore rejects any autonomy in the sense of thought that is lacking in consequences. For Brecht, literature either reinforces existing patterns of behaviour or contributes to their transformation; the latter is the preferred option, since the recovery of the transformative potential reminds humanity of its innate capacity to change its environment, otherwise obscured by routinised patterns of behaviour in the service of a status quo. The thrust of Brechtian criticism is directed against established literary and theatrical practices, including the insistence on the value of the auratic character of art and its implied call for an appreciative rather than a critical recipient, as represented for example by Gundolf (to pick a conservative example). However, Brecht's argument for engagement would also find critics on the left, for example Adorno, who, drawing on the utopian element in autonomy aesthetics since Kant, Goethe and Schiller, could cast Brecht's 'intervention' as a slide towards an accommodation with the given order: a trenchant criticism, to the extent that it sheds light on Brecht's own inability to articulate a public critique of Stalinist terror, despite his many private doubts.

In a wider context, Brecht's interventionism can be seen as an aesthetic corollary to the emergence of twentieth-century pragmatism. For all his theoretical reflections, Brecht surely never engages in strict philosophy; on the contrary, his deliberations retain an ineradicable scepticism towards all thought that purports to be pure. The significance of literature, and thinking, lies in their results, not in any illusions about 'eternal values', a constant target of Brechtian polemics.

His insistence on the social nature of action has a double character. The primary significance involves his ongoing interrogation of the category of the 'individual'. Like other twentieth-century thinkers (notably Freud), Brecht harbours grave doubts regarding the legitimacy of the notion of a coherent individuality as the basis of social organisation. Yet while Freud dissolves the individual into several psychic functions and into family history, Brecht treats the category of the individual as an ideological illusion, masking the general social nature of our being. Individualism is, ultimately, merely an artefact of Western culture after the decline of the pre-modern collectivism of the Middle Ages (on this point, Brecht would agree with Mann's Naphta); socialism promises a return to collective structures in the future, and hence a supersession of the individualist legacy. This individualism found its highest expression in the literature of the turn of the century and especially in expressionism, with its hypertrophic subjectivity. In stark contrast, Brecht intends his theatre to explore the integration of the individual in a network of social exchanges.

Despite Brecht's hostility toward individualism or individual subjectivity, his understanding of the social nature of action led him to search for nothing more adamantly than agency, albeit collective rather than individual. While the isolated subject disappears, the subject reappears in the group, as the audience, the class or the party. The project of his 'epic theatre' involved a rejection of the 'Aristotelian' precepts of existing drama – seen as addressing isolated viewers in ideological terms – and their replacement with thought structures intended to elicit a critical stance from the collective subject of the theatre public. The implied recipient of the work of art ceases to be the affective individual, cast derogatorily as connoisseur, Romantic or philistine, who is displaced by the potential collective subject, drawn from council communist notions of the revolutionary working class. It is the project of Brechtian theatre to call that group subject into being through the specific stratagems of dramaturgical representation, understood to elicit certain responses on the part of the audience, in which a critical and activist sensibility might be awakened.

Brecht's primary device to achieve this result is the so-called 'Verfremdungseffekt' ('alienation effect'). Instead of structuring theatrical performance in such a manner as to evoke an emotional identification of the audience with a figure on stage, Brecht aspires to underscore a distance between audience and actor, precisely in order to encourage the audience to develop a critical distance to the representation, and this distance is in turn seen as prerequisite to the emergence of an independent critical stance. Of course, as different as Brecht's insistence on engagement may be from a Schillerian account of aesthetic autonomy, both models share the basic assumption that aesthetic experience – whether as the encounter with Kantian disinterested pleasure or as the challenge of the 'alienation effect' – is the school in which the subject is formed and educated to a social and political maturity. Thus while interventionist poetics differ from autonomy aesthetics in the particular assumptions regarding reception patterns, both accounts, both Brecht and Schiller, impute to aesthetic experience an immanent teleology toward ethical community.

The relationship between Brecht's theoretical claims and the character of his literature *per se* is by no means transparent. Critics debate whether the quality of Brecht's plays was achieved because of his theoretical frame or despite it. There can be no doubt that, for Brecht at least, the literary works are themselves locations for theorisation and reflection on his philosophy and its Marxist inflections. In fact, the conceptual problematics are thought through more effectively in the literature itself than in his poetological or philosophical essays. Literature appears to address the philosophical problems more effectively than the philosophical writing addresses the literature.

His most famous stage work, for example, *Die Dreigroschenoper* (1928; *The threepenny opera*), is framed by the ballad or 'Moritat' introducing the central figure, Mackie Messer. This foregrounded, explicative voice is symptomatic of the project of epic theatre, in so far as it focuses the recipient on the key issues, undercuts any affect of suspense or identification, and calls for a critical perspective. Each stanza of the song announces a different case study for reflection, a different example of a crime, suggesting an agonistic world of culprits and victims, Brecht's description of capitalism. More importantly, it underscores the elusiveness of the culprit in order to invite the audience to adopt a heightened awareness of crime around them. The real criminals, so Brecht suggests, remain invisible. What, however, is the result for the audience? Brecht's intention was surely to generate a social-critical suspicion of capitalist institutions: 'What is a bank robbery, when compared with founding a bank?' he asks in the course of the play.[22] Yet the distancing provided by the 'Verfremdungseffekt' may not be as effective as he had hoped, for the audience may end up with an adulatory fascination for Mackie, who combines tough-guy charm with Robin Hood romanticism. Similarly, in his late play *Mutter Courage und ihre Kinder* (1939; *Mother Courage and her children*) performances elicit sympathy for and identification with the heroine, rather than the critical distance which the theory had prescribed. This *de facto* ambivalence becomes especially prominent in the most political plays, for example *Die Maßnahme* (1931; *The measures taken*), which masterfully works out the authoritarian potential of communist political behaviour while leaving unclear whether Brecht approves.

This ambivalence of the aesthetic work is itself worth philosophical reflection. For it surely demonstrates how the political writer cannot escape the dynamics of an autonomy aesthetic that inherently resists tendentious statements. Precisely because of the literary status of the texts, the political message cannot be one-dimensional. For Brecht, drama became the location for experiments in the social realm, the outcome of which would necessarily be unpredictable. Yet it is the aesthetic work, rather than the frequently tendentious theoretical gloss, which succeeds in uncovering the complexity of the substance.

Thus despite the lucid assertions of allegiance and intervention in the programmatic statements, Brecht's literary works are frequently poised in a delicate balance between cynicism and hope, between conformism and resistance. Forced to flee Nazi Germany, he traversed Scandinavia and the Soviet Union, eventually arriving as an exile in Los Angeles, where he remained until returning to East Berlin in 1948. His quatrain on 'Hollywood' catches both the specific situation of the exile as well as the Brechtian problematic more broadly:

> Jeden Morgen, mein Brot zu verdienen
> Gehe ich auf den Markt, wo Lügen gekauft werden
> Hoffnungsvoll
> Reihe ich mich ein zwischen die Verkäufer.[23]
>
> Every morning, to earn my bread
> I go to the market where lies are sold
> Full of hope
> I get in line among the sellers.

The description of the economic condition, sharp and analytic, conveys criticism while at the same time representing a bitter acquiescence, a sense of the inescapability of the situation. What happens to the hope as he stands 'among' the sellers? The image suggests a merging with the mass, a bitterly ironic conclusion to the project to overcome subjective individuality. Yet the preposition 'zwischen' remains irksome to the extent that it holds onto a residual difference: he is between the sellers, but perhaps not of them. The choice between hope and refusal is left, at best, to the recipient, who is confronted with an existential alternative which the aesthetic work formulates but cannot resolve.

The question whether such ambivalence should be judged a failing or, alternatively, a necessary component of aesthetic complexity underlay two crucial literary-critical debates, in which the left-wing avant-garde (including Brecht) confronted the proponents of the emerging doctrine of socialist realism and, later, the politics of the popular front. Politicised debates over aesthetic categories took place both in a series of articles during 1929–30 in the journal *Linkskurve* (*Left turn*), the organ of the 'Association of Proletarian Revolutionary Writers', and, nearly a decade later in 1937, in *Das Wort* (*The word*), an exile journal. In both cases, proponents of an orthodox Marxism, closely aligned with the Soviet Union, denounced the Weimar-era efforts to develop a tentative alliance both between Marxism and modernism and between communist politics and conservative states in the international political system.

In the *Linkskurve* exchanges, Georg Lukács, who had by this point abandoned his earlier maverick Marxism and migrated close to the centre of the Communist Party, launched a series of attacks on communist authors, such as Willi Bredel and Ernst Ottwalt, who were unambiguously of the left but whose poetics diverged significantly from the realism which Lukács propounded. The controversial points involved formal aesthetic features of the works under question: the use of montage, the deployment of documentary material, and a complexity of perspectives (as was common in modernist literature more broadly). Rather than treating these aspects as indications of innovative literary developments, Lukács attacked them for their implicit epistemological tenets: montage suggests a lack of coherence, documentation undercuts the mission of literary narrative and fetishises facticity, while multi-perspectivism indicates that the author has abandoned his responsibility to provide a coherent world-view and succumbed to an ideological confusion incompatible with the scientific claims of Marxism-Leninism. Against these failings, Lukács sets as a norm for literature the representation of 'totality', a key term in his pre-Marxist *Theorie des Romans*, which, according to *Geschichte und Klassenbewußtsein*, is the defining category of Marxist thinking. The work of art should demonstrate the complex, internal dialectics of the social world, rather than isolating particular perspectives. A dialectical account of totality attains to an objectivity which Lukács contrasts with the 'subjectivism' and 'formalism' that characterise modern literature.

Nineteenth-century realism was preferable to modernism, according to Lukács, because of its superior epistemological capacity. Even if an author's specific politics were less than progressive, the artistic drive inherent in realism to create a totality would necessarily capture the internal development of a society and its ultimately irresistible progress, behind the backs of the characters. In this dismissal of tendentious art, Lukács is one with Marx and Engels, themselves admirers of a canon of literary greatness rather than of politically correct but poetically minor authors. More important than this specific literary taste, however, Lukács's critique of left-wing modernism conveyed an overarching philosophical account of society in which human cognition is considered fully compatible with the cohesiveness of social totality, and any dissonance is ultimately resolved as a component of an all-embracing dialectic. This social whole is objectively given, even if it is not always subjectively perceptible, due to varying class standpoints. It is the proletariat, and the party that represents its interests, that can best ascertain the dialectic of the whole, and it is the critic who relies on the scientific Marxism advocated by the party who is best positioned to judge the adequacy of the literary work. The Weberian problematic of the splintering of the world into distinct value-spheres, a problematic which Lukács himself had set at the basis of his own *Theorie des Romans*, appears to have been resolved – and not by Weber's irrationalist 'new prophets', but through Lukács's apodictic assertion of totality as always immanent in the social world. Later Adorno, in his critique of Lukács, would refer to this astonishing gesture of healing the fragmented world by *fiat* as an 'extorted reconciliation'.[24]

The so-called 'expressionism debate' which took place in *Das Wort* in 1937 again turned to modernism, but in a different political context and with an even greater judgementalism. The debate had been set off by expressions of dismay on the part of leftist authors, such as Thomas Mann's son, Klaus, that the expressionist poet Gottfried Benn, so admired in Weimar, had publicly aligned himself with the Nazi regime after 1933. Hence the designation 'expressionism debate': the narrow question involved the vicissitudes of expressionist thinking and whether it could easily slide into fascism. The broader question evaluated modernist literature in general, especially its anti-realist aspects, which gave rise to the accusation that it represented an escapist flight from reality or even an ideological effort to obfuscate the real. Lukács again played a major role, eliciting stinging comments from Brecht, who defended modernist literature and its experimental techniques as vehicles to achieve greater cognitive mastery of a social environment significantly different from that of the age of literary realism. While Lukács's epistemological agenda remained much the same as in 1929–30, the political agenda had become more apparent. The debate over literary forms and movements was primarily a debate over whether German authors and intellectuals could remain independent even in exile or whether they would be subordinated to the party-line Marxism from Soviet Russia.

Lukács's position is not without significant ambiguities, particularly with regard to its political standing. From the perspective of Brecht and other left-wing modernists, Lukács appeared to advocate a dangerously authoritarian and obsolete epistemology, and his perpetual reversion to notions of 'dialectic' and 'objectivity' had none of the political panache of Brecht's activist theory of drama. On the contrary, they regularly implied a loss of independence and an integration into collective discipline. From this standpoint, Lukács appeared to function as the leading theoretician of 'socialist realism'. Moreover, his insistence on the priority of criticism over literature, and 'science', i.e. Marxism-Leninism, over aesthetic experience, translated directly into an assertion of the primacy of the political party over artistic creation, leaving little room for notions of free creativity. Yet Lukács can also be viewed as arguing explicitly against the overly politicised, frequently propagandistic literature of the socialist world. Against any obligatory tendentiousness, Lukács invoked the achievements of the grand masters of earlier bourgeois culture, regardless of their political views. With this in mind, he can be judged a moderate within the communist camp, trying to use the residual literary-critical public sphere to articulate an alternative to the total politicisation of culture. Therefore, Lukács's philosophical apparatus, developed largely through his literary-critical writings, eventually contributed to the emergence of an oppositional Marxism in Eastern Europe during the Cold War era.

By the thirties, at the latest, Lukács chose to characterise his specific canon as 'realistic', but the rubric was broad enough to encompass both Goethe and Thomas Mann, as well as Balzac and Tolstoy. The literary criticism of the orthodox Marxist Lukács still depended, however, on the organising principle of the pre-Marxist period, the desideratum of a 'subject–object unity', by which was meant the particular integration of the individual into the social world. The tenor of the argument for the socialist-realist aesthetic had in fact little to do with the theories of realism that had been promulgated during the nineteenth century. On the contrary, the advocacy for realism ultimately represented a classicist philosophical stance derived from German idealism. Similarly Lukács's critical evaluation of modernist literature as subjectivist and therefore flawed echoed the classicist denunciations which Goethe and Hegel had directed against the Romantic literature of the early nineteenth century.

In contrast to this implicit classicism, Walter Benjamin developed a literary criticism combining aspects of Romanticism with Marxism and the contemporary avant-garde. While the Lukácsian aesthetic valorised the closed or organic totality of society, which it was the obligation of the work to reproduce within itself, Benjamin's aesthetic thinking derived from the critical practice of the Romantic era and its notion that the work of art is, in itself, fragmentary and incomplete. It is only through the process of criticism, that is, through the reception, that it can move towards its fulfilment and its own truth. This stance intertwines the desideratum of an activation of the audience, the fundamental principle of Brechtian aesthetics, with a more general shift towards an aesthetic of reception, rather than one of production. It is hardly self-evident that a Marxist literary philosophy would deflect attention from the conditions of production. Nevertheless, Benjamin has moved literary criticism away from determinations of authorial intent and towards the character of the recipient's response to the aesthetic experience. Thus the crux of Benjamin's literary criticism frequently involves positing particular relationships between features in the construction of the work of art and the imputed response to them by the recipient, and Benjamin pursues these issues, whether he is considering the Romantic Fragment, the modern novel, the avant-garde work replete with montage, or the work of art in the age of technological reproduction: cinema.

Benjamin assumes the work of art to be a quite tenuous construction, and although it may feign a symbolic unity or simulate internal coherence, it cannot withstand the passage of time, or history, that is, the real historical time in which its reception occurs. The veneer of aesthetic wholeness – that same totality in which Lukács vested the cognitive value of the aesthetic object – wears down, at least for the critical reader. With the disappearance of a symbolic aesthetic appearance, the work of art loses its capacity to seduce the recipient into accepting the illusion of beauty, and the truth content of the work of art comes to the fore. However, this emergence of truth takes place only through history and reception, fundamentally ethical forces contrasted with the deceptively natural appearance of the beautiful work.

This dynamic, which Benjamin finds inherent in a philosophical and social novel such as Goethe's *Die Wahlverwandtschaften* (1809; *Elective affinities*), holds all the more for the reception of cinema, the topic of his seminal essay on 'Das Kunstwerk im Zeitalter seiner technischen Reproduzierbarkeit' (1935; 'The work of art in the age of technological reproduction'). As art undergoes the industrialisation of its production, it loses the seductive aesthetic of an 'aura', and a post-auratic art emerges which, for Benjamin, has the capacity to elicit a critical audience. The greater the secularisation of the aesthetic sphere, the greater the emancipatory potential for an audience no longer subdued by authoritarian patterns of reception – Gundolf's 'reverence'. Benjamin's argument is frequently taken as an indication of the critical potential inherent not only in film but in modern mass culture in general, and it is no doubt the case that in his critical *œuvre* the question of the relationship between autonomous art and modern popular forms is posed most dramatically. His enthusiasm for the emancipatory potential presumably inherent in the cinema is the opposite of Adorno's scepticism regarding the allegedly democratic nature of mass-marketed commercialised culture. The enthusiasm with which Benjamin appeared to applaud the dissolution of the auratic work of art certainly reflected the technological utopianism of the era. He consequently spends little time querying whether the anti-aesthetic implicit in his argument, the preference for the politicisation of art in the form of the cinema, may not also lead to deleterious consequences of conformism or levelling.

Benjamin's Romantic poetics and epistemology frequently intermix with several other areas of philosophical concern. Benjamin rarely writes directly on politics in a strict sense, even though his criticism is full of Marxist borrowings. Nevertheless, there is a nascent political philosophy pervading his writings that confirms connections both to the conservative political thinker Carl Schmitt (especially the latter's *Politische Theologie* (1922; *Political theology*)) and to the Austrian playwright Hugo von Hofmannsthal. Developed in his study of the German Baroque drama, the *Ursprung des deutschen Trauerspiels* (1925; *Origin of German tragic drama*), a notion of sovereignty emerges in Benjamin's writings which sets the ruler, the sovereign, outside of everyday life, indeed he is specifically opposed to it. Politics ceases to be a matter of routine regularisation, developing a regime of normal processes, or establishing formally consistent procedures. On the contrary, politics is seen as deploying a unique power that is fully distinct from everyday forces or common-sense notions of justice. It is the authority to declare the moment of exception, the absolute power of the sovereign, or a divine intervention, be it as *deus ex machina* or as revolution. For Lukács, the work of art was measured in terms of its capacity to highlight the immanent development of historical forces; for Benjamin the work of art involves the sudden rupture, a peripatetic turn, that stands in absolute opposition to the normal order of things.

This fascination with the sudden intervention in history, a corollary to the epiphanic *unio mystica* in Hofmannsthal's writings, interlocks with Benjamin's proximity to the religious philosophy of the era. His close friend and interlocutor, Gershom Scholem, was the author of a seminal study of Jewish mysticism, and Judaic tropes punctuate some of Benjamin's key writings. Other religious thinkers of the era, such as Rudolf Otto or Karl Barth, are equally pertinent, even though there is no direct relationship to Benjamin: contemporary religious philosophy underscored the radical difference and absolute otherness of the godhead, viewed as fully and qualitatively different from the human condition. Benjamin's philosophical accomplishment involves transforming that religious difference into an account of art and a characterisation of revolution.

The record of this transformation is displayed, most prominently, in 'Über den Begriff der Geschichte' (1941; 'On the concept of history'). Jettisoning post-Enlightenment and especially nineteenth-century accounts of historical time as linear development and teleological progress, Benjamin demonstrates the illusory nature of that vision and its contribution to a politics of enervation. The stronger the assumption regarding the necessarily teleological character of history, the more irresistible notions of development become, which however can quickly elicit a quietistic, even fatalistic stance. Instead, Benjamin sketches a model of the radical caesura, the abrupt break in the empty flow of time, and he describes this break in a language that combines both a religious-philosophical messianism and a political-philosophical aspiration for revolution. This requires renouncing familiar notions of progress as somehow consistent with an immanent flow of time. Instead history appears as a single catastrophe, when viewed from the appropriate perspective, which Benjamin describes in an emblematic passage:

Es gibt ein Bild von Klee, das *Angelus Novus* heißt. Ein Engel ist darauf dargestellt, der aussieht, als wäre er im Begriff, sich von etwas zu entfernen, worauf er starrt. Seine Augen sind aufgerissen, sein Mund steht offen und seine Flügel sind ausgespannt. Der Engel der Geschichte muß so aussehen. Er hat das Antlitz der Vergangenheit zugewendet. Wo eine Kette von Begebenheiten vor *uns* erscheint, da sieht *er* eine einzige Katastrophe, die unablässig Trümmer auf Trümmer häuft und sie ihm vor die Füße schleudert. Er möchte wohl verweilen, die Toten wecken und das Zerschlagene zusammenfügen. Aber ein Sturm weht vom Paradiese her, der sich in seinen Flügeln verfangen hat und so stark ist, daß der Engel sie nicht mehr schließen kann. Dieser Sturm treibt ihn unaufhaltsam in die Zukunft, der er den Rücken kehrt, während der Trümmerhaufen vor ihm zum Himmel wächst. Das, was wir den Fortschritt nennen, ist *dieser* Sturm.[25]

A Klee painting named *Angelus Novus* shows an angel looking as though he is about to move away from something he is fixedly contemplating. His eyes are staring, his mouth is open, his wings are spread. This is how one pictures the angel of history. His face is turned toward the past. Where *we* perceive a chain of events, *he* sees one single catastrophe which keeps piling wreckage upon wreckage and hurls it in front of his feet. The angel would like to stay, awaken the dead, and make whole what has been smashed. But a storm is blowing from Paradise; it has got caught in his wings with such violence that the angel can no longer close them. This storm irresistibly propels him into the future to which his back is turned, while the pile of debris before him grows skyward. *This* storm is what we call progress.

For Benjamin the well-meaning trust in the progress of history has a debilitating effect, transfixing the angel and postponing indefinitely the redemptive action of revolution. Therefore the Enlightenment notion of perfectibility and the associated philosophy of history, which had been inherited by Marxism and which is at the root of Lukács's insistence on immanent development, fails on at least two scores. The blind faith in progress conceals the structures of permanence within the social condition, which have remained impervious to change; the optimism associated with progressivism is therefore based on an unwarranted illusion. In addition, the very confidence with which developmental progress is invoked contributes to a fatalistic inaction. Progressivism turns out to contribute to the epidemic conformism and the inability to act. Benjamin suggests an alternative to this passivity through the interventionist imagery, divine or revolutionary, and the imagined capacity for a full and radical change.

The Benjaminian structure of temporality, combining a rejection of progressivist developmental patterns with an awareness of the imminence of radical transformation, appears in the major novels of the period. Both *Der Zauberberg* and Alfred Döblin's *Berlin Alexanderplatz* (1929) profoundly revise nineteenth-century notions of development. In the former, repetition in history is figured in the usage of the leitmotif, borrowed from Wagnerian music; this contrasts with the overall plot which is still dependent on conventional notions of education (no matter how Mann may direct an ironic glance at those conventions). In the latter, Döblin goes further, in so far as *Berlin Alexanderplatz* is a *Bildungsroman* in which *Bildung* fails and growth does not take place. Permanence and repetition surround the hero, Biberkopf, overwhelmed by the city and the seemingly immalleable structures around him. Bourgeois models of autonomy, both individual and aesthetic, lose their validity, replaced by an emphatic aesthetics of montage. The nineteenth-century fiction of subjective development is replaced by the suspension of the hero between the permanence of his environment and a horizon of redemption. The significance of the individual shrinks in relation to aspirations for community.

While aesthetic theory within the left-wing culture of Weimar and the Hitler era – Brecht, Benjamin, Lukács – relativised individual subjectivity with reference to political-economic categories, psychoanalysis inquired into the lability of individuality, threatened both by external forces of society and internal libidinal pressures.[26] Many of the fundamental texts, especially Freud's *Die Traumdeutung* (1900; *The interpretation of dreams*), were written well before the outbreak of the First World War, and the grand contours of psychoanalysis had been firmly established: the Oedipal conflict, the developmental nature of sexuality, instinct theory, and – of particular pertinence to criticism – the hermeneutic apparatus implicit in Freud's work on dreams, an apparatus which he frequently demonstrated could be extended to works of literature. While the predominant lineage of philosophy in Germany since the eighteenth century concerned the status of the subject and consciousness, psychoanalysis became in effect a philosophy of the unconscious, building on the Romantic and post-Romantic undercurrent running from Goethe and Heine through Schopenhauer and Nietzsche.

While Freud uncovered the faultlines and internal contradictions within the psyche, the overall tendency of psychoanalytic theory involved an effort to foster subjectivity by promoting an expansion of rational understanding into the heretofore uncharted dimension of the unconscious. Yet for psychoanalysis too, the First World War represented a watershed, contributing to a pessimistic turn, the articulation of a dual instinct theory. Not only Eros, but Thanatos as well, a death instinct, is seen as holding sway in human life, and in the late, major cultural-critical works, Freud explores the role of repression and dissatisfaction within the process of civilisational rationalisation: *Das Unbehagen in der Kultur* (1930; *Civilisation and its discontents*) and *Der Mann Moses* (1939; *Moses and monotheism*).

Freud's own proximity to literature has often been noted: the plethora of literary references in his writings, despite his scientific aspirations; the several literary-critical essays; and especially the literary character of the case studies themselves. Nevertheless it is in contemporary literature itself that the psychoanalytic sensibility, particularly the exploration of the ambiguity of desire, is worked out in extraordinary complexity. This is above all the case for the writings of Arthur Schnitzler, Freud's contemporary in Vienna. Although the two did not collaborate, they did recognise the uncanny resemblance in their work. While Freud developed the technique of 'free association' for use in psychoanalytic practice, Schnitzler is the master of the narrative deployment of stream-of-consciousness writing in German, both in his early *Leutnant Gustl* (1901; *Lieutenant Gustl*) and in *Fräulein Else* (1924; *Miss Else*). The latter brings together both a recognition of the lability of the individual psyche and a sensibility for the dialectic of repression in society: repression preserves social order while restricting individual creativity, and this dialectical understanding of repression anticipates Freud's own theoretical account. On vacation in a mountain resort with her aunt and cousin, Else learns of her father's pending arrest for embezzlement; it can be avoided only if she is able to borrow funds from another guest, an older man, who takes the opportunity to make a sexual advance. His proposition, however, sets off a crisis that ends hours later in her suicide. In the course of the first-person narrative, Else reveals the complexity of her love and resentment towards her parents, itself a source of guilt, compounded by her confrontation with her own sexual energy. She succumbs to two pressures, the objective humiliation which her family's need and her presumed benefactor's prurience had elicited, and the subjective experience of her own torrential desire. Freud transformed the psychoanalytic reflection on pathological cases into a general theory of the human mind; Schnitzler's elaboration of Else's death is similarly much more than an individual circumstance, no matter how tragic, namely an analysis of the extreme tentativeness of any apparent ego cohesion. The setting in the Alps, and Else's repeated fascination with the natural beauty around her, take on the allegorical significance of a permanence outside the high life of the resort, gesturing towards an inescapable death and consequently quite parallel to the status of the city in Döblin's *Berlin Alexanderplatz*. Schnitzler's nature and Döblin's city both signal the absolute limits of the liberal world of individual subjectivity, the social forces that defeat the central figures in the two narratives. Those defeats are, ultimately, the verdict which contemporary literature pronounces on the possibility of the subject.

The initial Weimar-era project, the pursuit of a collective subject, had as its corollary and consequence an anti-subjectivism, a deep-seated doubting of the viability of the subject as it had been thought in prior philosophy. In various ways, established thinking, whether treated as science, as Western metaphysics or as Enlightenment, came to be viewed as crisis-ridden, in urgent need of a profound correction by a more effective philosophical stance. These fundamental rethinkings of the project of philosophy took place against the background of much widespread popular scepticism regarding science. Despite some lingering enthusiasm for technology, an undercurrent of polemical anti-scientific thinking, combining a hostility to the natural sciences with a more general anti-rationalism, coloured German intellectual life, leading to the emergence of a 'cultural despair',[27] the same despair which Weber attacked in his 1918 address. In this context, both Benjamin's argument regarding the rationalisation of the aesthetic sphere and Freud's insistence on the progress of rationality within the unconscious appear all the more indebted to an Enlightenment project.

Beginning with Edmund Husserl's *Logische Untersuchungen* (1900; *Logical investigations*), phenomenology developed into the leading new philosophical initiative in Germany.[28] Attempting to describe the phenomenon itself, free of any presuppositions, Husserl's initial goal was to redefine philosophy as a strictly scientific undertaking by separating it both from the historicist relativism of a cultural hermeneutic and from the 'naturalism' associated with a natural-scientific psychology. The operations of the mind are not seen as matters of empirical psychology, but involve instead the nature of thought *per se* and therefore aspire to a universal validity. Yet such sanguine assertions of the validity of a scientific philosophy became less credible, particularly after 1933 with Hitler's accession to power and the anti-rationalism associated with the Nazi movement. The situation became particularly acute for Husserl, since his own student, Martin Heidegger – who had dedicated his philosophical opus, *Sein und Zeit* (1927; *Being and time*) to Husserl – had joined the Nazis and had taken quasi-philosophical positions repudiating the project of science.

Husserl's answer came in his 1935 lecture to the Viennese Cultural Society, entitled, 'Philosophy and the crisis of European humanity'. The presentation entailed a major turn in Husserl's thinking, fully elaborated in his *Die Krisis der europäischen Wissenschaften und die transzendentale Phänomenologie* (*The crisis of European sciences and transcendental phenomenology*), published posthumously in 1954. Husserl's late work remains the most successful and consistent effort to think through the disappointing, frequently even destructive consequences of scientific technological culture, without however renouncing either science or Western thought more broadly. The breathtaking turn for the otherwise formal philosopher Husserl involved a historical reflection on the trajectory of philosophy since the Greeks and their discovery of the concept and theoretical thinking. For Husserl, the defining moment of Western philosophy is the imagination of a universal validity as the goal for science; the subsequent teleology of science, and especially philosophy, involves the constantly self-questioning pursuit of this universalism. Yet for the Greeks, scientific abstraction stood in a dialectical relationship to the concrete problems of the life-world, the pre-scientific environment of everyday tasks. Husserl invokes the notion of a life-world not in order to slide towards a cultural relativism, but to describe the context in which theoretical thinking emerges. Precisely this contextualisation is crucial, for later, Husserl continues, in the period conventionally designated as the origin of modernity, Galileo and Descartes substitute the theorised mathematical world for the specificity of the life-world. Philosophical science redefines its context as its object, and this objectification of the world consequently occludes the substance of the life-world and its particularities. Blind to its own surroundings, contemporary science becomes specialised and surrenders its original mission of guiding humanity towards validity; at the same time it provokes an anti-scientific reaction against its own practices of objectification.

For Husserl the solution involves retrieving this original mission of philosophy by rejecting the 'naturalism' and 'rationalism' which render the world a mere object for technical manipulation. The alternative is a 'heroism of reason', a capacity to continue science without objectifying either the natural or the social environment. Husserl's solemn programme had a particular poignancy in the face of the Nazi regime, but it is just as relevant today as Europe faces other crimes against humanity and nature:

Europas größte Gefahr ist die Müdigkeit. Kämpfen wir gegen diese Gefahr der Gefahren als 'gute Europäer' in jener Tapferkeit, die auch einen unendlichen Kampf nicht scheut, dann wird aus dem Vernichtungsbrand des Unglaubens, dem schwelenden Feuer der Verzweiflung an der menschheitlichen Sendung des Abendlandes, aus der Asche der großen Müdigkeit der Phoenix einer neuen Lebensinnerlichkeit und Vergeistigung auferstehen, als Unterpfand einer großen und fernen Menschenzukunft: Denn der Geist allein ist unsterblich.[29]

Europe's greatest danger is weariness. If we struggle against this greatest of all dangers as 'good Europeans' with the sort of courage that does not fear even an infinite struggle, then out of the destructive blaze of lack of faith, the smouldering fire of despair over the West's mission for humanity, the ashes of great weariness, will rise up the phoenix of a new life-inwardness and spiritualisation as the pledge of a great and distant future for man: for the spirit alone is immortal.

For Martin Heidegger, Husserl's student and eventual successor at the University of Freiburg, phenomenology, despite its success in ridding philosophy of empirical psychological residues, remained trapped in the inherited dichotomy of subject and object. In order to overcome naturalistic objectification, philosophy would have to leap beyond the subject as well and pose the question of Being ('Dasein') itself. Where the phenomenologist Husserl referred back to the origins of science in Greek geometry, the ontologist Heidegger invokes even earlier, pre-Socratic philosophers, prior to the emergence of the hegemony of the concept in ancient idealism and prior to the division of knowledge into the separate fields of philosophy, science and art. Late twentieth-century tendencies (often associated with deconstruction) to approach philosophy as literature or to redefine the study of literature as primarily a matter of philosophical aesthetics derive from this Heideggerian appeal to a pre-specialised mode of thinking. Such a re-totalisation contrasts with the account that proceeds from Kant's three distinct critiques, through Weber's description of separate value-spheres, to Habermas's description of modernity as dependent precisely on the legitimacy of distinct modes of knowledge: scientific, ethical and aesthetic.

Heidegger's diachronic move to the pre-Socratics ultimately bolsters the synchronic diagnosis of contemporary existence as one which has forgotten the ultimate status of Being, and replaced it with a world-view of isolated beings. Modern man (Heidegger uses the term 'das Man' – literally 'the one' – to convey a sense of trivialised anonymity) hides in chatter ('Gerede') and a vacuous everyday life. However, an anxiety in the face of death has the potential of eliciting the question about Being, just as it is also the specific capacity of the work of art to retrieve Being from the oblivion of our ontological amnesia ('Seinsvergessenheit').

Heidegger's 1935 lecture on the 'Ursprung des Kunstwerks' ('Origin of the work of art') proceeds by rejecting the notion that the work is comparable to other objects or things. The preponderance of objectified things, mere topics of our consciousness, is on the contrary a symptom of the problematic philosophical situation of the present. To attain to a truth pertaining to Being would require a clearing away of this clutter, and precisely this is the mission of art. Heidegger begins with the allegory of a Greek temple, an intentionally non-representational choice, since representation itself is implicated in the subject–object distinction. Rather, the temple sets up the 'world' of the community, disclosing its universe of possible meaning, while also setting that world in a physical cosmos, the 'earth', which meanwhile tends towards concealment. This simultaneity of setting up and concealment constitutes truth as a line of tension within every work of art. Truth is not some content which art might communicate, nor is it a matter of descriptive accuracy with reference to a set of isolated objects. On the contrary, truth emerges in the work of art as the recognition of an irreducibly agonistic situation of existence, which Heidegger finds expressed in the poetry of Rilke and above all Hölderlin. Genuine poetry recovers the sacred mission once assigned to it by Romanticism.

This Romantic redefinition of the poet as the source of an Orphic knowledge demonstrates the importance of a comparison with Benjamin, who also, as noted above, depended on Romantic paradigms. Both thinkers insist on the contiguity of literature and philosophy, although for Benjamin the specifically aesthetic work finds its fulfilment only in the subsequent critical discourse of its reception, in other words the two are in a sequential process, while Heidegger tends to dismantle the distinction between the two realms altogether: poetry is already philosophy rather than the topic of a later philosophical commentary. Furthermore both Benjamin and Heidegger examine art within the context of the larger problem of the period, the possibility of community. Just as Heidegger reflects on the relation of the temple to the life of the people, Benjamin turns specifically to modern popular forms, such as cinema, and investigates the relationships among aesthetic form, reception patterns and political consequences. However, while these similarities indicate how both thinkers grappled with common issues, their solutions for art and literature are quite distinct. For Heidegger, the genuine substance of art, its role in the emergence of truth, involves retaining and displaying its Orphic character, while for Benjamin the work loses its aura, permitting the emergence of a critical public through rational debate. If there is a call for criticism implicit in Heidegger, it involves a criticism of critical culture, the chatter of the modern world, and this demonstrates his proximity to the anti-modernism and anti-rationalism of contemporary cultural conservatism.

Heidegger was one of the most prominent German intellectuals, and surely the most prominent philosopher, to embrace the Nazi movement, and in 1934 he served briefly as the rector of the University of Freiburg, overseeing the initial execution of Nazi policy. His inaugural speech as rector and other addresses of the period are generally seen as evidence of his attempt to provide a philosophical defence of his political choice. The Nazi revolution was cast as an overcoming of the desiccation of modernity, i.e. Weimar democracy, and the recovery of an awareness of Being. He quickly retreated from academic politics, although he never provided a clear recantation of his engagement. Not even after World War Two did he ever offer a reflection on the crimes of the Nazi era, despite his prominence both in Germany and internationally. The extent to which Heidegger's philosophy in general can be viewed in the light of his role in the Third Reich and his inability to offer a critique of the period remains a topic of considerable controversy. Critics regard his political choice as evidence of the likely consequence of his philosophical anti-modernism, while more friendly readers are prepared to treat the episode as a separate matter which bears little relation to his major philosophical contributions.

Aside from the difficulty of a specific judgement on Heidegger's role in German politics, a general consideration of literature and philosophy in relationship to National Socialism is important. Yet here too a definitive characterisation remains elusive, in part because intellectual life in general faced extraordinary *de facto* limits after 1933. The police-state atmosphere, the bureaucratic intrusion, the purges in the university, the politicisation of cultural life and the impossibility of open discussion were hardly conducive to productive writing. Many writers fled into exile, and few significant authors remained. Gottfried Benn, a leading poet of the Weimar era (and included in the expressionist anthology *Menschheitsdämmerung*), was one exception; his staying provoked a protest from Thomas Mann's son, Klaus, and this in turn initiated the debate over the political ramifications of expressionism, discussed above. That the aged Gerhart Hauptmann decided to stay in Germany had to do with personal circumstances. In general, and excluding the serious literature that was still published in Germany during the initial years of the regime, before the full institution of its cultural policies, literature in Nazi Germany rarely achieved a significance worthy of philosophical reflection. The literature which supported the regime faced powerful criticism; the literature which the regime supported was mediocre. Serious literature was in exile; what remained was a matter of bureaucratic management, individual compromise, or private tragedy.

The most important literature from within Germany could not be published until after the war. Dietrich Bonhoeffer, one of the few leading Protestant theologians to participate in the resistance against Hitler, reflected on a rethinking of Christianity, secularism and ecumenicism. He was executed in 1945 for his political activities, and his *Auf dem Wege zur Freiheit: Gedichte und Briefe aus der Haft* (1954; *On the path to freedom: poems and letters from prison*) was published posthumously. Viktor Klemperer, a professor of French literature at the Technical University of Dresden, was removed from his position because of his Jewish background. Due to particular circumstances – his marriage to a non-Jew and his war record – he was not deported to a death camp but remained in Dresden, where he was subject to constant humiliation and abuse. Between 1933 and 1945 he kept a rich diary and a copious record of daily life in Nazi Germany, published as *Ich will Zeugnis ablegen bis zum letzten* (1995; *I shall bear witness to the last*). In their quite different accounts, Bonhoeffer and Klemperer both demonstrate a concern with the possibility for individual integrity and non-conformism in the face of a tyrannical force, in contrast to the critiques of subjectivity that pervade much of the literature and philosophy after 1918 and despite the various collectivist models which circulated in political discussion.

The dearth of serious literature in Germany during the Nazi era indicates that an inquiry into the question of a Nazi or more broadly fascist literature has to be posed with reference to material outside this period and outside Germany. It is important to note that the major works of right-wing popular or *völkisch* literature appeared earlier, during the Weimar Republic, for example Jünger's war accounts, such as *In Stahlgewittern* (1920; *Storm of steel*), or Hans Grimm's fascist *Bildungsroman, Volk ohne Raum* (1926; *People without space*), which in fact became a bestseller. Texts such as these combine specifically tendentious themes, which on occasion become propagandistic – militarism, colonialism, anti-Semitism, authoritarianism – with literary features that suggest a more expansive underlying agenda and the possibility of reconstructing a fascist aesthetic. Its features would include a structural iterativity involving a repetition of tropes and themes, devoid of developmental moments that might suggest a progress in history; an explicit refusal of aesthetic autonomy through claims to documentary status; and in Benjamin's phrase, an 'aestheticisation of politics', a representation of struggle as seductively fascinating rather than as a vehicle for the resolution of substantive differences. To argue that elements such as these constitute the foundations of a fascist philosophical aesthetic would however require inserting this sparse German material into a wider European context. In particular it is elsewhere, in French, Italian and Anglo-American literature, where major authors – Céline, Maurras, Marinetti, Lewis and Pound, for example – completed significant literary works which were implicated in their involvement with fascist politics. Yet writers' political allegiances or philosophical declarations do not always provide exhaustive understandings of their literature.

As the centre of German intellectual life moved into exile, the third major rethinking of the Western philosophical trajectory was written in the United States by the leading figures of the Frankfurt School for Social Research, Max Horkheimer and Theodor Adorno. Unlike Heidegger's rejection of conceptual thinking altogether, Horkheimer and Adorno's account sought to rescue Enlightenment from its own failing. Yet unlike Husserl, who diagnosed that failing in terms of the shifting relationship to the life-world, they identified the problem as lying within conceptual thinking itself. In their co-authored *Dialektik der Aufklärung* (1944, published 1947; *Dialectic of Enlightenment*),[30] Enlightenment, which had once overcome mythic thinking through science, is judged to have taken on mythic form in its refusal to direct criticism toward itself. Because it does not interrogate its own project of conceptual clarification, it cannot recognise that myth too was once a form of Enlightenment, offering allegorical explanations in order to attempt to control the violence of nature. By the twentieth century at the latest, it is Enlightenment that exercises violence by attempting to impose conceptual uniformity onto the particularity of experience, leading to policies of homogenisation: either violently as in Nazi Germany or Stalinist Russia, or more subtly through the cultural conformism emanating from the 'culture industry' in the United States. The tyranny of the concept becomes the bureaucratic administration which persecutes difference, be it in the form of the ethnic or cultural group that is liquidated or the individual of character – such as Bonhoeffer – who is not tolerated. The immanent teleology of Western thinking towards destruction elicits a deep-seated pessimism, facing a brave new world of genocide and bureaucracy. The only possible alternative would be a redirection of the Enlightenment to reflect on its own inconsistencies (instead of the Heideggerian option of stepping out of rational thinking altogether).

Frankfurt School writings are frequently referred to as 'Critical Theory', a reference to Horkheimer's programmatic essay on 'Traditionelle und kritische Theorie' (1937; 'Traditional and Critical Theory'), a binary relation in which the former option suggests a repetition of the same, while the latter envisions the qualitatively new and different. The co-authored *Dialektik der Auklärung* includes a *locus classicus* of critical-theoretical literary criticism, the reading of Homer's *Odyssey*, particularly the encounter with the Sirens. That the oarsmen, the lower classes, have their ears plugged with wax in order to save them from the Sirens' song is taken to indicate the inequity in the distribution of culture; that Odysseus, as the archaic image of the bourgeois individual, can hear the song, but only at the price of being bound to the mast, points to the very nature of autonomous art. The power of art is contingent on its hermetic separation from the practical concerns of life. Here and in his numerous other postwar writings on aesthetics, especially music (but also literature in his *Noten zur Literatur* (1958–74; *Notes on literature*), Adorno draws on a Hegelian Marxist lineage which he combines with the programme of autonomy aesthetics derived from Schiller and Kant, in order to insist on the emancipatory quality inherent in art: authentic art is revolutionary. However, it is not at all the tendentiously revolutionary or political art which interests him. Rather it is the serious art of formal accomplishment, in particular the difficult art of modernism in which the potential for a social freedom is inscribed: Schoenberg or George. It is the stringency of Beckett, not the exhortations of

Brecht which Adorno comes to regard as the vehicle for an emancipatory vision.

The philosophical re-evaluations of Western thought in Husserl, Heidegger and Horkheimer/Adorno resonated with encyclopaedic judgements on the era in a series of major novels from Austria. The first portions of Robert Musil's unfinished *Der Mann ohne Eigenschaften* (*The man without qualities*) appeared in 1930. Set in imperial Vienna, the novel's central concern is the problematic of modernity, the apparent preponderance of senseless activity, to which the only proper response is an ironic perspective. Thus the initial topic, plans for a celebration of the 1918 anniversaries of the emperors of Austria and Germany, is particularly revealing from a post-war perspective, which can recognise that date as marking the collapse of both regimes. The integrity of the novel does not derive from any cohesive plot, but from the ongoing discourse of the narrator, Ulrich, who recognises that modern meaning has shifted from individuals to things and relationships. This impoverishment of the individual explains the designation 'without qualities'. In this context, neither a pathos of subjectivity nor a heroism of development can provide an appropriate stance or a legitimate literary strategy; in their place, literature becomes extended essayism, ironic and conceptual reflections on shifting problems. The alternative, a synthesis of reason and emotion, is played out in the figure of Arnheim, modelled on the German writer and politician Walter Rathenau who had been assassinated by right-wing extremists in 1922 (Mann refers to him in 'The German republic'), and Ulrich himself delves into a mode of mysticism, the 'other state', which appears to resolve the fragmentation of modern experience but never does so conclusively. Rationalised civilisation has its discontents, particularly as it becomes increasingly fragmented and apparently pointless, but there is no self-evident counter-programme, except for the resigned stance of irony.

Hermann Broch's trilogy *Die Schlafwandler* (1931–2; *The sleepwalkers*) could equally be misunderstood as a historical novel, since each section associates a specific year, 1888, 1903 and 1918, with a fundamental cultural formation. Yet just as *Der Mann ohne Eigenschaften* should be seen not as a limited portrait of Habsburg Vienna but as a judgement on modernity in general, Broch's novels are not genuine period descriptions. Instead, the underlying concern that links the three novels is the continuous collapse of values and the consequent loss of orientation in the world. Broch's mastery lies in his capacity to adapt the rhetorical style of the different novels to their specific cultural problematics, but in general the narrator's perspective frequently overshadows the particular material, subsuming them into the singular concern with values. Broch's subsequent novel, *Bergroman (The spell)*, published posthumously in 1953, shifts attention from the urban material of *Die Schlafwandler* to an isolated village and the capacity of the community to succumb to fascinating demagoguery, in an explicit analogy to the rise of fascism.

The relationship of fascism to the structures of culture is also the topic of Elias Canetti's *Die Blendung* (1935; *Auto-da-Fé*), not however in the form of specific historical references but in the analysis of authority in relation to literary form. The central figure, Peter Kien, a renowned Sinologist, lives surrounded by the books of his library, assiduously avoiding human contact with others. It is this refusal of solidarity that blinds him to the proto-fascist resentment that is developing around him, while also trapping him in an iron cage of loneliness. When he cannot avoid succumbing to the request of his housekeeper to borrow a book, he chooses a novel for her, a choice which is accompanied by a moment of literary criticism:

Für sie kam bloß ein Roman in Betracht. Nur wird von Romanen kein Geist fett. Den Genuß, den sie vielleicht bieten, überzahlt man sehr: sie zersetzen den besten Charakter. Man lernt sich in allerlei Menschen einfühlen. Am vielen Hin und Her gewinnt man Geschmack . . . Jeder Standpunkt wird begreiflich . . . Romane müßten von Staats wegen verboten sein.[31]

A novel was the only thing worth considering for her. But no mind ever grew fat on a diet of novels. The pleasure which they occasionally offer is far too heavily paid for: they undermine the finest characters. They teach us to think ourselves into other men's places. Thus we acquire a taste for change . . . The reader learns to understand every point of view . . . Novels should be prohibited by the state.

In fact, *Die Blendung* makes good on this promise by incorporating into the novel a multiplicity of voices; far from regarding this discord as a problem of loss of cohesion, Canetti evidently deploys the narrative polyphony as a corrective to an overly hierarchical and homogenised culture, as figured by Peter. In other words, the decay of order, which appeared so problematic for Broch, becomes the precondition for a human solidarity for Canetti. In his postwar philosophical and anthropological study *Masse und Macht* (1960; *Crowds and power*) he continued to pursue related topics, especially mass behaviour and the relationship of the individual to it.

However, the singularly summative novel of ideas for this era of German literature, philosophy, and culture in general, is Thomas Mann's

Doktor Faustus (1947). Reworking the Faust material, the overriding literary figure of the German tradition, the novel borrows more insistently from the sixteenth-century chapbook than from Goethe's dramas, but it thereby suggests a single cohesive epoch from the Reformation to the Second World War, and the analysis of its cultural substance is simultaneously an interrogation of the German record. A first-person narrative placed in the mouth of the garrulous and frequently unselfcritical Serenus Zeitblom, it charts the biography of the composer Adrian Leverkühn, from his early childhood, through his musical career, to his death in 1940. Zeitblom is a Catholic and a humanist while Leverkühn is Protestant, and the pair suggests the divided soul of Germany. Moreover the name itself invokes Nietzsche (as do many other of Leverkühn's associations), echoing the Nietzschean exhortation to live dangerously. These multiple cultural-historical levels are reproduced, formally, in the temporal structure of the novel. The present of the narrator, during the Second World War, criss-crosses with Leverkühn's and his own paths from the late nineteenth century; there are also older historical reminiscences with regard to the cultural heritage, and Zeitblom refers explicitly to the future moment of the reader. Organised in a polyphonic simultaneity, these competing and intertwined time-lines suggest that moments of the past and the future are permanently present, rather than representing neatly separated moments in a linear trajectory of progress.

Leverkühn's central musical achievement involves the development of a method of serial composition, explicitly modelled on the twelve-tone theory of Arnold Schoenberg. The novel includes brilliant essays on musical pieces, some real, such as Beethoven's sonata opus 111, and some imaginary compositions of Leverkühn. The unfolding of this musical discussion frames a cultural-historical debate between Zeitblom and his friend, in which the former grows increasingly wary of Leverkühn's scepticism towards individual creativity. If irony or parody had become primary vehicles for composition, this seemed to suggest a sterile dependence on the past and the incapacity to reach qualitatively new ground, and this in turn would imply the demise of creative subjectivity. However, Leverkühn found his 'Durchbruch' ('breakthrough') in serial composition, the repetition of all twelve notes of the scale. While the conservative humanist narrator regards this solution as a frightening loss of freedom, Leverkühn, in contrast, regards the self-imposed order of serial composition as itself the precondition of freedom.

The particular achievement of the novel is the double exposure of a narrative about the emergence of modernist music with a reflection on

German politics in the early twentieth century. Reflection on artistic and cultural matters becomes an allegory for an inquiry into politics; thus the question of compositional freedom is very much a vehicle to think through the status of freedom in German culture. Leverkühn's progress in music, contingent on a brilliant pact with a devil who cites from Adorno's musicological writings, goes hand in hand with an alienation from human relations. The specifically non-communicative aesthetics of hermetic art seems to mirror the imperviousness of the dictatorial Nazi regime; yet at the same time, only that same rigorously hermetic art is capable of a mournful expressivity which can articulate suffering in an adequately uncompromising manner. The work of art, that is, both this novel and the musical works which it describes, eschews the outdated sentimentalism which Zeitblom might prefer, growing hard, structured and tough, but only because these difficult aesthetic structures are the only ones equal to the sorrow at hand. The problem of the subject, diagnosed to be so helpless in *Berlin Alexanderplatz* or so vulnerable in *Fräulein Else*, finds its ultimate formulation here. Through the renunciation of any sentimentalistic subjectivity, through the adoption of hermetic form, the work of art becomes the vehicle for a faint hope in the recovery of a new subjectivity in the future. The analogous message held for wartime Germany: only through renunciation and defeat might a future be possible.

NOTES

1 Bertolt Brecht, *Gedichte*, ed. Suhrkamp Verlag and Elisabeth Hauptmann, vol. VI of *Gesammelte Werke*, 8 vols. (Frankfurt am Main: Suhrkamp, 1967), p. 259. English modified from: Bertolt Brecht, *Selected poems*, translated by H. R. Hays (New York and London: Harcourt Brace Jovanovich, 1947), p. 61.

2 *Die protestantische Ethik und der Geist des Kapitalismus*, in *Gesammelte Aufsätze zur Religionssoziologie*, 3 vols. (Tübingen: J. C. B. Mohr, 1922), vol. I, p. 203.

3 *Die protestantische Ethik*, p. 204.

4 'Wissenschaft als Beruf', in *Gesammelte Aufsätze zur Wissenschaftslehre*, ed. Johannes Winckelmann (Tübingen: J. C. B. Mohr, 1968), p. 592. English translation: Max Weber, 'Science as a Vocation', in H. H. Gerth and C. Wright Mills (eds.), *From Max Weber: essays in sociology* (New York: Oxford University Press, 1958), p. 137.

5 Karl Marx, *Grundrisse: introduction to the critique of political economy*, trans. Martin Nicolaus (New York: Vintage Books, 1973), p. 111.

6 Peter Bürger, *Theory of the avant-garde* (Minneapolis: University of Minnesota Press, 1984), pp. 41–6.

7 'den kalten Skeletthänden rationaler Ordnungen ebenso völlig entronnen wie der Stumpfheit des Alltages', Max Weber, 'Zwischenbetrachtung', in *Gesammelte Aufsätze zur Religionssoziologie*, vol. I, p. 561. Compare Max Weber, 'Religious rejections of the world and their directions', in *From Max Weber: essays in sociology*, p. 347.

8 Oswald Spengler, *Der Untergang des Abendlandes: Umrisse einer Morphologie der Weltgeschichte* (Munich: C. H. Beck, 1979).

9 Kurt Pinthus (ed.), *Menschheitsdämmerung* (Hamburg: Rowohlt, 1959), p. 22.

10 *Menschheitsdämmerung*, p. 31.

11 'würden unsre Augen sich an Welt und Sonne satt und glühend trinken', *Menschheitsdämmerung*, p. 80.

12 'Es war süß, zu weilen und sich versäumen, / Von Wirklichkeit den Leib so wie von staubiger Rüstung zu entketten', *Menschheitsdämmerung*, p. 80.

13 'Warum stieg ich nieder? Warum lief ich den Weg? Wohin laufe ich noch? . . . Von morgens bis mitternachts rase ich im Kreis', *Von morgens bis mitternachts*, in Georg Kaiser, *Stücke* (Berlin: Henschel, 1972), p. 58.

14 Friedrich Gundolf, *George* (Darmstadt: Wissenschaftliche Buchgesellschaft, 1968), p. 1.

15 Gundolf to Karl Vossler, 4 May 1926, in *Gundolf Briefe. Neue Folge*, ed. Lothar Helbing and Claus Victor Bock (Amsterdam: Castrum Peregrini Presse, 1965), p. 216.

16 Ernst Bertram, *Deutsche Gestalten: Fest- und Gedenkreden* (Leipzig: Insel, 1934), pp. 51f.

17 Thomas Mann, *Der Zauberberg*, in *Gesammelte Werke*, 12 vols. (Oldenburg: S. Fischer Verlag, 1960), vol. v, p. 162. English: Thomas Mann, *The magic mountain*, trans. H. T. Lowe-Porter (New York: Vintage, 1969), p. 114.

18 Bertram, *Deutsche Gestalten*, p. 54.

19 Ernst Jünger, 'Der Kampf als inneres Erlebnis', in *Sämtliche Werke*, part II, vol. I: *Essays II. Betrachtungen zur Zeit* (Stuttgart: Klett-Cotta, 1980), pp. 72f.

20 Thomas Mann, 'Von deutscher Republik', in *Gesammelte Werke*, vol. XI, p. 835. For a different translation see 'The German republic', in *The order of the day: political essays and speeches of two decades*, trans. H. T. Lowe-Porter (Freeport: Books for Libraries Press, 1969), p. 45.

21 'Von deutscher Republic', in *Gesammelte Werke*, vol. XI, p. 852.

22 'Was ist ein Einbruch in eine Bank gegen die Gründung einer Bank?', *Die Dreigroschenoper*, in *Gesammelte Werke*, vol. I, p. 482.

23 Bertolt Brecht, 'Hollywood', in *Gesammelte Werke*, vol. IV, p. 848.

24 Theodor W. Adorno, 'Erpreßte Versöhnung', in *Noten zur Literatur*, ed. Rolf Tiedemann, *Gesammelte Schriften*, 20 vols. (Frankfurt am Main: Suhrkamp, 1974), vol. XI, pp. 251–80.

25 Walter Benjamin, 'Über den Begriff der Geschichte', in *Gesammelte Schriften*, ed. Rolf Tiedemann and Hermann Schweppenhäuser, 7 vols. (Frankfurt: Suhrkamp, 1974), vol. II, pp. 697f. Compare: *Illuminations*, ed. Hannah Arendt, trans. Harry Zohn (New York: Schocken, 1969), pp. 257f.

26 Compare Ritchie Robertson's remarks on Freud in chapter four above, pp. 174ff.

27 See Fritz Stern, *The politics of cultural despair: a study in the rise of the Germanic ideology* (Berkeley: University of California Press, 1961).

28 Compare Ritchie Robertson's remarks on Husserl in chapter four, pp. 189f.

29 Edmund Husserl, 'Die Krisis des europäischen Menschentums und die Philosophie,' in *Husserliana*, ed. Walter Biemel, 30 vols. (Haag: Nijhoff, 1962), vol. VI, p. 348. Compare *The crisis of European sciences and transcendental phenomenology. An introduction to phenomenological philosophy*, trans. David Carr (Evanston: Northwestern University Press, 1970), p. 299.

30 Compare Robert C. Holub's remarks on Horkheimer and Adorno in chapter six, pp. 248f.

31 Elias Canetti, *Die Blendung* (Munich: Carl Hanser Verlag, 1963), pp. 41–2. Compare *Auto-da-Fé*, trans. C. V. Wedgwood (New York: Continuum, 1982), p. 42.

Coming to terms with the past in postwar literature and philosophy

Robert C. Holub

THE TROUBLED LEGACY

From 1945 until at least reunification in 1989 German intellectual and cultural life, including philosophy and literature, was dominated by the endeavour to come to terms with the past. At the conclusion of its second military defeat in less than three decades, Germany was morally exhausted and physically devastated. In contrast to the First World War, when Germany surrendered before it was invaded by foreign armies, the Second World War brought tremendous losses for Germans both on the battlefield and at home. Three and a half million German soldiers lost their lives fighting for Adolf Hitler and his Reich, and just as many civilians perished; ten million German soldiers were taken as prisoners of war, some never to return. The economic destruction was immense: Germany, reduced in size by about a quarter, experienced a loss of about a third of its national wealth, along with fifteen percent of its available housing. Hardest hit were the major cities, which were the primary targets in the Allied air attacks. Shortly after the end of hostilities another pressing problem arose: the refugees from the East began pouring into a country that could not even take care of its own population. It is estimated that up to twenty-five million Germans lost their homes because of evacuation, flight or bombing. The situation was most dire in the eastern portions of Germany, where the battles between the German and the invading Soviet armies had been severely contested.

The defeat of Germany was total and devastating, but the intellectual preoccupation with the past resulted not so much from Germany's discredited military tradition or its desperate economic situation. Indeed, as the postwar years have demonstrated, Germany was able to overcome its authoritarian tendencies, developing into an exemplary democratic nation, and a scant decade and a half after its unconditional surrender it had become one of the leading economic powers in the world. But it was not able to overcome two legacies that have haunted its cultural life for the last half century. The first of these legacies is Nazism, which has come to be synonymous with absolute evil. National Socialism and Adolf Hitler hold a special place in German as well as world history; they transcend the militarism and authoritarianism that nurtured their emergence and have long since been regarded as a permanent blemish on the German character. After the war German intellectual and literary historians had to account for how their nation, apparently so cultured and advanced, could fall prey to the brutality and barbarity of the Third Reich. Georg Lukács's *Zerstörung der Vernunft* (1954; *Destruction of reason*), which traced the rise of Nazism back through the German philosophical tradition, was perhaps rightly criticised for its distortions of seminal texts, but several works produced in the West, for example Friedrich Meinecke's *Die deutsche Katastrophe* (1946; *The German catastrophe*) or Alfred Martin's *Geistige Wegbereiter des deutschen Zusammenbruchs* (1948; *Intellectual precursors of the German collapse*), or even Thomas Mann's *Doktor Faustus* (1947; *Doctor Faustus*), with slightly different emphases, likewise found Hitler's rise prepared by the German intellectual tradition. Central preoccupations for the authors and philosophers of the postwar period were how Germany could fall to the depths of Nazism and what was necessary to remove its renegade status and to preserve respectability among the nations of the world.

The second and more important legacy with which Germany has had to contend in the postwar period was the Holocaust or Shoah. Although Germany perpetrated many criminal actions against its own citizens during the period 1933–45 and against other peoples during the Second World War, and although under National Socialist rule many religious, ethnic and political groups – the Sinti and Roma, the mentally ill, homosexuals, Jehovah's Witnesses, Eastern Europeans, communists and socialists – were severely persecuted, the German genocide of the Jewish people occupies a special place in history. The enormity of the undertaking – over five million Jews were murdered – the systematic nature of the annihilation and the recognition that these acts of mass murder were planned and carried out by a nation formerly considered among the most civilised on earth are factors that make the Holocaust remarkable and almost unfathomable. Postwar writers and philosophers were faced with the impossible task of explaining how a nation could allow such acts to be committed in its name and how to deal with the pressing issues of guilt, responsibility and expiation. But they were also confronted with a series of practical and theoretical issues arising from the Holocaust. A central concern of several intellectuals immediately after the war and for the ensuing decades was how to ensure that the Holocaust would not recur again in Germany. Philosophers, writers and critics asked themselves what kinds of cultural, political and institutional reforms were needed to eliminate anti-democratic attitudes, to ensure an informed, critical and autonomous voting public and to prevent xenophobic and racist sentiments. With regard to more theoretical matters intellectuals found that the assumptions they made prior to the Holocaust were no longer valid. Progress and enlightenment had to be considered dubious notions; the connection between morality and civilisation seemed tenuous; indeed, all explanations of human history, all precepts of modernity appeared to be called into question by the horrific crimes of National Socialism against the Jewish people of Europe.

The demise of National Socialism and its attendant barbarity was necessarily accompanied by a new consciousness and a new mission for German intellectuals. Because the four years of Allied occupation in 1945–9 and the establishment of self-sufficient German states appeared to represent a radical break with the Third Reich, critics have often hypothesised a zero-point (*Nullpunkt*) or 'clear-felling' (*Kahlschlag*) of German culture in the postwar era. Further evidence for such a new beginning comes from the discontinuity of intellectual life from National Socialist Germany to the Federal Republic and the German Democratic Republic. Although older writers and philosophers emerged from so-called inner emigration and, particularly in the GDR, several prominent authors returned from exile, literary and intellectual life, especially in the West, found new and important contributors. The establishment of *Gruppe 47* (Group 47), a loosely structured West German writers' organisation that served as a showcase for young authors, set an ideological agenda that was clearly anti-fascist and individualistic, in short, a rupture with the cultural politics of the preceding years. Similarly in East Germany the tone was resolutely against Nazism, and although a collectivist spirit soon engulfed all purely intellectual activity, there was an unmistakable endeavour to distance culture from its past trappings. New journals were another sign of a fresh start – *Der Ruf* (*The call*), *Die Sammlung* (*The gathering*), or *Die Wandlung* (*The transformation*) in the Western zones, *Ost und West* (*East and west*) or *Sinn und Form* (*Meaning and form*) in the East – and before the cold war divided Germany into camps culturally at war with one another, a similar spirit of renewal pervaded both East and West. Especially important were foreign influences. In a certain sense West Germany caught up with the rest of the Western world in the initial postwar period, and the reintroduction of abstract art, atonal music and an existentially informed literature and philosophy were signs of its reintegration into the family of civilised nations.

Despite efforts to forge a new cultural climate, relying on foreign rather than corrupted German traditions, intellectual life was not entirely free from continuities either. With the advent of the cold war, the communist enemy seemed more important than the National Socialist past, and as a result many former Nazis or fellow travellers were able to regain power in the cultural sphere. Especially in the Federal Republic, university life continued to be dominated by professors active under Hitler, and many governmental and bureaucratic offices, including much of the juridical system, soon saw former National Socialists again in leading positions. More importantly, however, the new generation of democratic writers acknowledged their own affiliation with the traditions of a 'better' Germany. Often they reached back to the artistic and intellectual heritage of the Weimar Republic, or to other democratic figures or periods in German history for their inspiration. After the trauma of the war and the Holocaust it was necessary to recreate German philosophical and literary history in a reflective fashion to enable a new orientation. But many intellectuals soon recognised that it was not really possible to separate out a 'good' German tradition from its 'evil' perversion; a complex dialectic informs aesthetic and philosophical development. Indeed, the tension in postwar German philosophy and literature from the end of the war right through unification comes from the collective effort to escape the long shadow of the past, on the one hand, and, on the other, the constant need to recall, represent, reinterpret, repudiate Germany's troubled legacy.

PHILOSOPHICAL SOLUTIONS

German intellectual responses to National Socialism and the Holocaust were varied, but three philosophically informed perspectives can serve as paradigms for the way in which the Germans have mastered their past. The first viewpoint is represented by a text composed in exile even before the close of hostilities. One of the most subtle and engaging reflections from the forties, *Dialektik der Aufklärung* (*Dialectic of Enlightenment*) by Theodor Adorno (1903–69) and Max Horkheimer (1895–1973) employed a sociological analysis informed broadly by psychoanalysis and the tradition of Western Marxism.[1] Composed during the last year of the war and published in a limited edition in Amsterdam in 1947, this book eventually became one of the most influential works of the postwar years, although its enormous impact came only during the 1960s with the appearance of the student movement. The authors, two Jewish intellectuals who returned to Germany after the war and occupied university posts, are among the most celebrated members of the Frankfurt School of Social Research, a group devoted to interdisciplinary study that arose in the late 1920s in Frankfurt and, because of its leftist and Jewish profile, was forced to leave Germany after Hitler's assumption of power. The book was therefore written while Adorno and Horkheimer were in exile in the United States; the preface, completed in May 1944, bears the place designation Los Angeles, California. The framework for *Dialektik der Aufklärung* is much larger than Hitler or the Holocaust: the authors' purview encompasses the course of the Western world since the Greeks. The central thesis, succinctly stated, is that Enlightenment turns back on itself. Conceiving Enlightenment in its widest sense as a pattern of human domination over nature or as instrumental rationality, Adorno and Horkheimer demonstrate how this domination, which was originally emancipatory, eventually turns into hegemony in various spheres of human existence. They argue that the endeavour to control the forces of nature forms a seamless continuity with the suppression of human nature and oppression of human beings; thus what we originally conceive as emancipation becomes enslavement to others or to ourselves. The initial chapter in *Dialektik der Aufklärung* deals with the 'concept of Enlightenment' in fairly abstract terms; the two famous excursuses to this chapter take up Odysseus as the prototypical Enlightenment figure and Juliette, the character created by the Marquis de Sade, to show how enlightened morality turns into something rather less than ethical conduct. In a chapter relating directly to the experiences of the Frankfurt School in the United States, Horkheimer and Adorno then turn to the culture industry. Here they are intent on showing how popular culture in the Western world performs a function analogous to political oppression on other parts of the globe. Their vision is thus one of a totally administered world. In Germany and much of Europe fascism reigns; in the Soviet Union the population is subjugated by an oppressive state socialism; in the United States the culture industry gives us only the illusion of freedom.

Perhaps the most relevant section of *Dialektik der Aufklärung* for understanding the Third Reich is the chapter entitled 'Elements of anti-Semitism'. Like the book as a whole, this chapter treats contemporary events as part of a larger philosophical reflection. We are not given a history of anti-Semitism, or an analysis of anti-Jewish traditions in

Germany, but rather the general mechanisms that account for anti-Semitism and by which anti-Semitism functions. Initially Adorno and Horkheimer reject the view that anti-Semitism is a distortion of the social order; for a society based on fascist principles it is a prerequisite and necessity. The liberal account, which considers Jews individuals and not different from other peoples, does not recognise the exigencies of power, and in this sense the fascist perspective on the Jews is just as true as the liberal interpretation. What allows anti-Semitism to insinuate itself in the twentieth century is the total domination to which we as citizens of modernity are subjected. In essence, people living under a system of domination are deprived of choice, autonomy and subjectivity. Unfortunately these same people are then set loose as 'individuals' (which they are not) to act or at least to perform actions in a social order. What results are 'senseless reflexes' in the behaviourist mode, ritualised behaviour, non-thinking, non-reflective responses to situations and the reduction of groups to stereotypes. Adorno and Horkheimer associate anti-Semitism with totality, a total response that does not admit of critique, reflection, or differentiation. In this totalised situation people can readily believe that Jews are parasitic elements of a fundamentally sound economic order, and they can be held responsible for the exploitation of the dominant system of production. Distortions and abnormalities of all types are ultimately projected onto the Jews, who function as the repository for the psychotic nature of modernity. For Adorno and Horkheimer, anti-Semitism is not an essence of the fascist system, but one interchangeable plank in a party platform, something that may desist, only to be replaced by another pernicious prejudice. Only with the cessation of domination as our mode of relating to the world and each other can we rid ourselves of the root cause of anti-Semitism.

As Jews living in exile, Adorno and Horkheimer observed events in Germany and Europe from the outside. They did not and could not speak directly to the most pressing issues confronting most Germans, who suddenly found themselves indicted in the eyes of the world because of their implicit complicity with the Hitler regime. Among the few intellectuals who addressed these concerns in the immediate postwar period was Karl Jaspers (1883–1969), whose essay on *Die Schuldfrage* (1946; *The question of German guilt*), more than any other text in the postwar epoch, established the official agenda for Germany with regard to Nazism and its crimes.[2] Like Adorno and Horkheimer, Jaspers had his philosophical training and initial reputation from activities prior to 1945. Originally a student and then a professor of psychology and psychiatry,

Jaspers became during the Weimar Republic a noted professor of philosophy and, along with his colleague Martin Heidegger (1889–1976), one of the founders of existentialism. Although he remained politically naive throughout the 1920s, once the Nazis came to power he refused cooperation, and in 1937 he lost his teaching position, in part because of his marriage to a Jewess. After the war his central concern was to restore the integrity of the German system of higher education, and most of his writings in the pivotal years 1945–6 focus on issues at German universities. Indeed, the preface to *Die Schuldfrage* makes it clear that this essay as well was conceived as part of his personal pedagogical programme: after a period in which higher education had been instrumentalised for such nefarious objectives, he was proposing an attitude and a method for the entire nation that could move it towards a spiritual renewal.

Jaspers's essay is a response to several postwar exigencies. In suggesting ways to approach the topic of guilt, Jaspers is competing with two contemporary occurrences: denazification and the Nuremberg Trials. Denazification was the Allied method for dealing with the enormous number of Germans implicated by membership in the Nazi party or related organisations, or by non-military activities during the war; its goal was to cleanse dangerous elements from positions of responsibility. Administered first by the occupying powers and later by the Germans themselves, denazification was by all accounts a failure. The questionnaires Germans were asked to complete became objects of ridicule – as evidenced in the satirical novel by Ernst von Salomon (1902–72), *Der Fragebogen* (1951; *The questionnaire*) – and eventually the vast majority of Germans received pardons or outright acquittal for all crimes. The initial Nuremberg Trials, which were taking place while Jaspers was writing *Die Schuldfrage*, were meant to adjudicate the guilt of the more prominent Nazi officials and the leaders of industry who were implicated in high crimes. Somewhat more successful than denazification in their rigour, the Nuremberg Trials also served an exemplary function and demonstrated to the native populace and to the world that the rule of law had returned to German soil. Indeed, Jaspers's text, which was completed before the end of the first of the eleven Nuremberg Trials, is a German defence of the legitimacy of the trials, a legitimacy that many other Germans called into question on a number of technical and substantive grounds. In arguing that Nuremberg is not simply victor's justice, and that the actions of certain officials, although not violations of statutes existing at the time, were still offences that could be legitimately tried, Jaspers sanctioned the Allied undertaking.

But Jaspers also challenged an opinion prevalent in certain circles in the Allied powers that would hold all Germans equally accountable for the crimes perpetrated by National Socialism. One of the main functions of *Die Schuldfrage* is to refute the collective guilt hypothesis. In doing so, Jaspers was opposing factions that would have favoured the complete de-industrialisation of Germany, and relying on more moderate opinions, in particular those of Hannah Arendt (1906–75) and Dwight MacDonald (1906–82). Arendt, whose thesis on totalitarianism was to became a cornerstone of Western ideology in the 1950s, and whose report on the Eichmann Trial in Jerusalem in 1961 achieved notoriety for its 'banality-of-evil' thesis, contended in 1945 that guilt cannot be fairly determined by an outside agency. MacDonald, even more radically, maintained that the most heinous crimes were carried out against the will and without the knowledge of the German people. Jaspers, as part of the vanquished, could not be quite so defensive about his country or compatriots, but he did suggest categories that mitigated the guilt and the responsibility of most Germans for the crimes committed in their names. Only criminal guilt, he asserted, could be tried before a court of law and punished. All other forms of guilt had different adjudicative authorities and consequences. Political guilt belonged in the hands of the victors; the appropriate punishment was a loss of sovereignty; the Third Reich can thus be found guilty in a political sense because of the actions of the state, but this guilt holds no direct consequences for individuals. For individuals not guilty in the criminal sense Jaspers develops the categories of moral and metaphysical guilt. One's conscience and one's God, respectively, are the authorities that determine these classes of guilt, and the consequences are such vaguely religious notions as penance and the transformation of oneself before the Supreme Being. The application of Jaspers's four categories of guilt would produce a small number of criminally guilty; but the vast majority of the population would be called upon to engage in moral cleansing and spiritual renewal.

Jaspers's *Die Schuldfrage* was the most important postwar intellectual response to Nazism and the Holocaust. Because it readily admitted the criminal activity of the fascist regime, yet exonerated most of the German people from direct punishment, and because it relied on a moralistic rhetoric that involved humility, contrition and atonement, it functioned well throughout the postwar epoch as a framework for German attitudes towards the past. Jaspers's text set the tone for the official political culture of the Federal Republic, establishing a moral consensus for confronting Germany's troubled legacy. From discussions of reparations and

commemorations of the 'night of broken glass' ('Kristallnacht') to relations with Israel and Willi Brandt's kneeling gesture at the Warsaw ghetto,
West Germany adhered to a high ethical path that resonates in Jaspers's
discussions. Jaspers himself, however, was hardly satisfied with the impact
of his essay in the immediate postwar era or in the ensuing two decades.
It is a curious and sobering fact of intellectual life in West Germany that
Jaspers's work stands virtually alone; outside of a few official proclama-
tions from the church and an occasional remark by a politician, there was
no intellectual response to the questions concerning German guilt and
responsibility, even as the extent of German atrocities became widely
known. There was no general discourse, no public sphere for the issues
Jaspers raised, and even in 1967, two years before his death, Jaspers was
to lament that the spiritual reversal he had deemed necessary if Germany
was to redress its grave transgressions had not occurred.

A third philosophical figure must be conjured to account for a variety
of response that was neither sociological and political, nor religious and
moralistic. Martin Heidegger, whose involvement with National Socialism in the 1930s was well known, represents another mode of dealing with
the past. Philosophically he shared with Jaspers, at least in his early work
around *Sein und Zeit* (1927; *Being and time*), a concern with the existential
predicament of the individual; like Adorno and Horkheimer, he posited
an overarching critique of Western man since the Greeks. But perhaps
because of his own association with National Socialism as rector of the
University of Freiburg in 1933–4, he was silent about Nazism and the
Holocaust after the war. The scant remarks he did make were defensive
and equivocal. In one instance he compared the Nazi genocide to mech-
anised agriculture; in another he likened the Shoah to the expulsion of
ethnic Germans from Eastern Europe and their detainment in reloca-
tion camps. His only public interview on the topic of his Nazi affiliation
was carefully staged and edited by Heidegger himself and was allowed
to appear only after his death.[3] In the interview he portrays himself as a
victim of National Socialism and downplays any significant involvement
or intellectual affinity with the party. At best Heidegger can be accused
of a moral failing. But it is less a personal fault than a structural flaw that
one encounters in Heidegger's mendacity and prevarication. Heidegger,
like many of his fellow intellectuals, sought to ignore the past and escape into a realm of existential concerns or linguistic play. In this sense
he represents an amoral strand of German literature and philosophy,
one that occupies a marginal position until the 1980s, when it emerges
in the guise of postmodernism, challenging the moral and political

consensus set primarily by Jaspers and those who implicitly adhered to his message of remorse and atonement.

LITERATURE OF IMMEDIATE EXPERIENCE

For young authors, coming to terms with the past meant trying to understand their own actions as combatants in World War Two. Perhaps the most common figure in postwar literature was the soldier, either involved in battle or returning home. Because these men were overwhelmed by the war and by the utter collapse of the value system under which they had lived, the initial postwar efforts were largely records of experience. But unlike the militaristic and nationalistic war novels of the Third Reich that praised warfare and the warrior, the prose of the returning soldiers was sober and subjective, looking inward. In more than one sense the label 'literature of the rubble' characterises well these endeavours to confront the horrors of the battlefield. With Germany lying in ruins, a new generation of authors found that they could no longer rely on the ideology with which they had gone to war, or the language formerly used to express feelings and emotions. They were compelled instead to seek from the fragments of their existence and their language a means to construct some meaning for their behaviour and the actions of the German nation. In the initial decade following the Second World War most writers were unable to comprehend the larger issues that informed their lives. Reacting against ideology as a general evil, they took solace in a private and moralistic view of humanity. The purview of much of this writing is limited; the narrative voice is often a first-person account or filtered through a single subjectivity; the descriptions are sparse, and there is an effort to convey candour and simplicity. The German soldiers in postwar literature are contrite, but they themselves are victims of Nazism, not perpetrators of crimes.

No writer typifies this postwar mood more than Heinrich Böll (1917–85). The recipient of the Nobel Prize for literature in 1972, Böll was an author whose writings charted the developments in West German literature for over three decades. A critic of the smugness accompanying the 'economic miracle' in the 1950s and an ally of progressive forces during the turbulent 1960s and 1970s, he began his career with a series of moving portrayals from the lives of common soldiers. *Der Zug war pünktlich* (1949; *The train was on time*) is exemplary in this regard.[4] It depicts the train ride of a reluctant common soldier named Andreas from his furlough in Cologne to the eastern front in Poland. On his journey he befriends two soldiers whose experiences have made them victims of the war: Willi returned home to find his wife sleeping with another man; the blond soldier, who is never identified by name, has been raped by his sergeant on a lonely outpost on the eastern front. Andreas has not been violated by the war in such a direct fashion, but since the narrative consists largely of his thoughts and observations, we know that he suffers pangs of guilt for his involvement in brutality he can neither comprehend nor prevent. All three are weary, carrying out actions mechanically without any commitment to the cause they serve. Although the war seems ubiquitous, the Nazi party and Adolf Hitler are never mentioned by name; they are not part of Andreas's consciousness. For the most part the Holocaust is also absent; Andreas prays for the Jews, but they are only one group among many that weigh upon his conscience, and none of the characters acknowledges the Nazi policy of genocide or its implementation.

Böll's novel illustrates well the moral imperatives initiated by Jaspers's essay. Jaspers's message was one of individual, spiritual values, and by focusing on the reflections of a young, naive and innocent figure, the narrative structure precludes any analysis of larger issues surrounding the war and its attendant barbarity. The political or social dimensions of the Third Reich are beyond the grasp of all agents; the characters relate to their situations directly and sensuously without distance or reflection. The sole purpose of Andreas's prayers is to attain personal peace with himself, to atone for any wrong-doing in his life. His previous actions, however, cannot be categorised as criminal; at most they consist of minor moral or 'metaphysical' failings for which he is determined to atone. He is thus exemplary of the type of person required to fulfil Jaspers's call for a renewal in the postwar era. Both Jaspers and Böll derive their conceptual framework and their imagery from the Christian, religious sphere. Böll's Andreas is transparent as a wartime Christ figure, praying for the sins of all humanity, those perpetrating crimes and those deceived by Nazi propaganda, as well as the war's many victims. He is a soldier with no weapon but prayer – he has left his rifle at home – who is delivered up to death by a Polish prostitute trying to rescue him and his two companions from the bloodshed. Böll's characters in his early works, like Andreas, represent the goodness remaining in Germany. Themselves defiled and violated by a war they did not countenance, they function to reassure Germans of their basic decency despite their implication in horrific occurrences. Providing metaphysical solace in a devastated nation, they suggest that the German past could be best confronted with moral reform rather than institutional or social change.

Similar in this regard is *Draußen vor der Tür* (1947; *The man outside*), the most important play of the immediate postwar period.[5] Its author, Wolfgang Borchert (1921–47), was a war veteran who, like his hero Beckmann, had served on the harsh eastern front and who returned physically and emotionally damaged. Using techniques borrowed from the expressionist epoch, Borchert portrays the anguish experienced by a soldier, obviously a type of German Everyman, trying to adjust again to civilian life. The play is structured around Beckmann's encounters with persons in postwar society; in successive scenes he meets a girl whose husband has not yet returned from the war, his former commanding officer, a theatre producer and Frau Kramer, who informs him of his parents' suicide. Interspersed are surrealistic dialogues between Beckmann and 'the Other One'. Each encounter demonstrates his difficulty in regaining a place in postwar Germany. Indeed, the very title indicates that estrangement defines Beckmann's existence. Even if the outer accoutrements of war are stripped away – and Beckmann's never are – the psychic damage remains, causing Beckmann to be perceived as a freak and to consider himself foreign. To an extent this play is also based on individual and moral premises reminiscent of Jaspers's essay. Beckmann, like Andreas, is in no sense criminally responsible for the suffering of the war; both are victims rather than perpetrators, Germans who were opposed or indifferent to the political forces of Nazism, and who were innocent of racist prejudice. Like most initial confrontations with the fascist legacy, *Draußen vor der Tür* is less concerned about the violence inflicted on others by Germans than about the debilitating impact of battle on the native population. As if overwhelmed by the war and the callousness of the postwar era, Beckmann wanders zombie-like through German society, unable to end his own life, but with no direction.

Beckmann's predicament obviously reflected the situation of thousands of soldiers who found themselves in a state of material and spiritual depravity. His drama is existential not simply because it includes healthy doses of existential themes such as individuality, dread and anxiety, the finitude of existence and a reliance on human subjectivity, but because it presents these themes at a time when existence itself was a real question for the German populace. In contrast to Böll's Andreas, for whom God was the focal point of a more human world, Beckmann finds himself abandoned even by the Supreme Being. As striking as Nietzsche's reflections on the death of God is the opening prologue, in which an undertaker, who metamorphoses into Death, confronts an old man who reveals himself as God. Death wins the dialogical battle when God confesses that he is powerless to alleviate the suffering of the world, and at the close of the play Beckmann cries out in vain for succour from a silent and impotent deity. Inside this existentially tinged frame, however, Borchert includes a good deal more social critique than one finds in the early Böll. The colonel who gave Beckmann responsibility for eleven men who eventually perished suffers no pangs of remorse; he is enjoying a meal with his family and cannot identify with Beckmann's inability to adjust to peacetime. And the producer rejects Beckmann's strange and frightening performance, advising him to practise further, and that truth has nothing to do with real art. Like Böll's novel, Borchert's play rarely mentions Nazism and only alludes obliquely to the Holocaust. But it raises philosophical, social and aesthetic issues in a troubling fashion, presenting problems for which postwar experience had no solutions.

Although postwar literature and philosophy focused on the moral, social and psychological problems confronting Germans, another type of experience was responsible for perhaps the most famous poem composed in German in the entire century, 'Todesfuge' ('Death fugue'). Written by the Romanian and later French citizen Paul Celan (1920–70) probably at the close of the war, it appeared first in 1948, but it became known only in 1952 when it was included in the collection *Mohn und Gedächtnis* (*Poppy and remembrance*). A haunting lyrical cadence that employs chant-like repetition and striking imagery, 'Todesfuge' adapts the techniques of a Baroque fugue, weaving motifs together and altering them slightly when they reappear. It opens with the paradoxical image of 'black milk', evoking a sinister nurturing as well as the billows of smoke ascending towards the heavens from the crematorium. The Jewish prisoners imbibe this milk all day; it is simultaneously sustenance and bane:

> Schwarze Milch der Frühe wir trinken sie abends
> wir trinken sie mittags und morgens wir trinken sie nachts
> wir trinken und trinken
> wir schaufeln ein Grab in den Lüften da liegt man nicht eng[6]

> Black milk of morning we drink it at evening
> we drink it at noon and at daybreak we drink it at night
> we drink and we drink
> we shovel a grave in the skies there is room enough there

A contrast to the miserable existence of the Jews, who are never named as Jews and who are always presented in the plural, is provided by a German SS guard; the German lives in a house, plays with serpents and writes letters home to Germany. His interaction with the Jews is violent and humiliating: he forces them to whistle and dance for his amusement; he threatens them with dogs; he shoots them with bullets. Interwoven in these lines are references to a typically German woman, Margarethe, whose blond hair is implicitly contrasted with the ashen hair of Shulamite from the Song of Solomon. The eeriness and stark imagery in this poem resemble techniques in Borchert's surrealist drama, but here the experience is not of a German soldier but of the Jewish victims of Nazi genocide.

Celan's poem became important because it was an unusually evocative effort to depict the Holocaust, an event at once so incomprehensible and of such enormous proportions that it appears to thwart representation. Indeed, Adorno was thinking specifically of this poem when he declared that writing poetry after Auschwitz was barbaric. Obviously Adorno could not have been accusing poets like Celan or Nelly Sachs (1891–1970), whose postwar lyrics also dealt with the Holocaust, of the barbarism their poetry was attempting to expose. Adorno's concern came first from the dangers of an aestheticisation of something beyond the pale of humanity. If an author composes a poem about any subject, he must employ an aesthetic form or veneer that threatens to direct us away from the experience, the history, the reality. The rhythms and figures that Celan has woven into his 'Todesfuge' may deflect from the very theme of the poem, distancing us, or bemusing us, enchanting us, rather than drawing us into reflection and critique. They may also suggest, as Adorno wrote in another context, that something about the event makes sense, so that the horror is removed and the victims are done an injustice by art.[7] But Adorno is also concerned about the social order in which such a poem could be written; the essay in which his provocative remark appeared bears the title 'Kulturkritik und Gesellschaft' ('Cultural criticism and society'), and his characterisation of the postwar world as a place of absolute reification suggests that there is no location or standpoint from which criticism or culture could cope with the exigencies of post-Holocaust modernity.[8] Although Adorno was later to modify his dictum on poetry after Auschwitz, the predicament of how to represent the Holocaust – and what such representation meant for cultural criticism – would figure prominently in the activist literature of the 1960s.

BREAKTHROUGH AND RE-ORIENTATION

The literature of immediate experience ceded in the 1950s to a complacency with regard to the German past. The theoretical and literary reflection inclined towards an existential mood, which did not exclude consideration of the war, but did not further a working through of the trauma of Nazism and the Holocaust. In the German-speaking world Swiss writers were more widely recognised and innovative than their German counterparts. The novels of Max Frisch (1911–91), *Stiller* (1954; *I'm not Stiller*) and *Homo faber* (1957), with their focus on outsiders, are not without social commentary, but their main concerns are questions of identity and self. The plays of Friedrich Dürrenmatt (1921–90), in particular *Besuch der alten Dame* (1956; *The visit*), employ techniques of the grotesque and the absurd to uncover the hypocrisy of the postwar recovery. From Germany the writings of Wolfgang Koeppen (1906–96) expressed deep regret about the direction taken in the Adenauer restoration, but in general literary works left the larger questions of guilt and responsibility unexplored. Amid the remarkable economic recovery known as the 'economic miracle' German intellectuals appeared content to quibble with some social developments and to wonder about issues of being and essence, but they remained largely insensitive, publicly, to the wrongs committed by their nation during the Third Reich. Recognising the tendency in the Federal Republic to deny or minimise past wrongs, Adorno ascribes it to a psychic mechanism of repression. Similarly Alexander and Margarethe Mitscherlich analysed *Die Unfähigkeit zu trauern* (1967; *The inability to mourn*) as a collective German neurosis. Neither Adorno nor the Mitscherlichs, however, recommend traditional Enlightenment to alleviate anti-Semitic sentiments in postwar Germany. Rather, they advocate a programme that will strengthen subjectivity so that individuals can resist fascist ideology.

The turning point for German prose literature on the issue of coming to terms with the past occurred with the publication of Günter Grass's *Die Blechtrommel* (1959; *The tin drum*), a novel that also put Germany on the map again in world literary circles. Grass belongs to the generation of writers and intellectuals that have contributed most to the moral consensus that developed around Nazism and the Holocaust. Born in 1927, Grass and all his generation spent their formative years under National Socialism and fought in the war, but because of their youth were rarely in positions of responsibility. When they emerged as young men and women, the more reflective among them endeavoured to account and atone for the crimes committed by Hitler's Germany. After the war Grass studied art at the Düsseldorf Academy, and began also to compose poems, short prose pieces and plays, but although encouraged by members of the *Gruppe 47*, his initial efforts achieved only modest success. *Die Blechtrommel* was a phenomenal breakthrough, and Grass has been one of the focal points of the German literary scene ever since. *Katz und Maus* (1961; *Cat and mouse*) and *Hundejahre* (1963; *Dog years*) followed quickly after *Die Blechtrommel*, and the three works, which are set in Grass's birthplace, became known as the *Danzig trilogy*. Since the 1960s Grass has also been an important figure in German politics. As an outspoken member of the Social Democratic Party, he has lent his support to political candidates and causes on many occasions. Most controversial was his position on German unification, which he initially opposed, in part because of the legacy of Auschwitz. His most important novels, though complex and multi-dimensional, reflect his political commitment: *Der Butt* (1977; *The flounder*) traces women's contribution to culture from prehistory to the present, while his most recent work, *Ein weites Feld* (1995; *Too far afield*), casts a critical eye on German history of the twentieth century, especially in light of recent developments. In 1999 the Swedish Academy recognised him with the Nobel Prize for literature.

In *Die Blechtrommel* Grass employed a unique narrative means to view the past.[9] His narrator and hero, Oskar Matzerath, who was born in Danzig in 1924 and has refused to grow since the age of three, relates retrospectively his exploits from a mental institution in the Federal Republic on his thirtieth birthday. His standpoint is thus at once that of a child and that of someone able to see under and through the machinations of the adults around him. Growing up in Danzig in the late twenties and early thirties in a mixed Polish-German family, Oskar offers the reader a grotesque perspective on the petit-bourgeois milieu before the war and during the Nazi occupation of Poland. He himself is at first not enthralled by the Nazis: at a mass demonstration he transforms their marches into waltzes and thus thwarts their nationalist and militarist celebration. But he later joins a travelling theatre group, composed of midgets like himself, that entertains at the front, contributing there to raising the morale of the troops. Significant is not so much Oskar's allegiances and conscious desires, or the exact nature of his adventures, which leave many dead people in his wake. Rather, important for the course of postwar German literature is the linguistic virtuosity with which Grass weaves together various motifs, while criticising implicitly the mentalities that allowed the rise of fascism. *Die Blechtrommel* is an antithetical *Bildungsroman*; Oscar does not grow and mature into a paragon of humanism, but, like the German people, remains immature and unable to view the past except as a deformed and deranged dwarf. Perhaps not coincidentally Siegfried Lenz (1926–) utilised a similar formula almost a decade later for his extremely successful *Deutschstunde* (1968; *The German lesson*).[10] In a more directly critical view of the ideals that led to National Socialism, Siggi Jepsen, imprisoned in a reformatory, relates how his father's zeal in carrying out his duty as a policeman destroyed a family and a friendship. In both Grass's and Lenz's novels the reader is forced to view National Socialism and its aftermath from within the mind of a limited narrator. But in both cases this puerile perspective reveals the absurdity of the Nazi mentality. Important is not immediate experience, but the filtered narrative viewpoint of someone unable to fathom the very events that he is relating.

Grass perfected this technique in the second part of his trilogy, *Katz und Maus*, which remains a pivotal text for understanding the way in which Germany confronted its troubled past.[11] The novella is apparently about a teenager, Joachim Mahlke, and his youthful exploits in Danzig during the war. Son of a deceased Polish railway worker, Mahlke is at first an awkward and unathletic boy, who then develops great physical prowess and some unusual quirks of character. With a group of peers he swims regularly to a half-sunken Polish mine-sweeper, and Mahlke soon becomes the fastest swimmer and the most proficient diver; he is even able to make his way into a secret hideaway, the radio room of the boat that can be accessed only by a long and complicated dive. He drags almost all of his belongings into the hideaway and sets up there a veritable chapel to his religious obsession, the Virgin Mary. He also becomes obsessed with the knight's cross, a military honour for special valour and achievement, and he even pilfers the medal from a distinguished visitor to his high school, which results in his expulsion. Although still a teenager, Mahlke changes his mind suddenly about military service and enlists; he soon distinguishes himself in battle, blowing up enough tanks to win a knight's cross himself. When his former principal, the ardent disciplinarian Klohse, refuses to allow him to address the school because of his former transgression, Mahlke stalks and then strikes him. Mahlke fails to return to his regiment, seeking shelter instead in his sanctuary on the mine-sweeper. But he never resurfaces.

Like the writings of immediate experience, this novella is about a victim of the war years. Although Mahlke becomes an exemplary soldier, he is the prototypical outsider, unable to adapt to the exigencies of a regimented order. His relationship to National Socialist organisations and to the official ideology thus remains ambivalent. He is dismissed from a Nazi youth group because he refuses to become a squad leader: his attendance at church would have conflicted with his leadership duties. He thinks his schoolmates are crazy for wanting to enter the military, and his own accomplishments as gymnast, swimmer and soldier appear to be personally rather than ideologically motivated. Grass had the chance here to present the education of a National Socialist, but he chose not to. Instead, he presents us with a misunderstood teenager trying to cope with the difficulties of growing up under conditions that he himself considers normal. Mahlke and his friends do not question National Socialism or its ideology; it is the only governmental system that they have ever really known. Indeed, the frightening aspect of the novella is how easily the youth of Danzig has internalised militaristic vocabulary and aspirations. They fit in with the system, however, not because they are convinced Nazis like their principal Klohse, but because they are unable to think outside of the parameters set for them. Only Mahlke remains an individual whose actions arbitrarily coincide with or contest the prevailing order.

The novella is about more than Mahlke. It is also, and perhaps even primarily, about the narrator, a man the reader eventually learns is named Pilenz and who was Mahlke's boyhood friend. Pilenz is connected with the church; two-thirds through the novella the reader learns that he has been encouraged to write his account by Father Alban, who advises him 'to get it off his chest'. Pilenz also mentions casually that he admires St Augustine's *Confessions*, and that the story he tells is about, among other things, 'mea culpa'. The attentive reader soon realises that Pilenz is writing a confession, and that his descriptions of Mahlke's actions, which he stylises into a veritable saint's life, are part of a personal atonement. Indeed, the very title of the novella and the opening episode suggest that the story is structured according to a framework of guilt and victimisation. In the opening chapter and several times thereafter Pilenz relates an incident on a playing field; Mahlke was lying in the sun and his enormous Adam's apple, perpetually in motion, attracts the attention of a cat, which, the reader comes to recognise, Pilenz places on Mahlke's unsuspecting throat. Pilenz, in short, is not only a narrator who idealises Mahlke and his exploits, but also Mahlke's tormentor; his friend, but simultaneously his persecutor. The reader is thus repeatedly invited to see through Pilenz's narrative and to discover the adolescent ambivalence towards someone who is different. Eventually we catch Pilenz lying to Mahlke, or perhaps to the reader; in particular Pilenz's description of his actions when Mahlke goes into hiding raises questions about his honesty and the nature of his relationship to his alleged friend.

Like the works of the 1940s and the theme of Jaspers's seminal work, *Katz und Maus* is about guilt. But unlike these earlier works that helped create an individualistic moral consensus, Grass makes the assignment of guilt and responsibility more difficult. Perhaps the main way in which he unsettles the question of morality is by unsettling the narrative: if we remain uncertain whether what we are reading is a true account, we may be unable to delineate with clarity motives and accountability. While on one level the novella is about the relentless effort to reduce life to conformity, in particular to a conformity that maintains a veneer of Germanness and German values, it is also about how postwar Germans, left with guilt for actions they cannot directly admit and perhaps do not even understand, fail to come to terms with their past. Pilenz is exemplary in his prevarication and his obfuscation of his true relationship with Mahlke, whom he assists but also betrays. Significant is an incident related in the novella about a teacher named Brunies, who obviously held liberal views opposed to Nazism. Eventually he is arrested and imprisoned on what appears to be a trumped up charge of eating vitamin tablets designated for students. Actually he was denounced, and Pilenz's remark – 'I hope I didn't testify against him' – captures well the mental state of a nation fifteen years after the war unable to attain any certainty about its past, hoping that it is not guilty of actions for which it must be ashamed. *Katz und Maus* is not a work about immediate reactions, about recent experiences; it is about contemplation and the inability to reflect upon the past as a mature and autonomous subject. Pilenz tries to write himself free, but he remains a childlike narrator, unable to comprehend or to admit the implications of his own actions.

POLITICISING THE PAST

The 1960s were a time of questioning in many Western nations. The generation growing up in the 1950s, discontented with the complacency of its parents, rebelled against the values and norms of bourgeois society. In Germany there were special dimensions of this rebellion. The 1950s represented not only a growing prosperity and the reintegration into the Western family of nations, but also repression of the past. Other Western nations emerged from the war without any collective trauma; the youth of the student movements therefore rebelled against a vaguely defined establishment, but rarely against anything connected with the Second

World War. German activists of the sixties, however, were concerned not only about the reinstallation of traditional values by their elders, but also about the avoidance of a thoroughgoing and candid confrontation with Nazism and the Holocaust. The generational conflict in West Germany had special meaning; sons and daughters called into question not merely the life-style of their parents, but also their involvement in the Third Reich. The outstanding literature of the 1960s thus tends to be less the grotesque and playful writings of Grass or the satire of petty bourgeois life associated with a novel like Martin Walser's (1927–) *Halbzeit* (1960; *Half-time*), than works of direct confrontation and overt engagement. We are no longer concerned with coming to terms with one's own experience and involvement or overcoming personal psychic malfunction, but with accusing others of complicity and responsibility for some of the most horrendous acts of world history. For the first time German literature takes note of the Holocaust in works that are not personal, but attempt to be objective; that literature became increasingly involved during the sixties with documentation, especially of the Holocaust but also of other world occurrences, and contrasts sharply with the writings of the first two postwar decades.

The most important play of the German postwar period – although not necessarily the most aesthetically accomplished – was undoubtedly *Der Stellvertreter* (1963; *The deputy*) by Rolf Hochhuth (1931–).[12] The stage production in Berlin created a sensation not only in Germany but around the globe, because its theme was the role of the Vatican in the Holocaust, and because it contained an implicit accusation that Pope Pius XII could have and should have done more to prevent the loss of Jewish lives. The main plot is rather convoluted and at times slightly melodramatic. Riccardo Fontane, a young Jesuit priest and son of an influential papal adviser, meets by chance the SS Officer Kurt Gerstein, who tries in vain to convince the Vatican's German representative to ask the Pope to intercede on behalf of the Jews. Gerstein, whose duties as an engineer afford him access to the extermination camps, plays the role of a double agent, working apparently for the Nazis in sensitive positions, yet secretly conspiring with anyone who will help him retard the machinery of death. Eventually Riccardo has a session with the Pope, but it is evident that Pius XII cares more about world politics, Vatican investments and Hitler's opposition to communism than he does about the destruction of European Jewry. Riccardo decides to take on the responsibility that the Pope will not assume: he travels to Auschwitz to be among the victims. Riccardo dies at the hands of 'the doctor', an obvious fictionalisation of

Josef Mengele, and when Gerstein's machinations are exposed, he and the Jewish person he endeavoured to rescue are also murdered.

The bold act of putting the Pope on trial before the eyes of the world made this play notorious, but it also signalled an important shift in the way writers dealt with the troubled German past. Hochhuth made extensive use of documentation and research to compose his drama; the plot is original, but most of the characters are either historical or based on historical persons. The book version includes elaborate stage directions containing information on the figures in the play, the Holocaust and other issues the author wishes to promulgate in print; in a lengthy appendix Hochhuth discusses his sources in detail. These cited materials give an insight into Hochhuth's practice as a playwright and set a tone for both documentary literature of the 1960s and the desire to remain objective about the past. It is obvious that Hochhuth had studied the memoirs, biographies, diaries, letters, speeches and legal protocols that pertain to the Jewish question under the Third Reich before framing his play. What he has written is therefore thoroughly documented in the sense that every major scene and action, every reference and allusion has some basis in historical reality. Rather than publish a history of the Jewish question with regard to the Catholic Church or an examination of Pius XII's positions on the extermination of the Jews during the Second World War, Hochhuth fashions his 'facts' into dramatic form, insisting that he used invention only in order to transform the raw material into a form suitable for the stage. We might conceive of Hochhuth's method, therefore, as different from, but somewhat analogous to previous writers. Instead of experience – the primary source for Grass, Böll, and Borchert – Hochhuth employs history, but he, like they, adds something to it to make it a literary work. What comes to dominate Hochhuth's drama are facts and arguments such as one might encounter in a historical study, not necessarily a piece of art. His way of confronting the past thus becomes qualitatively different from previous attempts because he is interested in two things that had been previously separated: a public and accessible statement such as one finds in literature, film and drama, and a historical argument based on documents, such as one might find in a piece of scholarly writing.

Two aesthetic problems inhere in *Der Stellvertreter*. The first relates to the representation of the Holocaust. In the final act Hochhuth situates the action in Auschwitz, and he is well aware of the artistic minefield he is trying to traverse. Documentary realism, the representational approach he had used throughout, is inadequate to depict an event that exceeds human imagination, but he also contends that Celan's 'Todesfuge' is an equally unsuccessful representation because it resorts to metaphors and thus mitigates the horror. Although he is able to recognise the dilemma facing an author wishing to represent the Holocaust, he is unable to arrive at a solution. The stylised poetic first scene of Jews in boxcars and the naturalist dialogue for the remainder of the act simply replicate the two alternatives Hochhuth found unsatisfactory. Indeed, this inability to reach an aesthetically adequate form is at the heart of the second problem. Hochhuth's drama is structured around a series of dialogues; in most cases a representative of the forces attempting to obtain a stronger intercession from the Pope debates with someone articulating the papal position; in other scenes Gerstein spars with the incarnation of evil, the doctor. The action moves towards a climax; good and evil are clearly delineated; personal decisions, informed by autonomous individuals and their chosen moral values, are presented as the forces that can thwart or sustain the Nazi genocide. In short, Hochhuth's approach to the Jewish question and the involvement of the Vatican in Nazi genocide is traditional, reminiscent of a classical drama. Hochhuth retains and develops the moral imperative implicit in Jaspers, but removes it from personal experience, placing it on a world-historical stage. Friedrich Schiller's historical tragedies appear to be Hochhuth's model: *Der Stellvertreter* is ultimately a drama of ideas, a modern morality play, and many questioned whether the form and the structure were adequate in postwar Germany of the 1960s to deal with the complexities of historical events.

The intellectual climate of the 1960s, although buoyed by Hochhuth's drama, favoured slightly different, more ideological and more systemic explanations for the atrocities committed in the past. Exemplary in its innovative form and its implicit political argumentation was *Die Ermittlung* (1965; *The investigation*) by Peter Weiss (1916–82).[13] Its subject was the trial of twenty-two Germans active in the concentration camp at Auschwitz-Birkenau. Beginning on 20 December 1963, the trial lasted over a year and a half. The most important proceedings involving German war crimes to take place in Germany since the initial Nuremberg Trials in 1946, and rivalled in notoriety only by the Eichmann proceedings in Israel in 1961, the Auschwitz trial was the first major action taken by Germans against former concentration camp guards and the first result of inquiries by the Central Office for Investigation of National Socialist Crimes, established in Ludwigsburg in 1958. The sensation caused by the lurid testimony and the reactions of the defendants created a lasting impression on the German political and intellectual scene: the trial was responsible, in part, for ensuring that the statute of limitations on Nazi crimes would not expire. Perhaps more importantly the court proceedings in Frankfurt contributed to a new public consciousness concerning the Nazi past, marking a turning point in the society's willingness to confront the past and try to understand how Germans could have perpetrated such horrendous crimes.

In attendance at the Auschwitz trial on 13 March 1964 was Weiss, whose play *Marat/Sade* (1964), then in the midst of rehearsals, was to become a German and then an international success. Born into a Jewish family that converted to Protestantism, Weiss was nonetheless forced to flee Germany in 1934 after the Nazis had come to power. He became a Swedish citizen in 1945, and although he acquired considerable fame in Germany, he maintained his residence in Sweden until his death in 1982. His initial literary endeavours were composed in Swedish, but he eventually settled on German as his language for literature. His early work, influenced to a degree by Franz Kafka and relating primarily to his experiences in exile, was part of the existentialist, autobiographical mode of the postwar era. By the mid-sixties, however, Weiss, like many writers of that period, had turned to more political concerns. His breakthrough work, *Marat/Sade*, recasts the mind–body contrast in terms of social revolution and sexual pleasure. After *Die Ermittlung* Weiss continued with documentary works that supported his leftist political commitment: plays thematising anti-colonial struggles in Angola and Vietnam were followed by dramas dealing with Hölderlin and Trotsky. Weiss's masterpiece in prose was his monumental, three-volume *Ästhetik des Widerstands* (1975–81; *Aesthetics of resistance*), a novel about working-class resistance, participation in the Spanish civil war and the Second World War, and the place of art in modern societies.

Like Hochhuth, Weiss was confronted with an immense amount of documentation. But *Die Ermittlung*, in contrast to *Der Stellvertreter*, integrates factual materials in novel and imaginative ways. Hochhuth constructs a story based on conventional dramatic structures: exposition, complication, climax, dénouement and tragic end. He employs his documents as ammunition in the speeches of the various characters, in stage directions, or in his lengthy prose conclusion. Weiss abandons traditional dramatic structure and constructs his drama around a creative citation and adaptation of the documents themselves. He does not aim to reconstruct or invent a narrative of events, but instead seeks to recount in systematic form various aspects of the concentration camp. His eleven 'acts', called 'songs', start with testimony on the ramp and the physical structure of the camps, proceed through accounts of various persons, procedures, and instruments of death and end with the crematorium. Instead of recreating a possible historical occurrence during the war, as Hochhuth does, Weiss allows the reports taken from the Auschwitz trial to reflect on the past, and his drama consists almost entirely of the speeches of the accused, witnesses, prosecutors, defence attorneys and judges. There are almost no stage directions, and Weiss provides only a short authorial note at the beginning of the play. The method he uses is one of condensation, a 'concentration' ('Konzentrat') of statements, as Weiss himself writes, playing eerily on the word concentration camp ('Konzentrationslager'). The 409 witnesses are reduced to an anonymous nine; eighteen of the original twenty-two defendants appear in the play; the year and a half of testimony totalling thousands of pages is condensed into fewer than 200 pages of unrhymed, unpunctuated and largely arrhythmic verse. To ensure a variety of response, Weiss often takes testimony from different parts of the trial, sometimes relating to different historical persons or occurrences, and adopts it for a more coherent event involving a single individual. The condensation and simplification are justified because Weiss believes that the experiences of the concentration camp inmates were largely interchangeable. In the brief introductory note he argues that there is no need for names or differentiation, since they were treated anonymously by their tormentors. Although the defendants retain their identities, they too are more important as vehicles for establishing facts than as illustrations of the moral depravity or gross disregard for human life in Auschwitz. Weiss is uninterested in the individuals, in individual psychology and in personal histories. Rather, he examines how people function as parts of a system and as means for conveying the nature of the system to which individuals belong.

There is thus a tension present in Weiss's play between empirical reality as recorded in documents and supra-individual structures and ideologies as constructed in Weiss's creative use of documents. It is important to note that Weiss does not recreate the trial itself; the play includes no opening statements, no sentencing, no conclusion to the proceedings. Indeed, the title of the play indicates well that the drama aims at examination and understanding, not at guilt and condemnation. The subtitle, 'Oratorium in elf Gesängen' ('Oratorio in eleven songs'), makes the spectator aware of the constructed nature of the drama and, perhaps, by extension, of the constructed nature of the camps and the events that occurred there. An oratorio is a musical production using voice and orchestra that usually deals with a sacred story. It is dramatic, in the sense that it recounts a tale with various parts and personae, but in contrast to an opera, for example, it narrates without the use of scenery, costume or actions on stage. Together title and subtitle reflect the dual use of the raw materials for the play: to document the facts of history and to construct a new and non-mimetic reality different from that same history. In a sense Weiss has not written a play about Auschwitz, even though he has taken all his documentation from the Auschwitz trial. The fact that the words 'Jew' or 'Jewish' do not occur in his play provides evidence that he is not concerned with the Holocaust as a genocide against the Jews. Rather, he is interested in exploring how the Holocaust was a logical extension of the inhumanity inherent in modern capitalist societies. His emphasis on the positions the accused now hold in the Federal Republic and the seamless integration of alleged criminals into the postwar world point to his concern, echoed also by Adorno, that the extermination camps were an extreme manifestation of an order based on oppressed and oppressors, a limit case for what occurs every day in societies based on exploitation. Weiss is thematising more than the banality of evil about which Hannah Arendt wrote after the Eichmann trial. He is connecting the logic of fascism with an underlying inhumanity in the capitalist order of Germany and the industrialised world.

The critical, anti-fascist spirit so evident in the dramas of Hochhuth and Weiss can be understood as an implicit warning against the persistence of National Socialism in postwar society. According to this politicised appropriation of the past, Nazism did not necessarily perish with the demise of Hitler, even though the Third Reich would appear to have been completely discredited after the war. Rather, essential, albeit less virulent features of fascism continue to adhere even in liberal democratic orders. Adorno's concerns since the 1940s thus parallel and inspire the dominant literary production of the 1960s. In the arena of philosophy and theory, however, the task of detecting and exposing vestiges of anti-democratic tendencies was best performed by the most outstanding and prolific student of the Frankfurt School, Jürgen Habermas (1929–). His first major work concerned the public sphere, and in a sense all of his subsequent efforts have been conceived in an effort to open up debate around issues central to a democratic society. Habermas disagrees with his mentors Adorno and Horkheimer about liberal democracy and the culture industry. Although he has not been blind to the deficiencies of postwar Germany and the Western societies, he distinguishes clearly among fascist, communist and liberal regimes. Critical of orthodox proclivities in leftist thought, he has opposed dogmatic thinking wherever it has appeared. He allied himself with Adorno in an early controversy against positivism and empirical reductionism in the social sciences – the opponents in the debate were Karl Popper and Hans Albert – but he also opposed a few years later tendencies in the student movement that would have eliminated debate and free speech. His stance against 'leftist fascism' among student leaders was perhaps phrased in a regrettable way, but it was consistent with his antagonism to non-reflective and non-critical thought.

In the late sixties Habermas found fault with aspects of two popular theoretical models. The first was the hermeneutics of Hans-Georg Gadamer (1900–). The major proponent of the ontological turn in hermeneutics in the twentieth century, Gadamer, drawing on the early work of his teacher Heidegger, posited understanding as our way of being in the world. His most original contribution to hermeneutic theory is the notion of a horizon, the standpoint that limits our vision, but which is also the prerequisite for any interpretation. The concept of a horizon also became a popular notion in literary theory during the late sixties in Hans Robert Jauss's (1921–97) aesthetics of reception. In Gadamer's and Jauss's theory understanding takes place as a fusion of horizons; historical interpretation thus involves a willingness to open one's own perspective to the other. As openness and willingness to enter into dialogue Habermas had no objection to Gadamer's hermeneutics. What disturbed him, however, was the lack of a critical edge to understanding and interpretation if one conceives of hermeneutics as all-encompassing and the interpreter as a passive recipient of tradition. If one accepts Gadamer's framework, there would seem to be no way to distinguish among different types of texts according to ideological criteria; ontological hermeneutics has no emancipatory trajectory. In challenging the preferred notions of the Enlightenment, Gadamer claims that authority exists because it has been accepted, rather than imposed; prejudices are not something to be avoided, but the prerequisite for all interpretation; the classics are works that have persevered in the face of variable tastes and changing times, and as such are beyond criticism. Habermas defends the Enlightenment precisely because it posited a reflective ability to challenge authority, to question prejudices, and to criticise the canonical works of the past. In keeping with the radicalism of the sixties and the legacy of the Frankfurt School, Habermas advocates that tradition must continuously be subjected to critique, and that a hermeneutic theory that does not postulate some means of escaping the hold of our flawed heritage is ultimately a conservative enterprise.

Habermas detects a similar conservative penchant in the theories of Niklas Luhmann (1927–98), the most important sociologist of the postwar period and the advocate of an approach called systems theory. As in the case of Gadamer, Habermas was attracted to aspects of Luhmann's work and anxious to enter into dialogue with him. The book he and Luhmann jointly published in 1971 contains the results of a seminar to which Habermas had invited Luhmann in Frankfurt. At the centre of Luhmann's thought is the notion of a social system, which reduces environmental complexity and establishes an equilibrium, as well as a boundary between itself and its infinitely more complex exterior environment. Social systems, in contrast to organic systems or cybernetic systems, reduce complexity through meaning; selectivity inside a given social system is controlled by antonymous pairs such as transcendence/immanence (for the religious system) or truth/falsehood (for scientific systems); these conceptual dualities are responsible for the reduction of complexity that occurs when elements enter a system from the environment. In a sense systems theory thus represents the anti-hermeneutic stance *par excellence*: if we understand Gadamer's magnum opus *Wahrheit und Methode* (1960; *Truth and method*) as a text that sought to establish the encompassing nature of hermeneutic truth over natural scientific method, we could view the systems-theoretical approach as an assertion of the very opposite, the hegemony of method as science over truth conceived as hermeneutic understanding. Although it is the polar opposite of hermeneutics in some regards, Habermas detects in systems theory a similar deficiency in the place accorded to critique and reflection. Perhaps the most damaging claim that Habermas makes involves the notions of truth and ideology in Luhmann's work. If truth is defined functionally, as Luhmann suggests, as a mode of selectivity within scientific systems, then theories and facts are no longer susceptible to critique and invalidation outside of this particular arena. Habermas, who advocates a consensus theory of truth, believes that Luhmann's position has rather pernicious consequences for social theory. Luhmann's reduction of truth to its function of producing certainty denies us the possibility of evaluating ideologies other than in their role of maintaining systems. There can be no critique of ideology without a criterion of truth to determine which statements represent interests that are grounded in asymmetrical relations (power, status, etc.) and which statements are the expression of a genuine, unforced consensus. Luhmann's theory, Habermas implicitly contends, prohibits any emancipation because it does not allow us to criticise the regressive nature of domination in individual social systems or in the social system as a whole.

Habermas's debates thus reinforced in practice what they advocated in theory: they functioned to open and keep open a public dialogue on issues important to a democratic order. In the case of Gadamer and Luhmann, Habermas detected theoretical implications that threatened emancipatory directions in philosophical and social thought. Habermas was thus coming to terms with the past in a less direct fashion than the literature of the period, which confronted Nazism and the Holocaust directly. For Habermas the defence against fascism and racism involves the theoretical struggle with tendencies that would deny the full and unencumbered participation of the citizenry in matters that affect their lives and happiness. Gadamer's suggestion that we are all passive recipients of historical traditions, even if these traditions have been established on the basis of power and prejudice, and Luhmann's notion that the subject is irrelevant for sociological analysis violate Habermas's democratic ideal in which an informed populace, putting aside private interests, decides collectively on matters pertaining to the public weal. This participatory hypothesis, articulated in various forms in his writings – from the early work on the public sphere to notions of an ideal speech situation or a decolonised life-world in his later *Theorie des kommunikativen Handelns* (1981; *Theory of communicative action*) – was developed as a reaction to a National Socialist heritage characterised by distorted speech and a non-existent public sphere. Like the literature of the 1960s with its implicit challenge to the status quo and its exposure of fascist remnants in the Federal Republic, Habermas's work can be viewed as a ruler by which West Germany could measure its distance from the troubled past.

THE OTHER GERMANY: THE GDR AND WOMEN

The moral consensus that evolved into politicised confrontations was a phenomenon of the Federal Republic and was not matched at all by developments in the East. Indeed, on the issue of coming to terms with the past West and East Germany diverged radically. While many in the West tended to identify National Socialism with a more encompassing totalitarianism that included Eastern bloc communism, the GDR associated Nazism with capitalism, claiming that fascism perseveres in a somewhat less virulent strain in the liberal democracies of the West. Since the GDR had eliminated capitalism and its attendant exploitation of the working class, it had also eradicated all remnants of National Socialism. Both sides of the iron curtain believed that they represented the true anti-fascist legacy, but the vigilance necessary to prevent the return of National Socialism assumed radically different forms. In the West, where political forms and racist ideologies were emphasised more than economics, there was a focus on the state and, especially in the 1960s, anti-Semitism. In the East, the state enforced a concentration on economic features and on ideologies it deemed implicated in or contributing to capitalism. Perhaps the central feature separating the intellectual outlook of the two German states, however, was the control over cultural production. The official moral agenda in the West was set to some degree by state officials, but one encountered a wide response, ranging from indifference to a perspective like Weiss's, which had many similarities with the positions in the GDR. In the East the government and its various agencies played an active role in setting the anti-fascist agenda as anti-capitalism, and often divergence from this view could lead to the accusation of promoting fascism.

In the years directly after the war, East and West had not differed very much in their cultural output and intellectual views. Lessing's *Nathan der Weise* (*Nathan the wise*), with its message of religious tolerance, and Goethe's humanistic play *Iphigenie* were favourite selections in theatres in all parts of Germany. The first feature film in the postwar period, Wolfgang Staudte's (1906–84) *Die Mörder sind unter uns* (1946; *The murderers are among us*), was produced in the Soviet zone and resembles in many regards Borchert's *Draußen vor der Tür*: both feature heroes who were emotionally destroyed by the war; both criticise from a moral perspective the officers who are now able to adjust so readily to postwar life. But with the advent of the cold war, the physical and ideological separation became firmly established. Since the GDR considered itself by definition anti-fascist, it did not have to deal with vestiges of Nazism. The writings of the 1950s focus on building a socialist nation; plays like Erwin Strittmatter's (1912–94) *Katzgraben* (1953) or Harald Hauser's (1912–94) *Am Ende der Nacht* (1955; *At the end of the night*), or novels like Eduard Claudius's (1911–76) *Menschen an unserer Seite* (1951; *People on our side*), are concerned with workers and farmers in the present, not with Nazis of the past. The so-called 'novels of arrival', which appeared around 1960, presented history as an unproblematic transition from Nazism to the socialism of the GDR. Under the anti-fascist mantra the Jewish question was non-existent. Although some returning communists recognised that all Germany owed a debt to the Jews of Europe, and although even some communist leaders were Jewish, the cosmopolitan campaign of the early 1950s made talk of Jewish compensation or restitution practically a crime. The Holocaust was almost completely absent from literary and theoretical discourse for the first three decades of the GDR's existence. Inmates of concentration camps, such as in Bruno Apitz's (1900–79) *Nackt unter Wölfen* (1958; *Naked among wolves*), were usually political prisoners or Eastern Europeans; the resistance, for example in the film *Stärker als die Nacht* (1954; *Stronger than the night*), consisted of the communist working class.

Literary texts dealt occasionally with the Jewish question and thereby provided something of a vehicle for discussion of the Holocaust. Johann Bobrowski's (1917–1965) *Levins Mühle* (1964; *Levin's mill*), for example, presented a historical case of anti-Semitism in Germany. But only with Jurek Becker's (1937–) novel *Jakob der Lügner* (1968; *Jacob the liar*) do we find a work that achieved widespread acceptance dealing exclusively with the persecution of the Jews during the Third Reich. Becker himself was familiar enough with this persecution: he grew up in the ghetto and spent time in two concentration camps. Filmed by director Frank Beyer in 1974, the novel tells the story of Jacob Heym, who lives with his fellow Jews in a crowded Polish ghetto. Jacob is commanded to enter a guard house, where he overhears a radio report concerning the advancing Soviet army. Miraculously he is allowed to leave unharmed. The next day he relates the news to a friend about to risk his life for a few potatoes, but his friend only believes his story when Jacob tells him that he has a hidden radio. Thereafter Jacob unwillingly becomes the source of hope for the entire ghetto, and he is forced to fabricate daily reports about the military situation. There is a black humour in the situation, and the comic elements are heightened by Becker's narrative technique, which relates even horrific events in a straightforward fashion without pathos and contrived melodrama. Becker supplies two endings: in the first everyone is rescued and lives happily ever after. But the narrator tells us that this is not the real ending, since in reality the ghetto was liquidated and everyone, including our hero, perished. Much like the writers of the immediate postwar period, Becker was writing from experience; the reflective level of the narrator is used for humour, not for confrontation with the past. And since Becker was himself a Jew and a victim of the Holocaust, he was perhaps ill suited to aid the Germans in coming to terms with the past.

Although many writers had touched upon National Socialism and had written about experiences during the Third Reich, for nearly three decades GDR authors had employed mostly clichés rather than reflection and analysis when they wrote about the National Socialist past. For this reason the appearance in 1976 of Christa Wolf's *Kindheitsmuster* (*Patterns of childhood*) marks a turning point in East German confrontation with the past.[14] Wolf was herself largely a product of the GDR literary scene. Born in 1929 in Landsberg an der Warthe, like the heroine of her novel she had a childhood under National Socialism. She earned her Abitur in 1949, the same year she joined the Socialist Unity Party. After studying German literature at Jena and Leipzig from 1949 to 1953, she began work in the publishing industry, also writing essays and reviews for various GDR publications. Her first endeavour in belletristic writing, *Moskauer Novelle* (1961; *Moscow novella*), was pretty much in the paradigm of socialist realism, the official cultural doctrine in the GDR. Her next work, the novel *Der geteilte Himmel* (1963; *Divided heaven*), established her reputation in East and West; the story of two lovers torn apart by the Wall, it employed subjective compositional elements that departed significantly from the objective narrations of the 1950s. *Nachdenken über Christa T.* (1968; *The quest for Christa T.*) went further in its validation of subjectivity and individualism. The eponymous heroine is an outsider in a society that demands conformity; her story, which ends in her death, is told in the reflections of her friend, the narrator, and in scraps from her own memoirs. Wolf, whose name had been struck from the candidacy list for the Central Committee of the SED in April of 1967 for her protest against the censorship of a novel by Werner Bräunig, was severely criticised in the GDR for *Nachdenken über Christa T.*, which was hailed by Western critics as a breakthrough in style and theme. Although Wolf continued to be a respected author in the GDR, until 1989 she appeared to be, like her heroine, an outsider to the literary establishment.

The appearance of *Kindheitsmuster* thus continued two tendencies Wolf had already established. As in her earlier works, she continued to explore, thinly veiled under a fictional mantle, her own life. The central character, Nelly Jordan, grew up in a town formerly in Germany, now in Poland; she is about the same age as Wolf and was exposed to similar institutions and events. The reflective narrator writing the story has daughters who are about the age of Wolf's actual daughters. Like earlier works, *Kindheitsmuster* also touches on sensitive topics for GDR public opinion. Formerly fascism was treated with socialist platitudes about economics, but Wolf is interested in showing how National Socialism used insidious mechanisms to insinuate itself into people's lives. To expose these mechanisms, yet not tell a story from the perspective of Nazism, Wolf employs a sophisticated multi-layered narrative that operates on a number of different but interwoven levels. The first is the tale of Nelly, a young woman growing up in a town identified only as 'L'. The story begins in the early thirties with the narrator's earliest memories as a young child; at one point the narrator includes an event that occurred before Nelly's birth, but most of the novel concentrates on happenings between 1933 and 1947. We are, therefore, taken through the years of the Third Reich, 1933–45, and shown some of its aftermath, at least what Nelly sees of it. In this narrative line there are some aspects of the novels of arrival, but significantly there is no turning to socialism; Nelly never fully arrives. The second narrative line – and it is simultaneously the occasion for the writing of Nelly's story and an interruption of that narrative – is the two-day journey the narrator, obviously Nelly as an adult East German, takes with her husband H., her brother Lutz and her fifteen-year-old daughter Lenka to visit her place of birth, formerly Landsberg, now Gorzów Wielkopolski, in Poland. This trip occurs on 10 and 11 July 1971, and it leads the narrator to reflect on her youth in the Third Reich. The third narrative level is that of the actual writing of the novel. It occurs from November 1972 until May 1975. Included here are various changes in the narrator's life, including a trip to the United States, which again has an autobiographical dimension: Wolf was Max Kade German Writer in Residence at Oberlin College in Oberlin Ohio in the spring of 1974.

These narrative levels allow Wolf a great flexibility with regard to her confrontation with the past. Like the writings of direct experience composed after the war, Wolf's novel explores what it was like to live in the Third Reich. But it does not permit this experience to be unmediated: instead, we are afforded two temporal points from which the events of the past are evaluated, criticised and comprehended. Like the plays of the 1960s, the reader is invited to find continuities between the past and present. But continuities in Wolf's novel are never simple. Indeed, at various points the socialist regime in the GDR, or even in the Soviet Union, is found to exhibit similarities with Hitler's Germany, though socialism is not portrayed as simply another variant of totalitarianism. More important than global issues, however, is the dialectic of continuity and discontinuity in personal development. The fact that the narrator of the 1970s objectifies her own life history, that she does not identify with the person she was, that she feels Nelly to be foreign and unsympathetic, indicates that Wolf is dealing with the past not only to condemn the present, but to distance herself from that past. She distances herself, however, in order to examine her former self, to understand how people became what they were, how they have outgrown their former selves and how their childhood may still inhere in what they have become. What ultimately concerns Wolf is how National Socialism continues to exist in her, and by extension in people's subjective beings. The novel is obviously about the maturation of a young girl, and it thus falls into the tradition of the German *Bildungsroman*. But when the maturation process has been one in which the person you were was a fascist, or a believer in an inhumane ideology, when you look back at your past and see someone who is a stranger in terms of ideology and beliefs, then this coming to terms with your own past is simultaneously a coming to terms with the German past. The significance of Wolf's novel for postwar literature is that she manages to confront both her personal past and the fascist past as intertwined; she approaches both with candour and insight, with the mixture of curiosity, terror and trepidation that accompanies the gradual disclosure of an unwanted identity.

With regard to the Holocaust *Kindheitsmuster* is less concerned with the actual events and facts – to which the protagonist could not have been exposed as a girl – than with the way prejudice becomes part of Nelly's ideological worldview. Chapter six, which is devoted centrally to anti-Semitism, demonstrates that the mechanism by which racism is inculcated in young minds is not necessarily direct indoctrination, but a process that operates with hints, associations and even silences. In the first half of this chapter the narrator relates Nelly's experience with Lori Tietz, the daughter of a rich factory owner. Significant in this relationship is that for the first time Nelly perceives herself as a split consciousness; she is able to witness herself acting. The self has here become bifurcated; under social conditions infused with hierarchy and power, subjectivity is damaged. In countering the falseness of the Tietz family, who only want Nelly to visit Lori so that the brighter girl can help her slower classmate with homework, Nelly finds herself acting in-strumentally. She opposes the hypocrisy that emanates from the Tietz family, but her only weapon is imitation of their mendacity. Thus, in a gesture that is typical for Wolf's works, a potential opposition becomes an identification. Nelly does not counter falsehood, she participates in it. The resulting damaged subjectivity reveals itself as a necessary prelude to her introduction to anti-Semitism, which is not a sudden revelation, but a series of occurrences with various dimensions and implications. Her most direct experience of anti-Jewish attitudes results from a visit by the bookseller, Leo Siegmann, an ardent Nazi who relates his expe-rience with an unnamed Jewish child in secondary school. While the Jewish child would sit innocently at his place, his classmates would file by him and punch him for no reason; it was just the natural thing to do. Despite the incoherence of his account, Siegmann's tale obviously leaves an impression on Nelly. Her fantasy involves her in a similar incident, which she embellishes with clichéd details gleaned from her racist environment. She imagines a Jewish child; she will have to punch him, because he speculates that she may not; all Jews are speculators. She convinces herself that the Jewish child is making her hit him. It is really his fault; she is doing her duty. Nelly's fantasy is then stimulated by the recollection of a man who exposed himself to her and by her disgust at reptiles and insects, which she associates with the man's naked member. The chapter closes with an incident in which the Aryan heritage of Nelly's father Bruno is questioned. When Nelly, only about eight years old at the time, hears of the inquiry, she blurts out that she does not want to be Jewish; her mother Charlotte wonders how Nelly knows anything at all about Jews. What the chapter has shown is precisely how Nelly comes to her knowledge about Jews. The paths of prejudice, of irrational hatred and racism, are certainly not elucidated with the descriptive logic that we find in historical accounts. But Wolf's chapter is probably closer to the reality of National Socialism as it was experienced than the typical accounts of anti-Semitic propaganda. And it also accords well with Adorno's theoretical model: National Socialist ideologemes function by processing dubious 'facts' through fantasy to alter damaged subjectivity.

Kindheitsmuster was a path-breaking work for the GDR in its coming to terms with the fascist past, but it was also pioneering for Germany as a whole. Its focus on subjectivity fitted well with the so-called 'new subjectivity' of the 1970s, but it was also the first major work to depict in such detail women's involvement with National Socialist ideology. In the West until the appearance of Wolf's novel, women's role in the Third Reich had been largely trivialised: in most of the prominent cultural products women were viewed either as adjuncts and aids to male protagonists or as flighty, impressionable fellow travellers of fascism. Olina in Böll's novel is a vehicle for Andreas; the woman in Borchert's play is clearly unimportant in comparison to Beckmann; the focal point for Grass is always his male protagonist and author. In Hochhuth's drama the only woman is a helpless but willing plaything for the doctor's amorous advances. If women were implicated in Nazism, they swooned and were impressed by the shiny buttons on the uniforms; but they were never treated seriously as participants in the ideology of National Socialism. During the immediate postwar period women therefore could function more readily, at least in literature, as a source of humanism, Iphigenie-like in their purity, undefiled by ideology and war. Matters were, of course, a bit different in the GDR. Especially in several early plays – Strittmatter's *Katzgraben* or Friedrich Wolf's (1888–1953) *Bürgermeister Anna* (1950; *Mayor Anna*) – women were more often portrayed as agents of change as the SED recruited them for the new socialist society. But behind this more positive portrayal is the same stereotype that was operative in the West. Women, because they were apparently inactive politically, because they were involved solely with the home and the family, were somehow considered instinctively anti-fascist. Wolf's novel, however, altered the stereotypical views of women and National Socialism radically, showing that their involvement with fascism and racism was different from men's, but that it was a deep and insidious participation nonetheless.

Wolf's *Kindheitsmuster*, like her earlier works, thus participates in the growing feminist consciousness and literature of the late 1960s and 1970s in both parts of Germany. Although writers such as Ilse Aichinger (1921–), Hilde Domin (1912–), Luise Rinser (1911–), Nelly Sachs (1891–1973), Ingeborg Bachmann (1926–73) and Anna Seghers (1900–83) had published notable works dealing with women's issues, in some cases both before and after 1945, a consciously feminist movement arose only in the 1970s. In the West the appearance of a feminist literature coincided with the increased emphasis on subjectivity: fiction often contained autobiographical accents and personal accounts. The most radical work in this movement was Verena Stefan's (1947–) *Hautungen* (1975; *Shedding*), in which the narrator turns from heterosexual relations, in which she received no validation, to lesbianism, which is portrayed as harmonious and supportive of women. The GDR had a quite different feminism. Since women's problems were supposedly solved with the transition from capitalism to socialism, no movement existed, and writers developed various creative means to deal with issues facing women. Sometimes writers employed a documentary mode, for example Sarah Kirsch (1935–) in *Die Pantherfrau* (1973; *The panther-woman*) or Maxie Wander (1933–77) in *Guten Morgen, du Schöne* (1977; *Good morning, beautiful*); other authors preferred a fantastic, science-fiction-like style, for example Irmtraud Morgner (1933–90) in *Leben und Abenteuer der Trobadora Beatriz* (1974; *Life and adventures of troubadour Beatrice*), or in the collection *Blitz aus heiterem Himmel* (1974; *Lightning out of the blue*), in which three prominent women authors wrote short stories about a woman who becomes a man. The feminist movement in German literature rarely thematised the Nazi past, as Wolf had done, but it was important nonetheless for an overcoming of the vestiges of National Socialism. In its essentialist variant it alleged that patriarchy was somewhere at the foundation of fascist behaviour; in less extreme form it suggested that a genuine anti-fascism involves working towards a society in which gender discrimination no longer exists.

THE TURN IN THE 1980S

The moral consensus around the German past that had been articulated by Jaspers, accepted as the official stance for political culture in the West, politicised in the 1960s by a generation questioning its parents and the foundations of the Federal Republic, and explored subjectively and psychologically in the 1970s, began to show signs of attenuation in the 1980s. The return to a CDU-led government under Helmut Kohl after a decade and a half of Social Democratic rule brought with it a new atmosphere in politics, as well as in culture. Kohl expressed the notion of the 'grace of late birth', a clear reference to his belief, shared by many, that those who were too young to have participated in the war and the Holocaust were exonerated from blame and responsibility. The most important symbolic event of Kohl's chancellorship, until unification presented itself in 1989, was undoubtedly the ceremony at Bitburg in 1985. Staged as a reconciliation on the occasion of the fortieth anniversary of the end of World War Two, the ceremony at the military cemetery in Bitburg, where members of the SS were also buried, was to feature an appearance by United States President Reagan and was meant to relegate to the past Germany's troubled legacy. To a certain extent Kohl was merely reflecting a political reality of the Federal Republic: after forty years of semi-official contrition, Germany yearned to be accepted as a nation equal with others, and many felt its good conduct had earned it this right. Moreover, the generation of people responsible for or even involved in the Third Reich was rapidly dying off; by the mid 1980s the vast majority of people in West Germany had only second-hand knowledge of Hitler or the Holocaust. There were still obvious signs that the moral consensus held sway: Richard von Weizsäcker's moving speech on 8 May 1985 or the resignation of Philip Jenninger from the German parliament because of a faux pas regarding 'Kristallnacht' (the 'night of broken glass') indicated the resilience of an ethical resolve. Especially in the area of culture, however, there were indications of a transformation. The left joined the right in trumpeting themes of nationalism, and the focus on daily life, psychological and personal issues, and post-activist subjectivity led intellectuals away from a reckoning with the past. The American TV series *Holocaust* did elicit a great deal of compassionate response when it was shown in 1979; but Edgar Reitz's (1932–) rejoinder in his epic film of the mid-twentieth century, *Heimat* (1984; *Home*), which gave more air time to panoramic sweeps of German landscape than to the crimes of National Socialism, was even more popular.

Peter Schneider (1940–) was able to convey the ambivalence in the prevailing German sentiment about its past in the short story *Vati* (1987; *Dad*).[15] Since the 1960s Schneider had been one of the most perspicacious commentators on Germany. A former leader of the oppositional movement, he excelled in polemical essays from the left. In 1973 his novella *Lenz* correctly diagnosed the downfall of student activity and became one of the founding works for the 'new subjectivity' that dominated the ensuing decade. In the early eighties his *Der Mauerspringer* (1982; *Wall jumper*), based on an East–West love affair, gave voice to the widely felt frustration concerning the division of Germany. *Vati* participated in the large production of works during the 1970s and 1980s dealing with the relationship between children, now mature and reflective, and their parents, usually the father and sometimes implicated in a silence about former activities in the Third Reich. From Peter Handke's (1942–) *Wunschloses Unglück* (1972; *A sorrow beyond dreams*) and Brigitte Schwaiger's (1949–) *Lange Abwesenheit* (1980; *Long absence*) to Bernward Vesper's (1938–71) *Die Reise* (1977; *The journey*) and Ruth Rehmann's (1922–) *Der Mann auf der Kanzel* (1980; *The man in the pulpit*), sons and daughters observed, questioned, and often suffered from their parents' involvement with the National Socialist regime. Schneider, however, selected an extreme case for his story: Josef Mengele. In 1985 the family of Mengele announced that he had died in Brazil, and it eventually became known that he had maintained communication with his family while in exile. Mengele's son Rolf, whom Schneider knew personally, had published some remarks about his father, and Schneider, borrowing from these memoirs, constructed a fictitious first-person account in the form of a letter of justification written by Rolf Mengele to a friend, in particular about his visit to his father in 1977.

The book was not well received, and it is probably not Schneider's best work, but it does capture well the ambivalence of a generation towards its past and towards its responsibility for a legacy it neither affirms nor wants. The first-person narrator is a typical German of his generation, an average citizen with normal feelings and desires. That he is the son of one of the most infamous criminals in German history is depicted throughout as a cruel stroke of fate. The narrator, a decent person, deserves better. His moral integrity is tested throughout the story, and in a certain sense he fails these tests because he never turns his father over to the authorities or notifies anyone of his whereabouts. He displays more familial loyalty than commitment to tenets of abstract humanism and is therefore not beyond reproach. But no one can really blame him for this shortcoming. His justification, though perhaps not without misgivings on the reader's part, is understandable. That on the last few pages of the story he is more upset about a man who has stolen five hundred dollars from him than about his father's role in Auschwitz is no doubt a bitterly ironic comment on Schneider's part, but it is paradigmatic for the normality surrounding the figure. In contrast to earlier portrayals, this story reveals sentiments that many in Germany had held, but that were only now included in public discourse: in contrast to the accepted view of the moral consensus, the Holocaust is a source of discomfort, not contrition. Comparing photographs of his family and concentration camp survivors, the narrator feels as if he must choose between loyalty to his father and compassion for his victims. Although the choice remains unclear, the shift in victimisation is evident. The son has suffered enough for the sins of the father; in comparison his own faults are minor and all too human. From the German perspective of the 1980s it is the children of the Nazis who are the victims of their fathers' crimes, not the people who were tortured, maimed and killed.

By taking an extreme case of generational conflict about past misdeeds, Schneider was able to give voice to the sentiment of exhaustion in dealing with the German past. Indeed, aside from Weiss's *Ästhetik des Widerstands*, the 1980s produced few works that occupy themselves with the moral and political issues so important for the preceding decades. Instead, literature in Germany was dominated by a turn to postmodern forms and directions; aesthetics and playfulness became more valued than ethics or politics. A literature focusing more on linguistic and formal elements had long been a staple of Western postwar writing. An experimental and consciously avant-garde perspective had long been part of the Austrian scene, from the Vienna Group, whose most prominent members were Oswald Wiener (1935–), Ernst Jandl (1925–), and H. C. Artmann (1921–2000), to the Graz Group, which included noted writers such as Handke and Elfriede Jelinek (1946–), and the nihilistic loner of postwar Austrian literature Thomas Bernhard (1931–89). In the Federal Republic the writings of authors such as Arno Schmidt (1914–79) or Helmut Heißenbüttel (1921–96) likewise exhibited an emphasis on literariness and experimentation. Even in these authors, however, the German past insinuated itself occasionally, such as in Bernhard's acerbic play *Heldenplatz* (1988; *Heroes' square*), composed for the fiftieth anniversary of the Austrian annexation to Germany, or Heißenbüttel's collection of stories entitled *Wenn Adolf Hitler den Krieg nicht gewonnen hätte* (1979; *If Adolf Hitler had not won the war*). In the 1980s there was still an element of social critique in the works of writers such as Botho Strauß (1944–), perhaps the most prominent writer of the decade, but the general feeling was one of ennui and hostility towards what was perceived as the moralism of the previous decades. Aestheticism seemed to go hand in hand with conservatism: in 1982 Ernst Jünger (1895–1998), whose associations with the right and occasional anti-Semitism had made him anathema during the postwar period, was given the coveted Goethe Prize. Jünger's work had been championed by Karl Heinz Bohrer (1935–), the editor of the influential journal *Merkur*, who became known as an advocate of an increasingly fashionable aesthetic anti-modernity that sometimes went under the name of postmodernism. In most countries postmodernity was associated merely with playfulness in form, with pastiche and collage; in Germany it was tantamount to anti-utopianism. Hans-Magnus Enzensberger (1929–), the founding editor of *Kursbuch*, a renowned poet and author, and a prominent voice of the left during its heyday, anticipated the 1980s symbolically in his narrative poem *Untergang der Titanic* (1978; *The sinking of the Titanic*), in which both Cuba, the third-world leftist utopia, and technological progress, the Marxist hope for the future, are depicted as chimeras of an era whose demise has already occurred.

With the advent of postmodern art and thought in Germany, many intellectuals rose to the task of defending modernity, or at least trying to understand what it was and why it appeared to be faltering. Hans Blumenberg (1920–96) spent considerable effort examining the origins of the modern age, its major theoretical presuppositions and its mythic structures. But unquestionably the most vehement, prominent and controversial defender of modernity was Jürgen Habermas. As always Habermas's defence was connected with his perception of a theoretical threat to democracy and openness. Postmodernism as a cultural phenomenon was less important for him than philosophical attempts to transcend modernity. In his initial observations on the issues of modernity and postmodernity, Habermas makes it clear that modernity is an unfinished and emancipatory project that merits continuation, while postmodernity is an outgrowth of a neo-conservative manner of thought.[16] Modernity is characterised by the separation of three types of activity – science, morality and art – into individual spheres. This scheme, drawn from Max Weber, is ultimately related to Kant's three critiques, which circumscribe the same general topics from the perspective of human subjectivity. With the disintegration of a unified religious or metaphysical world-view, each sphere obtains an autonomy and is assigned a particular question and domain: truth, conceived as an epistemological matter, is ascribed to natural science; normative rightness, formulated in terms of justice, is relegated to morality; and the determination of authenticity or beauty is ascertained through judgements of taste in the realm of art. Habermas continues these tripartite divisions by identifying a specific rationality with each sphere: cognitive-instrumental for science, moral-practical for ethics, and aesthetic-expressive for art. Only with the advent of modernity do we witness an immanent history for each of these three realms; only in the modern era do these spheres begin to operate under internally developed laws and imperatives. In this schema postmodernists are characterised as anti-modernists who embrace only the aesthetic side of the modernist project. They counter the instrumental rationality of science by recourse to spontaneity, the archaic, the anarchic, the emotional and the irrational.

Habermas provided a slightly more refined and extensive response to postmodernists and poststructuralists in his monograph *Der philosophische Diskurs der Moderne* (1985; *The philosophical discourse of modernity*).[17] In this book he treated postmodernity as part of a post-Hegelian response to the central problem of modernity. Emancipating itself from the dogmas of religion and the past, modernity sets itself the task of creating its normativity out of itself. With Hegel the central problem for philosophy is subjectivity, defined as a structure of self-relation, or in Hegel's formulation, self-consciousness. In turn this awareness of the necessity for the modern age to ground itself in self-conscious subjectivity leads Hegel to a paradoxical deprecation of the individual and critique, especially in his theory of the state, and Habermas views subsequent philosophy as a series of attempts to cope with this Hegelian legacy. The left and right Hegelians are two sides of the same coin: the former group seeks refuge in critique, materiality and a philosophy of praxis; the latter reaffirms the Hegelian notion of the state and religion. Thus while the left Hegelians endeavour to counter the pernicious effects of modernity by revolutionising society, the right Hegelians, all the way down to the neo-conservatives of our era, advocate tradition and values as the remedy for social ills. A third option, and the one thematised extensively in *Der philosophische Diskurs der Moderne*, seeks to reject the Hegelian problematic in its entirety, opposing reason and Enlightenment as the essence of modernity that must be overcome. Nietzsche is the most original thinker of this ilk, whose later adherents include Heidegger, Adorno and Horkheimer (at least in *Dialektik der Aufklärung*), Foucault and Derrida. In Habermas's narrative of the philosophical tradition, fundamental ontology, negative dialectic, poststructuralism and deconstruction are only variants of the dead end of the post-Hegelian philosophy of the subject. The outside, other or 'post' that is envisioned as an opposition to Hegel is thus always just the irrational mirror image of reason conceived as self-contained subjectivity. Habermas's alternative 'solution' to the Hegelian problematic involves a rejection of subjectivist philosophy in favour of intersubjective thought, an abandonment of rationality reduced to instrumentality for a communicative variety. The greater part of *Der philosophische Diskurs der Moderne*, however, is concerned with criticising the false path propagated by those putatively 'radical' thinkers who would oppose reason with 'non-rational' alternatives.

For the first three decades of the postwar era Nietzsche was politically suspect because of his great popularity in the Third Reich. Heidegger was recognised as at best a naive political opportunist, at worst a convinced Nazi, who had supported the Hitler regime and refused to recant his affiliation after its demise. The philosophical foundation of poststructuralism was thus tainted, and Habermas's criticism of these French philosophers and their heritage has to be understood as part of coming to terms with the past in the Federal Republic. A more differentiated view was provided by the early writings of Manfred Frank (1945–). The poststructuralists existed on the fringes of academia until the 1980s, although their books were generally available in translation. With the publication of *Was ist Neostrukturalismus?* (1983; *What is neostructuralism?*), Frank made them a widespread topic of discussion. Like Habermas, Frank viewed poststructuralism as a response to a German tradition. Indeed, one of his main contentions is that poststructuralists unwittingly repeat arguments made by German idealists, or that they do not really go beyond the philosophical positions of their German predecessors. Most important for Frank are Schelling, in particular for his positing of a non-reflective subjectivity, and Schleiermacher, who recognised that a general code must be paired with an individual interpreter in order to have a cogent philosophical view. Although Frank was sympathetic to the general poststructuralist enterprise, he also perceived political liabilities. In contrast to many French theorists, Frank sought to redeem a humanist position, to save the individual as an autonomous and moral agent, and to oppose the potential totalitarianism of a ubiquitous and omnipotent code. He too recognised the politically precarious foundations of poststructuralist thought, and he criticised even more incisively than Habermas the perils of an irrationalist penchant in some writers. By the second half of the 1980s, his views on poststructuralism soured considerably, and at one point he cautions students against re-imbibing the intellectual tradition of the Third Reich simply because it now appears cleansed of its former nationalist detritus.

Although the 1980s witnessed the first public questioning of the moral consensus, then, it was still very much alive in the writings of Habermas and Frank. Significant, however, is that for the first time there was a public struggle over the meaning of the past and how it related to the future. For Frank and Habermas, the poststructuralists and their adherents in Germany threatened to smuggle in fascist ideologemes in the guise of oppositional values. A more direct menace to the implicit moral agreement about Nazism and the Holocaust was the historians' debate, perhaps the central ideological event of the decade. Once again Habermas was the central figure. At issue were remarks made by Ernst Nolte, a student of Heidegger's who wrote on theories of fascism, Michael Stürmer, a historian and speech writer for Helmut Kohl, and Andreas Hillgruber, a professional historian; although the approach of each was very different in character, Habermas detected a common thread in their endeavour to reinterpret the German history of the Third Reich in order to make it normal or unexceptional. The motivation, Habermas presumed, was to legitimate a new conservatism and a potential nationalism in the Federal Republic. Despite the enormous number of essays and books about the historians' controversy, a debate never really occurred: the historians who opposed Habermas almost uniformly questioned his views on history and his credentials as a historian. There was a great deal of discourse debating the singularity of the Holocaust. But Habermas's central concerns had to do with identity formation and the illicit use of a sanitised history to make possible a positive identification with nation and state. The pivotal point for both sides was thus their respective understanding of the Holocaust. For the conservative historians Auschwitz was an obstacle to a new German identity; for Habermas, as for Jaspers, it remained its prerequisite.

EPILOGUE: POST-WALL PERSPECTIVES

The sudden and unexpected dismantling of the Berlin Wall in November of 1989 and the rapid movement towards German unity initially brought with it a recrudescence of nationalist sentiment. In the German Democratic Republic the drive for unification was fuelled in part by the prospects of acquiring economic security, while in the Federal Republic the conservative majority, sensing the culmination of their nationalist aspirations, was relentless in pushing the process towards completion. The rapidly achieved unification seemed to bring closure to postwar efforts to come to terms with the National Socialist past. The initial act of the first freely elected GDR parliament in 1990 was a resolution, Jaspers-like in its official posture of contrition and its willingness to accept responsibility for past crimes, asking forgiveness from the Jews for actions committed by Germans during the Third Reich and for the GDR's hostile policies toward Israel. But this parliament lasted barely half a year, and the official focus of government soon turned to more pressing economic and political matters. The intellectual scene in the early 1990s was dominated by the controversies around Christa Wolf, first centred on her novel *Was bleibt* (1990; *What remains*), which appeared to many to be self-serving as a first-person account of a woman writer under surveillance by the Stasi (State Security Police), and then focused on the disclosure in 1993 that Wolf had herself been engaged by the Stasi as an informant from 1959–62. One of the most celebrated essays on Wolf, penned by Ulrich Greiner, went beyond her life and works to condemn postwar literature in East and West because, informed by an ethic of convictions, it purportedly focused on extra-literary pursuits and was controlled by external agencies: conscience, the party, politics, morality or the past.[18] In the cultural sphere unification appeared to reinforce the emerging conservative ideology of the 1980s. The turn or 'Wende' of 1989 completed the 'Wende' of 1982. And in this climate coming to terms with the Nazi past receded into the background, as East Germany began to confront its SED legacy, and West German commentators relegated the 'literature of conviction' to the historical dustbin.

The National Socialist past, however, was more resilient than anyone expected. As the dust settled from unification, Germany once again resumed its preoccupation with the most horrific aspects of the Hitler regime. Stephen Spielberg's *Schindler's list* (1993) was seen by millions of Germans; the publication of the wartime diary of Viktor Klemperer, a Jewish scholar of romance literature who survived the Third Reich in Germany, was a surprise bestseller. The favourable reception of Daniel Goldhagen's book *Hitler's willing executioners* (1996), which accused Germany of a widespread ideology of eliminationist anti-Semitism that caused normal citizens to be willing participants in the Holocaust, indicated that Germans in the 1990s had not yet jettisoned Jaspers's basic tenets. The controversial exhibition concerning the German military participation in the Holocaust – the prevailing myth was that only the

SS perpetrated the mass killing of Jews – and the debate about a Holocaust memorial in Berlin are further indications that in the new Federal Republic the moral consensus of the pre-Wall era perseveres. Amid this renewed concern with its crimes against European Jewry, the Federal Republic experienced a surprising renaissance of German-Jewish literature. Jewish authors were not unknown during the postwar years – Paul Celan and Peter Weiss are two notable contributors to German literature – but in the 1980s and 1990s one finds a second generation of Jewish writers, born after the war and raised in Germany. Two of the most notable in recent years have been Rafael Seligmann and Esther Dischereit. Seligmann, born in Palestine in 1947 and raised for ten years in Israel, moved to Munich when he was ten and received an education as a political scientist. His first novel *Rubensteins Versteigerung* (1989; *Rubinstein's auction*), written in the style of Philip Roth's *Portnoy's complaint*, dealt with the experience of being a young Jew in contemporary German society. Esther Dischereit (1952–), born and raised in the Federal Republic, has authored *Joëmis Tisch* (1988; *Joëmi's table*) and *Merryn* (1992); both are composed in a disjointed, postmodern style and deal with the alienation involved in being a Jew and a woman in Germany today. For both writers the Shoah exists as an undeniable background, but their concerns appear to be with the establishment of a new, postwar German-Jewish identity.

If there was any question that German-speaking writers were just as preoccupied with the legacy of the Third Reich after the fall of the Wall as before, the year 1995 should have sufficed as evidence. One of the finest, one of the most popular, and one of the most controversial books of the decade all appeared that year, and each dealt with issues of mastering the past. The Austrian novelist Christoph Ransmayr (1954–) published *Morbus Kitahara* (*The dog king*), a surrealist story whose fictional premise is that postwar Germany deteriorates further from its wartime devastation because there was no Marshall Plan and thus no economic miracle. The reader follows the fate of three loners in a desolate setting whose climate is characterised by penitence, restitution and revenge. In the same year Bernhard Schlink's international bestseller *Der Vorleser* (*The reader*) appeared. It relates the tale of a young man who has an affair with an older woman, Hanna Schmitz, who turns out to have been a concentration camp guard. The novel partakes in the shift in victimisation of the 1980s, because the reader is made to feel compassion for Hanna. In the course of her trial, the narrator comes to learn that Hanna is illiterate: when she was a camp guard, she had young Jewish women read to her, and it is suggested that she had them killed to cover her shame; at the trial she receives the greatest prison sentence because she does not want to admit her illiteracy. The narrator corresponds with her in prison, and she eventually learns to read, but she commits suicide just prior to her release. The German concentration camp guard is the unfortunate victim of the war in this tale, not the persons who perished under her charge. A final work from 1995 brings up the question of victimisation from a very different perspective. *Fragmente* (*Fragments*) by the Swiss author Binjamin Wilkomirski relates in memoir-like fashion from the perspective of a child the dispersed memories of a Polish boy, born in 1939, who lost his family in the Holocaust but himself survived the ordeal. The memoir/novel also relates postwar experiences from orphanages in Poland and Switzerland, as well as the narrator's eventual adoption and his difficulties integrating into a normal social order. A controversy arose when it was revealed that the author, whose real name is Bruno Doesseker, was born illegitimately in Switzerland in 1941. Wilkomirski insists that his tale is genuine and that it is based on the deep memories made conscious only through extensive psychotherapy; but its publication would seem to demonstrate only the extent to which German-speaking authors strive to be themselves included among the victims. The year 1995 thus witnesses a continuation of the confrontation by German-speaking writers with the Nazi legacy. As in previous years, the various attempts to come to terms with National Socialism and its crimes – and to avoid doing so – have brought out the best and the worst in postwar Germany. And although these endeavours have taken different forms in the past five decades, as we head into a new century and a new millennium, the 1990s offer no indication that German intellectuals have exhausted their engagement with their unmasterable past.

NOTES

1 Theodor W. Adorno, *Gesammelte Schriften*, ed. T. W. Adorno, Gerschom Scholem, Rolf Tiedemann and Hermann Schweppenhauser, 20 vols. (Frankfurt am Main: Suhrkamp, 1997), vol. III. Compare Russell Berman's remarks in chapter five above, pp. 237ff.
2 Karl Jaspers, *Die Schuldfrage* (Zürich: Artemis, 1946).
3 Martin Heidegger, '"Nur noch ein Gott kann uns retten": Spiegel-Gespräch mit Martin Heidegger am 23. September 1966', *Der Spiegel* 30 (31 May 1976), pp. 193–219.

4 Heinrich Böll, *Der Zug war pünktlich* (Munich: dtv, 1949).
5 Wolfgang Borchert, *Das Gesamtwerk* (Hamburg: Rowohlt, 1949), pp. 99–165.
6 Paul Celan, *Gesammelte Werke*, 5 vols. (Frankfurt am Main: Suhrkamp, 1983), vol. I, pp. 41–2.
7 'Was bedeutet: Aufarbeitung der Vergangenheit', in *Gesammelte Schriften*, vol. XI, pp. 555–72.
8 Adorno, *Gesammelte Schriften*, vol. XI, pp. 11–30.
9 Günter Grass, *Die Blechtrommel* (Neuwied: Luchterhand, 1959).
10 Siegfried Lenz, *Die Deutschstunde* (Hamburg: Hoffmann und Campe, 1968).
11 Günter Grass, *Katz und Maus* (Neuwied: Luchterhand, 1961).
12 Rolf Hochhuth, *Der Stellvertreter* (Reinbek bei Hamburg: Rowohlt, 1963).
13 Peter Weiss, *Die Ermittlung: Oratorium in 11 Gesängen* (Frankfurt am Main: Suhrkamp, 1965).
14 Christa Wolf, *Kindheitsmuster* (Berlin: Aufbau, 1976).
15 Peter Schneider, *Vati* (Darmstadt: Luchterhand, 1987).
16 See Jürgen Habermas, 'Die Moderne – ein unvollendetes Project', *Die Zeit*, 19 September 1980. A slightly modified version of the essay appeared in *Kleine politische Schriften I–IV* (Frankfurt am Main: Suhrkamp, 1981), pp. 444–64.
17 Jürgen Habermas, *Der philosophische Diskurs der Moderne* (Frankfurt am Main: Suhrkamp, 1985).
18 Ulrich Greiner, 'Die deutsche Gesinnungsästhetik. Noch einmal: Christa Wolf und der deutsche Literaturstreit', *Die Zeit*, 2 November 1990.

Bibliography

PRIMARY TEXTS

Adorno, Theodor W., *Ästhetische Theorie*, ed. Gretel Adorno and Rolf Tiedemann, Frankfurt am Main: Suhrkamp, 1970.

Gesammelte Schriften, 20 vols. in 23, Frankfurt am Main: Suhrkamp, 1971–86.

Adorno, Theodor W. and Max Horkheimer, *Dialektik der Aufklärung* (1947), Frankfurt am Main: Fischer, 1979.

Anderson, Edith (ed.), *Blitz aus heiterem Himmel*, Rostock: Hinstorff, 1975.

Apitz, Bruno, *Nackt unter Wölfen*, Halle (Saale): Mitteldeutscher Verlag, 1958.

Arendt, Hannah, *Eichmann in Jerusalem: a report on the banality of evil*, New York: Viking, 1963.

Bahr, Hermann, *Zur Überwindung des Naturalismus: Theoretische Schriften 1887–1904*, ed. Gotthart Wunberg, Stuttgart, Berlin, Cologne and Mainz: Kohlhammer, 1968.

Barth, Karl, *Der Römerbrief*, Munich: Chr. Kaiser, 1922.

Becker, Jurek, *Jakob der Lügner*, Berlin: Aufbau, 1968.

Beer-Hofmann, Richard, *Gesammelte Werke*, Frankfurt am Main: Fischer, 1963.

Benjamin, Walter, *Gesammelte Schriften*, ed. T. W. Adorno, Gerschom Scholem, Rolf Tiedemann and Hermann Schweppenhauser, 5 vols., Frankfurt am Main: Suhrkamp, 1974–82.

Bernhard, Thomas, *Heldenplatz*, Frankfurt am Main: Suhrkamp, 1988.

Bertram, Ernst, *Deutsche Gestalten: Fest- und Gedenkreden*, Leipzig: Insel, 1934.

Bloch, Ernst, *Der Geist der Utopie*, Munich: Duncker und Humblot, 1918.

Blumenberg, Hans, *Die Legitimität der Neuzeit*, Frankfurt am Main: Suhrkamp 1966.

Die Genesis der kopernikanischen Welt, Frankfurt am Main: Suhrkamp, 1975.

Arbeit am Mythos, Frankfurt am Main: Suhrkamp, 1979.

Bobrowski, Johann, *Levins Mühle*, Frankfurt am Main: Fischer, 1964.

Böll, Heinrich, *Der Zug war pünktlich*, Munich: dtv, 1949.

Bölsche, Wilhelm, *Das Liebesleben in der Natur*, 3 vols., Leipzig: Diederichs, 1903.

Bohrer, Karl Heinz, *Die Ästhetik des Schreckens*, Munich: Hanser, 1978.

Bonhoeffer, Dietrich, *Auf dem Wege zur Freiheit: Gedichte und Briefe aus der Haft*, Berlin: Lettner, 1954.

Borchert, Wolfgang, *Das Gesamtwerk*, Hamburg: Rowohlt, 1949.
Brecht, Bertolt, *Gesammelte Werke*, 10 vols., Frankfurt am Main: Suhrkamp, 1967.
Breitinger, Johann Jakob, *Critische Dichtkunst*, 2 vols., Zürich: Orell, 1740; facsimile reprint, ed. Wolfgang Bender, Stuttgart: Metzler, 1966.
Brentano, Clemens, *Werke*, ed. Wolfgang Frühwald, Bernhard Gajek and Friedhelm Kemp, 2nd edn, 4 vols., Munich: Hanser, 1973–8.
Broch, Hermann, *Die Schlafwandler, eine Romantrilogie*, Zürich: Rheinverlag, 1932.
Büchner, Georg, *Sämtliche Werke und Briefe*, ed. Werner Lehmann, 2 vols., Hamburg: Christian Wegner, 1967.
Canetti, Elias, *Die Blendung*, Munich: Hanser, 1963.
  Masse und Macht, Hamburg: Claassen, 1960.
Celan, Paul, *Gesammelte Werke*, 5 vols., Frankfurt am Main: Suhrkamp, 1983.
Chamberlain, Houston Stewart, *Die Grundlagen des neunzehnten Jahrhunderts*, Munich: Bruckmann, 1899.
Chamisso, Adelbert von, *Sämtliche Werke*, 4 vols., Berlin-Leipzig: Knaur, n.d.
Claudius, Eduard, *Menschen an unserer Seite*, Halle: Mitteldeutscher Verlag, 1951.
Dilthey, Wilhelm, *Der Aufbau der geschichtlichen Welt in den Geisteswissenschaften*, Leipzig: Teubner, 1927.
  Gesammelte Schriften, ed. Georg Misch, 10 vols., Stuttgart, 1958.
Dischereit, Esther, *Joëmis Tisch*, Frankfurt am Main: Suhrkamp, 1988.
  Merryn, Frankfurt am Main: Suhrkamp, 1992.
Döblin, Alfred, *Berlin Alexanderplatz: die Geschichte von Franz Biberkopf*, Zürich: Walter, 1996.
Dürrenmatt, Friedrich, *Der Besuch der alten Dame*, Zürich: Verlag der Arche, 1956.
Durkheim, Emil, *Suicide: a study in sociology*, trans. John A. Spaulding and George Simpson, ed. George Simpson, London: Routledge and Kegan Paul, 1968.
Enzensberger, Hans Magnus, *Der Untergang der Titanic*, Frankfurt am Main: Suhrkamp, 1978.
Fichte, Johann G., *Bestimmung des Menschen*, Berlin: Voss, 1800.
  Werke, ed. I. H. Fichte, 8 vols., Berlin: de Gruyter, 1971.
Fontane, Theodor, *Romane, Erzählungen, Gedichte*, ed. Walter Keitel, 6 vols., Munich: Hanser, 1962.
  Sämtliche Werke, ed. Walter Keitel, 20 vols., Munich: Carl Hanser, 1969.
Frank, Manfred, *Das individuelle Allgemeine*, Frankfurt am Main: Suhrkamp, 1977.
  Was ist Neostrukturalismus?, Frankfurt am Main: Suhrkamp, 1983.
Freud, Sigmund, *Gesammelte Werke*, London: Imago, 1940–52.
  The standard edition of the complete psychological works of Sigmund Freud, ed. James Strachey, 24 vols., London: Hogarth Press, 1953–74.
Freytag, Gustav, *Soll und Haben*, 2 vols., 23rd edn, Leipzig, Hirsel, 1888.
Frisch, Max, *Stiller*, Frankfurt am Main: Suhrkamp, 1954.
  Homo Faber, Frankfurt am Main: Suhrkamp, 1957.
Gadamer, Hans-Georg, *Wahrheit und Methode*, Tübingen: Mohr, 1960.
Garve, Christian, *Popularphilosophische Schriften über literarische, ästhetische und gesellschaftliche Gegenstände*, reprint, ed. Kurt Wölfel, 2 vols., Stuttgart: Metzler, 1974.

Gellert, Christian Fürchtegott, 'Abhandlung für das rührende Lustspiel', in *Die zärtlichen Schwestern*, ed. Horst Steinmetz, Stuttgart: Reclam, 1988.

George, Stefan, *Werke*, 2 vols., Düsseldorf and Munich: Küpper, 1958.

Goethe, Johann Wolfgang von, *Werke* (Hamburger Ausgabe), ed. Erich Trunz et al., 14 vols., Munich: Beck, 1948–60.

Gottsched, Johann Christoph, *Versuch einer critischen Dichtkunst* (1730), facsimile reprint, 4th edn (1754), Darmstadt: Wissenschaftliche Buchgesellschaft, 1962.

Grass, Günter, *Die Blechtrommel*, Neuwied: Luchterhand, 1959.

Katz und Maus, Neuwied: Luchterhand, 1961.

Hundejahre, Neuwied: Luchterhand, 1963.

Der Butt, Neuwied: Luchterhand, 1977.

Ein weites Feld, Göttingen: Steidl, 1995.

Grillparzer, Franz, *Sämtliche Werke*, eds. Peter Frank and Karl Pörnbacher, Munich: Carl Hanser, 1964.

Günderrode, Karoline von, *Sämtliche Werke und ausgewählte Studien*, ed. Walther Morgenthaler, Karin Obermaier and Marianne Graf, 3 vols., Basle and Frankfurt am Main: Stroemfeld, 1990–1.

Gundolf, Friedrich, *George*, Darmstadt: Wissenschaftliche Buchgesellschaft, 1968.

Habermas, Jürgen, *Strukturwandel der Öffentlichkeit. Untersuchungen zu einer Kategorie der bürgerlichen Gesellschaft*, Neuwied: Luchterhand, 1962; Frankfurt am Main: Suhrkamp, 1991.

Theorie des kommunikativen Handelns, 2 vols., Frankfurt am Main: Suhrkamp, 1981.

Der philosophische Diskurs der Moderne, Frankfurt am Main: Suhrkamp, 1985.

Habermas, Jürgen and Niklas Luhmann, *Theorie der Gesellschaft oder Sozialtechnologie – Was leistet die Systemforschung?*, Frankfurt am Main: Suhrkamp, 1971.

Handke, Peter, *Wunschloses Unglück*, Salzburg: Residenz, 1972.

Hardenberg, Friedrich von, *Novalis. Schriften*, ed. Paul Kluckhohn, Richard Samuel et al., 6 vols., Stuttgart, Berlin, Cologne and Mainz: Kohlhammer, 1960– .

Hauser, Harald, 'Am Ende der Nacht', in *Sozialistische Dramatik: Autoren der Deutschen Demokratischen Republik*, Berlin: Henschelverlag, 1968, pp. 37–104.

Hebbel, Friedrich, *Werke*, ed. Gerhard Fricke, 5 vols., Munich: Carl Hanser, 1963–7.

Hegel, Georg W. F., *Sämtliche Werke* (Jubiläumsausgabe), ed. Hermann Glockner, 20 vols., Stuttgart: Friedrich Frommann, 1964.

Werke, ed. Eva Moldenhauer and Karl Markus Michel, 20 vols., Frankfurt am Main: Suhrkamp, 1970.

Heidegger, Martin, *Sein und Zeit* (1927), Tübingen: Niemeyer, 1993.

' "Nur noch ein Gott kann uns retten": Spiegel-Gespräch mit Martin Heidegger am 23. September 1966', *Der Spiegel* 30 (31 May 1976), 193–219.

Heißenbüttel, Helmut, *Wenn Adolf Hitler den Krieg nicht gewonnen hätte*, Stuttgart: Klett-Cotta, 1979.

Herder, Johann Gottfried, *Sämtliche Werke*, ed. Bernhard Suphan, 33 vols., Berlin: Weidmann, 1891; repr. Hildesheim: Georg Olms, 1967.

Hermand, Jost (ed.), *Das Junge Deutschland: Texte und Dokumente*, Stuttgart: Philipp Reclam, 1966.

Der deutsche Vormärz: Texte und Dokumente, Stuttgart: Philipp Reclam, 1967.

Hochhuth, Rolf, *Der Stellvertreter*, Reinbek bei Hamburg: Rowohlt, 1963.

Hölderlin, Friedrich, *Sämtliche Werke und Briefe*, ed. Michael Knaupp, 3 vols., Munich and Vienna: Hanser, 1992–3.

Hoffmann, E. T. A., *Werke*, ed. Walter Müller-Seidel, 4 vols., Darmstadt: Wissenschaftliche Buchgesellschaft, 1984.

Hofmannsthal, Hugo von, *Gesammelte Werke in Einzelbänden*, ed. Bernd Schoeller, 10 vols., Frankfurt am Main: Fischer, 1979.

Husserl, Edmund, *Husserliana: Gesammelte Werke*, Haag: M. Nijhoff, 1950ff.

Jacobi, Friedrich Heinrich, *Werke*, 7 vols., Leipzig: Fleischer 1812–25.

Jaspers, Karl, *Die Schuldfrage*, Zürich: Artemis, 1946.

Jauss, Hans Robert, *Literaturgeschichte als Provokation der Literaturwissenschaft*, Konstanz: Universitätsverlag, 1969.

Jean Paul (Johann Paul Friedrich Richter), *Werke*, ed. Norbert Miller, 6 vols., Munich: Hanser, 1959–63.

Jelinek, Elfriede, *Die Klavierspielerin*, Reinbek bei Hamburg: Rowohlt, 1983.

Jünger, Ernst, *Sämtliche Werke*, Stuttgart: Klett-Cotta, 1978–80.

Kafka, Franz, *Schriften, Tagebücher, Briefe*, ed. Jürgen Born et al., Frankfurt am Main: Fischer, 1982– .

Kant, Immanuel, *Werkausgabe*, ed. Wilhelm Weischedel, 12 vols., Frankfurt am Main: Suhrkamp, 1977.

Political writings, ed. Hans S. Reiss, Cambridge: Cambridge University Press, 1990.

Philosophical writings, ed. Ernst Behler, New York: Continuum, 1992.

Keller, Gottfried, *Sämtliche Werke*, ed. Jonas Fränkel, 22 vols., Zürich-Munich: Eugen Rentsch, 1927.

Kiesewetter, J. G. C. C., *Grundriß einer allgemeinen Logik nach Kantischen Grundsätzen*, 2 vols., 2nd edn, Berlin: Lagarde, 1795–6.

Gesammelte Briefe, ed. Carl Helbling, 4 vols., Bern: Benteli, 1950.

Kirsch, Sarah, *Die Pantherfrau*, Berlin: Aufbau Verlag, 1973.

Kleist, Heinrich von, *Sämtliche Werke*, ed. Helmut Sembdner, 2 vols. (1952), Munich: Hanser, 1993.

Klemperer, Viktor, *Ich will Zeugnis ablegen bis zum letzten. Tagebücher 1933–1945*, Berlin: Aufbau, 1995.

Kraus, Karl, *Schriften*, ed. Christian Wagenknecht, 20 vols., Frankfurt am Main: Suhrkamp, 1989–94.

Lasker-Schüler, Else, *Gedichte*, ed. Karl Jürgen Skrodzki, 2 vols., Frankfurt am Main: Jüdischer Verlag, 1996.

Lenz, Siegfried, *Die Deutschstunde*, Hamburg: Hoffmann und Campe, 1968.
Leibniz, G. F. W., *Philosophical writings*, trans. Mary Morris and G. H. R. Parkinson, ed. G. H. R. Parkinson, London: J. M. Dent, 1997.
Lessing, Gotthold Ephraim, *Lessings Werke*, ed. Kurt Wölfel, 3 vols., Frankfurt am Main: Insel, 1967.
Loewenthal, Erich, and Lambert Schneider (eds.), *Sturm und Drang. Kritische Schriften*, Heidelberg: Verlag Lambert Schneider, 1963.
Ludwig, Otto, *Shakespeare-Studien*, ed. M. Heydrich, Leipzig: Hermann Gesenius, 1872.
Lukács, Georg, *Die Theorie des Romans: ein geschichtsphilosophischer Versuch über die Formen der großen Epik*, 3rd edn, Neuwied: Luchterhand, 1965.
  Geschichte und Klassenbewußtsein: Studien über marxistische Dialektik, Neuwied: Luchterhand, 1970.
  The destruction of reason, trans. Peter Palmer, London: Merlin Press, 1980.
  The historical novel, trans. Hannah and Stanley Mitchell, London: Merlin Press, 1989.
  German realists in the nineteenth century, trans. Jeremy Gaines and Paul Keast, ed. Rodney Livingstone, London: Libris, 1993.
Mach, Ernst, *Die Analyse der Empfindungen und das Verhältniss des Physischen zum Psychischen*, 2nd edn, Jena: Gustav Fischer, 1900.
Mann, Thomas, *Gesammelte Werke*, 13 vols., Frankfurt am Main: Fischer, 1974.
Marx, Karl, and Friedrich Engels, *Werke*, Institut für Marxismus-Leninismus beim ZK der SED, 42 vols., Berlin: Dietz, 1983.
Mauthner, Fritz, *Beiträge zur Kritik der Sprache*, 3 vols., Stuttgart: Cotta, 1901–2.
Mitscherlich, Alexander, and Margarete Mitscherlich, *Die Unfähigkeit zu trauern*, Munich: Piper, 1967.
Morgner, Irmtraud, *Leben und Abenteuer der Trobadora Beatriz nach Zeugnissen ihrer Spielfrau Laura: Roman in dreizehn Büchern und sieben Intermezzos*, Berlin: Aufbau, 1974.
Müller, Adam, *Kritische, ästhetische und philosophische Schriften*, ed. Walter Schroeder and Werner Siebert, 2 vols., Berlin and Neuwied: Luchterhand, 1976.
Musil, Robert, *Gesammelte Werke*, ed. Adolf Frisé, 9 vols., Reinbek: Rowohlt, 1978.
Nietzsche, Friedrich, *Werke*, ed. Karl Schlechta, 3 vols., Munich: Hanser, 1956 (later edn: 6 vols., Munich: Hanser, 1980).
  Umwertung aller Werte, ed. Friedrich Würzbach, 2 vols., Munich: Carl Hanser, 1969.
  Sämtliche Werke, ed. Giorgio Colli and Mazzino Montinari, 8 vols., Berlin and New York: Walter de Gruyter, 1972.
Otto, Rudolf, *Das Heilige: über das Irrationale in der Idee des Göttlichen und sein Verhältnis zum Rationalen*, Munich: Beck, 1979.
Pinthus, Kurt (ed.), *Menschheitsdämmerung*, Hamburg: Rowohlt, 1959.
Plato, *The collected dialogues of Plato including the letters*, ed. Edith Hamilton and Huntingdon Cairns, Princeton, NJ: Princeton University Press, 1961.
Raabe, Wilhelm, *Sämtliche Werke*, ed. Karl Hoppe, 20 vols., Freiburg im Breisgau and Braunschweig: Hermann Klemm, 1951–94.

Ransmayr, Christoph, *Morbus Kitahara*, Frankfurt am Main: Fischer, 1995.
Rehmann, Ruth, *Der Mann auf der Kanzel: Fragen an einen Vater*, Munich: Hanser, 1979.
Remarque, Erich Maria, *Im Westen nichts Neues*, Cologne: Kiepenheuer und Witsch, 1962.
Rilke, Rainer Maria, *Werke*, 4 vols., ed. Manfred Engel et al., Frankfurt am Main and Leipzig: Insel, 1996.
Rosenzweig, Franz (ed.), '*Das älteste Systemprogramm des deutschen Idealismus. Ein handschriftlicher Fund*', *Sitzungsberichte der Heidelberger Akademie der Wissenschaften*, Philosophisch-historische Klasse (1917), 5. Abhandlung.
Rousseau, Jean-Jacques, *Émile ou de l'éducation*, Paris: Garnier Flammarion, 1966.
Ruprecht, Erich (ed.), *Literarische Manifeste des Naturalismus 1880–1892*, Stuttgart: Metzler, 1962.
Schelling, F. W. J., *Werke*, ed. Manfred Schröter, 12 vols., Munich: C. H. Beck, 1946–59.
    Schriften, ed. Manfred Frank, 6 vols., Frankfurt am Main: Suhrkamp, 1985.
    Philosophie der Offenbarung 1841–42, ed. Manfred Frank, Frankfurt am Main: Suhrkamp, 1993.
Schiller, Friedrich, *Werke* (Nationalausgabe), ed. Benno von Wiese, 42 vols., Weimar: Böhlau, 1962.
    Sämtliche Werke, ed. Gerhard Fricke and Herbert G. Göpfert, 5 vols., 6th edn, Munich: Hanser, 1980.
Schlaf, Johannes, *Frühling*, Leipzig: Verlag Kreisende Ringe, 1896.
Schlegel, Friedrich, *Kritische Friedrich-Schlegel-Ausgabe*, eds. Ernst Behler, Hans Eichner and Jean-Jacques Anstett, 35 vols., Paderborn, Munich, Vienna and Zürich: Schöningh, 1958– .
Schleiermacher, Friedrich D. E., *Hermeneutik und Kritik. Mit einem Anhang sprach-philosophischer Texte Schleiermachers*, ed. Manfred Frank, Frankfurt am Main: Suhrkamp, 1977.
Schlink, Bernhard, *Des Vorleser*, Zürich: Diogenes, 1995.
Schmitt, Carl, *Die geistesgeschichtliche Lage des heutigen Parlamentarismus*, 6th edn, Berlin: Duncker & Humblot, 1985.
Schmitt, Hans-Jürgen, *Die Expressionismusdebatte: Materialien zu einer marxistischen Realismuskonzeption*, Frankfurt am Main: Suhrkamp, 1973.
Schneider, Peter, *Lenz*, Berlin: Rotbuch Verlag, 1973.
    Der Mauerspringer, Darmstadt: Luchterhand, 1982.
    Vati, Darmstadt: Luchterhand, 1987.
Scholem, Gershom Gerhard, *Major trends in Jewish mysticism*, Jerusalem: Schocken, 1941.
Schopenhauer, Arthur, *Sämmtliche Werke*, ed. Julius Frauenstädt, 6 vols., Leipzig: Brockhaus, 1923.
Schubert, Gotthilf Heinrich, *Ansichten von der Nachtseite der Naturwissenschaft*, Dresden: Arnold, 1808.
    Die Symbolik des Traumes, Bamberg: C. F. Kunz, 1814.

Schwaiger, Brigitte, *Lange Abwesenheit*, Wien: Zsolnay, 1980.
Seligmann, Rafael, *Rubinsteins Versteigerung*, Frankfurt am Main: Eichborn, 1989.
Spengler, Oswald, *Der Untergang des Abendlandes: Umrisse einer Morphologie der Weltgeschichte*, Munich: C. H. Beck, 1979.
Spielhagen, Friedrich, *Vermischte Schriften*, Berlin, 1864.
Spinoza, Baruch de, *Ethics*, trans. Andrew Boyle, rev. G. H. R. Parkinson, London: J. M. Dent, 1995.
Stadler, Ernst, *Dichtungen*, ed. Karl Ludwig Schneider, 2 vols., Hamburg: Ellermann, 1954.
Stefan, Verena, *Häutungen*, Munich: Verlag Frauenoffensive, 1975.
Stifter, Adalbert, *Gesammelte Werke*, 14 vols., ed. K. Steffen, Basel and Stuttgart, 1967–72.
Strittmatter, Erwin, *Katzgraben*, Berlin: Aufbau, 1953.
Thomasius, Christian, *Vernunftlehre*, in *Deutsche Literaturdenkmäler des 18. und 19. Jahrhunderts*, vol. LII/2; New Series 2/3, Nendeln: Krauss, 1968.
Trakl, Georg, *Dichtungen und Briefe*, ed. Walther Killy and Hans Szklenar, 2 vols., 2nd edn, Salzburg: Otto Müller, 1987.
Tucholsky, Kurt, *Deutschland, Deutschland über alles; ein Bilderbuch von Kurt Tucholsky und vielen Fotografen; montiert von John Heartfield*, Berlin: Neuer deutscher Verlag, 1929.
Vesper, Bernward, *Die Reise*, Frankfurt am Main: März bei Zweitausendeins, 1979.
Wagner, Richard, *Ausgewählte Schriften und Briefe*, ed. Alfred Lorenz, 2 vols., Berlin: Bernhard Hahnefeld, 1938.
Walser, Martin, *Halbzeit*, Frankfurt am Main: Suhrkamp, 1960.
Wander, Maxie, *Guten Morgen, du Schöne*, Berlin: Buchverlag Der Morgan, 1977.
Weber, Max, *Gesammelte Aufsätze zur Religionssoziologie*, 2nd edn, Tübingen: J. C. B. Mohr, 1922.
   Gesammelte Aufsätze zur Wissenschaftslehre, 3rd edn, ed. Johannes Winckelmann, Tübingen: J. C. B. Mohr, 1968.
Weininger, Otto, *Geschlecht und Charakter* (1903), Munich: Matthes & Seitz, 1980.
Weiss, Peter, *Die Verfolgung und Ermordung Jean Paul Marats, dargestellt durch die Schauspielgruppe des Hospizes zu Charenton unter Anleitung des Herrn de Sade*, Frankfurt am Main: Suhrkamp, 1964.
   Die Ermittlung: Oratorium in 11 Gesängen, Frankfurt: Suhrkamp, 1965.
   Ästhetik des Widerstands, Frankfurt am Main: Suhrkamp, 1975–1981.
Wieland, Christoph Martin, *Werke*, 5 vols., ed. Fritz Martini and Hans Werner Seiffert, Munich: Hanser, 1964–6.
Wilkomirski, Binjamin, *Bruchstücke: Aus einer Kindheit 1939–1948*, Frankfurt am Main: Jüdischer Verlag, 1995.
Wolf, Christa, *Moskauer Novelle*, Halle: Mitteldeutscher Verlag, 1961.
   Der geteilte Himmel, Halle: Mitteldeutscher Verlag, 1963.
   Nachdenken über Christa T., Halle: Mitteldeutscher Verlag, 1968.
   Kindheitsmuster, Berlin: Aufbau, 1976.
   Was bleibt, Berlin: Aufbau, 1990.

Wolf, Friedrich, *Gesammelte Werke*, 6 vols., Berlin: Aufbau, 1960.
Vischer, Friedrich T., *Ästhetik oder die Wissenschaft des Schönen*, ed. Robert Vischer, repr. of 2nd edn (Munich 1922–3) 6 vols., Hildesheim: Olms, 1996.

SECONDARY TEXTS

Améry, Jean, 'Aufklärung als *philosophia perennis*', in Paul Raabe and Wilhelm Schmitt-Biggemann (eds.), *Aufklärung in Deutschland*, Bonn: Hohwacht, 1979.
Anz, Thomas, *Literatur der Existenz: Literarische Psychopathographie und ihre soziale Bedeutung im Frühexpressionismus*, Stuttgart: Metzler, 1977.
Aschheim, Steven E., *The Nietzsche legacy in Germany 1890–1990*, Berkeley: University of California Press, 1992.
Auerbach, Erich, *Mimesis: Dargestellte Wirklichkeit in der abendländischen Literatur*, Bern: Francke, 1946.
Bakhtin, Mikhail M., *The dialogic imagination: four essays*, ed. Michael Holquist, trans. Caryl Emerson and Michael Holquist, Austin: University of Texas Press, 1996.
Barker, Andrew, *Telegrams from the soul: Peter Altenberg and the culture of fin-de-siècle Vienna*, Columbia, SC: Camden House, 1996.
Barner, Wilfried (ed.), *Geschichte der deutschen Literatur von 1945 bis zur Gegenwart*, Munich: Beck, 1994.
Beiser, Frederick C., *The fate of reason. German philosophy from Kant to Fichte*, Cambridge and London: Harvard University Press, 1987.
The early political writings of the German Romantics, Cambridge: Cambridge University Press, 1996.
Black, Max, *Models and metaphors. Studies in language and philosophy*, Ithaca, New York: Cornell University Press, 1962.
Blumenberg, Hans, 'Nachahmung der Natur. Zur Vorgeschichte der Idee des schöpferischen Menschen', in *Wirklichkeiten, in denen wir leben. Aufsätze und eine Rede*, Stuttgart: Reclam, 1985, pp. 55–103.
Boa, Elizabeth, *The sexual circus: Wedekind's theatre of subversion*, Oxford: Blackwell, 1987.
Böhme, Hartmut, and Gernot Böhme, *Das Andere der Vernunft. Zur Entdeckung von Rationalitätsstrukturen am Beispiel Kants*, Frankfurt am Main: Suhrkamp, 1985.
Bohn, Volker, *Deutsche Literatur seit 1945*, Frankfurt am Main: Suhrkamp, 1995.
Bohrer, Karl-Heinz, *Ästhetik der Plötzlichkeit. Zum Augenblick des ästhetischen Scheins*, Frankfurt am Main: Suhrkamp, 1981.
Borchmeyer, Dieter, 'Fontane, Thomas Mann und das "Dreigestirn" Schopenhauer–Wagner–Nietzsche', in Eckhard Heftrich et al. (eds.), *Theodor Fontane und Thomas Mann*, Frankfurt am Main: Klostermann, 1998, pp. 217–48.
Bowie, Andrew, *Aesthetics and subjectivity. From Kant to Nietzsche*, Manchester: Manchester University Press, 1990.
Schelling and modern European philosophy. An introduction, London: Routledge, 1993.
From Romanticism to Critical Theory. The philosophy of German literary theory, London and New York: Routledge, 1997.

Boyle, Nicholas, 'Kantian and other elements in Goethe's "Vermächtniß"', *MLR* 73 (1978), 532–49.

Goethe. *The poet and the age*, vol. I: *The poetry of desire*, Oxford: Oxford University Press, 1991.

Braungart, Georg, *Leibhafter Sinn. Der andere Diskurs der Moderne*, Tübingen: Niemeyer, 1995.

Braungart, Wolfgang, Gotthard Fuchs and Manfred Koch (eds.), *Ästhetische und religiöse Erfahrungen der Jahrhundertwenden, II: Um 1900*, Paderborn: Schöningh, 1998.

Brinkmann, Richard, *Wirklichkeit und Illusion. Studien über Gehalt und Grenzen des Begriffs Realismus für die erzählende Dichtung des neunzehnten Jahrhunderts*, Tübingen: Niemeyer, 1966.

Brinkmann, Richard (ed.), *Begriffsbestimmung des literarischen Realismus*, Darmstadt: Wissenschaftliche Buchgesellschaft, 1969.

Bürger, Peter, *Theorie der Avantgarde*, Frankfurt am Main: Suhrkamp, 1974.

Burrow, J. W., *The crisis of reason: European thought, 1848–1914*. Cambridge: Cambridge University Press, 2000.

Cassirer, Ernst, *Heinrich von Kleist und die Kantische Philosophie*, Berlin: Bruno Cassirer, 1919.

Philosophy of the Enlightenment, trans. Fritz C. A. Koelln and James P. Pettegrove, Boston: Beacon Press, 1966.

Ciafardone, Raffaele, *Die Philosophie der deutschen Aufklärung. Texte und Darstellung*, ed. Norbert Hinske and Rainer Specht, Stuttgart: Reclam, 1990.

Cohn, Dorrit, 'Freud's case histories and the question of fictionality', in Joseph H. Smith and Humphrey Morris (eds.), *Telling facts: history and narration in psychoanalysis*, Baltimore and London: Johns Hopkins University Press, 1992.

Critchfield, Richard, and Wulf Koepke (eds.), *Eighteenth-century German authors and their aesthetic theories: Literature and the other arts*, Columbia SC: Camden House, 1988.

Danto, Arthur C., 'Philosophy as/and/of literature', in *The philosophical disenfranchisement of art*, New York: Columbia University Press, 1986, pp. 135–61.

Derrida, Jacques, *Marges de la philosophie*, Paris: Minuit, 1972.

During, Simon, *Foucault and literature. Towards a genealogy of writing*, London and New York: Routledge, 1992.

Eagleton, Terry, *The ideology of the aesthetic*, Oxford: Blackwell, 1990.

Eggert, Hartmut, Erhard Schütz and Peter Sprengel (eds.), *Faszination des Organischen. Konjunkturen einer Kategorie der Moderne*, Munich: Iudicium, 1995.

Ellenberger, Henri, *The discovery of the unconscious: the history and evolution of dynamic psychiatry*, New York: Basic Books, 1970.

Emrich, Wolfgang, *Kleine Literaturgeschichte der DDR*, Leipzig: Gustav Kiepenheuer, 1996.

Engel, Manfred, *Rainer Maria Rilkes "Duineser Elegien" und die moderne deutsche Lyrik*, Stuttgart: Metzler, 1986.

Feuerlicht, Ignace, *Thomas Mann und die Grenzen des Ich*, Heidelberg: Winter, 1966.

Fick, Monika, *Sinnenwelt und Weltseele. Der psychophysische Monismus in der Literatur der Jahrhundertwende*, Tübingen: Niemeyer, 1993.

Finney, Gail, 'Revolution, resignation, realism 1830–1890', in Helen Watanabe O'Kelly (ed.), *The Cambridge history of German literature*, Cambridge: Cambridge University Press, 1997, pp. 272–326.

Fliedl, Konstanze, *Arthur Schnitzler. Poetik der Erinnerung*, Vienna, Cologne and Weimar: Böhlau, 1997.

Fohrmann, Jürgen, and Harro Müller, 'Einleitung. Diskurstheorien und Literaturwissenschaft', in Jürgen Fohrmann and Harro Müller (eds.), *Diskurstheorien und Literaturwissenschaft*, Frankfurt am Main: Suhrkamp, 1988.

Foucault, Michel, *Die Ordnung des Diskurses*, Munich: UTB, 1974.

'Was ist ein Autor?', in *Schriften zur Literatur*, Frankfurt am Main, Berlin and Vienna: Ullstein, 1979, pp. 7–31.

Fox, Thomas C., *Stated memory: East Germany and the Holocaust*, Rochester: Camden House, 1999.

Frank, Manfred, '"Intellektuale Anschauung". Drei Stellungnahmen zu einem Deutungsversuch von Selbstbewußtsein: Kant, Fichte, Hölderlin/ Novalis', in Ernst Behler and Jochen Hörisch (eds.), *Die Aktualität der Frühromantik*, Paderborn, Munich, Vienna and Zürich: Schöningh, 1987, pp. 96–126.

Einführung in die frühromantische Ästhetik, Frankfurt am Main: Suhrkamp, 1989.

Futterknecht, Franz, *Infantiles Bewußtsein. Johann Karl Wezels Kritik der Moderne*, Munich: Iudicium, 1999.

Gaier, Ulrich, 'Mythologie der Vernunft. Grenzüberschreitungen der Philosophie im 18. Jahrhundert', in Klaus Bohnen and Per Øhrgaard (eds.), *Aufklärung als Problem und Aufgabe. Festschrift für Sven-Aage Jørgensen*, Munich: Wilhelm Fink Verlag, 1994, pp. 65–76.

Gay, Peter, *The Enlightenment: an interpretation. The rise of modern paganism*, New York: Random House, 1968.

Weimar culture: the outsider as insider, New York: Harper and Row, 1968.

Geuss, Raymond, *Morality, culture and history. Essays on German philosophy*, Cambridge: Cambridge University Press, 1999.

Gilman, Sander, *Jews in today's German culture*, Bloomington: Indiana University Press, 1995.

Ginsberg, Robert (ed.), *The philosopher as writer: the eighteenth century*, London and Toronto: Associated University Presses, 1987.

Goetschel, Willi, *Constituting critique. Kant's writing as critical praxis*, Durham and London: Duke University Press, 1994.

Goldman, Harvey, *Politics, death, and the devil: self and power in Max Weber and Thomas Mann*, Berkeley: University of California Press, 1992.

Greiner, Bernhard, '"Die neueste Philosophie in dieses . . . Land verpflanzen". Kleists literarische Experimente mit Kant', *Kleist-Jahrbuch 1998*, Stuttgart: Metzler, 1998, pp. 176–208.

Grimminger, Rolf (general ed.), *Hansers Sozialgeschichte der deutschen Literatur*, 12 vols., Munich and Vienna: Carl Hanser, 1980–99; vol. V: *Zwischen*

Restauration und Revolution 1815–1848, ed. Gert Sautermeister and Ulrich Schmid, 1998; vol. VI: *Bürgerlicher Realismus und Gründerzeit 1848–1890*, ed. Edward McInnes and Gerhard Plumpe, 1996.

Hampson, Norman, *The Enlightenment*, Baltimore: Penguin, 1968.

Harrowitz, Nancy A., and Barbara Hyams (eds.), *Jews and gender: responses to Otto Weininger*, Philadelphia: Temple University Press, 1995.

Heller, Erich, *The disinherited mind: essays in modern German literature and thought*, Cambridge: Bowes & Bowes, 1952.

The ironic German: Thomas Mann, London: Secker & Warburg, 1958.

Herf, Jeffrey, *Divided memory: the Nazi past in the two Germanys*, Cambridge, MA: Harvard University Press, 1997.

Hermand, Jost, *Kultur im Wiederaufbau: Die Bundesrepublik Deutschland 1945–1965*, Munich: Nymphenburger, 1986.

Die Kultur der Bundesrepublik Deutschland 1965–85, Munich: Nymphernburger, 1988.

Hermand, Jost, and Frank Trommler, *Die Kultur in der Weimarer Republik*, Munich: Nymphenburger Verlagshandlung, 1978.

Holub, Robert C., *Reflections of realism: paradox, norm and ideology in nineteenth century German prose*, Detroit: Wayne State University Press, 1991.

Jürgen Habermas: critic in the public sphere, London: Routledge, 1991.

Horch, Hans Otto, 'Fontane und das kranke Jahrhundert. Theodor Fontanes Beziehungen zu den Kulturkritikern Friedrich Nietzsche, Max Nordau und Paolo Mantegazza', in Hans-Peter Bayerdörfer, Karl Otto Conrady and Helmut Schanze (eds.), *Literatur und Theater im Wilhelminischen Zeitalter*, Tübingen: Niemeyer, 1978, pp. 1–34.

Houlgate, Stephen, *Freedom, truth and history. An introduction to Hegel's philosophy*, London and New York: Routledge, 1991.

Johnston, William M., *The Austrian mind: an intellectual and social history*, Berkeley: University of California Press, 1972.

Kaes, Anton, Martin Jay and Edward Dimendberg (eds.), *The Weimar Republic sourcebook*, Berkeley: University of California Press, 1994.

Kafitz, Dieter, *Johannes Schlaf. Weltanschauliche Totalität und Wirklichkeitsblindheit*, Tübingen: Niemeyer, 1992.

Karpenstein-Eßbach, Christa, 'Zum Unterschied von Diskursanalysen und Dekonstruktion', in Sigrid Weigel (ed.), *Flaschenpost und Postkarte. Korrespondenzen zwischen Kritischer Theorie und Poststrukturalismus*, Cologne, Weimar and Vienna: Böhlau, 1995, pp. 127–38.

Kelly, Alfred, *The descent of Darwin: the popularization of Darwinism in Germany, 1860–1914*, Chapel Hill: University of North Carolina Press, 1981.

Kleefeld, Gunther, *Das Gedicht als Sühne. Georg Trakls Dichtung und Krankheit: Eine psychoanalytische Studie*, Tübingen: Niemeyer, 1985.

Kool, Frits, *Die Linke gegen die Parteiherrschaft*, Olten: Walter Verlag, 1970.

Koopmann, Helmut, 'Thomas Mann und Schopenhauer', in Peter Pütz (ed.), *Thomas Mann und die Tradition*, Frankfurt am Main: Athenäum, 1971, pp. 180–200.

Korff, Hermann August, *Geist der Goethezeit. Versuch einer ideellen Entwicklung der klassisch-romantischen Literaturgeschichte*, 4 vols., Leipzig: Weber, 1923; Leipzig: Koehler und Amelang, 1953.

Kowalik, Jill Anne, *The poetics of historical perspectivism: Breitinger's 'Critische Dichtkunst' and the neoclassic tradition*, Chapel Hill and London: University of North Carolina Press, 1992.

Le Rider, Jacques, *Modernity and crises of identity: culture and society in fin-de-siècle Vienna*, trans. Rosemary Morris, Cambridge: Polity, 1993.

Liebrand, Claudia, *Das Ich und die Andern. Fontanes Figuren und ihre Selbstbilder*, Freiburg: Rombach, 1990.

Luft, David S., *Robert Musil and the crisis of European culture, 1880–1942*, Berkeley and Los Angeles: University of California Press, 1980.

'Schopenhauer, Austria, and the generation of 1905', *Central European History* 16 (1983), 53–75.

Lyotard, Jean-François, *La condition postmoderne*, Paris: Minuit, 1979.

McCarthy, John A., *Crossing boundaries: a theory and history of the essay in German 1680–1815*, Philadelphia: University of Pennsylvania Press, 1989.

'Aufklärung des ästhetischen Scheins – die Ästhetisierung der Aufklärung', *Das achtzehnte Jahrhundert* 15/2 (1991), 147–69.

Madland, Helga, 'Imitation to creation: the changing concept of mimesis from Bodmer and Breitinger to Lenz', in Richard Critchfield and Wulf Koepke (eds.), *Eighteenth-century German authors and their aesthetic theories*, Columbia SC: Camden House, 1988, pp. 29–43.

Manning, Susan, 'Literature and philosophy', in H. B. Nisbet and Claude Rawson (eds.), *The Cambridge history of literary criticism*, vol. IV: *The eighteenth century*, Cambridge: Cambridge University Press, 1997, pp. 587–613.

Martens, Gunter, *Vitalismus und Expressionismus. Ein Beitrag zur Genese und Deutung expressionistischer Stilstrukturen und Motive*, Stuttgart, Berlin, Cologne and Mainz: Kohlhammer, 1971.

Martens, Wolfgang, *Die Botschaft der Tugend. Die Aufklärung im Spiegel der deutschen Moralischen Wochenschriften*, Stuttgart: Metzler, 1968.

Michler, Werner, *Darwinismus und Literatur. Naturwissenschaftliche und literarische Intelligenz in Österreich, 1859–1914*, Vienna, Cologne and Weimar: Böhlau, 1999.

Molnár, Géza von, *Romantic vision, ethical context. Novalis and artistic autonomy*, Minneapolis: University of Minnesota Press, 1987.

Goethes Kantstudien, Weimar: Hermann Böhlaus Nachfolger, 1994.

'Goethe and critical philosophy: the *Wissenschaftslehre* as supplement to his Kant-Studies', in Clifford A. Bernd, Ingeborg Henderson and Winder M. McConnell (eds.), *Romanticism and beyond. A Festschrift for John F. Fetzer* (New York: Peter Lang, 1996), pp. 57–77.

Müller, Wolfgang G., 'Rilke, Husserl und die Dinglyrik der Moderne', in Manfred Engel and Dieter Lamping (eds.), *Rilke und die Weltliteratur*, Düsseldorf and Zürich: Artemis & Winkler, 1999, pp. 214–35.

Mullan, John, 'Sensibility and literary criticism', in H. B. Nisbet and Claude Rawson (eds.), *The Cambridge history of literary criticism*, vol. IV: *The eighteenth century*, Cambridge: Cambridge University Press, 1997, pp. 419–33.

Murphy, Richard, *Theorizing the avant-garde: modernism, expressionism, and the problem of postmodernity*, Cambridge: Cambridge University Press, 1999.

Nehamas, Alexander, *Nietzsche: life as literature*, Cambridge, MA: Harvard University Press, 1985.

Nehring, Wolfgang, 'Möglichkeiten impressionistischen Erzählens', *ZfdPh* 100 (1981), 161–76.

Neumann, Gerhard, '"Kunst des Nicht-lesens". Hofmannsthals Ästhetik des Flüchtigen', *Hofmannsthal-Jahrbuch* 4 (1996), 227–60.

Nivelle, Armand, *Literaturästhetik der europäischen Aufklärung*, Wiesbaden: Athenaion, 1977.

O'Brien, William Arctander, *Novalis. Signs of Revolution*, Durham and London: Duke University Press, 1995.

Pascal, Roy, *The German novel: studies*, Manchester: Manchester University Press, 1956.

  From naturalism to expressionism: German literature and society 1880–1918, London: Methuen, 1973.

Pasley, Malcolm (ed.), *Nietzsche: imagery and thought*, Berkeley: University of California Press, 1984.

Perry, Douglas Lane, 'The institution of criticism in the eighteenth century', in H. B. Nisbet and Claude Rawson (eds.), *The Cambridge history of literary criticism*, vol. IV. *The eighteenth century*, Cambridge: Cambridge University Press, 1997, pp. 3–31.

Pietzcker, Dominik, *Richard von Schaukal: Ein österreichischer Dichter der Jahrhundertwende*, Würzburg: Königshausen & Neumann, 1997.

Pütz, Peter, *Die deutsche Aufklärung*, 4th edn, Darmstadt: Wissenschaftliche Buchgesellschaft, 1991.

Reed, T. J., *Thomas Mann: the uses of tradition*, Oxford: Clarendon Press, 1974.

  'Nietzsche's animals: idea, image and influence', in Malcolm Pasley (ed.), *Nietzsche: imagery and thought*, London: Methuen, 1978, pp. 159–219.

Reichmann, Eberhard, 'Die Begründung der deutschen Aufklärungsästhetik aus dem Geist der Zahl', *Monatshefte* 59/3 (1967), 193–203.

Ricœur, Paul, *The rule of metaphor. Multi-disciplinary studies of the creation of meaning in language* (1975), Toronto and Buffalo: University of Toronto Press, 1977.

Riedel, Wolfgang, *Die Anthropologie des jungen Schiller. Zur Ideengeschichte der medizinischen Schriften und der 'Philosophischen Briefe'*, Würzburg: Königshausen & Neumann, 1985.

  'Homo Natura': Literarische Anthropologie um 1900, Berlin and New York: de Gruyter, 1996.

Rieff, Philip, *Freud: the mind of the moralist*, 3rd edn, Chicago: University of Chicago Press, 1979.

Ritvo, Lucille B., *Darwin's influence on Freud*, New Haven and London: Yale University Press, 1990.

Roberts, Julian, *German philosophy. An introduction*, Oxford: Polity Press, 1988.

  The logic of reflection. German philosophy in the twentieth century, New Haven and London: Yale University Press, 1992.

Rorty, Richard, *Philosophy and the mirror of nature*, Oxford: Blackwell, 1980.

Rutherford, Donald, *Leibniz and the rational order of nature*, New York: Cambridge University Press, 1998.

Ryan, Judith, 'Die "allomatische Lösung": Gespaltene Persönlichkeit und Konfiguration bei Hugo von Hofmannsthal', *DVjs* 44 (1970), 189–207.

The vanishing subject: early psychology and literary modernism, Chicago: University of Chicago Press, 1991.

Rilke, modernism and poetic tradition, Cambridge: Cambridge University Press, 1999.

Saine, Thomas P., *Von der kopernikanischen bis zur Französischen Revolution. Die Auseinandersetzung der deutschen Frühaufklärung mit der neuen Zeit*, Berlin: Erich Schmidt, 1987.

Saul, Nicholas, 'Aesthetic humanism. German literature 1790–1830', in Helen Watanabe-O'Kelly (ed.), *The Cambridge history of German literature*, Cambridge: Cambridge University Press, 1997, pp. 202–71.

Saul, Nicholas (ed.), *The body in German literature around 1800*, Special number of *German Life & Letters* 52/2 (1999).

Scaff, Lawrence A., *Fleeing the iron cage: culture, politics, and Modernity in the thought of Max Weber*, Berkeley: University of California Press, 1989.

Schings, Hans-Jürgen, *Der mitleidigste Mensch ist der beste Mensch. Poetik des Mitleids von Lessing bis Büchner*, Munich: Beck, 1980.

Schlant, Ernestine, *The language of silence: West German literature and the Holocaust*, New York: Routledge, 1999.

Schmidt, James (ed.), *What is Enlightenment? Eighteenth-century answers and twentieth-century questions*, Berkeley CA: University of California Press, 1996.

Schnädelbach, Herbert, *Philosophy in Germany, 1831–1933*, trans. E. Matthews, Cambridge: Cambridge University Press, 1984.

Schneider, Helmut J., 'Naturerfahrung und Idylle in der deutschen Aufklärung', in Peter Pütz (ed.), *Erforschung der deutschen Aufklärung*, Königstein im Taunus: Hanstein, 1980, pp. 289–316.

Schneiders, Werner, *Hoffnung auf Vernunft. Aufklärungsphilosophie in Deutschland*, Hamburg: Meiners, 1990.

Das Zeitalter der Aufklärung, Munich: C. H. Beck, 1997.

Schneiders, Werner (ed.), *Aufklärung als Mission. La mission des Lumières. Akzeptanzprobleme und Kommunikationsdefizite*, in *Das achtzehnte Jahrhundert*, Supplementa, vol. 1, Marburg: Hitzeroth, 1993.

Schnell, Ralf, *Geschichte der deutschsprachigen Literatur seit 1945*, Stuttgart: Metzler, 1993.

Schulz, Walter, *Metaphysik des Schwebens. Untersuchungen zur Geschichte der Ästhetik*, Pfullingen: Neske, 1985.

Seel, Martin, *Die Kunst der Entzweiung. Zum Begriff der ästhetischen Rationalität* (1985), Frankfurt am Main: Suhrkamp, 1997.

Sheppard, Richard, 'Unholy families: the œdipal psychopathology of four Expressionist Ich-Dramen', in Richard Sheppard (ed.), *New ways in Germanistik*, New York, Oxford and Munich: Berg, 1990, pp. 164–91.

'The problematics of European modernism', in Steve Giles (ed.), *Theorising Modernism*, London: Routledge, 1993, pp. 1–51.

'Insanity, violence, and cultural criticism: some further thoughts on four Expressionist short stories', *Forum for Modern Language Studies* 30 (1994), 152–62.

Spörl, Uwe, *Gottlose Mystik in der deutschen Literatur um die Jahrhundertwende*, Paderborn: Schöningh, 1997.

Sprengel, Peter, *Geschichte der deutschsprachigen Literatur 1870–1900. Von der Reichsgründung bis zur Jahrhundertwende*, Munich: Beck, 1998.

Stahl, August, '"ein paar Seiten Schopenhauer" – Überlegungen zu Rilkes Schopenhauer-Lektüre und deren Folgen', *Schopenhauer-Jahrbuch* 69 (1988), 569–82; 70 (1989), 174–88.

Stern, Joseph P., *Re-interpretations. Seven studies in nineteenth-century German literature*, 2nd edn, Cambridge: Cambridge University Press, 1981 (1st edn 1964).

Idylls and realities: studies in nineteenth-century German literature, London: Methuen, 1971.

On realism, London: Routledge and Kegan Paul, 1973.

The dear purchase. A theme in German modernism, Cambridge: Cambridge University Press, 1995.

Sulloway, Frank J., *Freud, biologist of the mind: beyond the psychoanalytic legend*, 2nd edn, Cambridge, MA, and London: Harvard University Press, 1992.

Swales, Martin and Nicholas Boyle, *Realism in European literature: essays in honour of J. P. Stern*, Cambridge: Cambridge University Press, 1986.

Tatar, Maria, *Lustmord: sexual murder in Weimar Germany*, Princeton, NJ: Princeton University Press, 1995.

Taylor, Charles, *Sources of the self. The making of modern identity*, Cambridge: Cambridge University Press, 1989.

Timms, Edward, *Karl Kraus, apocalyptic satirist*, New Haven and London: Yale University Press, 1986.

Troeltsch, Ernst, 'Aufklärung', *Realenzyclopädie für protestantische Theologie und Kirche* 2 (1897), 273.

Uerlings, Herbert, *Friedrich von Hardenberg, genannt Novalis. Werk und Forschung*, Stuttgart: Metzler, 1991.

Van Cleve, John W., *The merchant in German literature of the Enlightenment*, Chapel Hill, London: University of North Carolina Press, 1986.

Vietta, Silvio, *Neuzeitliche Rationalität und moderne literarische Sprachkritik*, Munich: Fink, 1981.

Literarische Phantasie. Theorie und Geschichte – Barock und Aufklärung, Stuttgart: Metzler, 1986.

Die ästhetische Moderne. Eine problemgeschichtliche Darstellung der deutschsprachigen Literatur von Hölderlin bis Thomas Bernhard, Stuttgart: Metzler, 1992.

Wagner-Egelhaaf, Martina, *Mystik der Moderne. Die visionäre Ästhetik der deutschen Literatur im 20. Jahrhundert*, Stuttgart: Metzler, 1989.

Weyergraf, Bernhard, *Literatur der Weimarer Republik 1918–1933*, Munich: Hanser, 1995.

Wiggershaus, Rolf, *Die Frankfurter Schule: Geschichte, theoretische Entwicklung, politische Bedeutung*, Munich: Hanser, 1986.

Willet, John, *The new sobriety, 1917–1933: art and politics in the Weimar period*, London: Thames and Hudson, 1978.

Wolff, Hans M., *Die Weltanschauung der deutschen Aufklärung in geschichtlicher Entwicklung*, Bern: Francke, 1949.

Wunberg, Gotthart, *Der frühe Hofmannsthal. Schizophrenie als dichterische Struktur*, Stuttgart, Berlin, Cologne and Mainz: Kohlhammer, 1965.

Zelle, Carsten, *'Angenehmes Grauen'. Literaturhistorische Beiträge zur Ästhetik des Schrecklichen im achtzehnten Jahrhundert*, Hamburg: Meiner, 1987.

Ziolkowski, Theodor, 'James Joyces Epiphanie und die Überwindung der empirischen Welt in der modernen deutschen Prosa', *Deutsche Vierteljahresschrift* 35 (1961), 594–616.

Index

Index prepared by Valerie Elliston.

NOTE: titles of works appear under author's name, with the initial article ignored for alphabetisation.

absolute, the: and art, 93–4; the constructed, 71, 84; and empiricism, 92–3; as highest point of knowledge, 81, 92; nature as product of, 81; and the Romantic Fragment, 73
abstinence, 22
acceptance of inevitable, 35
accessibility of texts, 52
accountability, 60
action and movement of nature, 20
activism, 22, 36
Addison, Joseph, 19, 38
Adorno, Theodor, 8, 9, 209, 212, 237, 238–9, 258; *Dialektik der Aufklärung*, 248–50; and Habermas, 269–70
aesthetics, 2, 18–21, 58, 80, 106; aesthetic discourse, 88; 'aestheticisation of politics', 237; ambivalence of aesthetic work, 221–2; autonomy, 82, 105, 115–16, 134, 146, 202, 220, fascist refusal of, 237; conservatism (1980s), 283; construction, 20, 71; and Dadaism, 207–8; in drama on Holocaust, 265–6; and ethics, 52; ideology of the aesthetic, 104; influence over theories of cognition, 82; Kant on, 58, 64, 66; Kleist's scepticism, 88; Mann's use of, 214; modernism, 69; the monstrous, 19, 21; ontological immanence, 123; overlap with political theory, 218; in post-Second World War poetry, 258; power over the self, 63; primacy of aesthetic in Nietzsche, 135–6; problem of sense of smell, 185–6; productive reception, 20, 37, 42; purposiveness, 66; of reception, 270; reception of stimulus, 19–21; Schiller, 64, 68–9; of *Sturm und Drang* movement, 44–5; three modes of expression, 94; transfiguration 132; utopian consensus,

87; value of aesthetic pleasure, 41, 66; Weber's argument, 202; the wondrous, 38–9, 44; *see also* art; intuition
affinities, 87
agency, 220
Aichinger, Ilse, 279
Albert, Hans, 270
Alexis, Willibald, 121, 128
alienation: Brecht on, 220, 221; from source of being, 62; *see also* fragmentation
allomatic process, 192
Altenberg, Peter (pseudonym of Richard Engländer), 185
Das älteste Systemprogramm des deutschen Idealismus (unidentified author), 80, 81
altruism, 49, 157
American War of Independence (1776), 18
Améry, Jean, 22
anamnesis, 77
Andreas-Salomé, Lou, 159, 168, 189
androgyny, 78, 84, 187–8
animals, 82–3, 86, 159–60
anthropology and Christianity, 109
anti-logocentrism, 7, 206
anti-rationalism, 200
anti-Semitism, 10, 126, 128–9, 236, 258, 259; in *Dialektik der Aufklärung*, 249–50; in GDR (1960s), 273–4, 277–8; *see also* Holocaust (Shoah)
antiquity as model for culture, 46, 69
Apitz, Bruno, 274
appearances, 3, 59, 60, 66, 136
apperception, 60, 61
architecture, gothic, 47
Arendt, Hannah, 252, 269

307